THE CRYS
An Ess

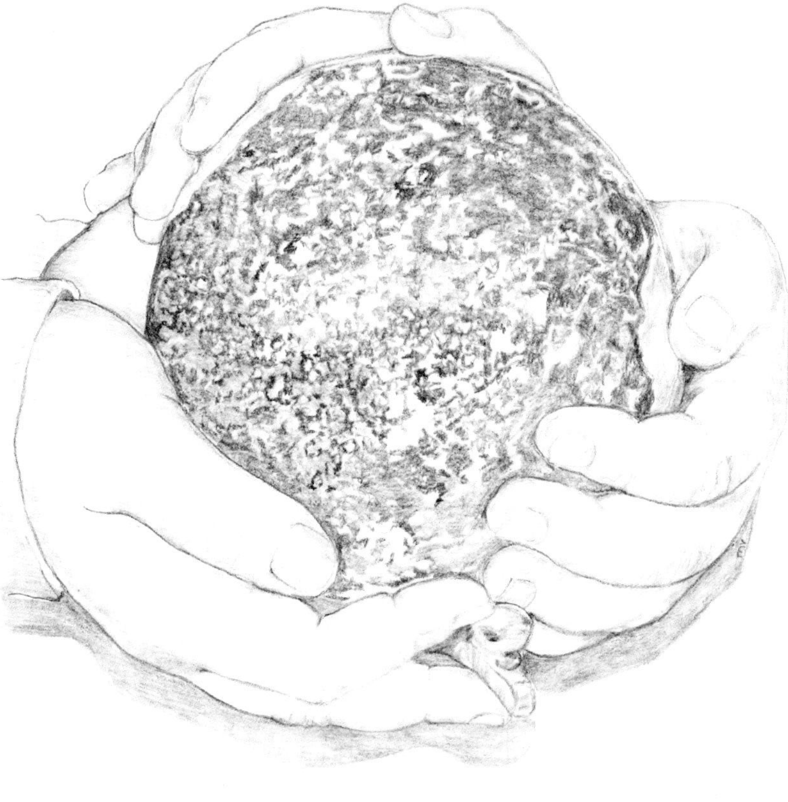

Crystal Healing Teacher Katrina Raphaell & margherita in Hawaii 1998.

Thank you for the gift of your teaching.

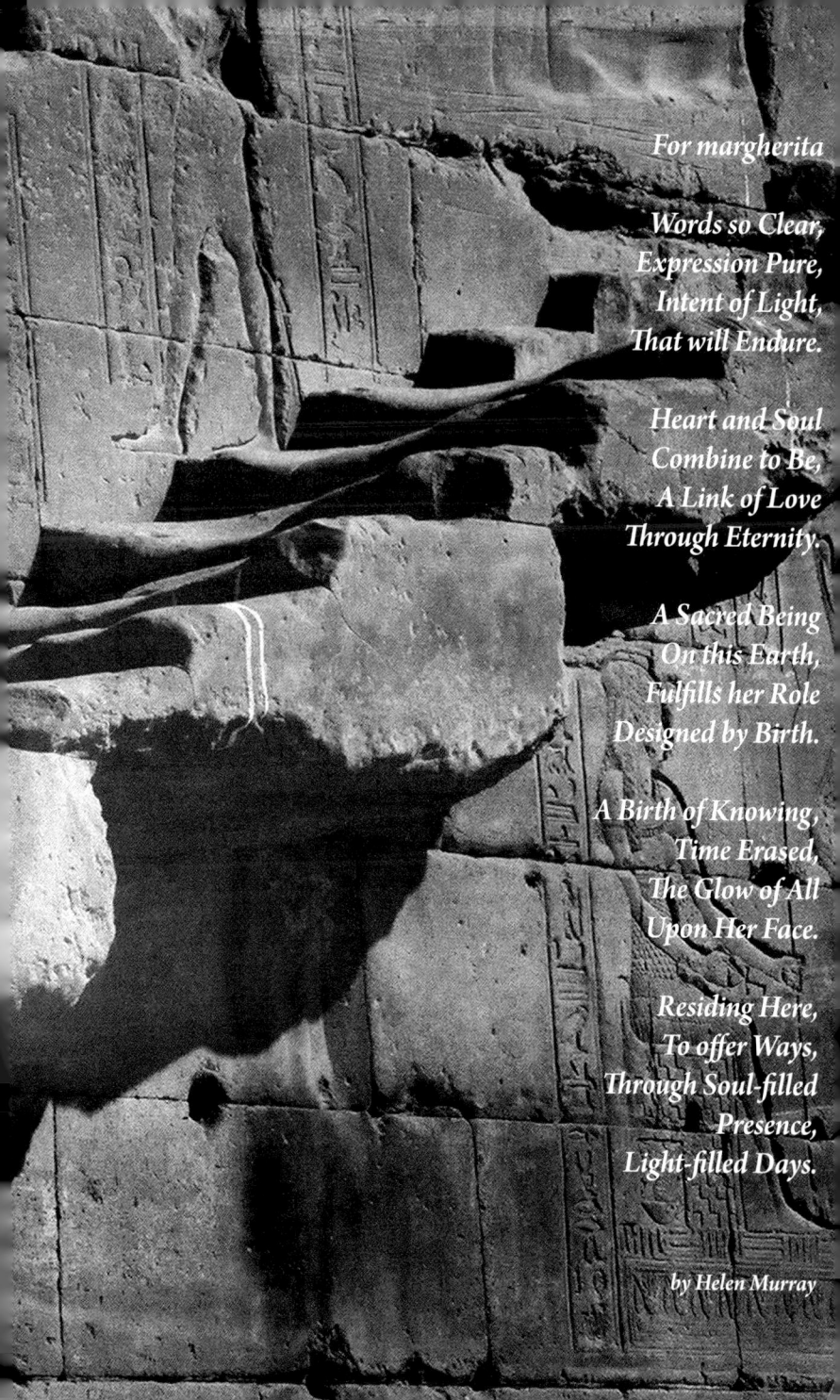

For margherita

Words so Clear,
Expression Pure,
Intent of Light,
That will Endure.

Heart and Soul
Combine to Be,
A Link of Love
Through Eternity.

A Sacred Being
On this Earth,
Fulfills her Role
Designed by Birth.

A Birth of Knowing,
Time Erased,
The Glow of All
Upon Her Face.

Residing Here,
To offer Ways,
Through Soul-filled
Presence,
Light-filled Days.

by Helen Murray

In honour of the Crystal Dakini,
and Her Team of Devas,
seen in the Light of the Crystals on Earth

THE CRYSTAL LOTUS HANDBOOK
An Essential Guide to Crystals

Cover & book design, drawings & crystal images by Margherita
Cover painting and author photos, © darinka blagaj www.darinka.com
Photos (Landscapes) © Jiri Vondrak www.jirivondrak.com
Photo (Condor) © Hilary Slater www.hilaryslater.weebly.com
Painting (Love Tree) © MiSun Kim-Hunter, www.misun.ca
Earth image on page: 51, courtesy of Uppsala University.
Poem on page 3 © Helen Murray, www.crystalsource.com

ISBN 978-0-9784683-0-9
ISBN 978-0-9784683-1-6

Published by:
The Crystal Lotus
RR# 2, Tamworth, Ontario, Canada, K0K 3G0
www.thecrystallotus.com
613-379 2225

Printed in China

This book is published and printed as a direct result of the generous finanscial support from the following sponsors:

Abigail van Clieaf, Andrew McKay, Ann Wrona, Brita Ball, Carol Heath, Caroline Denby, Dianne Jeffrey, Doreen Sullivan, Gwen Wannamaker, Helen Masters, Helen Sladden, Helen Will, Ingrid Fejer, Jaqueline Henley, Johanna Koeslag, Jiri Vondrak, Joe Sokolsky, Judy Derrett, Julei Busch, Julia Dietz, Katherine Salnek, Kathryn Shumelda, Laurie Clark, Lena Hammar, Linda Bingley, Louise Gallotta, Louise Nault, Maria Fatima Barros, Marika Huska, Marli Joy, Mary Florence, Mary McCandless, Maryan Milsom, Nicki & Marc Sheriff, Ohannes Bedrossian, Pam Polley, Paula McClintok, Rebecca Fuller, Susan Kern, Tawlia Chickalo, Tom Wojdylo, Triz Remedios, Zintra Zarins Imrie.

Supporting Sponsors: Albina Vanin, Anna Koushinsky, Barbara Turner, Darinka Blagaj, Debbie Purvis, Deborah Vaughan, Dorota Lisewski, Flavia Angelletta, Ginette Micheline, Heather Gurd, Heather Outhwaite, Jane Black, Jean Posche, Linda Morey, Lisa Houpt, Luciana Stan, Lucy Sousa, Lydia Vanin, Maura Ryan-Smith, MiSun Kim-Hunter, Pamela Love, Pooka Ness, Robin Lee Crowell, Shirley Nadenau, Sue Gunter, Tara Brox, Teresa Fischer, Terry Wolfert, Tyeb & Razia Sachee, Ursula Robinak, Vera Ketter.

Drawing shows hands pouring out prescious Lapis Lazuli, which is called the Stone of Wisdom. Welcome to the wondrous world of Crystals. May your journey be fruitful.

Acknowledgements

TEACHERS *Crystals:* Katrina Raphaell, Marilyn & Tohmas Twintrees, Melody, JaneAnn Dow, Helen Murray. *Life Wisdoms:* Anthony Templer, Whitecloud & Vairocana, Joy. *Hatha Yoga:* Ann Marie Edwards. *Healing:* Betty Tersigni, MarliJoy. *Flower Essences:* Andrea Mathieson.

WORK TOGETHER Helen Sladden, Laurie Clark, Tara Brox, Julei Busch, Pamela Polley, Roger Calverley, Anastasia Goodman, Ed Pierce & Susan Leeder and darinka blagaj.

CONTRIBUTORS Susan Kern, Mary Davis, Marc & Nicki Sheriff, Pam Polley, Savitri/Brahmani, Paula McClintock, Nancy Peel, Joanne and Karish.

PROFESSIONAL SUPPORT *Editing/Proof Reading:* Nancy Peel, Jean Poche, Roger Calverley, Hilary Slater and Peter Polley. *Core training for the Web:* Tomas Hammar. *The Crystal Lotus web site:* Sohee Kim-Schut. *Computer fix-it-all wizard:* Tom Wojdylo. *Web Marketing for Crystal Healing Club:* Tasneem Sachee. *Retail experience/advice:* Debbie Purvis. *Publishing advice:* Cherie Sohnen-Moe. *Printing technology training:* Doris Chung. *Photography expertise:* Jiri Vondrak. *Energy Work:* Allaine Nordin. *Vedic Astrology:* Alan Anand. *Facetting/Gemology:* Jan & Al Manestar. *Music:* Michael Moon. *Shiatsu:* Sher. *Hellerwork:* Jeff Weisman. *Professional development:* Helen Verhovsek. *Copy service in Kingston:* Julie, Deb and Sue.

CRYSTAL FRIENDS (in addition to those mentioned above or on the sponsor page) Adolphina Herrera Barinas, Adela Barbier, Adriana Ionescu, Adriana Killens, Adriana Satriya, Alani Galbraith-Kuzma, Alberto Kelly, Alexandra Ossova, Alicija Aratyn, Alison Cooke, Alla Lhnda, Allison Pope, Angela Adamson-Viola, Andrea & Tim Coulson, Andrea Mcleod, Andrew Owens, Andy Chan, Angela Greco,

Angela Ramsaran, Angela Smyth, Angela Thorne, Angelina Roza Brown, Ann Baka, Anne Murphy, Ann Imrie-Howlett, Anna Peruschek, Anne Marie Hodges, Barbara Brendemuell, Barbara Cambell, Barbara Keshwar, Barbara Smith, Barbara Stromberg, Bella Martins, Beth Gallas, Beth Schat, Bev Bazinet, Bharangi, Bonnie Smith, Bonnie Vanclief, Brenda Adler, Brenda Cordier, Bridget McFarthing, Brigitte Schwarzer, Carmen Beoughellette, Carmen Noseworthy, Carol Ebbitt, Carol Saint-Marie, Carole Seens, Carol Taylor, Carol Viau, Caroline Cloutier, Carolyn Buchanan, Cathy J. Jonathan, Cecilia Gano, Chantal Andrews, Celeste S. Vermette, Charlotte Harris, Cheryl Da Costa, Cheryl Dineley, Cheryl R. Dickson, Catherine Kennedy, Catherine McLaren-Tupling, Catherine Vigna, Cheryll Earle-Wills, Cheryl Uprichard, Christel Sjöheim, Chris Oliphant, Christian Ouimette, Christiane Aubin-Dinnoo, Christine Gross, Christine Pike, Christine Richards, Cindy Hempmill, Cindy Poon, Cindy Tanner, Colleen Miskov, Cynthia Gall, Cynthia Logan, Cynthia & Tim, Dana Katic, Daniel Rombough, Danielle Lam-Kulczak, David Bartlett, David Berger, David Hickey, Dawn Braden, Dawn Fairbairn, Dawn Munro, Dawn Price, Deanna Louise Riley, Debbie Periera, Deborah Ballon, Deborah Weiss, Debra Grose-Russell, Debra Joy Eklove, Dee Kruck, Deede Preston, Dennis Cooper, Diana Atherton Davis, Diane Brown, Diane Demidow, Diane Nall, Diane Tait, Donna Prymok, Donna Sahlberg, Doris Comtois, Diane Young, Domenic Rotolo, Donalda Loucks, Dr. Beverly Verpaelst/Johnson, Dynyasha, Effie Roderos, Elaine Moiton, Elana Millman, Elisa MacMillan, Elisabeth Schneider, Elise Thrasher, Ellen Allan, Ellen Simpson, Emily Spagnolo, Erin Daprato, Eva Dudas, Eva Lindstal, Eva Zelenka, Evan Hill, Eve Blake-Davis, Evelyn Moran, Fiona Young, Flor Hurtado, Fran Brunke, Franka Tiralongo, Gerry Cassidy, Gloria Ranney, Grace Rasmussen, Grecel Nepomuceano, Georgina Bayd, Glenys Lusk, Gloria Ranney, Grace Rasmussen, Gus Saltis, Harry Johnston, Harvey Harrison, Heather Bilz, Heather Harton, Heather Jansen, Heather Oerlemans-Cuyler, Heidi McBratney, Helen Garrison, Helen Jardine, Helen McLellan, Helen Roditio, Hildegard Gmeiner, Hulda Gislason, Ida Morra, Ingrid Cryns, Iris Scmidt, Irene Zonta, Isobel Provan, Jackie Green, Jackie Sedgwick, Jacqui Shaw, Jalanna Lloyd-Smith, Jan Benham, Jan Garvey, Jane Boyle,

Janellen, Jane Graham, Jane Scott, Jane Stephen, Janet Miller, Janet M. Zahodnik, Janice Stephens, Jaqueline Claire, Jaqui Michells, Jean Larsen, Jeanette Sweet, Jeannine Bolohan, Jennifer Dunstall, Jessie & Steve Godland, Jill Horne, Jill Ledden, Joan Dykens, Joan Rutherford, Joanna Parris, Joanne Johnston, Joanne Mathlin, Joe Hosick, Jodi Anderson, John W. Downs, Joyce Threlkeld, Judith Rothwell, Judy Malin Oronato, Karen Dermody, Karen Dickson, Karen Sheppard, Karen Scott, Kat Atsik, Kathie Smith, Kathy Forestall, Kathleen Switzer, Kathy Micheler, Kathy Ong, Kathy Ryndyak, Kayla Busch, Kelly Ritchie, Kerry McLeaod, Ken Forsyth, Kim Burns, Kim Templeton, Kimberly Wilson, Members of Kingston Gem & Mineral Club, Kirill Garkusha, Kirsty Naray, Krissy Richards, Kristina Goetting, Krystyna Ceinyak, Laura Taylor, Laura Weinberg, Lauren Bernstein, Lauren Burkley, Laurie D'Ascenco, Laurie Huston, Lee-Ann Steven, Leah Ann Wright, Lianne Graham, Ligia Feroiu, Linda Devine, Linda L. Brown, Mrs. Linda Hamilton, Linda McMahon, Linda Smith, Lin-Lin Chou, Lisa Murzin, Liz Evans, Liz Reinholds, Louise Brodie, Lorenna, Lori Ann Ouswald, Lori Burkley, Lorraine Beutler, Louise Brodie, Louise Edwards, Luana Harrison, Lynda Hester, Lynn Kranyak, Lynn Moore, Margaret & Kees, Margaret Campbell, Margaret Dalman, Margit Dehnicke-Templeton, Margaret Joan Gilmoure, Margaret Küntz, Margaret MacIntosh, Margaret Woolsey, Margot Levitt, Maria Victoria Miguez, Marie Axler, Marie Larson, Marilyn Allpress, Marilyn Gang, Marilyn Harding, Marilyn Mayo, Marilyn Symes, Marina Zlat, Marion Jutzi, Mark Langan, Mars Islamov, Martha Fauteaux, Martha Lucier, Martina Giblin, Mary Grant, Mary Magilsen, Mary Stajan, Maryann Cockburn, Maureen McBride, Mavis Moss, Maya Maer, Mel Killens, Megan O. Ross, Melinda Glew, Melvin Killens, , Mercedes Cobham, Michael & Sylvia, Michael O'Connell, Micheline Kourmi (Crystal Song), Michelle de Moel, Mila, Moira Graham, Molly Misra-Loeb, Monika McCominskey, Munira Khambata, Myrna Poolton, Najna Pilgrim, Nadja Grace Wingert, Nancy McGregor, Nicolas & Ingie Massicotte, Nicholas Giannetti, Nicholas R., Nita Hill, Noelle Kemmler, Nora Anderson, Norm Grant, Olga Gel, Pam Busch, Pam Lacek, Pam Schneider, Pamela Gamache, Pamela Tarek, Pat James, Pat Rigby, Pat Vallejo, Patti Bayley, Paul Chester, Paula Laing, Paula van Sickle, Penny

Williams, Peggy Williams, Peter Duchemin, Petra Norris, Pina Carriero, Rachel Strauss, Rae Henhawk, Randall Fox, Renate Katharina, Rick Goguen, Rita Goncalves, Riverstar Luke, Rob Floodgate, Robert & Betty Hall, Robert Simmons, Robin Cargill, Robynne Tennant, Ron, Ron Cross, Ronna Smithrin, Rose Ann Kulyk, Rose Marie Barker, Rosemary Lee, Rosemary Tayler, Rosetta Kopping, Ruth Brainis, Ruth Piercy, Ruth Z. Bolchim Morgan, Ruxandra Stefanescu, Sabina Pampor, Sandra Callender, Sandra Cureton, Sandra Lachance, Sandra Richmond, Sandy Rempel, Sandy White, Sanjive Jain, Sarah Kern, Scarborough Gem & Mineral Club Members, Scott Zimmerman, Selina Kahn, Shari Sali, Sharin Silver Nadlar, Sharon Mollaret, Sharon Russel, Shawn Gallagher, Shawna Robertson, Sheila Mawji, Shelley Dagorn, Shelley Paul, Shelley Underhill, Sherene Clark, Sheri Lots, Sherill Allard, Sherrill Richmond, Sherry Essnashari, Sherry Shaw, Sheryl Bassett, Shirley Allsworth, Smadar Lorie, Snow, Starr & John Harrison, Stella Maguire, Stephanie Dixon, Sue Graham, Susan Graham Guddat, Susan Madden, Susan Stortini, Susan Trotter, Susanne Schmidt, Suzanne Mastragostino, Suzane Proulx, Svetlana Bezuna, Svetlana Liberla, Svetlana Yufest, Syd and Shari Sali, Sylvia Garratt, Sylvia White, Tamara Penn, Tammy-Lynn Porter, Tanya, Cameron, Tanya Hughes, Tanya Ruben, Tanya Sukhar, Tatiana Kalinovska, Tatiana Tminkovski, Terry Langevin, Theresa Wasowicz, Tia Sahlberg, Tillane Beaulieu, Timothy Lennox, Tom Kennedy, Tony Hoogeven, Tony Uberoy, Tracey Epitropu, Usha Makan, Usha Ramsaran, Valerie Crozier, Valerie Smith, Vanda Cordier, Vanda Komorovski, Vena McKay, William Oulton, Visnya Linardic, Yulia Jitkova, Yvonne Browning, Yvonne Connell, Yvonne Woods, and All others including clients, crystal suppliers, fellow vendors and my family in Canada and Sweden, who have supported my work, I value your friendship.

MODELS FOR THE PHOTOS & DRAWINGS Ann Perrera, Anna Koushinsky, Brahmani, Bob Jackson, Carol Heath, Carolin Denby, Elin Hammar, Erin & Emma, Gunilla Hammar, Gunnel Liljefors, Helen Masters, Ida Hammar, Ingie, Jarmila Thea, Johanna Koeslag, Judy Derrett, Julei Busch, Julia Dietz, Julia Potter, Karen Gellman, Karish, Katherine Salnek, Laurie Clark, Lily Brox, Linda Bingly, Louise Gallotta, Luciana Rocha, Marilyn Twintrees, MarliJoy, Pam Polley, Rebecca Fuller, Susan Kern, Tara Brox, Tawlia Chickalo, Terry & Theresa, The Azez, Ulymar Rocha, Yulia Jitkova and Anonymous Models.

Thank You!

List of Contents

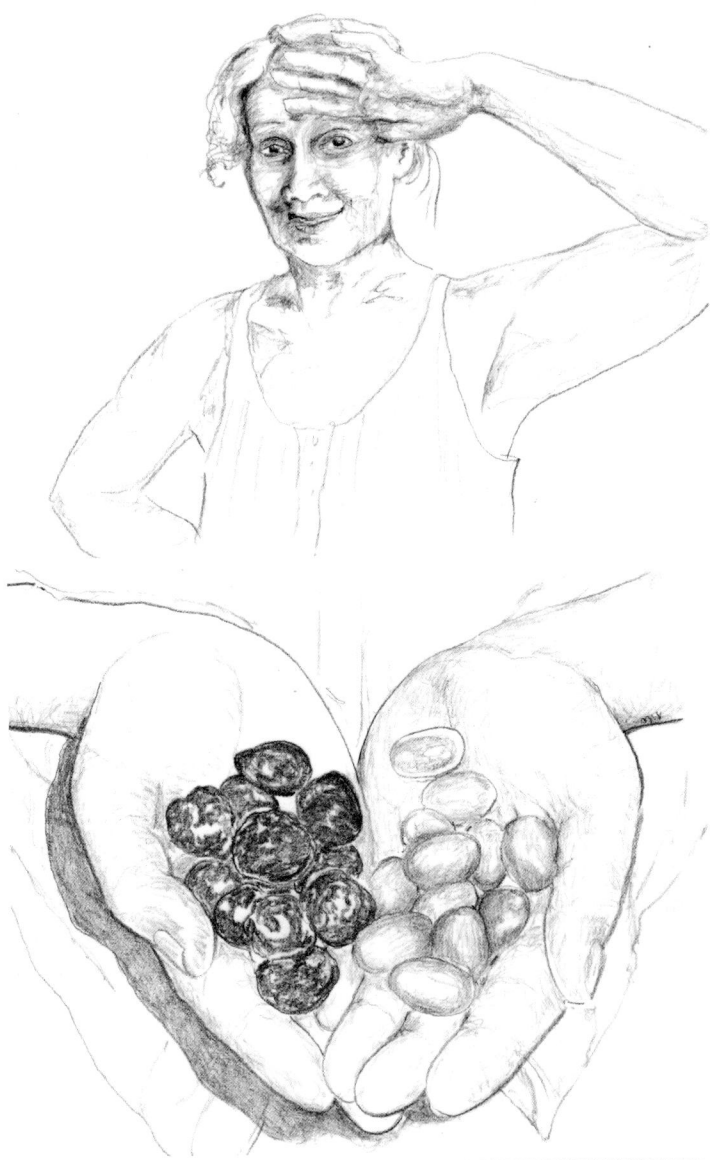

Figure 1 On the lookout for happiness, we may have to deal with both the good and the bad. Smokey Obsidian and light blue Angellite help us to deal with the dark and the light side of ourselves.

Beginning the Journey

To Love is to Know Intimately.
That is why we are here.

In ancient scripture[1] written in India some 5000 years ago, there are the discourses between Lord Shiva[2] and his beloved consort, Devi. Within these pages, many methods of achieving self-realization and liberation are shared. Devi asks Shiva questions, and he answers. One question in particular relates to the topic of this book: the question about how to deal with duality. Duality describes the polarities of good and bad, wealthy and poor, the multitude of opposites prevalent throughout all of life. The precise answer given to the question of polarities is that people should aim to be in the middle, walking a happy medium between the opposites. By being in this middle place, we are constantly moving towards the centre of our being. This is perhaps the root of what the Buddha[3] taught concerning the "middle way," around 500 BC in India. To illustrate this, he talked about how a stringed instrument was to be tuned: to produce a beautiful tone, the strings must be neither too taut nor too loose.

The crystals described in the list at the end of this book follow the format of two extremes with a resolving middle, the Crystal Key. Before we get there, however, I invite you on a journey that thoroughly answers the question: How can we use crystals for awareness, inner development and healing?

Crystals Mirror Our Story

Every particle in the Universe holds a certain vibration, a resonance of the energy of its initial creation. Crystals, as individual minerals, retain their original energetic birth patterning for extremely long periods of time - often hundreds of millions of years. Crystals therefore are considered to be the most reliable retainers of the original Divine Vibration of creation. The energetic messages from the beginnings of this planet can now be accessed via the beautiful crystals available today. By using crystals to assist aligning energies during the healing process, we are able to return to health and well-being and discover answers to many of the questions that now trouble humanity.

My intent with this book is to assist in the process of individual and group healing, allowing each individual to find a unique way to invite peace, love and abundance into his or her life. Unless you belong to the small group of people who were born completely self-realized, most of us struggle and cannot understand why we are not fully happy within ourselves or with our lives. Many of us spend a good portion of our lives yearning for and wanting to achieve things that we do not have, or struggling unsuccessfully to rid our lives of undesirable elements. An in-between stage occurs when all has failed and we just stay stuck, or when we are too comfortable to make any changes whatsoever. The result is that there is no movement and no potential for change. Boredom, struggle and challenge are growth-producing, (spiritually), and they give us an impetus to try to move out of a given situation. My belief is that we have come here to Earth in order to learn. Each life experience is an opportunity to gain greater understanding of what we are here to learn this time around. Any event that we have experienced in the past causes an imprint or memory within our systems. Strong emotional imprints cause bigger imprints than neutral ones. The imprints can be of a negative or positive character. It is important to note that imprints of extremely harmful or negative situations seem

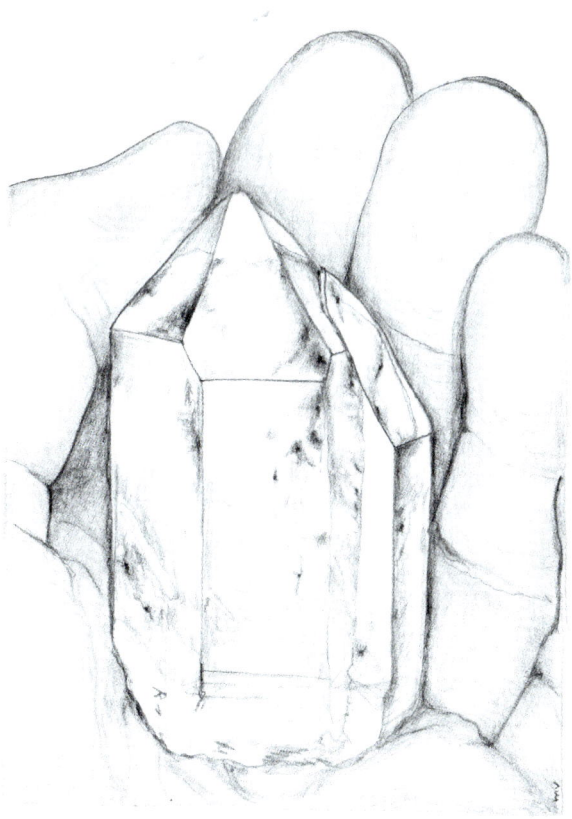

Figure 2 Quartz Crystal. To just be with a crystal and look into its depth is a meditation in itself. By allowing the natural world to speak to us, we may learn to appreciate the beauty and splendor around us, and begin to care about our planet more.

to stick with us more doggedly than positive imprints. The unhappy emotions take precedence over the pleasurable ones. It is easy to understand that when our ego[4] has experienced a situation perceived to be very dangerous, this experience strongly imprints subconsciously in order to avoid a repeat of that situation in the future. This phenomenon allows us to survive, to avoid harm, and to remain safe. From any particular event, we may construct a concept of what life is and how to best interact with that kind of situation in the future. As time goes by, we accumulate a vast database of responses to various events and situations that we think we need to have in order to live safely. All of this information is not necessarily available to us from our conscious memory, but it is nevertheless stored in various parts of our body and subconscious. Why is this so important to know? As long as there is a desire for something we do not have, suffering and unhappiness will be present in our lives. There are

Figure 3 A child collecting rocks on the beach. Notice how absorbed she is in the task of bringing them all home. She is naturally engaged in a moving meditation.

times when we believe that we are totally happy and have everything, and then all of a sudden something happens: an accident, a death, or some other unpleasant occurrence - and we are no longer happy. The seeds[5] of unhappiness remain dormant until triggered. Such imprints from the past cause us to react in the same way over and over again, even though those reactions may no longer be necessary or even helpful in our lives today. Our sub-conscious programs or imprints tell us that this is the way to feel and act in specific situations, yet they are solely going on what has happened in our past.

The Human Mind

A computer program that is slow or doesn't function properly is updated or replaced. This is normal common sense. The brain and memory functions work similarly to a computer's operating system and other installed programs. Any thought-form[6] present will engage when triggered. Non-beneficial thought-forms and resulting beliefs can be updated or replaced, just as a mal-functioning computer program can be. This process may not be so clear to most people. If the cultural programming from parents or society is very strong, there will be a strong reluctance to change a belief or habitual way of reacting, even though extreme harm can come from adhering to it. Beliefs that actually support life should, of course, be left in place. An original imprint (thought-form) contains a sort of hologram that has every detail remembered on all levels, including colour, scents, sensory information and the way to respond. These patterns are so ingrained in us that we no longer notice them. For example, we simply blink an eye when a speck of dust gets into it; we do not consciously think about doing it. These unconscious patterns are based on the past, and cause us to engage in both positive and destructive behaviours. Positive patterns give us life-affirming interactions and health, while negative ones may result in addictions or violence. If a memory pattern is very negative one tends to cover it up and store it away somewhere. It is still there, but we have forgotten about it. The response-pattern, however, is ready to be engaged when the right trigger comes. Boom! Think about what makes you angry and usually the person or situation triggering you will be blamed. Nevertheless, the response pattern is yours, and you are responsible to make the inner change.

Crystals can assist us in accessing our subconscious memories or scripts. You will see many examples of this in coming chapters. When we see our patterns for what they really are, we are able to create a future not from our past conditioning dictating our action, but from a place of choice. From this place, we can choose how we are going to feel or react to a situation in the present. This book is for you, as a help along the way to retrieve what I believe is our birthright: complete happiness. Crystal Healing and the practice of Crystal Yoga offer access to these imprints or thought patterns that may be causing illness or mental-emotional conditions.

How I Came To Know Crystals

In the past, I chose to explore extremes. I strove to have and be the best, and I tried to avoid the life circumstances that I didn't enjoy. Naturally, the worst happened in spite of my best efforts to avoid unpleasantness. Many good and pleasant situations also materialized, but at the time I was not balanced or centred. I have come to understand the balance of striving and struggling more clearly now. This is the process which actually leads us away from our centres. I began to see that the further I journeyed away from my centre, the more pain and suffering I experienced. In the process of doing so, I learned a great deal about my inner world, valuable self-knowledge that I can now apply to life. Like most children, I loved collecting rocks. My real connection with crystals, however, came into my life quite by chance. A friend took me to a gem show, and I was mesmer-

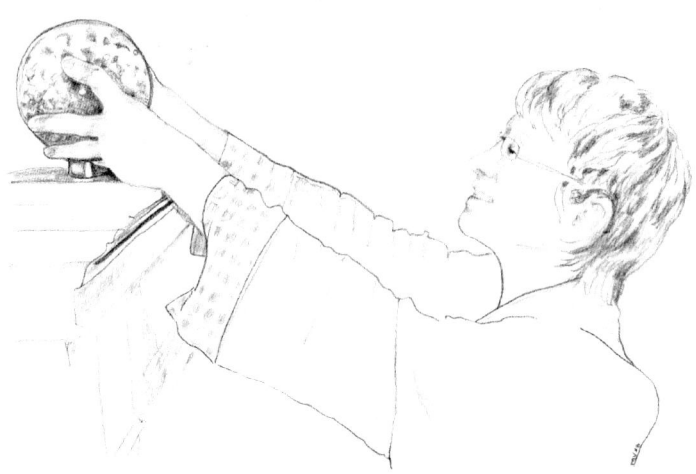

Figure 4 A sphere of Labradorite - the Stone of Magic.

ized by the variety and beauty of the stones. I became a collector right then and there. Eventually, I wanted to set the stones so that they could be worn as necklaces. In order to accomplish this, I also attempted to learn how to cut and polish stones and set them into jewellery.

My initiation into the deeper realm of the world of crystals came after I had purchased a rough piece of Labradorite at a silent auction in December, 1996. It was a small and quite inconspicuous piece that cost me roughly fifty cents. I began polishing it with the machine that I had rented for one month, from the gem club. It didn't take more than an hour and I remember feeling quite impatient to finish the stone. Afterwards, I sat down and looked at it, submerging myself in the layers of the deep luminescent blues displayed on its surface. I felt pulled into the stone, and I knew something in me was truly activated. I could not turn back from that moment. I felt compelled to explore all the aspects of the pull that I had felt. It was as though the stone itself or something within it, was calling me. It felt very much as if Alice[7] was calling to me from the other side of the looking glass: "I know something and I can share it with you. If you'd like to know, just follow me here." Within that small piece of Labradorite, I perceived an entire world of which previously I had had no conscious awareness. I was drawn to explore further. I began reading anything and everything I could get my hands on that would explain what I had felt.

A few months later, in the spring of 1997, I met my first real mentor in the field of the unexplained and unseen worlds, Betty Tersigni. I had found my inner calling. As I began working with her, layer after layer of my protective shielding lifted, as well as many personality traits that I no longer needed. My personal work is still ongoing, but the difficult process of letting go has become easier. I realized that all of us are going through a process of either ascension or descension, depending upon where we are within an unfolding consciousness. With the help of this little piece of Labradorite, I had literally scratched the surface of a magnificent realm. I had somehow become privy to a dimension of reality that I had not consciously known of before. In a very short time, new people and things began appearing in my life, and I began moving into a very new way of seeing. With the painful passing of my father and the ending of my marriage, I entered into a more self-sufficient phase of my life and into new relationships as well. Crystals became my modus operandi. I then studied with Katrina Raphaell in Hawaii. During my first stay on the beautiful island of Kauai, I entered a true purging stage where my emotions were flying very high. It became clear to me that many of my beliefs about life were obstacles to my growth and needed to be discarded. I am truly grateful for the initiations, guidance and help that I received there. Soon after, I began a Crystal Healing Practice and was asked to teach about crystals.

Summary

Duality is the view or condition from which we experience life. Events judged as opposites, either good or bad, are responded to either negatively or positively. If nothing happens we may be bored or feel stuck. We base our feelings on how we judge something, instead of accepting life as it is. In any person there are many subconscious programs that can be compared with a computer's operating system or program, which are dictating most responses and behaviour. When such patterns become harmful or destructive, a person suffers; however, it is possible to change this suffering by becoming aware. Crystals are containers for the divine creative vibration that made their form manifest. Crystals act as mirrors that may assist in detecting, reprogramming or erasing destructive patterns in the process of healing and self-realization. Thus, our life becomes increasingly freer and more enjoyable.

Figure 5 Crystals are beacons of light transmitting the divine facets of ourselves that we have forgotten, so that we can remember who we are. This is a huge pink Kunzite - the Love Commitment Stone.

Why Use Crystals?

Seeing Joy in a pebble is the delight of a child;
Become like a child, join in her delight!

Children know about the miracle of nature, especially stones and crystals. Whenever I attend an event with my stones, the children come to touch them in a state of wonder, not only one time but over and over until their parents get tired of it. Thea states:

> If we would see the crystals in their most rarefied state, we would see the true frequency of the entire creation which we live in.

The mineral kingdom is said to be the first density, or discrete vibratory level within the frequency spectrum of creation[1]. The plants are second and the animals third, continuing with further refined levels including angels up to the Godhead, as the least dense. It follows that the mineral kingdom is the furthermost extension of the Spirit in form. Crystals formed of individual minerals are the most evolved manifestation in their domain of matter. Essentially crystals are natural tools, given along with many other tools available to us, to aid us on our journey on Earth. People in the past have used crystals in a variety of ways: as external symbols of stature, as ritual items/icons, as tools for particular purposes, and in practices for manifesting wisdom

Definitions of terms used in this book:

Stone - can be a mineral or part of a rock. We use the word "stone" as synonymous with "crystal."

Rock - this is a formation consisting of several minerals, or mineral families together. For example, Granite comprises: Feldspar, Quartz and Basalt.

Mineral - individual member of a family that is defined by its chemical composition and structure. For example, Blue Lace Agate or Ruby.

Mineral family - Quartz is a vast family of minerals basically consisting of Silicone dioxide. Many minerals belong to this family: Amethyst, Rosequartz and Smokey Quartz to name a few.

Crystal - is a mineral which has manifested terminations. Here we use "crystal" as meaning any natural stone which may be used in healing and self-development. It can be in raw, polished, tumbled or naturally-terminated form.

and consciousness. The main reason for using a crystal is its specific helpful properties.

Let us look a bit deeper into the area of properties. They are either widely known or accepted, or unknown and sometimes questioned. We have:

> Measurable Properties
> Extra-Normal Properties

Firstly, the known properties are those which can be measured by a device or procedure accepted by conventional science. For clarity I name those "Measurable Properties." Secondly, properties that cannot be measured in traditionally accepted ways, I

will call "Extra-Normal Properties." These can fall into two categories: subjective and objective. "Subjective" relates to a person's
inner experience of the external brought inside, and the "objective" relates to something that is valid outside of any person's
individual perception of it. In this book I have explored my own
experience (hence subjective) of the properties of crystals. Just
because something is unknown at the moment does not mean
that it does not exist. History shows us proof of this. For in-
stance, during the Middle Ages, the Earth was believed to be flat,
because that was what could be seen by the eye. There was great
resistance to any replacement of this view. With humanity entering the space age, we can "prove" that the Earth is round because
we can "see" pictures of the Earth from space, showing clearly
that the Earth is really spherical. There is a tendency to reject
the unknown as dangerous, and thus we deny ourselves possible
benefits. My sincere intention, in this book, is to reveal what
is hidden so that it can be seen/felt/experienced/researched in
plain view for the benefit of a person's personal growth. Let me
quote the father of Gallileo, Vincenzo Galileo[2]:

*It appears to me that those who rely simply on the weight of author-
ity to prove any assertion, without searching out the arguments to
support it, act absurdly. I wish to question freely and to answer freely
without any sort of adulation. That well becomes any who are sincere
in the search for truth.*

A Crystal is self-contained and does not need anything outside
of itself: it is totally surrendered to its environment. It is, however, connected to its own species in the same way that a red rose
belongs to the family of roses. If one rose is picked and enjoyed,
the species of roses will still produce more roses if the nutrients
and conditions are favourable. Its life-time is short compared
to a crystal, whose lifetime may span aeons of time, from small
seeds of mineral conglomerations to fully blooming crystals, (as
terminated specimens) to their decay/destruction or erosion
and possible metamorphosis into a new life as other minerals or

other beings, until they again decompose into dust within clay and soil as a continuing cycle of "birth and death." Crystals are in this respect no different than other parts of creation, including ourselves as humans. We all have our purpose. Minerals are also essential as nutrients for higher life forms. Without minerals, plant and animal life could not exist.

How Did Crystals Appear?

Liquid water can be imprinted with information: it is shown[3] that only when the vibration is beneficial to life can such imprinted water solidify as snowflakes (crystals) when frozen. As a

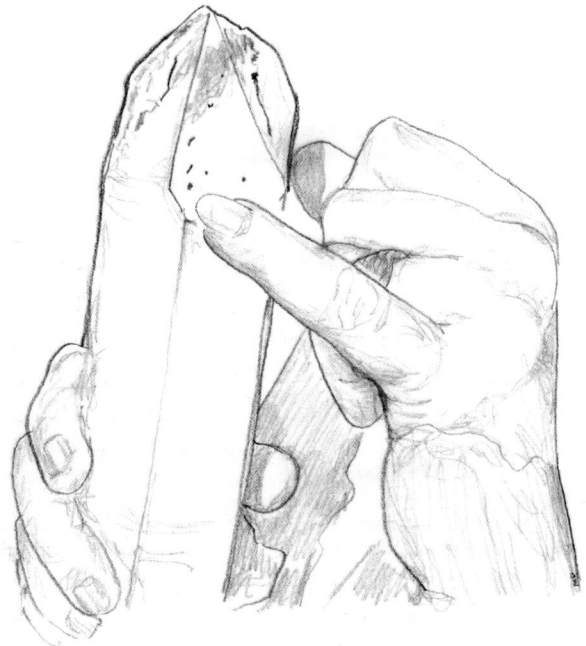

Figure 6 Record Keeper Crystal with small raised triangles showing on the main face. The records may be read by the keeper.

child I watched a saturated solution of regular table salt crystallize: as the water evaporated salt crystals would appear, if left undisturbed for a few days. The calmer the surroundings, the bigger the crystals would be. Other liquids or nutrient solutions create a vast array of crystals in the Earth following the same principle. In fact, crystals cannot physically form when the environment is physically or energetically unsuitable. Perhaps one might say that within molten magma, the environment is harmful to humans, but favourable to gestating crystals. Upon cooling, the molecules reach the required 'stillness' to manifest into crystal form. An example would be the Record Keeper[4] crystal, upon the surface of which one may discern tiny triangles - the records. A tuned-in person may decode such records from the crystal's creation. I would venture to say that crystals, like ourselves, are in fact the manifestation of the Creator's Love on Earth.

How Have Crystals Been Used?

Crystals have coexisted with humanity since the birth of mankind. Using crystals as objects of power, their keepers knew that their value was more than what could be seen on the surface. The magician's powerful crystal-tipped staff described in fairy tales and myths as a secret 'weapon' could indeed be very attractive to have in one's possession to use for either selfish or altruistic purposes, such as gaining increased awareness and control of one's world. The wise persons, however, knew that the magic is only within, and that becoming conscious is the only real way to gain true fulfilment. The crystals in their care provided a transformational focus to awake the sleepy mind. Crystals may allow the thought-oriented mind to relax into peace. From a place of serenity a person may be more able to let go and simply be. Habitual ways of thinking with which we have become identified prevent us from becoming our true selves. Crystals can provide a fruitful way to access inner worlds and change our conditioning. This was well understood by many ancient cultures that developed rituals for spiritual growth using crystals. For example, the Bible[5] describes the Breast-plate of Judgement worn by the high priest that included 12 crystals representing the 12 tribes.

Properties of Crystals

In the following summary I have attempted to illustrate some of the subtle properties exhibited in crystals. A crystal may act as one or more of the following descriptors.

The Anchor - grounding, containing, calming, holding, storing, creating boundaries, stability, binding

An anchor holds a boat from floating away and limits something from being dispersed. Most crystals are extremely stable compared to a living cell, and can in some cases withstand extreme conditions of time, pressure and heat, which are challenges to human life, and thus provide a template of stability. Our multidimensional spirit-soul is anchored in the third dimensional physical body. Being fully grounded helps us to function properly in normal life. A crystal may draw our attention to the lack of boundaries and grounding so that we may bring ourselves to be present and aware of what is going on. An example of an anchor is Black Tourmaline, which is used in the practice to improve balance and become more grounded.

The Sponge - absorbing, buffering, balancing

A sponge absorbs: we use it to clean up spills to be discarded or to retain moisture. After use we rinse it and squeeze out the liquid before reuse. Aragonite and Hematite act as a sponge. They absorb erratic energies from the environment, especially hot or violent emotions. This property is helpful in healing work where a person may release such energies or need to be protected from them.

The Shutter - filtering, cleaning, streamlining, sorting, harmonizing

 A shutter is used to filter unwanted light from a window. Energy or light may in the same way be filtered or streamlined though a crystal. The function of this type of crystal is to stream light precisely onto a target. This is used in a laser, facilitated by a ruby. The crystal structure functions as a filter. It streamlines the light and allows the laser to focus with such precision that it can cut though metals and can be directed to the moon or the far reaches of the solar system. Lasers have wide industrial, military and medical uses. The streamed light can be made so intense and focused as to melt and cut thick slabs of metal, or hair-thin tissue for delicate surgery. The lattices within certain crystals are able to be a conduit for an energy source in a similar way. Such crystals can be used by a person who is able to send healing energy such as a master of Reiki, Prana or Chi.

The Lens - amplifying, stimulating, expanding, opening, penetrating, strengthening, focusing.

 Scientists have found that a light beam is caused to bend or refract across a crystal surface, both on the way in and out of the crystal. If a transparent crystal is cut in a certain way, objects behind the lens become enlarged to the viewer. Lenses for microscopes, binoculars and early telescopes were made out of rock crystal (Clear Quartz) because of its ability to amplify and provide clarity, and for its consistency in structure. The image can be focused or enlarged

by the use of several lenses. In early man-made gems and glass, however, one might find waves, streaks and bubbles which would distort the path of the light and thus give a distorted image[6]. In navigation, a crystal's ability to refract was used in ancient times by seafaring Vikings, to discern the height of the sun over the horizon on cloud-filled days. The stone used was the Sunstone, which gives a colour flash only at certain angles[7].

For some spiritual traditions, prayer and devotional rituals often include preparing altars with icons painted with mineral pigments and sacred objects, made from various crystals. Crystals are placed inside certain religious statues/icons in order to concentrate and amplify their proposed powers. I once purchased a beautiful statue. Later, I had the pleasure to travel with a Tibetan Lama for a few hours. He blessed the statue for me and said to put crystals inside it to further empower it. By praying or practicing with a particular deity, the practitioner may aspire to embrace the virtues or the favours of that deity. Interestingly enough, that particular statue has on several occasions had bills of money manifest under it. The simple solution may have been that I had forgotten about putting money there, but the money was really needed when I found it.

Prayer can also take the form of reciting affirmations which would be amplified in the same way. The use of the Internet and computers has given rise to almost instantaneous co-ordinated prayer activity all around the globe. Any type of prayer, even that contrary to peace and the well-being for all, will be amplified in the same way. Users should be wary of the fact that what is going out will come back. In healing on a subtle plane, certain crystals can be used as a lens to amplify detrimental energy locked into our bodies and thereby facilitate its release. Generator Quartz and Elestials are examples of amplifiers.

The Mirror - reflecting, mirroring, clarifying, reminding

A mirror simply reflects a light or energy source. The moon is a good example. She reflects the sun's light for us to see to varying degrees during the lunar cycle. The ancient Chinese practice of Feng Shui also includes Crystals in its methodology. These Crystals are usually cut into fancy shapes and are intended to reflect and harmonize the energy inside a home or building, thereby enhancing the health and prosperity of its residents. Many people now draw on Feng Shui as a tool to harmonize their lives and their homes, and to contain and avert non-beneficial influences. In healing, a crystal may be used to detect troubled areas so that they come into focus. Healthy tissue will reflect more vitality than a blocked area. Crystals like Clear Quartz can be used to detect these areas by reflecting back to the viewer the level of energy present.

The Medium - impressionable, recordable, retrievable

The famous Emerald tablet was a green stone inscribed with letters relating to the wisdom of Thoth. The stone was used as the medium to store information. Computer technology does the same: by 'inscribing' small impulses into tiny Silicon chips within the computer, vast amounts of data can be stored and retrieved. This is similar to carving, except that it is on the level of energy, since we cannot see the imprints, even with a microscope. Ancient people knew that Quartz held energy and could be primed to release an energy charge. This can be felt as an energy jolt or a lightning flash. When exposed to mechanical pressure, electricity is produced[8]. This capability of Quartz Crystals has made them invaluable for modern technology, in radios, computers and watches. A Crystal may retain an energy imprint of its surrounding vibration. These imprints can be retrieved and transmitted as well. On a mental-emotional level it is also feasible to imprint and 'program' a crystal. For example, my teacher Betty had at one time programmed a Selenite crystal to assist in spinal alignments, for use in some healing sessions I received. The program placed within the crystal was later activated during the healing session. As the recipient, I experienced the energy as a piercing through of the blockages within my body.

The Window - illuminating, protecting

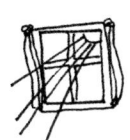 A window protects us from the wind and snow while being able to let light in. An external barrier like our skin or clothing also protects us. By adding additional items, like jewellery or cosmetics, we add further barriers to other people so that they are focused on seeing the outside first, and then they can make their decision on how to proceed with any interaction. At the dawn of civilization early humans also used stones and natural objects to adorn and protect themselves. Mineral pigments were used for murals and body decoration. Materials used included clays, chalk, alabaster, quartz, limestone, orpiment, charcoal, graphite, malachite, azurite, lapis lazuli and various metal oxides.

The Magnet - blending, absorbing, balancing, attracting, magnetizing, inspiring, aligning, harmonizing, healing

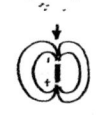 The Earth is surrounded by a magnetic field, caused by the occurrences of massive amounts of magnetic iron minerals within its core. Iron filings placed in proximity to a bar magnet will physically move to align themselves around it in a pattern following the Earth's magnetic field, and a freely suspended magnet will point to the poles. Seafarers used the magnetic property of lodestone for navigation, by simply floating an elongated piece on a cork in a bowl of water. Non-beneficial energies such as electromagnetic radiation, high

or low sound frequencies, light pollution and chemical toxins or geopathic stress, can contribute to ill health and unhappiness. From a healing point of view, certain placements of crystals in a grid may be established to address problems with erratic or destructive energy fields, in a space or in a house. The Grid would establish a new, more harmonious field by absorbing, deflecting or aligning such detrimental energies in the same way that iron filings would place themselves around a magnet. The grid becomes the magnet for the new situation. Intentional jewellery also sets up a grid that can draw to its user the intended result. By simply wearing a Crystal, one becomes bathed in its refraction and embraced by its energy. For example, if one's intent is to become beautiful, by using a Crystal, the mind is focused on being beautiful and the result is feeling beautiful. If the mind has that idea in place, the person emanates the beauty energy and others can see it too. This can be applied to other states such as being peaceful, forgiving, and focusing. Crystals assist us by maintaining the original intent over long periods of time. As a result, we are supported in our ability to achieve our purpose and the desired intent.

The Lighthouse - emitting, broadcasting, radiating, vibrating, pulsing

Gems present us with a splashing display of brilliant colours. What we see as colour is a precise part of white light that a crystal reflects, a veritable lighthouse in miniature. Lighthouses[9] are located to warn seafarers of dangerous areas, to guide them by broadcasting light or radio signals with unique signatures. When a traveller detects this signal, she knows she is on the right path. Each crystal also has its own unique signature that can guide us on our inner journey. Its source is both reflected energy and its own inner vibration that is emitted. All matter on Earth consists of molecules in very specific configurations. Within this structure of atoms, subatomic particles move constantly, as has been proposed by modern science. These subtle movements create a resonance or vibration that can be measured. In fact, scientists can tell us the composition of the elements in a distant star across the galaxies, by analysing the light it gives off[10]. These notable characteristics can be used for practice in healing by letting a crystal 'emanate' its vibration and thereby tune into or harmonize with the surrounding environment, such as personal space or a medium like water. Crystal Waters and Gem Elixirs can thus be created to assist in self-development and healing. Biodynamic farmers[11] are using crystals to broadcast nutrients into soil to enhance and harmonize their food production. This technique was common in past cultures as well. The ancients knew that Crystals were part of the makeup of fertile soil and they made up part of the inorganic materials needed for plant growth. Garden lovers will be pleased to learn that placing crystals near their plants may help them to grow more healthily and more beautifully.

The Portal - channelling, transporting, communicating.

 A portal, or tube connecting two places, may be used for transport from one place to another. In the modern radio it is, in fact, a crystal that picks up the radio signal so that we can hear sounds that are sent from a distant place. An inner portal can be established to finding answers to questions, and crystals may initially stabilize the ability to do so. Good examples of this are Labradorite, in whose luminescent layers I was allowed to access, and the Channelling Crystal[12] which allows for communication between places. Standing stones and labyrinths pose another example of portals between places separated by time and space.

Crucible - purifying, rarefying, transforming, moving, transmutation

 A crucible[13] is a place or situation in which concentrated forces interact to cause change. Wet clay is fired in a kiln, to be transformed into porcelain. Prevalent in the West are life styles that support accumulation of things and as a result, clutter and garbage are generated easily and unnecessarily. Clutter may create a lack of direction and clarity, as well as the inability to move forward. In some extreme cases there are so many things that there is no place to live. To reverse a clutter pattern, the offending clutterer must change his or her thinking and release the specific fears or unresolved emotions associated with holding onto the cluttering things. Crystals may assist in creating such a change within when we are ready. Even one minute of 'tuning in' can infuse fiery energy and the motivation for change. When the need to 'have' is diminished in a practitioner, more space is created and more energy is available to create satisfying effects, including money and fun. Examples of crucibles are Amethyst, Eudialyte and Garnet.

Summary

All life is based on crystalline structure. Models for crystal properties are described to enhance the understanding on the basis for using crystals for inner growth and healing. Because of the properties of crystals, the externally used inorganic minerals we call crystals have been used by humans since the earliest times of known history and for conventional uses in modern technology, including watches, radios, computers, data storage and navigation, as well as for extra normal (or unconventional) purposes such as: divination, scrying, healing, protection, gathering or managing energy and consciousness raising.

Figure 7 A benevolent presence beside us. Two crystal students in front of the 'Crystal Dakini' wall hanging. She models the placement of crystals used in healing.

The Teacher

Without Guidance,
I am truly alone...

One night many years ago I experienced the dark night of the soul. I intensely longed to come home. It was not just to go see my childhood home, but a deeper feeling that there was a place somewhere in the universe where I actually belonged, and where I could not lose my sense of peace. In the midst of that terrible night, I heard the word 'method' whispered in my ear from somewhere. I could not understand what to do at first, but it cut the emotional turmoil enough for me to begin to think clearly. Then, I just started to repeat the word over and over until I had come though the crisis I was in. I became curious as to what had happened to me that night. In the days that followed, I began to search for knowledge. I discovered that 'method' meant that I was to find a way by which I could become more aware of how things really are. My lower self's convenient comfort zone had been ripped open by my emotional havoc during that 'dark' night experience. This was the very place where guidance could be heard. My journey back home had begun in that very moment.

A true teacher can lead us to this place of peace. For some, Fear is the teacher. In a state of fear, one will make any effort necessary to either deal with it or avoid it. We may not like it, but when we can accept that any challenge or discord is really a teacher in disguise, the process of dealing with it becomes second nature.

By your side you have guidance to help you. Cultivating a state of surrender and humility may open you to be aware of your own personal adjuster or guardian angel. I suggest the name "Higher Self Guide," because it describes the division between a lower and a higher self, where the higher self is an extension of our source of existence, and the lower self is our inner child in training. When one pays attention to these impulses of guidance, one may experience the flavour of synchronicity and more ease. Staying connected continuously is the way to achieve the mastery one seeks to attain, in the process of self-realization. The integrating consciousness (our ego), on the other hand, is like a driver directing the child self by trying to predict how the road travelled will unfold in the future by means of looking in the rear view mirror. The great gift of attuning to guidance may be a permanent connection where the lower self is tempered and joined with the higher self. This is the goal for the work presented in this book.

Writing this book has been a tough teacher, as writing was my absolute worst subject at school. This is what I learned from doing it:

* Honour all my teachers who taught me all I know
* Always listen to my inspiration, my guidance
* Ask for help when I really need it
* My work should truly benefit others, and then it will benefit me also
* Love myself and all that I do
* When I face my fears, I go beyond what I believed I could do or be.

Listening to Guidance

What are spirit guides, non-physical teachers and channelled entities? To answer this question we might have to expand our mind to include the possibility of such beings. I feel there are beings that can teach us from beyond the barriers of physical reality. Some of those beings (that are channelled) are simply entities in the astral realms that may not be particularly enlightened. Others are bona fide masters, but if you are not sure, the best option is to find a living person who can teach you. You must verify that the teacher you seek is authentic and knows what he or she is teaching. A mere certificate on the wall may not count for very much: true experience and wisdom do, however.

What I propose here is that you seek your own direct connection with your source of being. It is an attempt to establish a direct link with your own higher self, since it is you yourself who is talking from a place of responsibility. It is not very wise to hand over power to another being. If you are sure that it is the divine part of yourself who speaks to you, then trust in the guidance you receive. A sure sign of true guidance is an uplifting feeling, triggered by joy and the awareness that what is said is always to the benefit of you and others. Negative actions against yourself or others are not true guidance at all. If you doubt, look deeply at your doubt, and then find something that you know is true and ask about it. You might want to keep a journal and compare entries over time. Common sense is always better than lofty words. Remember your higher self is directly connected with that which created you, and that can never harm you. Would a loving mother harm her baby?

Why: To be connected to real guidance, in my experience, is the most fulfilling feeling I have known. In spite of great challenges, it is a feeling of great trust and knowing. This inner feeling is prompting us to make choices to serve a higher good for all involved, but we might have to adjust some of our ways. There

Figure 8 Placement of the crystal Petalite, in the practice of connecting with inner guidance. Your stone will act like a lens and a magnet to draw out your heart's intent to have the loving vibration of true communication. Danburite or Angelite can be used in this practice as well.

must be a willingness to follow the advice given. If you ignore or discard what you receive it obviously will not help you or anyone else. In the beginning there are no questions to be asked, but allow for a state of mind that permits you to listen deeply without judgement. I have learned the gifts of the crystals by working with them. Crystals suitable in this way are: Angelite (the Angelic Guardian Stone), Petalite (the Spirit Guide Stone), and Danburite (the Spirit Heart Stone).

How to begin: Find an undisturbed place away from others, at home or in nature. Bring one crystal that strongly resonates with your search for guidance. I suggest picking one of the three stones above. Place it near your throat, which is the place of choice-making and truth. Make yourself as comfortable as possible in a seated position. State what you want, breathe it, feel your intentions strongly, and speak them out, even loudly, if the location permits. Use one or more of these affirmations:

I am open to receive my Higher Self's guidance,
I know your presence, communicate with me now!

I call upon my Celestial Guides and Teachers,
I feel your presence, as I listen to you now!

I call for my Guardian Angel to communicate with me.
I trust in your guidance, remove my barriers to hear you.

I am ready to listen to my Spirit's Guidance,
My heart knows your presence, communicate with me now.

Use at least 20 minutes to an hour, then become totally quiet and let yourself be open to receiving and to feel. At this second phase, allow at least 10-20 minutes. You may visualize how you want your guidance to look. The easiest is perhaps an angelic being such as a guardian angel. Your stone will act like a lens and a magnet to draw out your heart's loving vibration of true communication. Do not let your mind trick you. If you feel scared or have strange thoughts, ask that energy to leave immediately, then continue to ask yourself what you want: to know true guidance. For the first while, doing guidance sessions, expect only to touch the surface of your own undigested issues, but as you continue these layers will fall away. At some point you will experience the awareness that your intention is very clear and without doubt, and you are able to hold that feeling for a length of time. Then there may manifest a relaxation within, and a flow of very peaceful energy descending from above your head, or in your heart.

Effects: Depending on each person's capacity, you may gain an understanding of what true guidance is, and you will come to know that true wisdom originates in your heart, and thereafter it can be expressed by the throat in an effortless sharing without obstructions.

Maintenance: Continue with daily sessions until connection is made.

Crystal Care: The crystal is the outer symbol for your sacred quest. Treat the stone lovingly and store it in a personal place. Petalite and Danburite can be placed in pure spring water to be cleansed and then bathed in the sun for a few minutes. Angelite can be rinsed briefly in water but not exposed to water for any length of time in order to maintain its colour and shine. Bathe in the sun for a few minutes to energize. All stones (and humans) are best served by being loved.

Summary

At a certain stage of our journey our inner teacher or guide may be revealed. An attitude of surrender and humility demonstrates our readiness for the appearance of our guide. Also, a challenging event may open us up to become aware of how things really are, and it will change our life experience when we discover our individual connection to the source of our existence, represented by our guardian angel or high self. The 'character role' that we play, or 'lower self' may be seen as our inner child in training, guided by projections of past experiences (ego). A living teacher is invaluable to have on the journey of life and essential for those who seek total realization. By paying attention to the teachers present in different situations and things that happen to us we may awake faster to how things really are and thus become less afflicted by suffering. Finding our truth can be done by attuning ourselves to our living environment, including plants and crystals; we may perceive our own perfect place within creation and this perception will allow us make better life choices.

Practice:
Listening to Guidance - using Petalite, Danburite or Angelite

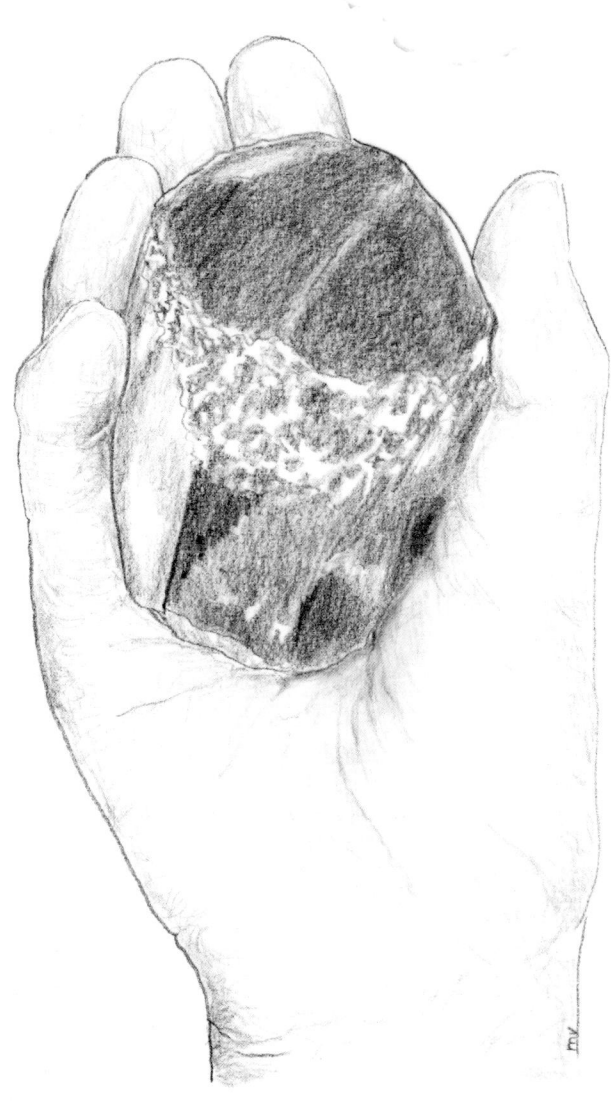

Figure 9 Black Tourmaline is a Spiritual Warrior Stone. It is helpful in practices to stay centred and grounded.

Ground Zero

*Earth is calling
Are you in?*

Airheads and space cadets on a coffee fix seem to move a lot of air, but do they get any real things done? And what are real things anyway? To answer this, one can look at how people work and what 'work' means. When I was young, we were not supposed to be lazy; working was the real thing, simply speaking, because when working one contributes, makes money, and is useful, and that is good. In school we were taught in physics that work is defined as matter moved against a gravitational pull[1]. This had to do with processes like carrying a load of bricks up a flight of stairs, but when dragging the bricks around on a cart on the same floor, no work was done. Returning to our airheads again, do they seem to run around in circles? Looking at them with the above definition in mind, we must conclude that no work is done and therefore their actions are useless. Is this true? In my experience from school, we were not taught to really relax or let our minds expand. Instead, we were programmed to be efficient and good at getting grades. This is not a bad thing in itself, but what was missing were some of the pieces that really matter, like knowing ourselves.

In order to find out who we are and to be true to ourselves, we may have to expand beyond socially-acceptable boundaries and not be 'working' so hard, as per the old definition. My grade school years pressed upon me the need to get the facts right and answer questions correctly. We very rarely got actual in-life situations to deal with, except at recess (I hated recess). Because of my particular needs not being met, I retreated into my head. Being in the head means being cut off or separated from other parts of one's being, such as the emotional and spiritual aspects, which consequently means being separate from others as well. Showing emotion was considered to be bad behaviour in general. I thought, as a child, that the spiritual was only something to do with church and preaching was something I didn't understand exactly. What I hadn't understood was that to be complete, one must connect all parts of one's being, including the body and the emotions. On a greater scale, that implies seeing the entire world as a vast interconnected being, where each part of creation belongs, including each one of us. If we are cut off in some way, we are not connected fully. In other words, we are neither centred nor grounded, which, in learning about consciousness, is vital.

Inside we have physical and subtle organs[2] that make the subtle connection possible. Within the spine is the spinal cord with nerves that relay bodily impulses to and from the brain. We also have subtle energy organs, undetectable by conventional means, yet they pick up on the emotional energy-environment around us. Most have experienced entering a room after a big argument; the air feels thick, sticky and unpleasant. Our separateness may manifest as withdrawal from others, from the Creator or parts of ourselves. When we do not fully reach down energetically into the Earth, but stay conscious mainly in the upper parts or even outside the body, we become "spacey" and unfocused. This is our vertical challenge. It is like a boat without an anchor in a storm. There is no control over where we might end up.

On the other hand we may be anchored in the Earth but horizontally displaced to one side or the other. In this case you will see a person with one-sided strong male or female attributes. Many women have been forced to live out of their male side in order to survive in the modern world. Such a woman does not easily access her feminine attributes or allow herself to be vulnerable. Intimate relations with others become difficult and challenging; her partners will inadvertently trigger those parts of her to become exposed. A man who cannot access his male side appropriately will have to use more of his female side to expresses himself. Such a man may experience being too vulnerable and having difficulties making decisions. Perhaps he becomes co-dependent, whereas the woman in this example strives to be independent.

The third alternative occurs when we have difficulty protecting ourselves. The reasons may be due to weak vital energy or lack of proper boundaries when interacting with others and their behaviours. The goal is to become balanced and take possession of our whole being, not just a limited part of ourselves. Crystals can be used to help us integrate our various parts energetically, to become grounded, centred and have clearer boundaries.

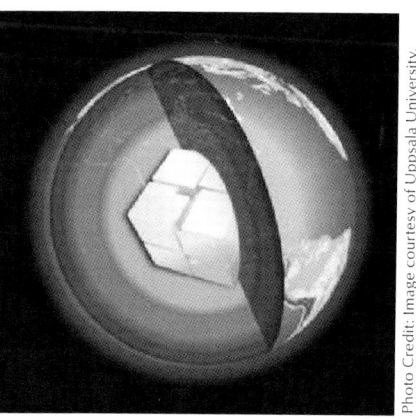

Photo Credit: Image courtesy of Uppsala University.

Figure 10 A proposed model of the earth's 1200 km massive core of iron to follow a defined crystal structure[3].

Setting Boundaries - Hematite Grid

Why: The central part of the Earth is said to consist of a molten metal core. Others say it is hollow, providing a place for other life forms. Recently a Swedish researcher proposed that the core of the earth consists of iron following a particular crystal structure. This actually supports my own experience on the topic. In either case, iron is a main constituent of the substances present there. It is logical to say that denser elements fall to the bottom (or centre in the case of a planet) and lighter materials such as gases go on the top. Since iron itself is rarely found in metal form because its nature is to rust in the presence of air (oxygen), one has to mine its oxides as a source. The red earth one can find in some sacred places is such rust, or iron oxides mixed with soil particles. This is mostly Hematite, which is considered to embody yin/feminine/receptive energy. Hematite feels heavy if held as a tumbled stone or naturally formed specimen. It has an absorbing quality and in this way extremely yin, or feminine. It is magnetic in nature and can be magnetized. Compare the effect a bar magnet has on iron filings. The filings form circular patterns around the magnet.

Tumbled pieces of Hematite[4] are used in healing to establish a boundary for the workspace much in the same way as a good fence prohibits an aggressor from entering. A person may use this stone to learn how to develop healthy boundaries. The benefits are that one may learn how to keep the energy in the personal environment harmonized and the outer boundaries of the aura well defined, and flexible to current situations. It is easier to manage a small area than a large area. This stone has been considered a great helper for persons who have a tendency to space out and get unfocused. Some even attach Hematite to their ankles for that reason.

How to begin: To work with Hematite, make a simple rectangular grid of four pieces of tumbled stones. They can be used around

Figure 11 Hematite grid with four tumbled stones around the body. Notice how much space this person allows herself to have.

a workspace, around a treatment table, around a bed or a sanctuary. In preparation for personal practice or meditation (in a seated position) or healing session (in a horizontal position, face up) place four pieces of Hematite around the intended space, making the area large enough to be comfortable. Then find a comfortable position. Close your eyes and let your body relax.

Take a few deep breaths and exhale slowly. Visualize the stones placed around you. Even if you might not feel their presence right away, you might use them as a point of reference for an imagined line of defence against anything that may intrude on you. Spend a few minutes visualizing this boundary line around you, then simply relax and allow your body to sense where the stones are placed, and discover how it feels. You might also find your thoughts wandering and sensations occurring in your body. Accept this happening without trying to control it. When you become aware of any distractions, quickly return to the visualization. Remain as long as you are comfortable, then open your eyes and look at the stones again. In the next step move the stones closer to you but at least the width of your palm away from your body, and repeat the process. You might experience the space as tighter and more confining. To finish this practice, extend the space out to create a rather large area, perhaps two arms lengths away from your body. Spend about 3 to 10 minutes in each step. Afterwards remove the stones and just remain in position. This may give you a sense of how far your personal boundary extends.

Effects: By practicing visualization, you are engaging your intuitive centre, located slightly above the midpoint between your eyebrows. By varying the distance to the stones you might observe a difference of feelings and sensations in your body. Discovering where you place your personal boundary may reveal to you how much private space you allow yourself. It may be too expanded and not very strong or too narrow and compact, letting nothing in. The choice is yours to change it in a way that serves you.

Maintenance: Repeat this preparation daily for a week or longer until you clearly feel your natural boundaries strengthen.

Crystal Care: Clean the stones often by placing them in pure spring water overnight. Hematite needs to be cleansed and cleared often because of its absorbing quality.

Dispelling Negativity - Black Tourmaline Warrior

Why: Black Tourmaline is a stone that terminates into very long shiny columns in favourable growth conditions. It is considered to embody yang/masculine/active energy. Visiting a mine in Brazil, I have personally seen black Tourmaline crystals, stretching out the height of three-story buildings within a rock face. This crystal is an excellent model for working with the spine and for anchoring the spinal energies into the Earth. This is helpful when one has to be active as well as interactive with one's

surroundings, while continuing with the inner focus. This practice is centering and grounding. The secret is in your tailbone. Some esoteric mystery schools taught their students to invisibly elongate the tailbone out from the body. This would give the practitioner a third leg to stand on, which in combat gave them extremely good balance. Masters of this technique would show no sign of disturbance, keeping their inner stillness, even during extreme or challenging outer circumstances.

How to begin: In a standing position, visualize your spine being a straight and very tall black Tourmaline. See it as a tall tower extending upwards above your head, and downwards below your feet into the earth. See yourself become invincible, your spine extended and firmly planted in the Earth like the long tap root of a growing oak. Then make your spine become wider and wid-

Figure 12 Practice with black Tourmaline visualized. Notice that the heart centre opens when both the top and the bottom of the aura connect.

er until it becomes like a full-grown tree, as wide as your torso. If you know the yogic Tree Pose, you may use it here, standing on one leg at a time.

Effects: Your personal energy goes where your thoughts go, so your auric skin becomes reflective and impenetrable like the sides of the Tourmaline. Aggressive or invasive energies directed at you will just bounce off without harming or affecting you in the least as you become proficient at it. In a line-up you may find that waiting times seem shorter and your mind is less stressed. Also, I have found multi-tasking is easier when the Tourmaline spine is activated.

Maintenance: Whenever you are standing, practice the Tourmaline Warrior Stance. Even when you do not have the actual crystal with you, maintain the visualization by seeing it cleansed and brightened by light and energy.

Crystal Care: Rinse your black Tourmaline in water as needed and place in the sun to energize often.

Protection - Black Obsidian Bubble

The image of a terrifyed child illustrate how we might have reacted to an event in the past. If we were not able to deal with the situation, the experience was frozen and encapsulated. What actually happened may be different than what we perceived, but it was deemed to be too much to handle at the time, so therefore a small part (or fragment) of us took it on, and is still holding it until healing or therapy can access and release it. These small fragments are safely tucked away somewhere, and are like three-dimensional video clips showing our age, how we were dressed and all the circumstances we believed to be accurate at the time of the event. Freeing up of such parts is the essence of healing.

When all parts of our being are reclaimed we are truly free.

Obsidian[5] is a brittle volcanic glass extruded as a product of fiery volcanic action. It is considered to model neutral/child/detached-observing energy. Rapid cooling creates a somewhat  transparent glass with a smoky lustre. A glass is a type of solidification that randomly places the molecules in the material extruded. It does not have time to make nicely-ordered layers, and thence it is a glass. Children growing up under perceived or real abusive or horrendous circumstances could be seen as having a similar growth patterns. Instead of dealing with and integrate their experiences properly; denial, fragmentation and other coping mechanisms appeared as viable alternatives. Obsidian, formed quickly in volcanic action, is therefore the ideal material, in my experience, to begin accessing and healing such past events without falling into destructive reaction patterns.

Why: Obsidian Bubble practice trains us to repair and engage our natural protective defence system. When such repairs are done one may be able to release encapsulated fragments without further harm.

How to begin: Find an undisturbed, safe and comfortable place. Gaze into a gold-sheen Obsidian sphere, or the picture of it. Then close your eyes and visualize the image clearly in front of

Figure 13 Reactions from traumatic experiences may cause us to fragment ourselves and then store such fragments under heavy shielding (encapsulation). Healing may revisit these events and free us.

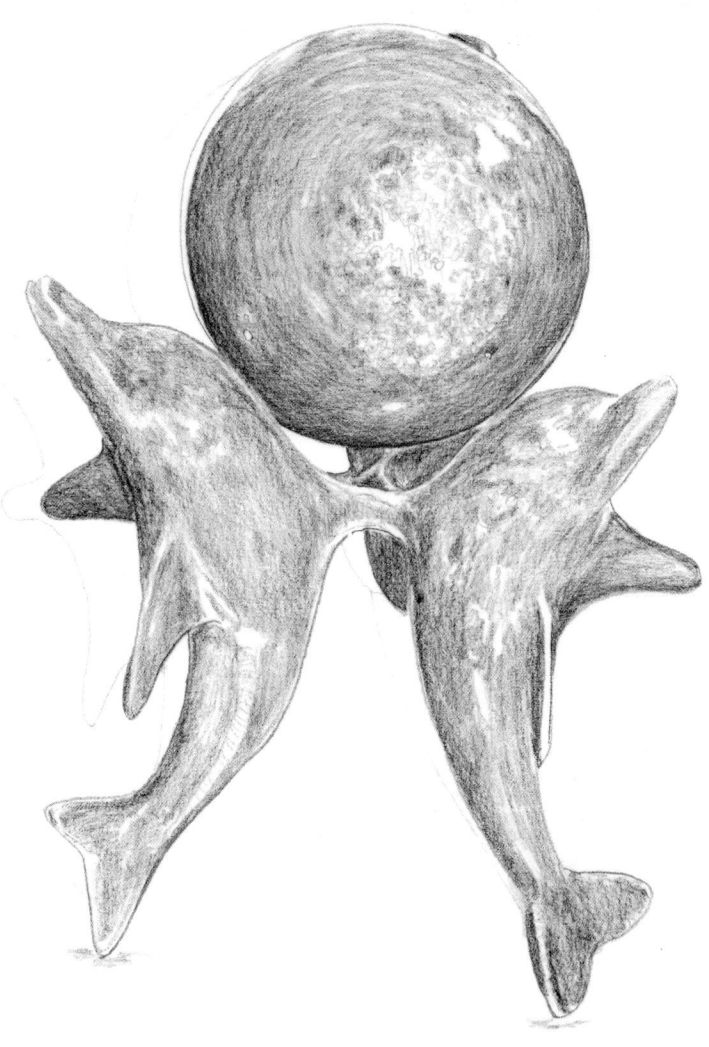

Figure 14 Black (gold-sheen) Obsidian Sphere - the Protection Stone, used in the practice of developing safety and confidence to heal traumatic experiences from the past. Top right: Visualized Obsidian Bubble with the silver-gold life support cord, connecting us to the physical and our source at the same time.

you. Continue by making this image larger and larger until it extends to the size
of your aura. Place yourself in the centre
of this bubble. The outside of the bubble is shiny and impenetrable, but from
inside you will notice how you can easily see to the outside. Any energy from
outside cannot penetrate inside to harm
you. Only healing light can reach you. It
comes through the bright shining gold-

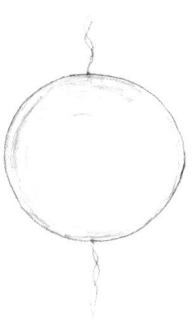

silver cord connecting your central channel via your Soul Star[6]
chakra, above you, to your Source, and extends via your Earth
Star chakra below, to the centre of the Earth. The feeling inside
the bubble should be visualized as that of being in a very resil-
ient soap bubble with the very thin and flexible gold-silver cord
going though it, holding it safely in place.

Breathe in brilliant light though this life support cord. Inhaling
from below and exhaling upward will bring expansion to your
thoughts and mind, while inhaling from above and exhaling
down will increase a sense of safety and grounded well-being. If
you are using the Obsidian Bubble protection for inner journeying, notice how you can direct your bubble with your breath.
You may navigate this as a ship, both in space and time.

Effects: Obsidian Bubble practice has proven helpful in energetically disturbing and stressful places. Anyone who is receiving
physical or verbal abuse can benefit by practicing being in a safe
bubble. One can then step by step build up a normal inner confidence of safety. The advantage with this type of exercise is that
one can begin to observe what is going on, instead of shutting
down. (If you are exposed to violent abuse, you should engage
your bubble immediately and physically remove yourself to a safe
place, and also take steps to seek help or therapy with a qualified
person you trust.)

Figure 15 Taking a stand for yourself and redefining old boundaries are essential for healing of traumatic experiences. In Obsidian practice one visualizes a flexible and permeable protective bubble that gives a small, but necessary distance to such events. Then one have a possibility to process and integrate them safely.

Maintenance: Try it on the subway or in a crowd of stressed people. As well, if you were to be energetically attacked or confronted beyond your comfort levels, engage your Obsidian Bubble.

Crystal Care: Obsidian is a soft stone easily scratched by metal. Place your obsidian sphere in the most sacred space you have created in your home. Let it be energized by the sun often.

Summary

In public school, work is taught as the means to foster good citizens but not necessarily to learn about consciousness. Learning to be grounded is a first step to become conscious and can be practiced three ways: vertically, horizontally or both at the same time. Hematite (yin/feminine/receptive), a common mineral in the Earth, assists in setting boundaries and making space for ourselves by energetically creating a safety grid around us. Black Tourmaline (yang/masculine/active) brings forth our ability to correct horizontal displacement. By practicing to stay centred and accepting each side of the body, the male and female sides can come to dynamic balance. The third option of staying centred with focus uses Obsidian (neutral/child/detached, observing), which helps us create a natural safe boundary so we may remain centred even when space orientation is unknown. This stone is also used in the practice of *Inner Journeying*.

Practices
Setting Boundaries - Hematite
Dispelling Negativity - Black Tourmaline
Protection - Black Obsidian Bubble

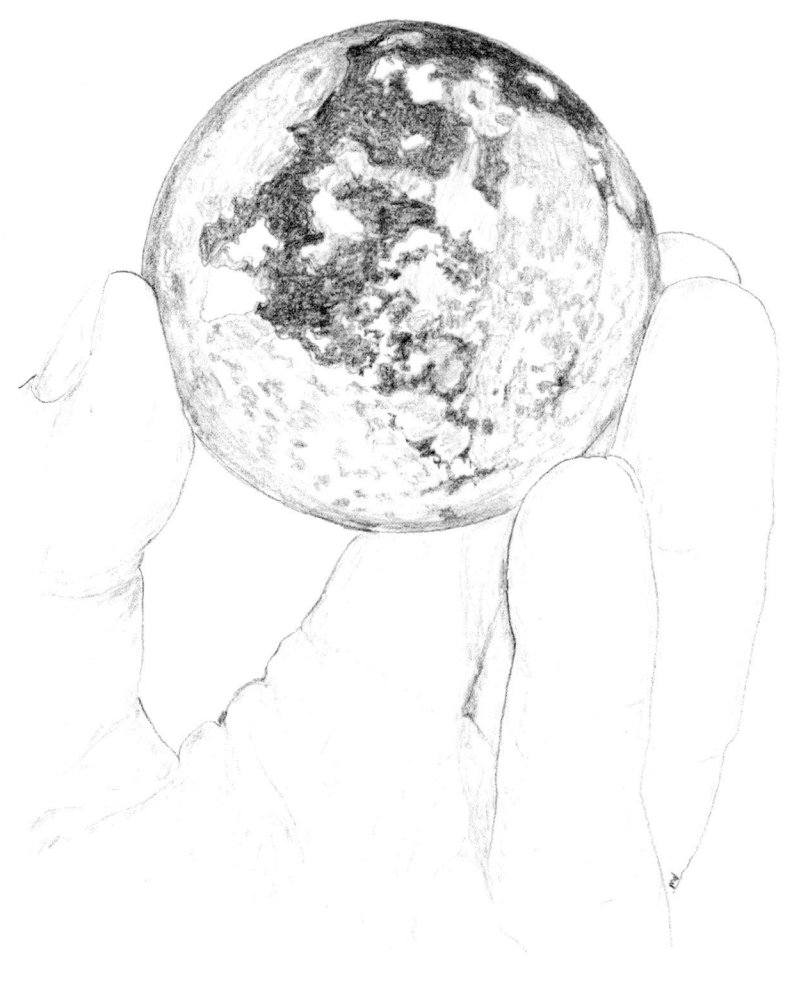

Figure 16 Eudialyte is a deep red complex silicate exhibiting black and white inclusions. It is an ideal stone for bringing anger and its related emotional states into proportion and resolution.

Crystal Touch

Having a Ball
Can't be missed

A lover's touch is beyond words; however, when the lover isn't here, we must take care of ourselves. Here are two practices using crystal balls as massage tools. All you need to begin with is a crystal ball and your hands. In reflexology it is taught that points on the feet, hands, and ears correspond to organs in the body. When these points are touched, impulses of healing are sent to the organs, and blockages in them are released.

To begin we will focus on the reflex points in the hands. Say that you arrive home feeling angry about traffic, the day, your boss, the weather, your family or all of the above at the same time. Instead of being disgruntled, enjoy a private and lovely healing time alone, using a crystal ball. In this example we can use an Eudialyte ball as it is a wonderful helper in emotional times. When we do not know what we want except what is missing, an Aquamarine ball is a great helper, as this stone gently assists us to find our truth by shifting what we thought was possible. For children and general relaxation we may use a sphere of Rose Quartz. The practice is done without any oils or lotions and is effective even through layers of clothing[1]

Hand Massage with Crystal Balls

Why: Using a sphere for massage is beneficial as we may have better control of where pressure is placed. The crystal may help you move stuck energy, thereby opening energy channels. It also teaches you to begin to notice your sensations in an organized way, which may lead to insights about causes of existing ailments. Crystal touch may provide a safe contact for persons who are over-sensitive to being touched.

How to begin: Select a small ball. Look at your hands, and tune in with the beauty and wonder of having hands. Visualize that along the skin are contact points to the rest of your body; there is no need to be too specific or worry about reaching the right points. Start at the lower corner of your palm, circling the small ball up to base of the little finger, then continuing to the tip, as shown in the drawing (top left). Move the ball in a circular motion up and down, so that you cover the entire surface of your palm, including in-between and the tops of your fingers and thumb. Then do the other palm and around the wrists, continuing with the back of the hands in the same way. You may find

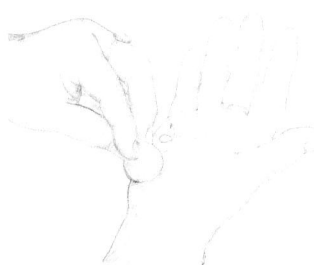

that certain points on your hands feel sore; in that case, make tiny gentle movements with the ball on that point until the soreness is released. Adjust the pressure so that you are comfortable, but keep it firm enough so that you do not drop the ball. When people drop the ball, it is usually because they are moving the ball too quickly. A slower pace is better, for then you may feel when the ball touches a reflex point, which some may also feel in the corresponding organ.

Effects: After a session people report being more relaxed, more centred, less stressed and happier. Touching the reflex points[2] is a balancing and gentle way of sending healing to your entire body. Sitting for a few minutes doing this practice is very calming and can be combined with other things like watching a movie or having a nice conversation with someone. When applied as a personal practice, it is an inroad to address one's life situation, and it introduces you to yourself. Hand massage is truly relaxing and reduces stress.

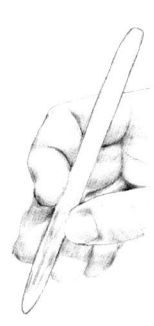

Maintenance: Invest your time in daily massages for at least a month. It is an ideal solution for busy people and for elders. Children love it (with adult supervision when necessary). Make it a pleasurable occasion to look forward to. Have your crystal

Figure 17 Laurie is showing how to use a small Aquamarine ball. This size is ideal for reaching in between the fingers, where you find the reflex areas for ears and eyes. The ball is slowly touching the entire surface of the hand in small circular movements. Reflexology Wands are also great for working with the points on the ear and hands as it provides more control over where pressure is placed.

Figure 18 Spheres can be used to relieve pain in the body. By applying gentle massage, you control the pressure and the speed with which the crystal is moved. A student said after being massaged: "It felt like a vacuum cleaner went over my whole body to whisk away my aches and pain." Another student said with obvious relief: "How could I possibly have missed this experience."

balls with you everywhere: on the train, waiting in line or in front of the TV. Why not do healing for yourself at any time you are able? Give a crystal hand massage to someone you love and appreciate!

Crystal Care: Wash your crystal balls regularly, to remove impurities from the surface, then rinse them with pure spring water. You may also energize your crystal balls in the sun for a few minutes when you feel the stones begin to look dull. To avoid burns or fire, never leave a transparent sphere in a window, as it acts as a lens!

Massage of Head, Neck and Shoulders

Why: This gentle and relaxing self-practice is an easy way to tend to aches and pains in the head, neck and shoulders. If assisted by a friend the entire back can be treated. One does not need to be an expert therapist to begin this practice, but if this is done for particular health reasons, deeper knowledge about your situation may be necessary. When the pressure is fairly light, the lymphatic system may be accessed, which may assist in reducing swelling and improve circulation.

How to begin: Sit in a comfortable position. Select a small-to-medium-sized ball for the head and shoulders. Start at the top of the head and roll the ball with tiny circular movements to the back and downwards to each side of the spine. Cover the entire area of the head down to the neck and shoulder, as far as you can reach, except the face. Make a short stop at the base of the skull, making tiny circles there before continuing down the neck as far as you can reach comfortably. Complete each stroke by circling on the endpoint for a while. Always massage on each side of the spine and never directly on it. Then bring the ball up to the top of the head again. Start at the top again slightly to the

Figure 19 A black Tourmaline sphere used in sphere massage is very relaxing and assists in grounding excited emotional energies. Persons who are stressed and exhausted might try it with success.

side of the centre back-line, paying attention to the lower edge of the skull. When you reach the side just behind the ear down to the corner where the neck meets the shoulder, stay at this point as long as you want, making circular movements before continuing to the sides along the top of your shoulder to the point where the arm is joined.

For the face, change to a smaller ball (one inch in diameter). Give yourself an incredible face-lift by moving the ball on the centre front line, from the base of the neck, where the collarbones meet, upwards over your face to your hair line and the top of your head. Then begin again, upwards along parallel lines toward the sides, until you reach the front of the ears.

The ears: If you'd like to include the ears you might use your smallest sphere (half-inch in diameter) or a reflexology wand. Gently roll the tiny ball around the entrance to the ear canal, moving the sphere gently outwards along the shape of the ear until you reach the outer edges. Then continue down the back of the ear, to where the ear meets the head. Do not massage inside the ear canal.

Effects: Crystal ball massage is one of the nicer things you can do for yourself, as it clears your head, may alleviate a headache, and in general, relaxes your system. It contributes to feeling refreshed and more alert. If you are working with a partner, make it into a special and loving treat.

Massage of Chest and Belly

Rib cage: Sit down comfortable on a chair. The centre front can benefit by sideways strokes in between the ribs and along the lower ribs and diaphragm.

Breasts: Start from the armpit and gently roll a 2" ball towards the nipple, but not touching it. Each stroke goes toward the nipple. Cover the entire surface of the chest. The region under the collarbones will especially benefit from this very gentle massage.

Belly: Start at the solar plexus and make circular movement, small first and then slightly larger, both clockwise and counter-clockwise. Then move to the navel and repeat with a larger ball. Include the entire belly, with larger circles moving toward your left side and downward, to aid digestion.

Crystals for Massage:

Rose Quartz (nurture & love) ideal for chest and front of body

Smokey Quartz (grounding and clarity) ideal for hips and legs

Aquamarine (purpose & relax) ideal for hands and upper body

Tiger-eye (uplifting and strengthening) ideal for belly

Black Tourmaline (negativity release) whole body

Eudialyte (emotional resolution) ideal for solar plexus and hips

Gold Calcite ball (being present) ideal for facial massage

Clear Quartz (for balance and attunement) whole body

Stones displayed above: Rutillated Quartz (energizing) centre, Angelite (calming and consoling) top right, and Fluorite (breathing room and mental space) left.

Hips and thighs: With a larger ball (3") you may access your hips and thighs. Start right behind the hipbone, with small circular movements, and move downwards. Next, start another downward movement further towards the back, until you have covered the entire surface, down the sides, and as far back you can reach.

Inner thighs and upper leg: Start in the groin area just inside the hip bone, moving the ball in small circles downwards toward the knee. Move each parallell stroke up and down, one outside the other, until the entire area of the thigh, side and back is covered.

Knee, lower leg and upper feet: With your right hand place the ball gently at the back of the right knee, and move the ball very gently in small circles touching the entire back of the knee, then make circular up and downward-strokes over your calf muscle from centre back ending at the out side of foot near the heel. Change hand, and continue massaging the right calf from the back centre line to the inside of the fot. Having done the back of the lower leg proceed to the front, first the outer and then the inner side in the same manner ending your downward stroke at each toe. Avoid the front bony part of the lower leg. Then switch to the other leg.

Soles of Feet: If you are able, put one foot up onto your knee and begin moving the small ball (1 - 1½") in the same way as was instructed for the hand. Cover the entire surface of the sole. If you prefer, place a medium ball on a towel on the floor and place your foot on top of it. Move one foot at a time in a circular way over the ball, thereby massaging the entire surface of the sole.

Full Back Treatment

With the assistance of a friend or a therapist, treat the entire back. The basic circular movement is the same as for the hands.

It is important not to massage directly on the spine; instead, move the ball slowly and gently up and down each side, in lines parallel to the spine, covering the entire surface of the back of the body.

Why: Anyone can benefit from crystal sphere massage. It is an easy and relaxing treatment that almost anyone can do.

How to begin: The person treated is positioned face down on a comfortable mat. Cover with a thin blanket if needed. Begin with a fairly large sphere, (even as large as 6 inches in diameter). Roll the ball very gently and slowly, from the base of the neck at each side of the spine down to the tailbone, then upwards and slightly to the side, so that the entire surface of the back a is covered. Continue with a smaller ball, on the back of each leg.

Our Crystal Tools

Size matters! A very small ball (¾") reaches the reflex point more precisely, especially in the ear. A larger ball is great to use on the back and large muscle areas. Try out which sizes you find easiest to work with, here are some suggestions:

½"	ears and between fingers
¾"	face, hands and arms
1-2"	neck and head
1½ - 2"	chest, breasts and diaphragm
2"	solar plexus
3"	navel and lower belly
3-6"	the back
3-4"	hips and thighs
2"	knee and lower leg
1 - 1½"	soles of the feet

Summary

Massage with crystal balls is fun and relaxing and may develop sensitivity to the needs of the body and its functions. This chapter describes how to do crystal ball massage for the entire body. Hand and foot massage may also access the reflexology points to vital organs in the body. The head and shoulders and entire surface of the front and sides of the body can be massaged while seated. The upper back and head massage can be used to connect with the meridians and opening the channels of the body. One may use different sizes of crystal balls from ½ - 6 inches in diameter, made from, for example Rose Quartz, Smokey Quartz, Aquamarine and Eudialyte, as well as golden Calcite.

Practices:
Hand Massage with Crystal Balls
Massage of Head, Neck and Shoulders
Massage of Chest and Belly
Full Back Treatment

Figure 20 A Healing Professional's set of crystal balls. From left to right: Black Tourmaline, Rosequartz, Clear Quartz and gold sheen Obsidian. In the hand a small transparent gold Calcite that may be used on the face.

Figure 21 Citrine Cathedral Lightbrary. A master crystal showing humanity its source of plenty and a new beginning for manifestation to be attracted. A practice with Citrine facilitates clearing ourselves for change. The cathedral form of Citrine provides, in addition, inner access to the wisdom of self-empowerment and purification.

How Did I Arrive Here?

Look to your body:
It reveals how you think

Close your eyes for a moment and see yourself in the ultimate place of happiness. What does that picture look like? If your picture differs from your present situation, you might ask: What caused my present situation of relative happiness, which changes moment to moment? And why am I still yearning for things I don't yet have?

Life will manifest according to how we think. That is how we arrived at this particular moment in time. To make change possible the crux is to invite other thoughts than those we are currently entertaining. Most of us are habitual thinkers, thinking the same thought forms over and over, causing mental-emotional freeways to be formed. The paths are so ingrained that a real clearing must happen before we can begin taking in anything new. Our bodies and homes are perfect repositories, and store the results of whatever we believe for ourselves. Similar to experience a cleansing diet that clears one's body of chemical toxins, one can also engage in a clearing of subtle mental emotional strata, including deposits of toxic feelings, hidden sources of much anguish and pain. It is well established that negative emotions contribute to physical illness, poverty and other unfavourable conditions.

Can crystals give me happiness and well-being? Well, no, they don't. You have to make that happen by your effort and mind power! However, the crystals provide perfect tools to help you along the way. In this chapter we will meet three crystals: Citrine, Tiger-eye and Pyrite. They are ready to assist you to make room for the new ways of life that you desire.

Breathing the Stone I - Citrine

The powerful vibration of Citrine is what I would imagine a supernova to feel like if it were to radiate through my solar plexus. Citrine has helped me trust and follow my intuition and feel confident about offering my gifts to the world.   Mary Davis

Why: A first step can be to clear yourself so that something new can come in. The Crystal to use is Citrine, the Clearing Stone. Citrine, with the elemental energy of airy fire, acts as a general clearing and purifying device, thus making room for whatever changes one may wish to make. Also, it prepares you for a fresh start with new inspiration.

How to begin: State what you are ready to change in your life, be it physical health, or any other condition that separates you from being happy. Find an undisturbed place where you can practice without interruption. Bring your crystal, or visualize an image of it. Breathe in its light-golden colour, and let yourself embrace the light and glow of it. Place your crystal so you can easily gaze into it. Seat yourself comfortably with your spine straight. Relax with a closed mouth, let the teeth separate slightly and place your tongue toward the roof of the mouth. Look deeply into your crystal with a soft relaxed gaze, and then focus on a single point within the crystal. Hold this relaxed focus during the entire session. Continue to 'inhale' the crystal through your eyes and

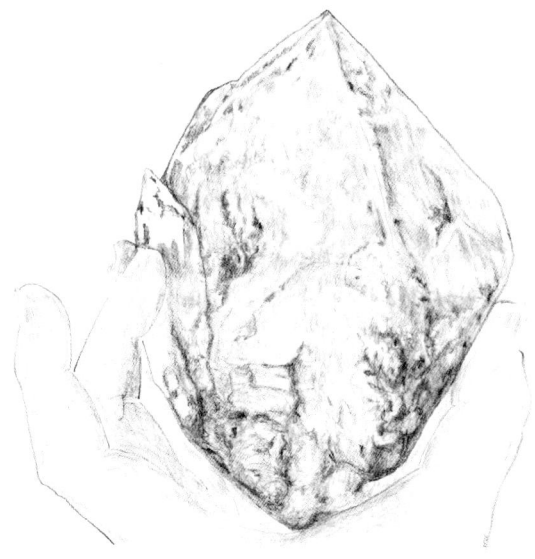

Figure 22 Citrine can be used in meditation as a perfect focal point for opening yourself to happiness and health.

fill yourself completely with its energy, and then exhale stale air out of your lungs. On the inhale, visualize the air being purified though the crystal. Continue like this for several breaths. Watch any thought that comes and let it go, like a small cloud that moves over a blue sky. You are the sky, an immovable observer. Treat any thoughts, regardless of whether they are pleasant or unpleasant, as passing air drifting away. Do not let your eyes wander as that is generating more thoughts. Remind yourself that they are only thoughts and that you do not need to interact with them. If distracted, simply return to the breath each time, and remain singularly focused on your crystal.

Maintenance: While you are working with the crystal, the energy patterns within your body may begin to align and to resonate with it. Continue with your focus and breathing, in spite of any sensations in your body. Remain the observer during the whole session. Over time, you may notice that you are not your thoughts and that you can choose your thoughts. Rather than having and experiencing predetermined 'tapes' or 'scripts' that you must follow, you can change your interaction with a script, either deleting it or changing it so that it fits your life choices better. Allow 10-20 minutes for each session. Continue the practice daily for at least 21 days or longer for best results.

In between your meditations: Find a picture, words or an item, to illustrate what you want. Then place a Citrine on or beside it. Make a sincere intention known to the Universe! When inspiration has room to be allowed in, the sky is the limit. When inspiration starts flowing, get yourself out of the way. Citrine helps you to clear out old ideas. Do not try to control how it should be done. Let the divine forces do their job; they are the experts. Your job is to see the opportunities, take action and receive the result. Keep your eyes open for the unexpected. Visualize the crystal (in this case Citrine with its bright gold or orange yellow colour) being placed in your body, surrounding your intention to change. Make it vibrant and glowing. See the new way of wellbeing that you desire, and assume it is already so. Affirm your intent as often as possible. Act as if you have already achieved your goal. Others will begin to treat you differently also. Involve your senses. Feel the crystal's energy vibrate in your inner being, allowing a different thinking to emerge. Let yourself clear out old ideas from your mental closet. Taste the difference of a new thinking and a new circumstance. Smell your victory over old thought patterns. Then go back to the meditation as described above, and let yourself clear the plate for change.

Effects: This practice allows for a fresh view of an old situation and the feeling of taking charge of the situation at hand. Also, when a situation is objectively evaluated one may discover resources that were forgotten or unavailable before. Communication may improve about personal needs, between partners and the family. A good look at the real cause behind any problematic situation may reveal its source.

Crystal Care: Citrine is good to go for any situation, and does not need to be cleared. Washing is sometimes good as a measure against dust. Express your care and gratitude to the Divine for the stones that are assisting you.

Journaling to Empty Ourselves

In conjunction with the Citrine practice this journaling technique can be utilized to great benefit. Journaling or automatic writing means to quickly write whatever comes to you without editing or censoring. This may reveal parts of you that are otherwise hidden on a conscious level. Journaling first thing in the morning[1] has proven effective in this aspect, as one is usually rested and is close to one's dream state (sub-conscious mind). The emotional and mental wastebasket can be emptied nicely by this process without dumping such garbage on others.

Personal Reflection: During a fragile time in my life I used Julia Cameron's method of journaling in the morning, three pages of longhand writing of anything that bothered me. I just wrote it down and it stayed on the page and left my mind free. I did this for almost a year. Now a decade and a half later, I still remember the relief I felt at having someone to listen to me. I was listening through my writing. My words were heard (by me). The letters on the page became the expression needed. I never read what I had written, but I still kept my journals, since they represented proof that I had actually worked through the difficulties that were going on, and that was very reassuring at the time. Painful separations resulted in friendships that I am very grateful for. Also I set the foundation to actually write. At the present time I now recognize that, in this simple exercise of writing, laid the foundation for enough skill and courage to write this book.[2]

Figure 24 Yellow Tiger-Eye is used in the practice of building strength. By stabilizing one's own vital energy, and beginning to build strength, one may regain the ability of take responsibility for one's own life more effectively.

Gaining Strength - Yellow Tiger-eye

Our precious body of living tissue has the capacity to repair itself to a high degree. Medical intervention may restore broken limbs, but unless we accept on a subtle level that healing is possible, treating symptoms will not remove a condition's cause. We may address the cause by removing ideas that we have of being powerless, helpless or victimized. Victims believe they are helpless and can do little to change their situation.

Why: The Tiger-eye practice is geared towards building up the energy field around the navel to gain more energy and repair failing support systems. As in building or repairing a house, such a project can only begin when enough funds and people are available to do it. In the human system it is the same: if not enough power and energy 'funds' are present, we do not get very far. The navel is the place where we were attached to our mother in the womb. The umbilical cord provided nutrients and oxygen to the growing embryo. After birth, the baby learned to breathe and take in energy by itself through the lungs and through the digestive system. On the subtle levels the navel area is the centre of the body. Japanese Sumo wrestlers demonstrate a powerful example of balance and strength. They train to use their belly[3] by concentrating their energy and power there. We are suggesting using a tumbled stone of Tiger-eye at the navel. Tiger-eye comes in at least three colours: yellow, red and blue. Here we will use the yellow variety. After completing this practice, you may add both the blue Hawks-eye, placed above the navel, and the red Bulls-eye, placed below.

How to begin: To gain strength personally, place a piece of Tiger-eye at the Navel. Some attach a small pouch to or in the clothing near the belly button. Intend to build your strength by inviting positively-empowering thoughts like:

As I build my strength on all levels, I have the means to fulfill my needs.

I take charge of my life, I now see myself as my own boss.
I am now opening my eyes to see a better world for myself.
I bide my time and prepare for change into a healthier life.
I see all that comes my way as an opportunity to improve my life.
My care for others includes taking care of my needs, too.

Maintenance: Pay daily attention to your belly and touch the stone often. Visualize a deep gold field of light surrounding you as you do this. Ask your inner guide to help you. Look for opportunities, and gather a list of things you can do. Make plans and preparation for projects to empower your situation. When you are ready you can act on them. This is the time to gather strength, so consider any actions carefully before you act on them. Continue the practice for at least one month.

Additional tool: A Tiger-eye Elixir can be used to support shifting the beliefs of being weak, powerless and victimized. When the breath is drawn into the belly area, energy is also directed there. Energy follows thought, so visualizing a strong energy flow being drawn into the navel actually brings energy there. To make Gem Water, place the cleaned stone in your water bottle. Sip all day. Tiger-eye is safe to be used in this direct method. Consult the chapter on Gem Elixirs for further details on handling and use.

Effects: After Tiger-eye practice one may experience feeling stronger and less tired. Tiger-eye works toward instilling strength. In a position of strength, one can make well-informed choices.

Crystal Care: Place your Tiger-eye in the sun often. Rinse every morning with spring water.

An extended yoga practice with Tiger-eye includes the visualization and creation of a spinning horizontal field of strength[4] around the body at the navel level. Energy is visualized spinning around you like two hula hoops moving in opposite direction.

Building a Wealth Foundation - Pyrite

Why: Poverty and abundance are states of mind. Pyrite (airy earth) may assist in balancing the mental body and the thinking processes to create abundance in the material world.

How to begin: Set a space conducive to meditation. Make space for undisturbed time for yourself. In a seated position with the spine straight, attach a piece of Pyrite to your forehead. You can use surgical tape or a thin scarf. If you are in a horizontal position, simply put the Pyrite on the Third eye. Invite your inner guidance. Begin to breathe in and out normally through the nose. Feel the air touching the sides of the nasal cavity and flowing down into your lungs. As you exhale, let stale air and obsolete energies be released. Keep breathing until the breath naturally assumes a relaxed pace. Count each breath and keep counting

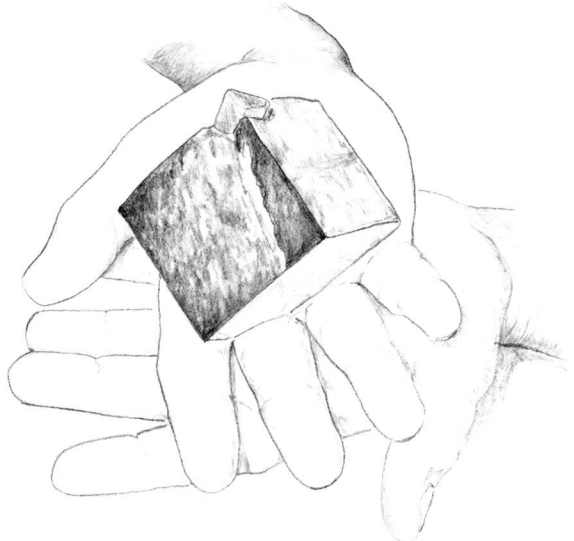

Figure 25 Pyrite, the Poverty Remedy Stone, can be used to achieving health in physical and material aspects of life and to develop the capacity to receive abundance.

your breaths until you have reached one hundred. Your body becomes relaxed and you may begin to feel all parts of your body. Let any thought flow out with each breath. Just let yourself come back to watching your breath.

When the breath has been established in this way, feel the Pyrite at your forehead; let it be a centre point to your thoughts. Cubic Pyrite is shaped in a perfect cube. Visualize this cube in space. Notice lightness and the colour gold. Make the cube radiate golden energy equally on all sides. Visualize placing the cube inside your head at the centre of the brain. Let the cube move and pulse golden energy into your thoughts, aligning them to shiny strings of coherence. Choose your affirmation among these suggestions:

> *I am supported on all levels of my being.*
> *I love the feeling of radiant golden light embracing my being.*
> *I have the clarity to see my inner shortcomings as guides to abundance.*
> *I am training my mind to think abundantly.*
> *I stabilize my mental capacity to include wisdom.*
> *I am a multidimensional being in a physical body.*
> *I am a timeless being, abundant by nature.*
> *All I truly need for me here is to accept and receive.*

Begin saying your chosen affirmations out loud. Feel the words resonate and sound strongly inside your brain and all parts of your body. Alter the voice to become a mere whisper towards the end, and then say the words silently. Continue to say the affirmations for at least 5 minutes in each session. Release any ideas about how your situation should change. Let yourself be the receiver of abundance and relax into a feeling of total abundance. After the session, thank the energy Pyrite and your Guidance team. Trust that you have now set in motion a change of circumstance. As I have been writing the meditations on Abundance and Grounding today, three things happened in rapid succession. First, my mother surprisingly called from overseas, offering to support me with a sum of money. Secondly, a cheque arrived in the mail. Thirdly, a new client called about what looks like a substantial crystal order. It was interesting as I had thought that I would be doing something else. It seems that everything happens in a natural order, in a way that I personally have little say in. What I do have say in is how I state my free will intentions. The Universe hears and responds with what I am asking for. All I am responsible to do is to receive it.

Maintenance: Continue this practice daily for at least 3 months.

Crystal Care: Pyrite is sensitive to water but you can wipe it with a moist cloth to clean it. Place it in the sun as often as possible for recharging.

ഇൻ

I Am My Own Money

For years I saw money as something outside of myself that I had to stress, struggle and strain to acquire. Moreover, there was always the danger that "it would run out" or that "there wouldn't be enough". Of course, these fears peaked when I quit my job to start my own business. Little did I know that part of my life's purpose would involve breaking through these illusions and helping others do the same! If I had to identify the single most significant shift relating to this, I would say it was the realization of author and spiritual teacher John Randolph Price's teaching, "you are your own money". Money, he asserts, is an acronym for "my own natural energy field", and I've found this to be 100 per cent true in my own experience. Working with crystals has allowed me to own this truth. Crystals are powerful tools that have helped me clear, balance and boost the natural energy frequencies of my chakras, while developing a prosperity consciousness. This has translated into attracting $100,000 in one year, starting a new and prosperous business aligned with my *authentic purpose and an abundance of other blessings. I've used crystals in a variety of different ways to help me with this process, and I continue to use them. Sometimes I place crystal layouts on my body, while doing chakra-balancing visualizations. Other times I use a specific stone in seated meditation or I wear a specific stone. I also have different configurations or "crystal grids" on my office desk... Since I started working and surrounding myself with crystals, I've experienced much transformation and many wonderful "improvements" in my life. Crystals have helped me embody the prosperity principles I teach; they've allowed me to experience money and abundance as an inherent part of myself, created by the flow of my own natural energy.*

By crystal healing graduate Mary Davis
- Coach and Prosperity Guide

Money is a token of trust; it is only a piece of paper saying that the amount on the bill can be exchanged for product or services.

Wealth is to have surplus of the resources on all levels that you need.

Poverty is a state of mind and is apparent when one manifests lack of resources available to live happily. Some need a huge resource of wealth to support them in order to feel secure enough. A millionaire in California was asked how much money would be enough for him to have available. The answer was that there was no limit; he could not really have enough. In this sense this millionaire was afflicted by poverty, even though he had millions of dollars.

Abundance is a way of being that supports life; it is a state that allows for the things one needs to manifest when they are needed. In this space there is a balanced flow of resources, with funds to provide well-being on all levels including the physical. People of abundance are open to receive and give freely, and are open to creating what they most dearly desire for themselves in spite of what others say is possible or not.

Summary

Being healthy and well in all areas is a way of thinking. To access a change of thought relating to health and abundance, a Citrine practice is proposed to clear the palate for change in all aspects of life. It will allow a change in attitude towards dis-ease and what it is possible to change. As a supporting technique one might use journaling to clear mental and emotional clutter. For patterns of helplessness and victim mentality, a strengthening discipline with Tiger-eye is introduced, stating that it is easier to act from a position of strength. Lastly a practice to establish a foundation of wealth with Pyrite is described, as the introduction to mental balancing.

Practices:
Breathing the Stone - Citrine
Journaling to Empty Ourselves
Gaining Strength - Tiger-eye
Building a Wealth Foundation - Pyrite

Mastering Manifestation

Wealth is all there,
As a seed in your Mind

Visualize all the resources imaginable being available to you. Could you accept that? This chapter attempts to make some clarifications about how to manifest well, and introduces the Crystal Orb as a tool to help you. As you might glean from the second question, even if the resources were available, some people may fail due to the fact that they didn't believe that their project could succeed. If the intention is clear and your heart is in it, there is no reason not to succeed.

The secret of manifesting lies deep within matter itself. To start, we may observe how life evolves. Within each form there is a structure and within the structure is an intention to direct it. In fact the structure itself is holding the intention for the form to manifest itself, as is the case in our own living DNA. The unique properties and our benefits of crystals described earlier, arise from their inner composition and structure meshed with our own intention and effort.

Figure 26 Illustration of the elements in Nature: water surrounding earthly forms of cliffs of rocks covered with lichens, plants and animal life. In the space of eternal sky behind the airy clouds shines our fiery sun.

Life as we know it began because physical form became stable and self-replicated successfully. Our entire body is composed of molecular structures that follow pure geometries. Atoms combine into molecules with high geometrical order because it economizes energy usage. Imagine trying to carry 5 books independently: one on your head, one in each hand, one on each shoulder - it is a juggling act, but if you tie them up in a stack, you might be able to carry them all in one hand.

Alchemists through the ages have pondered the elements, and the making of gold out of base metal. They provide us with some clues about how the elements make up our physical world. Perhaps our own bodies hold the answer to how the elements interact and become transformed. We are made of solid matter, liquids, neurological and gastric fires and gases that mix and interact with each other. We are a veritable metabolic laboratory, but we are more than that; there is also our voice and capacity to have conscious thoughts belonging to the element of ether/space. Even subtler elements may exist as consciousness itself. Recently Quantum physicists discovered that when one 'looks' at matter in its most minute subatomic components, it changes. In fact the very act of 'looking' alters it. This illustrates why 'manifesting with intention' works, as the very essence of matter is non-physical and can be affected by our thoughts. In short, our thoughts have the potential to alter our physical reality.

It is, best to try this out for yourself! Let us therefore explore further how the specific geometric structure, the Crystal Orb, can be used as an aid for manifestation. Technically it is called a cubatahedron. Each of the four rings of the Crystal Orb can be seen as a representation of the four elements: earth, water, air and fire. By realizing this we may direct the process by being conscious of it. The fifth element of space, at the centre, is our intention or new thoughtform. We state intention, and then weave the structure around it. Then we let the result be manifested.

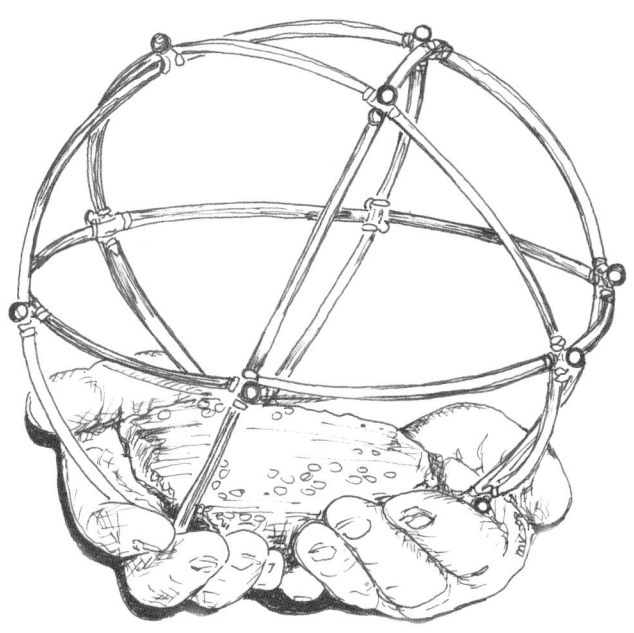

Figure 27 The Crystal Orb is made from four circles joined into a sphere. It is a model for how life evolves out of the prime Source. We use crystals to solidify our intentions of desired manifestations.

Examples of projects: Make a personal or communal project manifest, recover from an illness, create funds, start a business, find a team member, search for a mentor or teacher, find a new occupation, locate a new home, start a family - to name a few areas.

Personal Story: The Crystal Orb shown in the picture above was created as a sort of last resort to solve an interaction with another person. I was clear about what I wanted the situation to look like, but was not sure exactly how this could be manifested. Building the orb was quite easy, it as just flowed into being. I used white pearls at the node points to direct my thoughts to be more beautiful and clear in regards to the problematic relationship I was experiencing. Within its centre I placed a red tourmaline cluster in a matrix, given to me at the time. Since I was filled with gratitude, I saw this stone as perfect for my project. The crystals were aligned side by side very harmoniously, which fit my objective. I feel the effect of this orb still now, two years later, since it is an ongoing project. As an effect, I feel that my inner responses have gradually softened, and what I was upset about previously, I have come to see as a potential pearl given to me. I am truly fortunate to have gone through this powerful process.

Geometry Creates Energy Vortices

Any edge will collect energy; look at how dust bunnies always collect in corners and tight spaces as under the bed. That is an example of how things seek the most energy efficient place (the law of entropy). Removing corners helps energy flow. Geometric structures, such as geodesic domes that hardly have any corners, are very energy-efficient. They are easy to build and harmonious to live in.

By building a Crystal Orb with intention, one may learn about how life functions and about the mechanism of manifestation. Creating this structure with a particular intent in our mind, facilitates that intent/project to grow and become manifest[1].

The Crystal Orb may be viewed as sacred, as it contains all the platonic solids, which are the building blocks of all organic life. They are the basis for the structures exhibited within mineral crystals as well. In the practice to follow, we will build a Crystal Orb and add natural crystals to solidify the manifesting process, thereby building a stronger connection to Nature's potential abundance and to the Field of All Possibilities (or G-d). This dimensional field is also referred to as "the Source."

Cubatahedron: A polyhedron enclosed within a spherical structure made of 4 rings composed in a certain way that exhibit 8 triangles and 6 squares. It contains all of the platonic solids as well as the star tetrahedron. This construct of four rings held together in a particular way is an essential geometrical structure for life. It is called 'crystal' to signify its geometry in the same way as a mineral hold structure.

Platonic Solids include: Cube, Tetrahedron, Octahedron, Icosahedron and Dodecahedron that all fits within a Sphere.

Star Tetrahedron: two opposing tetrahedrons combined

Field of all Possibilities: this is the Womb of the universe where all creation emanates from.

Universal Providers: angelic or elemental beings assigned to carry out manifestation: bigger beings create galaxies, smaller ones are the building force behind, for example, a blade of grass. All beings serve the same supreme source.

Our challenge is to re-align ourselves with this field in order to receive. (We will discuss this further in the chapter *The Crystal Grid*.) Since part of the Crystal Orb structure contains an intrinsic Star Tetrahedron (the geometric shape yogis may see, surrounding the human body), it can be used in combination with meditation and yogic breathing to allow rapid progress on the path of self-discovery as well. In effect, it acts as an antenna that cleanses, balances, harmonizes and ultimately amplifies energies, and assists in aligning the physicality with the Field of All Possibilities. Antennae drink energy. Karish says:

Crystal Orbs accept all energy without judgment. As a charge builds, it begins to be broadcast as newly transmuted, harmonized energy. In this way they actually function as profound 'low-tech' energy purification devices.

Mastering Manifestation - the Crystal Orb

Why: The sooner we know what we want, the sooner we may manifest it. The ultimate reason for engaging in this process is to receive what we ask for. The Crystal Orb of Manifestation is a construct of four rings put together in a particular way. When activated, it magnetizes your intentions to become manifest by becoming your outer antenna that will be broadcasting them to the Universal providers. It can be applied to any project a person can think of, and it can be practiced by anyone who is willing to look within for answers to situations happening in outer life. The core of spiritual practice is the commitment to apply oneself, initially for the purpose of removing inner obstacles and then by putting the wisdom learned to use for the benefit of self and others. The reward is that we receive what we ask for. It is in the asking that we should pay some attention. This practice is directly about that.

How to begin: Make an Orb according to the instructions in the template section. We will bind our intentions to the structure by committing to what we want to receive. The Orb, when completed, is personally tuned to your project in question. You need to make one orb for each intention or project. I suggest you to start with one project. Two things are needed: gather material for your crystal orb and make a list of candidates for your first project. My first Orb was made out of paper towel and some tape, but my material of preference is copper wire, which can be sourced from a local building supply place. The results are not affected by the material. The only concern is if it is durable enough to be handled and that it is joined to create the geometry of the structure.

Selecting Project: To prepare your list of projects you can select a Pyrite, Imperial Topaz, Citrine or another stone you find suitable. Bring a pen and paper. Then lay down on your sofa with

Figure 28 Construction of the Crystal Orb by tying the nodes with wire and attaching crystals to solidify the intentions of the Crystal Orb keeper. Top left shows a model of the Star Tetrahedron.

the stone on your belly (navel). Relax and breathe deeply for at least five minutes to clear your mind. It is ideal to use a timer. Then sit up and begin writing your list. Try to write fast and do not dwell on each item too long. You should have at least ten items on your list before you go further. Then see if some of the items belong together. Make a new list of the combined entries: usually one will end up with 2-3 main intentions. Prioritize your entries. Select your first item as your project. Stick with it. Commit to do this project. Give your project a name. Create an "I am" affirmation that reflects having already received the desired result. Keep your work private and do not share the details with anyone unless he or she is doing it together with you. If you talk about it, it is like spreading your energy to the wind. Here you need that energy to go into manifesting your project.

Activation: Prepare a place for your Crystal Orb. It can be an altar or a movable tray. Take one item representing each of the elements: some earth, a bowl of water, a candle for fire and incense to represent air. Your crystals will represent space and be placed in the centre. Ask for each of the element's participation and your own inner guide to assist in the process. As you say your affirmation several times, focus on evoking a strong image and a strong feeling inside of having already received the result. Write the affirmation on a card as well, and place it with the Orb.

Maintenance: Touch your Orb several times a day and have many short Crystal Orb sessions every day. Begin with stating the affirmation several times while recalling a strong image and feeling each time. You may place pictures and flowers and thank you notes with your Orb, as well as recording any sign of success. Meditate on the state of ease and flow in all areas of your life.

Receiving: Watch for signs of results and immediately receive them fully. Thank everyone involved: Source and your inner guides (Heaven team), Nature's manifesting forces, other people and yourself (Earth team).

Figure 29 Activation of the Crystal Orb by using representation for the five elements: Air, Water, Earth, Fire and Space.

Effects: By tuning into Nature to communicate our intentions and wishes we may have an understanding of our role as a keeper of sacredness on the Earth. We are rewarded through the process with manifestations to our benefit. To have completed a Crystal Orb practice means you have stayed with the program until your intent is manifested. Crystal Orb Keepers report a sense of empowerment, love and lightness from having taken charge of their life. Apart from fulfilling inner desires, many other areas of life may be affected positively as well by this practice, since a positive attitude and light-heartedness spill over easily and make anything easier.

Summary

The secret of manifestation lies deep within matter itself. It is known that when 'looking' at sub-atomic matter, it changes. This explains in short why our intentions (our thoughts) create our reality. By building the Crystal Orb, a person may experience the effects first-hand. Intention is set, and then the structure is built around it. In the practice of working with the elemental forces symbolized by the four rings of the Crystal Orb, we may learn about the mastery of manifestation.

Practices:
Mastering Manifestation - the Crystal Orb

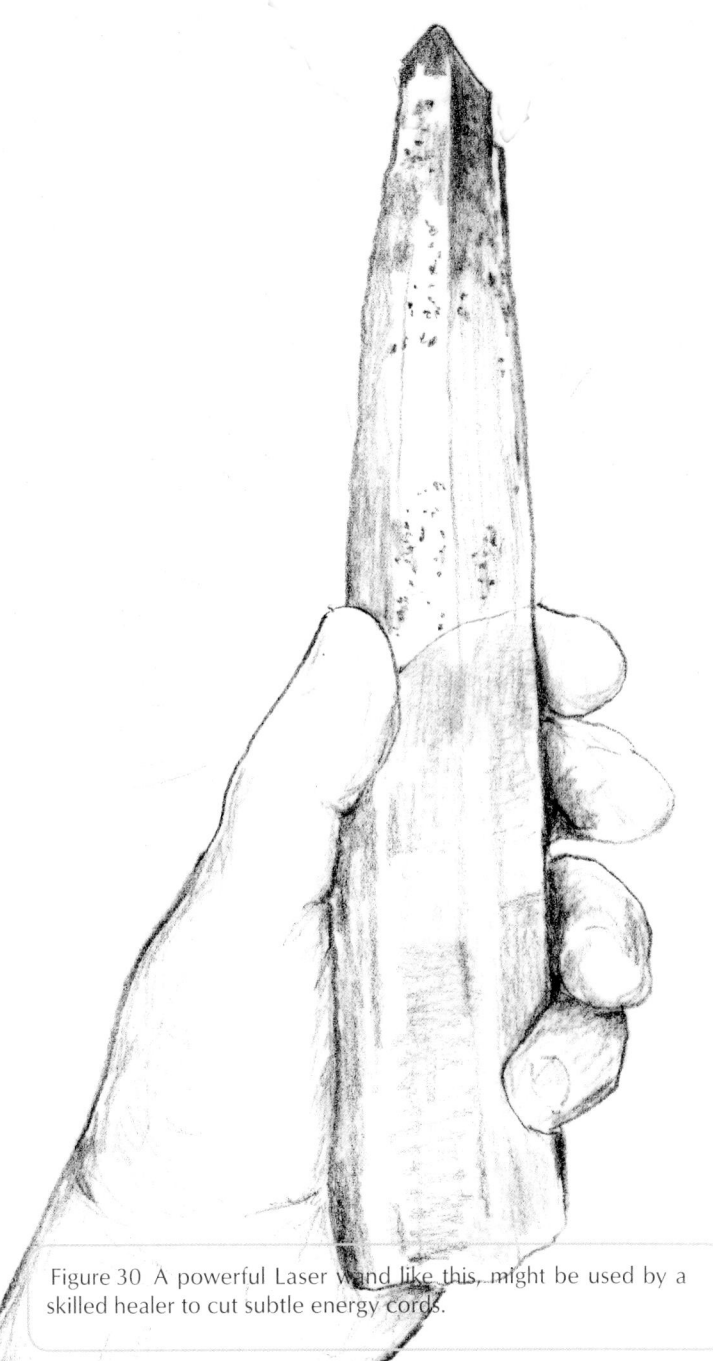

Figure 30 A powerful Laser wand like this, might be used by a skilled healer to cut subtle energy cords.

Crystal Wands

Stature reflects the power,
Wands its outer expression

A King holds a sceptre, the official presents his staff and the magician wields his wand. Historically, these objects were made of precious metals and gems, or executed in special types of wood, and used to signify stature and power. This may seem a tool of scarce attainability for the average person, especially the magical wand, which might be intriguing - a simply wave and your wish comes true! Such ideas belong perhaps to the category of fantasy! However, we may use a crystal wand in a variety of ways to develop our inner qualities. The sceptre, staff or wand may symbolize spiritual attainment: the rise of energy along our spine, resulting in awakening to our true potential and consciousness. The main use that we will explore here is firstly to learn how to direct energy in healing, and secondly to develop the inner capacity to hold more energy. The *Black Tourmaline Practice* is a good starting point for working further with crystal wands.

One may find natural crystal wands or wands cut entirely from various minerals. As we saw in a previous chapter, a wand can also be used as a tool for the crystal reflexologist. A fabricated crystal wand may consist of a copper tube or a wooden rod, adorned with several stones, and have a terminated crystal at the top. A personal healing wand is fairly easy to construct.

Make My Own Healing Wand

Why: Making a wand is a creative project that can inspire us to learn how find a way to move energy within. By working with natural materials - crystals, copper wire, wood, leather and fabric - we bind our energy into these materials and they remind us of our potential.

How to start: Collect natural or simple items: a stick of driftwood, feathers, soft leather, silk or cotton fabric scraps in fun colours, string or yarn, paint and some copper wire. You may smudge all the materials and yourself before assembly. Begin by centering yourself and then inspect the wood. See if you can find a piece that flows or elicits interest for you, and then trim the wood where needed. Perhaps ask for inspiration. The wood should feel good to hold. Find a crystal point and other smaller crystals to attach to the wood. One may attach the top crystal with copper wire or strips of leather. Sometimes I use fabric glue to secure the leather. You might feel inspired to paint part of the wood or decorate it with fabric. At the bottom end one may attach feathers on stings that hang down to act as a tail. Follow your creative impulses until you have completed your wand.

Selecting a healing purpose: The crystals you selected to be part of the wand, have significant meaning to you: otherwise, you wouldn't have picked them. Let them guide you further by holding your wand in front of you, let your work speak to you. Among the things you may choose are: standing up for yourself, setting boundaries, learning to speak up, learning to clear inner blockage to things you want to accomplish, working with your chakras, increasing your energy, facilitating healing, or how to be less distracted and more focussed. Look to the stones for answer. An Amethyst may prompt you to learn how to adapt and accept changes, Fluorite to help you focus, and Hematite to ground, etc. You might name your wand according to its healing purpose.

Maintenance: Set aside 15 - 20 minutes each day to work with your wand. Hold it to your heart and ask for guidance, and how you may attain what you need. Let yourself receive the answers. When you are complete, you can use the wand to sweep your aura which may assist any negativity to be released.

Store: Your wand is a tool for your intentions. Store it in a safe place or on an altar, dedicated to your personal progress. Continue daily for at least 12 consecutive days.

Effects: You may discover what your real needs are. When that happens you can address them more directly.

Categories of various wands for use in healing:

Natural Quartz Crystal Wands include the Laser Wand with very sharp tips and long body, the Generator Wand with a broad top and straight body that gives broad sweeps of energy, and the Goddess Wand that features a pear shaped body and open top to work with our earth connection.

Cut and Polished Wands made from massive crystal material. These are essential tools are useful for visualization and in layouts, as well as for accessing the reflex points on the body.

Composite Crystal wands provide a source for inspiration and may feature symbols and additional stones along its body.

Copper Wands are helpful in endeavours to connect energies, for example between chakras. The copper is providing additional conductivity. Copper tubing is easy to acquire and bends into almost any shape. Small crystals can be attached at the end. Usually copper wands are covered with cloth or suede. (See picture on page 106).

Wooden Wands provide a special challenge for the so inspired carver. Crystals may be added on the body or at the ends.

Staffs of Wood, are large wands that may serve as walking stick or for ceremonial use.

Figure 31 Lepidolite Wand made from blades of gemmy cleavage of Lepidolite. Notice the openings at the side where the crystals can be seen. Wands with Lepidolite, Kyanite and Selenite are ideal to use for sweeping and combing the aura.

Practice Inner Awareness with a Crystal Wand

Why: It is within each person to awaken to the inner potential. By using a natural or polished crystal wand we have a possibility to access that potential. By focusing on visualization along the physical spine, we may become aware of subtle channels that run vertically from the top of our head down to the base of our torso. These channels are key to our process of awakening. You can use this practice to train your ability to contain energy and then direct that energy through your wand.

How to start: Select a natural, polished or composite crystal wand to use for this practice. Make sure you resonate well with this crystal tool. Find a private space that you may be undisturbed and less distracted in. Sit comfortably in a chair and hold the crystal in front of you. Look at it deeply, then place it at your heart and close your eyes. Visualize it along your spine from your tailbone to the top of your head. Notice what you feel - just observe it, and afterwards write it down in your journal. Spend about 10 minutes or longer daily for 7 days.

Continuing practice: After looking at your wand, visualize it along your spine as before. Elongate it past your tailbone to 6" below your feet, and extend it to a foot above your head. The reason for this is that these places are the location for the out-of-body chakras: the Earth Star and the Soul Star. Watch with your inner eye how wide the wand becomes, then make the wand (and the vertical central channel) very thin like a pencil. You may use the *Dual Flow Breath* during the visualization, and then make it wider and wider until it is as wide as your body. Then make it thinner and thinner again until it is the width of a pencil once more. Do this twice daily, preferably up to 20 minutes in the morning and up to 20 minutes in the evening. Continue this for at least 7 days.

Store your wand in a silk cloth to protect it and clear negativity.

Effects: This practice may facilitate body awareness and the power of the spine and vertical channels. It is also energizing and helps to reduce mental distractions.

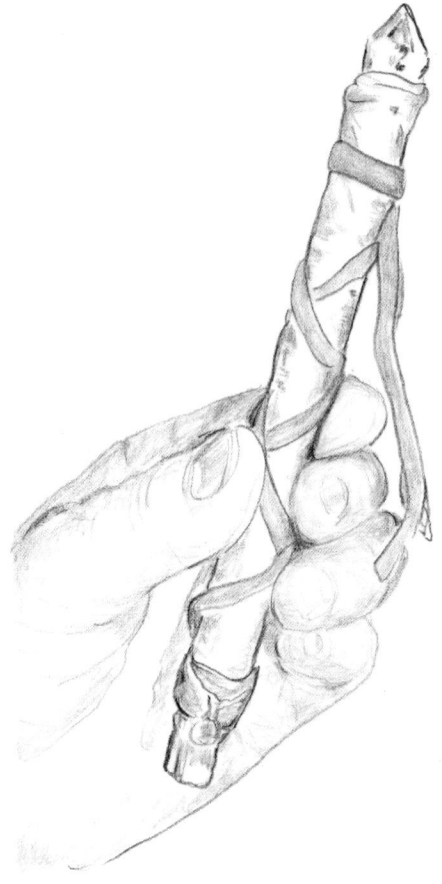

Figure 32 Copper wand with Amethyst and green Tourmaline. The crystals are inserted at the ends of a copper tubing that is covered with silk strips and suede lacing. Some fill the tube with tiny polished or raw crystals as well.

Summary

Wands have been seen historically as a symbol for stature and power. Much can be said for the use of wands for magical purposes. Here we propose to use wands to manage and direct our inner energies. Presented are two personal practices: making a personal healing wand to discover our real needs, and then a visualization with a natural or composite crystal wand to discover the power of our spine and the subtle energy channels at our vertical centre line.

Practices:
Make My Own Wand
Inner Awareness with a Crystal Wand

Figure 33 A Devic Temple, called so because of its inner appearance of a sanctuary. This crystal can used in the practice of learning how to access the intelligence within a stone.

Working with Nature

Divine helpers are ready when we are:
They have their mission, and we have ours

Most cosmologies include the presence of benevolent forces assisting humans. These forces might take the form of angels or other higher or lesser divinities. Contacting or collaborating with such beings has been an inspired goal for mystics and sensitive people who live close to Nature. It is known that children see them as fairies or elves, but they are usually told that they have too much imagination. Imagination is a faculty that one can use to be able to create with. Without it there would be no art and nothing new would ever be produced. By imagining something, dreaming about it, and then thinking it, that is how something can be manifested. Einstein used imagination to break the barriers of the known realities of his time. We benefit from this creative process every day. Of course, if one uses the imagination to mislead others for personal gain, that creates difficulties for everyone, but to express our inner world through art, the work speaks for itself. As I just wrote this sentence a huge rainbow appeared on my keyboard. Coincidence? I think not.... It does not matter if one believes in the extraordinary or not. If one is inspired, the secret door to the mystic realms of the heart can be opened.

The activity of talking to plants seems to improve their vitality and growth[1]. Modern biodynamic farmers[2] have found ways to

Figure 34 Creators of Crystal Fairies, Terry and Teresa are gifted artists who are able to depict how they see the living world around us, as expressed through their fairies. Shown: Amethyst fairy.

maintain the natural grid in their gardens by listening to[3] the intelligence behind nature. By being receptive to such energies one can receive their guidance. Believing in such intelligences or divine beings is one thing, but to have a deeper experience of this everlasting benevolent presence is another.

In nature where I go to rejuvenate myself, I feel totally alive. In fact, all is alive there. Every manifestation in nature, whether it is a blade of grass, an animal or a stone, has a living presence or intelligence of sorts. These 'nature intelligences' could be said to be the living blueprints behind the outer form of nature. Each species has its own deva[4] and each individual stone, plant or animal has its own elemental in charge of its growth and manifestation. These intelligences may communicate with humans who are capable of listening.

I have had the privilege of experiencing this communication firsthand, when working with crystals. First, one must tune in to the individual form and energy, and then focus on the intelligence behind the form. Honouring this process is vital. A deva working with plants in the well-known gardens at Findhorn states[5]:

"Each plant sounds a note which attracts its builders to it and calls substance to itself through the nature spirits. We devas know the individual notes for all in our charge, and we sound them, like tuning forks, to be picked up by each plant. When a seed is ready to germinate, moisture and warmth do not by themselves set its note vibrating. We do that. We set the seed on its way and hold out its note before it, to follow. That note changes with growth and stages, as does a man whose voice changes as he advances into maturity".

I feel that such a note can be perceived in each crystal also. It is that particular vibration that we can use, to come back to our own wholeness, or, in other words, to become healed.

Attune to Nature - Devic Temple

I was guided to go and pick up a certain crystal to illustrate how to access the intelligence within a stone. It was a beautiful crystal exhibiting lovely planes of shimmering light inside. It beckoned me: it is a Devic Temple[6]. It is shown on the previous page. I looked inside it and felt my brain start tingling; a whole world was shown to my inner eye that I could describe only as a flow

Fairies are defined as tiny mystical or imaginary beings in human form, usually less than human size and thought to be either helpful or harmful to humans. Other names are "elfs" or "sprites." They are depicted as clever, mischievous and having magical powers.

Deva (Sanskrit: 'divine') is defined as divine, or a being with divine powers mainly divided into sky, air, and earth divinities. In the ancient literature every tree, flower, river, and mountain was represented by a deva in charge of organizing its intelligence. Its mythological meaning is "god" or "goddess."

Elementals are beings responsible for individual life forms. They relate to the basic creative labour of building these forms, like an individual plant or crystal.

Stone beings may be other dimensional intelligences that use the stones as a contact point with humans.

of lights. I noticed that the entire room became very hot. "*Cut through to the essence,*" I am prompted. Yes... What I sense is a series of small impulses that may be described as a series of image-bits or parts of symbols or pictures. As I relaxed into them they formed themselves into a larger picture which my brain could interpret. When I stopped interfering in how these images had to be organized, the sender of these bits of information could complete the sending, and the entire painting became clear to me. What did I see? I saw a garden and within this garden the work of a gardener who cared for all that was in his garden, small and large alike. Nothing was extraneous - all parts had a place that was essential to the garden's function. The entire scenario was gloriously radiating with aliveness. 'She', (this Deva who is not seen), was showing me a template that I perhaps could use in my own life. Questions popped into my head: Is my life this beautiful? Is it functioning in all its parts and is it radiantly alive? I would have to answer no, not yet, although I felt close to it sometimes. I asked what to do! I felt the presence of this Deva, a miniature of a human's higher self, to which the crystal totally surrendered. A crystal does not have an ego as we do. I received a feeling or prompting that I had to connect to all parts of my-self, and then the living perfection would be manifest. I saw that I must consciously work on doing just that. I was deeply grateful for this insight.

An Unusual Meeting

I had been troubled by some pain in my shoulder and neck, and at this point the pain became worse. I had no idea that I would be given a piece of Azeztulite[7], but my anguish was deep. My concern was to overcome the dissonance I felt within. It had to do with my interaction with another person. I suspected that what I was dealing with was not the actual person but an influence that was harmful to both of us. I felt hooks in my own body that were hurting in specific locations at the sites of a couple of old injuries. A visiting friend handed me her two Azeztulites, a white sphere and a small golden point. I placed the sphere under my left foot, and the little golden point at the base of my skull behind my left ear. A circuit was engaged between the two crystals that pulled strongly on the pained ar-eas. I wanted to remove the harming energies and engage my *Crystal Orb Incinerator* (see chapter *The Crystal Orb*) to assist in the release. Lifetimes of old stuff tumbled around, and like an overfilled jar of molasses, I felt myself begging to be opened and to have the old emotions poured out of me. I felt a strong energy current in my body. It occurred to me to look into my mind. I had been engaged with critical thoughts and judgements against the other person. These thoughts quickly vanished as soon as I recognized them, and then I felt free of them. The injuries were not entirely healed, but temporarily sealed for entry, which was a great relief.

Then what happened next was truly remarkable. I saw a vision of a being, or rather a group of beings. I asked for confirmation from my friend and was told that it was not an attacking entity,

but some of the stone beings assisting me to release my old emotions. I was then given a remarkable gift of seeing them with my inner eye. I saw what they actually did. The image appeared at first as a head and chest of a green praying mantis, but this was no insect. It was the radiating Deva of the stones I was working with. The lower part of the body came to a point, like a thin icicle. It was draped in some form of wide brilliant green gown that turned out to be the field generated by the joint action. The head was crowned by an enormous headdress. As I later tried to draw this image, it appeared as a resonance chamber for a sub-audible voice (sound). The face was very peaceful and serene, totally absorbed in the activity of resonating a sound. I heard nothing but felt the strong current of the stone going through my body. It continued until all the pain was gone. So what was the result of my experience? I had opened my heart to the person I had carried judgement towards. I actually began feeling good and saw this person in a different light, I felt compassionate affection. It really did pop up into my heart spontaneously. The coming days showed me that I was not imagining this. It kept coming. I could detect a piece of myself that had been misaligned. It was corrected with this healing. I could now count the person I had struggled with as another friend on my list, as well as one less problematic person in my life. I hope to see everyone as friend in the future, and vice versa. I realized then that this was the place in me where I could personally start to make that happen.

Figure 35 Stone beings revealing themselves in a vision

Summary

Working with nature means to tune into the aliveness around us. What seems unreal to some will make a lot of sense to those who are able to ask for cooperation from the natural forces. In normal terms they are a product of the imagination. These beings are living in another dimensional plane, unseen by most, but they engage in important work for us in the physical world. Fairies are known mostly in the western world, and Devas in the East, but both are seen as part of the spectrum of life, with individual tasks and missions. Each living thing on the Earth (plants, animals and also crystals) is created from a subtle blueprint. Nature Devas activate the blueprint and the elementals build the physical form in accordance with their Deva's directions. A Devic Temple crystal may be an inroad to having a first-hand experience. Crystals may be a conduit for Devas and stone beings to share their energy with humans.

Practices:
Tuning in with Nature – Devic Temple

Figure 36 Role playing is the name of the 'game' in the course of 'normal life'. Whom do you really see, if not someone's mask? Rarely do we see someone who is willing to reveal his or her authentic self. Observe the convenient masks of: the 'air-head', 'pity-me-cry-baby', 'sweet-face' and 'raging bully'. When healing is evaporating our personas, the masks become obsolete. Notice the crystal talisman this practitioner is wearing to assist her in her healing.

Covered by Masks

A theatre play at the core
Runs idly around the store

Role-playing of young children is part of the natural growing process. One part after another is tried on the theatre stage of life. It is by playing and acting out games that a child learns to integrate life. As adults we may continue to play various roles as actors in a play, consciously or unconsciously, like being a mother, employer, servant, teacher, student, nurturer or victim, to name a few. Upon inner examination we may find several such actors on staff. All of them appear on cues according to their individual scripts, adapted to our personal situation, including the props or masks that go with the roles. These masks can be seen by others who accurately observe us, but not usually by ourselves. The play itself is supervised by the director, our ego,[1] who manages all scripts and calls in the actors. We get used to this as we are habitual creatures thriving on comforts. We might be enamored with certain roles to the point that we are totally identified with them; we believe these roles are who we are and thus they become our persona or identity. We try out the glamour girl, the lavish spender and the reckless adventurer. While this scenario is deeply embedded in our subconscious, we are attempting to live our daily life. It works fine when the good guys are playing, but we get into trouble when our archetypal shadows charge in and take over our stage without obvious consent

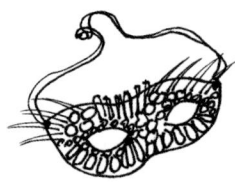

from our conscious mind. We may keep company with the tyrant, the abuser, the murderer or the criminal, without even knowing it. How is this possible? Early on, the child or young adult learnt the script that worked and handed over the responsibility to the director, as it was the easiest way to deal with what was going on at the time. The director is still carrying out our wishes. When a person reacts to someone's behaviour or a situation, it is usually not our authentic self who is doing the enacting and reacting, but one of our personas or actors. We are continuously receiving the consequences for this. The results can be seen as ill health, bad relationships, poverty, unhappiness or misfortune. To change this, we must intend on a more conscious involvement.

Healing means discovering our actors and their cues, and making beneficial changes to the scripts. What play do you want to be: a love story, murder mystery or glamorous soap opera? A play gets very interesting when unforeseen actors charge in and take over the show. A murder mystery would not be worth its name without a murderer and a dead body, I might add. Who wants to have a murderer at home? In the end we might get too exhausted to play roles. That may be a starting point for healing to become truly our free selves. The roles we play unconsciously or consciously are illustrated here by a participant at one of our weekend crystal intensives. The role she wanted to integrate was that of the princess. Consciously she knew that she was acting this role sometimes in her interaction with others in her life. What was attempted in a controlled and supportive environment was to fully experience how this role affected her and others around her. The exercise was to make a mask of the role to emphasize the script acted out. The masks were decorated and painted and crystals were selected, based on the participant's intuitive choice. Then the person got centre stage and was allowed to fully act out his or her script, wearing the mask he or she made.

Discover your personal Games & Payoffs

The Danburite Princess Mask. At this crystal intensive I had a unique opportunity to play out my princess persona. I was glad, excited and enthusiastic to be at the centre of attention. The group, as my trusted and loyal servants, was also eager to play along and fulfill any whim of mine. I sat front and centre of the room with as much pomp and airs as can be expected from a princess. I had my subjects dancing like ponies and they entertained me with a parade of funny antics. They quickly began to annoy me as they anticipated my next instruction. I began to feel very self-conscious and uncomfortable tossing around silly, self-serving commands. I realized my princess archetype was selfish, shallow and bored. As I sat quietly behind the mask, with no more enthusiasm for the game, the group waited while tears streamed. Within minutes I was empty and wanting to become invisible. I wanted to stop the drama but was held there as the spectacle I thought I wanted to be. It was an amazing process to connect with what seemed to be a fun and playful character. I can see how I have too often duped myself and tried to dupe others as the self-righteous Princess treating those around me like props to fulfill my fantasies. The integration was a deeply humbling experience. I found and comforted a piece of myself and found peace as myself. I uncovered that I really wanted to be real, an integral part of the whole, to respond appropriately when necessary instead of filling time and space with empty, useless frivolity, usually at the expense of others. The princess to me is now a symbol of codependency and immaturity, and since I've reckoned with this quality, I can more quickly come back to my authentic self.

Tara Brox

Make a Crystal Mask - Danburite

Why: Danburite, the spirit heart stone, demonstrated softly but with piercing clarity how the participant of the course was fooling herself by her playacting. By staying in the heart presently with what is, we find that games like this fall away as an ice cube melts in the sun.

How to begin: Make your Mask: You will need white paper, heavy craft paper (10 x 5"), glue, paint or crayons, an elastic band, fabric scraps, feathers, beads, crystals, and anything you might think could be used. Include also a piece of Danburite. Centre yourself by taking three relaxing breaths. Place the paper over your face, marking length and width and the centre of the eyes. Draw out the edges in the shape that comes to you, and the holes for the eyes. Glue the paper onto the heavier cardboard. Cut out the contours and the holes for the eyes. Make sure to test it on your face for fit and to ensure that you can see properly through it. Then take a moment to meditate on your situation. You may not know what persona is being illustrated - do not worry. Let yourself pick from your materials anything you can imagine that could be incorporated into your mask. Attach each component carefully until the front of your mask is complete and attach the elastic band to the sides so that you can wear your mask.

Working with your mask: Put your mask on, look in the mirror and then feel who you are in this mask. Stand up, move, and put on suitable music. Move with the music, and let the mask move you. Discover whom you are portraying. How does this part of you feel? What is this part of you expressing? Can you name it? Continue until you discover what this part of you represents.

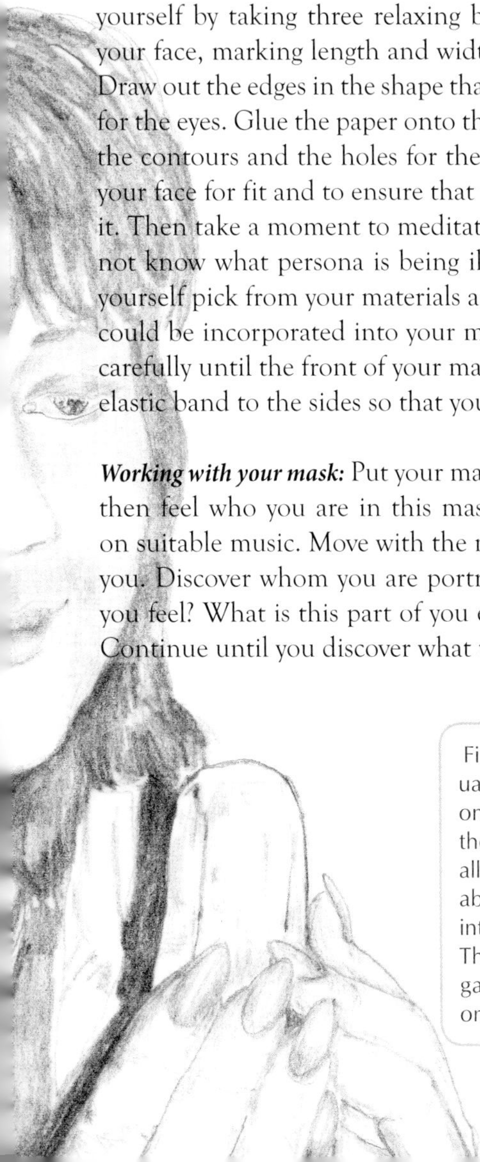

Figure 37 Danburite - the Spiritual Heart Stone. In meditation one can use Danburite to access the heart. The heart may open by allowing ourselves to be vulnerable. Then we may tend to the intimate needs of our inner child. This size of Danburite is great for gazing meditations or for placing on the heart in a healing session.

Maintenance: Repeat this 'dance' several times with a few days in-between until you are complete. To integrate this one might hang the mask on the wall in full view, and each time some new level of understanding may emerge. Keep this practice private to yourself or the people you are practicing with until the process is done.

Effects: In the actual playing out of the inner personas we may reveal to ourselves the games we engage in. This is a powerful self-healing technique. By stopping and removing our 'mask' we may discover our authentic selves and know better who we are.

Crystal Care: Pay attention to your mask as long as you need to continue with this practice. Place it in a prominent place where you may see it every day. After completed practice it may be disassembled, as it is no longer needed.

CRSO

Summary

By recognizing that everyone of us has played or is playing various roles as actors on the stage of our life, we may gain control over these subconscious characters and the directorship of our inner world. Acting out consciously the roles by means of a mask might trigger us to give up that game which really does not serve us in the long run. Making and working with a Danburite mask is a way of discovering hidden personas.

Practice
Make a Crystal Mask - Danburite

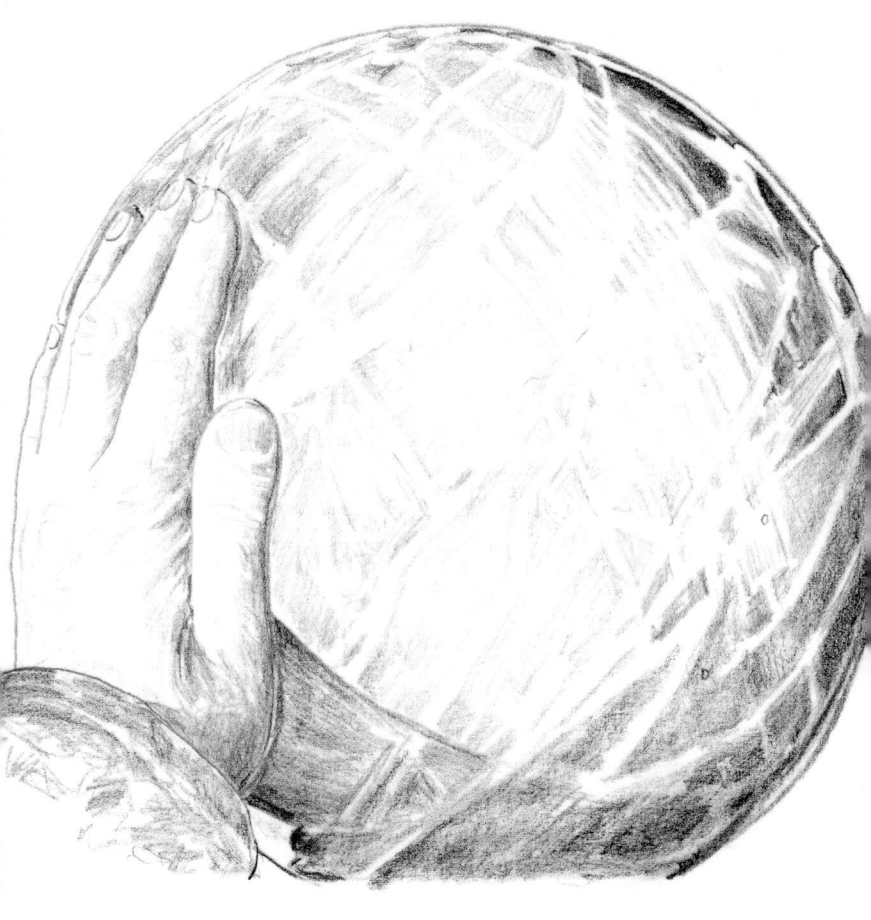

Figure 38 A massive Rose Quartz sphere. Rosequartz can be used to practice Self Love. To begin to love oneself is probably one of the most difficult tasks a person may have, next to releasing the need of being right. Rosequartz is one of the most popular stones, and perfect to give as a gift to anyone.

Love Illusion

If only there was Love
I would be Happy

Divine relationships: do they exist? You might have seen movies where the main theme is the love of two people. Usually they are unhappy and surrounded by unfulfilled love. Shakespeare's Romeo and Juliet came together only to die afterwards. We have very few role models to look up to in today's busy world. We are, in fact, scripted with a number of scenarios on how to live with others, and in particular with an intimate partner. Most of these scripts or programs may not serve us well. They are useful in either preserving our species in some way, or in benefiting and improving the control that some individuals, groups, or segments of society have over others. Do long eyelashes, perfect 'abs' or a size 6 body improve one's life? If one believes common advertising, one would think so. I have heard the sentiment: "If I only had that real soul mate, then everything would be great". Everyone wants Love, but do we know what that is? Most of us think that we do, but it may not be so. Our desires for love may arise from the sense that there is something "lacking." Without the desired object, we are not complete. When it is not there, we long for it and may even make ourselves sick over it. This is suffering, and some people are actually addicted to such patterns.

Let us see what the perfect love crystal, Rose Quartz, can pro-

vide. It is clearly the stone to work with in the case of low self-esteem, feelings of hopelessness and lack of love - regardless of the underlying causes.

Love recipe #1 Self-Love - Rose Quartz

It is only through true love that we can evolve as emotionally healthy beings. Without love, cruelty and mind-terror may ensue. Wars are started out of greed or hate for another. Violence and murders are committed because of a lack of empathy and a lack of understanding that, under the outer grisly appearance, there is a tender heart beating. It is said that one can only give something if one has it. This is particularly true of Love. If I love myself I can also give love to others and generate healthy relationships. Without self-love, the persons involved would only enact a co-dependent relationship, or, in other words, engage in game-playing. This does not provide the experience of truly fulfilling love but only continued misery and suffering.

Personal story: When I first approached Rose Quartz, I absolutely hated the stone. I didn't want it around me at all. I was actually revolted by the mere idea of being close to it. That was a reflection of how I felt about myself. I couldn't do or be enough. Only if I worked really hard and achieved lots of results (as in praise, acknowledgements or money) could I feel as if I was a good person. The colour might have reminded me of opinions about the colour pink, as in 'pink is for girls' - meaning good, pretty, and well-behaved little girls. I never felt that I was any good in doing the girl part. My interest was in other areas. Perhaps deep down I resented being a girl in the first place. The bottom line was that I could not be good enough to love myself very much. Instead of loving, I engaged in trying to prove to the

Figure 39 Placement of a crystal at the Heart centre.

world at large that I was lovable. This really never worked. The encounter with Rose Quartz put these feelings into focus. One of my friends wanted to go to a mine about three hours away from my home; she wanted to present a chunk of Rose Quartz to each person (children and adults) in her immediate family, as Christmas presents. I went along to go rock-hounding. It was great. I even got a few pieces, although I felt they were not very nice, appearing fairly pale and shattered. All I thought at the time was that I could at least sell them, meaning at least I did do some work there. God forbid that I should have enjoyed it as a social event. A couple of years went by with Spirit gently nudging me to start the inevitable process of me loving myself. It took an encounter with a ten-pound chunk of purple Rose Quartz scuffed under a scrap pile of rocks deep in the Brazilian hinterlands for me to get a whiff of what was going on. As they say, I had to have it! After that encounter I began to consciously work with this energy. Patterns of co-dependency going on within me were shot out of the emotional waters by the assistance of my then-excellent partner, who, of course, showed me no mercy. The universe wanted to make sure I got it this time. I did get it loud and clear. After I returned to Canada, that relationship ended with a bang and now I thank Spirit and everyone involved at the time for the help they gave.

Why: By identifying where one is co-dependent, we can begin the journey of personal freedom. Dependencies are seen in the acute need we may have for something or someone. By taking our power back we become more complete and sustainable as a person. Also, it becomes harder to control a person who has become free of co-dependency.

How to begin: To begin, commit yourself to practice self-love. Even if you have no idea about what it would feel like, you can still decide to do the practice. The results are really worth it. Then acquire a piece of Rose Quartz. It can be a tumbled stone or a small rough piece or a set stone in a necklace. A rose quartz

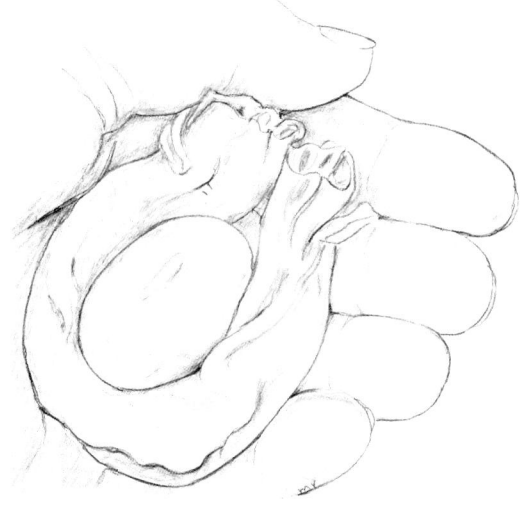

Figure 40 Tumbled Rosequartz and self-made medicine bag.

talisman[1] is ideal for this. It really does not matter as long as you can feel its pink energy and have clear intention. Place it on your heart. Using a medicine bag is an option. Wear it for 40 days. Touch your rose quartz lovingly and reaffirm your commitment to self-love throughout your waking hours. Attempt to place this intent foremost in your mind at all times.

Maintenance: Set aside a time each day to contemplate how you feel about yourself. It is a good idea to make notes of your findings in an I love Myself Journal. Discover new ways to appreciate yourself, and nurture your needs. You will also find that others reflect how you feel about yourself. Make a habit of giving something of yourself to others in the form of assistance, loving attention, service, or a material gift without expecting anything in return whatsoever. Notice how that makes you feel. Make a habit of accepting gifts or services from others with a sense of surrender. Notice how you feel when you are given a compliment. Share nothing about your practice and your findings except recording them in your journal. Only after the predetermined practice time has elapsed (in this case 40 days) should you share it with others. Not sharing this may be hard, but it is necessary to contain your own feelings and own them. Talking about them before consciously owning them dissipates the energy without anything having been learnt. Touch your crystal often. Thank it and the Divine every day for the assistance you are given. With this practice you can expect to encounter parts of yourself previously hidden. Loved ones will prove especially helpful in this regard, by being the most challenging they can be. Accept it and be joyful for your challenges. Only such trials will move the energy holding you back from yourself and real love.

Effects: By engaging in a longer practice, 40 days, you may find that you feel empowered in making better decisions in your relationships with others. Also, you can discover how much of your life is invested in trying to have others conform to your wishes without really liking it a whole lot (i.e. they feel the areas of your co-dependency). The same applies to you, too - you might see that others use you covertly as well.

Crystal Care: treat your stone lovingly, like a true treasure. Rinse it every other day in spring water, to keep the stone clear.

My Precious Body: Love recipe #2 - Red Garnet

Your body is an integral part of you. Existing without it would be difficult, unless you were an extremely accomplished yogi. An appreciated body is a healthy and happy body. Nourishing the physical is one way of accessing the inner self and your true heart. Perhaps an illness has afflicted you, more or less severely. If so, the practice is brought down into the physical in a very tactile way. Red Garnet assists humanity with its infusion of strong life force. The body is a physical warm-blooded bio-machine, which is there for you to use to fulfil your mission and your purpose. The body is your closest temple on Earth. A healthy body inspires beauty and love of life.

What is the cause of disease? *Toxemia and enervation are the underlying causes of all disease, whether acute or chronic. Toxins in the body originate from wrong choice, worn-out cells, drugs, unloving thoughts, polluted air and water. Enervation comes from over-activity, noise, radiation, extreme climate, overeating, sexual excesses, vaccination, toxins, stress or rapid detoxification*[2].

I find it interesting that unloving thoughts and wrong choices are mentioned in this quote as a cause of disease. Most would agree upon the compromising effects of toxins and detrimental life-style. Here we can address the area of healthy thinking. Garnet is the colour of the life-force fire. The Root Chakra in particular is a faculty that is concerned with physicality. Deep red energy stimulates circulation and vitalizes the lower chakras, and uses this vibration to run the body. The bottom part of the spine has been little appreciated in society and in some spiritual traditions. The Victorian era of shunning body parts as unclean and dirty has made a deep impact on our collective[3] psyche. It is perhaps time to be done with unhealthy thought forms about the body and its natural functioning. Blood is good for life! Other traditions have encouraged the renunciation of the 'impure' lower parts, especially the genitals and the bowel. Avoiding them altogether is considered best, but that cannot be done. You cannot separate the carburettor, wheels and exhaust mechanism from a car and then expect it to drive you places. Learning to love all parts of one's self, including the body, is essential for spiritual progress. Red energy is encouraging! If one rejects the body or parts of it, then negative red life force is energized. In that case, healthy passionate energy becomes aggressive and harmful to the self and others. Many have degrees of unresolved angers hidden in their body. They manifest as temper tantrums,

Figure 41 A Red Garnet This is a naturally terminated crystal, which we may use in making the Sacred Body Anointing Oil.

controlling behaviours, or pain and disease. When covered up they can turn into depression, poverty and other debilitating states.

Why: A healthy body provides a good home.

How to begin: Invite Garnet as a gentle but powerful healer. Begin by making a list of all the things you do not like about your physical situation and your body. Make it a Top 10 Body Parts List. Appreciate yourself for having the guts to begin a Sacred Body Practice. As in the treasure hunt of life, discover the gifts of pain and disease as a clue from Spirit. Reassess your situation. Think healthy thoughts, act in vibrant ways. Even the most severe condition has a possibility of healing. If you do not feel this is the case for your illness, shifting the attitude about it makes a whole world of difference. Dis-ease exists in the mind first. The physical experience of it is the last step. Make an oil infusion of Red Garnet, (see the chapter *Gem Elixirs* for complete instructions on how to make a crystal oil infusion). Use a carrier oil suitable for your needs. Put a couple of drops in your hand and apply a minute amount to each of your top 10 areas. Take great care to tune in with each area and say out loud to each area:

> *You are part of my Sacred Temple.*
> *Thank you for being part of me.*

If you are unable to apply the oil yourself, ask someone else to do it for you.

Maintenance: The physical part of touch makes this exercise very important. Expect to feel and see the results of your practice. Observe how the body responds to your care. Listen to what the body has to tell you. It has perhaps carried a huge load, and you are the only one who can remove it. If strong feelings are coming up, be grateful because that is the body's way of releasing its burdens. Sometime the burden is removed one tear at a time. Continue daily anointing of the Garnet oil for at least 12 days. In the case of a more serious condition, do the practice for up to 3 months or until it is not needed any more. Dowse[4] for the correct length of time for your situation.

Effects: I engaged in two instances of anointing practice, both with good results for myself. One was with a set of chakra oils, one for each of the chakras. I found that when applied before meditation or sleep, it was easier to relax and to have a restful night. The other one was as a long-term self-love practice. This oil was applied in the morning to the area needing most attention that particular day. After several weeks I began to notice how my application of the oil was beginning to make a difference. I began to look forward to applying the oil. It clearly let me feel and I got immediate feedback of how much my body enjoyed the attention. The result was a reduction of pain and discomfort, and natural adjustments of the spine, which, of course, were a great relief.

Crystal Care: Gem Oils should be stored in dark bottles and treated like valuable nectar for the skin.

Dealing with Pain - Two Stone Stories

Personal Story: The energetic impact of Boji Stones™ on the physical body is nothing short of spectacular. It opens and clears even the most blocked pathways and allows energy to flow. As a Mukti[5] Crystal Yoga teacher, I've had the opportunity to see some amazing results with a couple of students. One of the students in our class has had very bad arthritis in both of her hands. At the start of one of the yoga classes, she held a pair of Boji Stones™, one in each hand. Within ten minutes, the arthritic pain had completely left one hand and only a trace of it remained in two fingers of the other hand!! Needless to say, she was able to flow thru the yoga postures without any problems. She currently carries them in her pockets and holds them in her hands only when needed and has remained pain-free for over a year. Another student had total knee replacement on both knees 5 years ago and even though she is able to walk, she has had no feeling or sensation from the waist down. She worked with the Boji Stones™ during the entire class, sometimes holding them in her hands, or placing them on the upper thighs or on the knees. At the end of the class, she actually felt her legs for the first time in 5 years!!!

A personal experience with Mahogany Obsidian. Though I have had cysts in the breast for a long time, for the most part, they have never seemed to bother me. However, when I was going through a particularly stressful time in my life, the cyst in the left breast flared up and became very, very painful. The pain radiated to the shoulder and then down the left arm, leaving it with a very achy feeling. My entire awareness could not be distracted from this pain and discomfort, no matter what I tried. A couple of weeks after this started, when I went to visit my crystal teacher Margherita at a Gem & Mineral Show, a beautiful Mahogany Obsidian sphere on her display table caught my attention. Without giving it a second thought, I picked it up and held it while I sat talking to Margherita about crystals. After 15 minutes, all of a sudden I realized that the pain on my entire left side of the body had greatly, greatly subsided. As I mentioned this to Margherita, she wasn't the least bit surprised, for, she said, Mahogany Obsidian is "the pain remedy stone." Needless to say, it came home with me".

Savitri

Letting Go of Toxic Emotions - Malachite

Personal Story: All through childhood I had the deep longing to become a mother and to conceive a child like my mother did. I wanted an immaculate conception. I was 26 when I met my husband and we ignited this intent to become real. After we married we tried to conceive. Eighteen months later, still nothing happened. No pregnancy was on the horizon. I followed each menstrual cycle, feeling despondent and frustrated when it resumed each month without new life taking root. I sensed my child in the etheric perhaps waiting for me, and possibly my husband's, readiness. As time progressed, I got more and more impatient and increasingly focused on the question of what I would become if not a mother, so I increased and intensified my healing journey and began to feel crappy. A common release mechanism for me was vomiting. In my youth I was challenging and rebellious. I was unable to feel and wasn't connected to the power in myself; instead, I relied on external devices including sugar, coffee and smoking. The underlying cause, toxic thinking, was the real cause of physical challenges, which I was unaware of at the time.

Crystals came into my life as a curve ball and never left. My mom took me along to a crystal course and since that time, in 1998, crystals have been a part of my life. Each experience with the crystals has brought me closer and closer to myself, who I really am underneath my illusion of who I thought I was at the outset of my healing journey.

In 2002 during the advanced course in crystal healing, held at a remote retreat with close contact to nature, I came to do an Infusion procedure. An Infusion simply means that 'a single crystal energy' is applied to the body and around the aura. Many pieces are used, up to several hundred pieces in some cases. Normally 20-30 pieces of the crystal are used in the layout. The crystal chosen was Malachite. I was assisted by 3 facilitators in this process, which was a great help. I truly needed the extra support. My session began with setting the intent to purge any negative thoughtforms around being a mother as well as any other obstacles preventing me from conceiving. It was a very clear statement for me to proceed with. More than 25 pieces of Malachite were placed on and around me while adhering to the strict crystal healing protocol of protection and safety. I wasn't feeling well; as the process continued, I was sick to my stomach and vomited several times. Then there were moments in the session when I connected to my early childhood and feelings of light-heartedness and play. One memory in particular was as a little girl at a lake. I was swimming in the water with a wonderful sense of freedom, romping around and having a great time. I felt so relaxed and at ease in my physical body and in my mind in this memory. I had forgotten about that part of me. The session lasted for more than 2 hours in all. Many imprints and impulses seemed to be aligning and as a result made openings in my inner being. This happened all at once and my response was to retreat into my inner self to integrate the experiences occurring. I was purging, and as my fear of feeling emotions came to the surface, I had to rid myself of all the gory stuff as vomit and tears. Afterward, some amount of menses was also dispelled.

Figure 42 Malachite - the emotional purger stone. This powerful stone is of great help to anyone in transitional times.

After all of this, I was empty and needed rest and sleep. I had a deep knowledge that a new cycle was beginning.

The next day I was revived and appreciated some alone time. Later that day during the treasured field trip to a gem show where we had crystal assignments, I felt fine. It was not so odd that during the afternoon I met with a woman who announced to me that she just found out she was pregnant and told me about it. I was among the very first people she told this news to. Coincidence? I think not! I had purged, I was prepared, and the child took root within me, finally. Within days I had the confirmation that I was indeed pregnant. Wow! Intercourse aside, I had to become ready energetically to be fit and ready to bear a child. My child, now three and half years old, has a sweet sister born 2 years and one day later. My desire to be a mother was fulfilled. Thank you, Malachite!"

Tara Brox

Love recipe #3 - Malachite Elixir

Why: Purging does not have to be so dramatic. You can set the intention for the process to be gentler. This is up to you, but sometimes nothing but a spiritual two-by-four is used by Spirit to kick-start us along. A gentler form of purging can be done with a Malachite elixir, using the vibrational or indirect method.

How to begin: Set your Intent! Spend some time meditating on your intent. Write it down. Feel that this intent is what you want to achieve. Let yourself sleep with the Intent placed nearby in order to receive further clarification on the intention that would help you most. When you are clear, make it as a statement (affirmation or prayer). Write it on a card:

> *May I call and acknowledge*
> *The One Supreme Source of all creation and*
> *Accept my Divine Team guiding me.*
> *My Intent is: _____*
> *It is hereby affirmed!*
> *May this Process and this Elixir yield results,*
> *which assist the process of healing,*
> *for the highest good of all beings concerned.*
> *In Gratitude, So Be It!*

Protocol for a 7-Day Chakra Practice: Malachite Elixir with ascending dosage. State your intentions and make the elixir as outlined in the Gem Elixir chapter. Decide what your practice will involve. Notice if you need to take consideration of the New or Full Moon time. This example can be a guideline: the initial dosage should be dowsed as seven drops under the tongue once a day (alternatively seven drops in a water bottle each time the bottle is refilled.) Wait one hour from the time you took the elixir before ingesting any food. Use the elixir away from food, leaving at least thirty minutes before or after, for best effect.

Day 1 - Upon waking, take the elixir. Meditate for twenty minutes and journal any findings or thoughts. This will work on the root chakra and underlying foundation issues. Element: Earth. Aspects: Home, Family, Money, Sex, Survival. Physical areas: Feet, Knees, Legs, Hips, and Lower Back.

Day 2 – You will repeat Day 1's procedure except that you will make the elixir stronger, by reducing it by one drop. On Day 2, use six drops of elixir. The second day will focus on the sacral chakra and any issues related to the intention which may reside there. Element: Water. Aspects: Intimate Relationships, Creativity, Procreation, Sensuality and Emotions. Organs: Kidneys.

Day 3 – Use 5 drops. The Navel Plexus and Solar Plexus are addressed including the area of the stomach and digestion, gut feeling, power and ego. Be sure to keep journaling and from a detached place, address any things that come up. Own your own feelings. Note that challenges may arise at this point. Accept them and be joyful, for challenges move the energy that has been holding you back. Element: Fire. Aspects: Lack/Abundance, Action, Initiative, Power. Organs: Digestive tract, Intestine, Stomach, Liver and Spleen.

Day 4 – Use 4 drops. This is the mid-point addressing the heart of the matter. The heart is where the second layer of feeling is addressed. The heart centre in its lower aspect is sitting in the solar plexus region and in its higher aspect in the high heart at the thymus area in the upper chest. Stay with the process. You may want to increase your intake of water to support your process. Element: Air. Aspects: Sense of Feeling, Self-Worth, Capacity to Love, Co-dependencies, Attachment, Shielding/Protecting the Inner Child. Place of Intellect: Solar Plexus. Place of Prana/Life Force Intake: Lungs. Place of Love: Heart. To further support yourself, use the thymus thump[6]. Gently thump with two or three fingers on your breast bone in an area about 2" in diameter.

Day 5 – Use 3 drops. The throat centre deals with expression and making choices. Practice verbalizing, in your meditation and your journaling. Element: Space/Sound. Aspects: Expression, Vocation, Choice. Place of Stored Grief: Throat, Jaws, Teeth.

Day 6 – Use 2 drops. The intuitive centres can be blocked so you will not 'see' what is going on with yourself. To open the Third Eye, touch the space between your brows and ask that it will open for you to truly see. Attempt to stay in a calm state of mind and soon, as reasoning and thinking occur, begin to observe rather than being involved. Aspects: Intuition, Extra-sensory Perception, Thoughtform Creation, Guidance Reception, Integration. Place of: Beliefs, Thoughtforms.

Day 7 – Use 1 drop. The Crown chakra is the connection to source and the Divine. Allow a channel to be established to upper centres above the head. Use breath to bring in that energy and release obsolete fragments and thoughtforms. Be beyond a thinker. Aspects: Divine Connection, Guidance, Bliss. Access to Archetypal patterns stored in higher centres.

Maintenance: This completes the seven-day practice. Take at least two weeks to integrate the effects of the elixir. Maintain the daily meditations and journaling sessions.

Effects: You will experience a complete body overhaul, where pent-up emotional energies caused by toxic thinking may surface and be released. The benefit of spending at least one day each on the various levels and body areas gives a good insight into how your body functions and what that part of you needs.

Crystal Care: Gem Elixirs should be stored in dark tincture bottles, in the same way as other remedies.

Summary

The illusions of love cause much suffering. Our need for love and others' attention makes us become prey to co-dependent situations where freedom is cut short and unhappiness will eventually ensue. We can begin addressing this by engaging a rose quartz practice of self-loving. A simple talisman or stone is used in a longer practice of 40 days. The physical body is a precious vehicle in our life, but we may not treat it as well as it needs, causing pain and unnecessary illness. A practice with Garnet oil is explained, as well as how to work out undigested emotions and deep-rooted patterns within the various energy centres of the body, using Malachite: first as a layout, and then as a Gem Elixir.

Practices:
Love recipe #1 Rose Quartz - Self Love
Love recipe #2 Red Garnet - My precious body
Love recipe #3 Malachite Elixir - Release toxic emotions

The Lion's Roar

It is in the silence,
that you may hear what is spoken

How are your communication skills? Do you think that others understand the meaning of what you say? And, do you know what other people are trying to tell you? Ponder this example:

Personal Story: "I have only had a marginal benefit from what you have done for me," he said in his recorded message on her cell phone. With it came a few other similar statements loaded with hot emotions. In fact, she felt that this was the end of their relationship, and this was how he was able to deliver it to her. Upon seeing him on her return home, she asked him if he, in fact, wanted to split up. He said no, not at all, that was not what he meant; he had only wanted to get things off his chest. He had used the phone as some kind of deposit device (read toilet) for his emotions. She was stunned by his harsh words, as each time this had happened the emotional tone had grown rapidly worse.

Clearly, he was not communicating effectively to his partner. She was left hanging with a message that did not clarify or heal

Figure 43 Putting a crystal at the throat centre. It is the place where the mental stream from our head must align itself with the feelings of our heart, in order to have genuine communications.

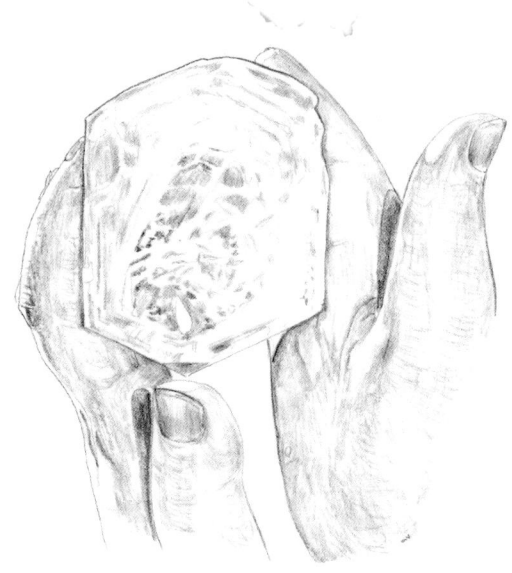

Figure 44 A larger blue Aquamarine - the Stone of Truth, can be used for making a simple 'gem water' in the practice of skillful communication. A tumbled stone can also be used with success.

their situation. She was not able to hear where he needed her. Instead she took the words as a personal attack. Both people in this testimonial seem to lack communicative and listening skills. Neither of them knew what was happening for the other. In such cases, communication becomes a sort of ping-pong game to be won or lost, rather than a genuine sharing of all available dimensions. A spiritual perspective would be to see a person involved with us as part of something bigger. Viewing the relationship as one body, perhaps regarding 'Her' as the left lung and 'Him' as the right, it is easy to see that no benefit comes from having conflict. One lung may be smaller than the other, but both are immensely helpful in the process of breathing. Without either one of them, the breathing capacity is reduced more or less by half. Many people on the planet are incapacitated in this way. We cannot change another person, since healing is only performed on the inside, by each individual. In both difficulty and in joy, any partner is truly mirroring something for the other. Two questions we can ask ourselves could be:

How can I change the way I speak, in order to be heard?
How can I learn to hear what is actually being said?

The Nature of Words

Written and spoken words shape how we live and interact with each other. Skillful communication clearly yields understanding, love and respect, which in turn enhance any relationship. Our spoken words spring from our thought-feeling process in the body and the brain, and are then manifested in the sounds uttered by the vocal cords. Our hearing, however, begins with the ear's perception, which is transmitted to the brain for interpretation and decision for appropriate response. In written communication, our eyes see the letters. The brain interprets them as words and sentences and meaning and gives response in accordance with the existing program it is operating with. The last three words are worthy of notice, as it is the inner operating program with all its subroutines that directs our responses. For example, loud excited words rapidly pronounced may be perceived as normal in some families, but as highly provocative and rude in others. Our style of speaking may be domineering and belittling or encouraging and tolerant by intention, or it may be perceived in such a way by those who hear us.

We can become aware of our style of speaking, and decide to speak in a style that seems more loving and affirming to others. Successful relationships are like a good sports game, only longer, and no winning or losing is needed. A great game is always enjoyed when each player acknowledges and plays fairly in accordance with the same rules. The task of communicating with an intimate partner is to express our own truth without negating[1] another person, and to come to a consensus on the terms of the issue. The fruit of a relationship should be something that both can enjoy and learn from. If one of the partners continuously refuses to participate in a positive way, abuse or damage of some kind is the outcome.

Communicating Skilfully - Aquamarine Water

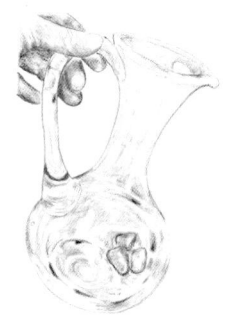

Why: Aquamarine, the Stone of Truth, together with Amazonite, the Stone of Personal Expression, holds the position of Airy Water in the Crystal Mandala[2]. Airy Water refers to the thinking or logical part of our emotions. We can use this quality of Aquamarine to practice skilful communication.

How to begin: Make a simple Gem Water by immersing a piece of clean Aquamarine in a clean carafe. Cover it and leave it in a sunny window for at least 30 minutes. You can extend it to the length of time appropriate for you. Put the energized water in a drinking glass or water bottle. The following morning, sit down with a pen and notebook and sip the water. Make sure you are undisturbed. Sip the water slowly. Whatever feelings come to your mind, write them down. Spend maybe ten minutes or up to a half hour on this or until you feel finished with what you have to say. Avoid analyzing, offering solutions, making to-do lists or projecting what could happen in the future, and just write what you truly feel right now about

Figure 45 Aquamarine or Amazonite Gem Water is made by submersing the gems in pure water. Place the carafe or glass container in the sun to energize the water. In this way the vibration of the stone is copied into the water. The water now carries the gem vibration for us to use in our practice.

your situation. This notebook is your personal listening ear and friend. Never read this to anyone or share what you have written. If you absolutely must read it, wait at least three to six months. In this way, you will have a better perspective[3]. The rest of the day: think about how you would like to feel. Decide to change your response to whatever is triggering any unhappiness.

Maintenance: Do Laugh Yoga! In situations that previously resulted in anger or argument, see if you could find something humorous. For example, in one situation with my own partner, my cat provided a comic relief by his acrobatics, so I decided to laugh, which changed a tense situation drastically. Know that almost all situations can turn out well, depending on one's perspective of it. You can support this practice with Coral Calcite Water[4] In the evening, as you make the next day's Gem Water, meditate on how your day went, and how many times you were able to change your response in a positive way. How many times did you feel joyful? Give yourself a great gold star in each case. Did you actually hear what your friend wanted to communicate to you? Keep this practice up for at least 3 weeks. You may find that your relationship and the way you communicate did change.

Effects: Aquamarine Gem Water practice may help to discover how to shift one's perspective towards hearing and understanding another person's view and also to hear and understand yourself. Journaling is a way to communicate any unspoken words. As soon as they are expressed on the paper, the vibration of that expression is also communicated on a vibrational level. The recipient will hear it with his or her subtle ear, when ready to open it. The subtle ear is the ear of the higher-self guide who does not engage in judgement or game playing, and therefore hears the authentic essence of any message.

Crystal Care: Make fresh gem water daily, using pure spring water. Cover the receptacle to reduce contaminants. Clean your stones each time and energize them in a sunny window.

Mantra and Affirmation

Many spiritual practices use mantras, sacred sounds or holy words in ancient languages like Sanskrit, in order to create change and transformation. The original Sanskrit language contains 50 sounds[5]. Each one of them is said to express an aspect of life depicted as petals on the flower image of each chakra[6]. Resonating at the head (Brow chakra) is the sound of AUM[7], which is said to be the root of physical manifestation; consequently, additional sounds may be viewed as the fine-tuning of Creation into the symphony of all life.

Mantras are chanted as individual sounds or as affirmations. One teacher once said to me that chanting is the 'Elevator to God'. All you have to do is go into the elevator (decide to practice); the energy generated by the chanting will move the car upwards (inwards). You decide which floor (level of consciousness) you desire (selected affirmation). Here we propose to select affirmative statements that are selected upon the basis of how well they resonate with your intentions. When affirmations are used correctly, we may alter our current inner program in effect[8]. Affirmation can be chanted, spoken, sung or written. What is important is that we thouroughly feel the words sink in, alternating with saying our chosen affirmation loudly then softly intil the words merge with our inner stream of consciousness. This is what we want - to install a better program for ourself. By doing this we replace beliefs we have that do not help us grow.

Personal story: My back went out a few times, and it was so painful that I had to stay in bed. Once it happened at work. I was moved from my regular workstation to a location that I had no choice about. I felt overpowered and helpless in my work situation. As I worked with the various issues to resolve those feelings, the problem in my lower back released and moved upwards. Some years ago, I experienced sharp pain in a point near the base of the neck during the night. At the time I decided to do a mantra practice to clear my mind because I couldn't figure out how to physically alleviate the pain. Prior to this event I had done a three-month practice with a particular mantra. After about ten minutes, the pain simply vanished and I could feel some of the energy return and the vertebrae moved to a better position. I hadn't expected this result, but the practice actually helped to relieve the physical pain. Mind over Matter! Until I resolve all of the issues[9] in my spine, I could use this method continually, especially in places such as at work, where it was difficult to stretch or lie down.

Later, in a healing session my intent was to fully correct and align my painful spine to release the cause. My facilitator laid out the

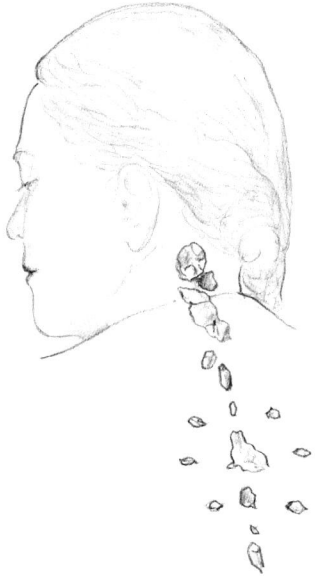

Figure 46 This shows a detail of an Extended Layout using many crystals around the body and on the body. The Layout included Pink Calcite, Elestials, double terminated Quartz, Citrine and Andalusite.

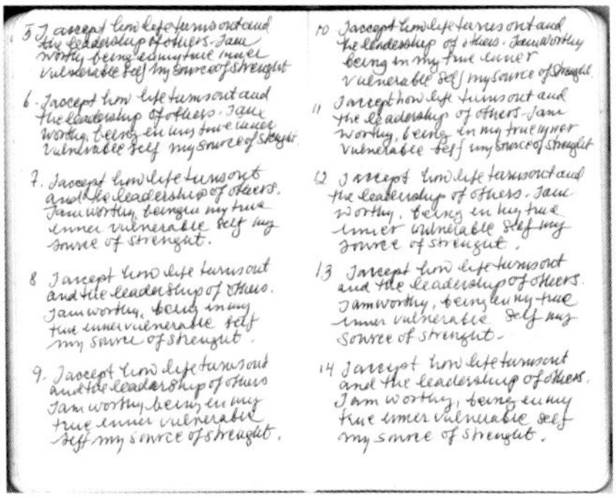

5 I accept how life turns out and the leadership of others. I am worthy, being in my true inner vulnerable self my source of strength.

6. I accept how life turns out and the leadership of others. I am worthy, being in my true inner vulnerable self my source of strength.

7. I accept how life turns out and the leadership of others. I am worthy, being in my true inner vulnerable self my source of strength.

8 I accept how life turns out and the leadership of others. I am worthy, being in my true inner vulnerable self my source of strength.

9. I accept how life turns out and the leadership of others. I am worthy, being in my true inner vulnerable self my source of strength.

10 I accept how life turns out and the leadership of others. I am worthy, being in my true inner vulnerable self my source of strength.

11 I accept how life turns out and the leadership of others. I am worthy, being in my true inner vulnerable self my source of strength.

12 I accept how life turns out and the leadership of others. I am worthy, being in my true inner vulnerable self my source of strength.

13 I accept how life turns out and the leadership of others. I am worthy, being in my true inner vulnerable self my source of strength.

14 I accept how life turns out and the leadership of others. I am worthy, being in my true inner vulnerable self my source of strength.

selected crystals on my back as can be seen in the drawing. I could feel the stones as she was placing them on the most painful areas close to my neck. I intensely knew that I was touching on very sensitive issues that I had previously avoided. They had to do with self-worth and setting reasonable boundaries with others. If I did not set the limits, others would do it for me, especially in intimate relationships. The inner resulting pressure from allowing such violations had physically crinkled my spine. The whole process of unfolding this particular issue first became evident in my twenties as lower back pain, but not until now, more than 30 years later, was I able to put the pieces of this painful puzzle together. With the help of my facilitator, a re-programming practice was suggested. To my surprise there were thoughtforms (programs) in place that forced me to choose to engage in self-damaging behaviour. I had, in fact, taken on a steel straight-jacket to protect myself a long, long time ago. The centre of protection was around my femininity and my expression of my needs. This was the source of my pain. My affirmation words included: acceptance, worthiness and being vulnerable. The 24-word affirmation was really hard to do, especially writing the word "vulnerable" but I persisted and as the days progressed I felt I was on track and it helped me. Now I let any pain guide me instead of putting it away somewhere. The ensuing months showed me where I had gone wrong, and I was now in a position to make changes that had previously been impossible. My past ego persona of 'she who handles everything (for everybody)' is now gone.

Figure 47 Written Affirmation Practice. Numbering each entry makes it easier. I also wrote the date and the day number at the beginning of each session.

Written Affirmations Practice

Why: Practicing silently with our inner voice can be a very successful way of changing non-beneficial beliefs (programs).

How to begin: The chosen Affirmation is written down in a notebook 21 times every day for 21 days[10]. If one misses a day, start over from day one again until complete. By repeating the words in written form the effect seems to me to be far more powerful, as the hand, the eyes and the thinking processes must be engaged simultaneously, and must be sustained during the time-frame it takes to write it. Also, as you are writing, you are documenting your own efforts.

Maintenance: Even though you are not speaking out loud in this practice, you are speaking and commanding your new program to be installed in your mind, and this process allows your inner self to correct the situation you want to remedy. Attempt to write with a sense of positive enthusiasm and belief that this will be true for you. The stones you may have used to formulate your affirmations can be put on top of your notebook in between sessions.

Effects: This practice addresses deeply embedded beliefs that are hidden from your conscious mind. The source of pain and other conditions may be addressed. If the cause is accessed and corrected, symptoms will disappear.

Crystal Care: Your affirmation notebook represents your new program and a new way of thinking, so treat it with respect.

Crystal Sounds - Singing Bowls

Sounds of pure Crystal Singing Bowls are transformative and divinely wonderful to listen to. They assist in helping us to be silent. It is in the silence of the mind where the thoughts are stilled that you may know yourself. I first came to hear such sounds in a workshop in the early nineties given by a gifted dance movement healer. As she started to sound the beautiful crystal bowl that she had displayed on a piece of fur, together with a few crystals, I remember how my whole being was changed by the sounds. How did it change me? I can only say that I found myself opened in a way that I had not experienced before. The tones resonated to the core of my being, shaking me up and allowing me to feel and to move more easily. It was a very transformative moment of my personal journey. Many healers now incorporate a variety of sounds in their therapies. One does not have to understand what or how crystal resonance works to receive its benefit. The Crystal Key for singing bowls relates to Tuning of the polarities of Discord and Harmony.

Why: The singing bowl practice teaches us to listen and to silence our mind. By their vibration they directly tune our system on both physical and subtle levels. Listening helps us to discover the crystal notes which vibrate on levels unavailable to the physical ear. By starting with the physical sounds, we may also develop our inner hearing. As well, it also offers training of the vocal cords to begin expressing energy that was blocked, or after that is accomplished, the expression of pure joy.

How to begin: For this you can use a singing bowl, or listen to a recording. The intention is to first listen and then free up your voice. Find an undisturbed place by yourself or with a group of like-minded people who also like to work with their voices. Set up the instruments and make yourself comfortable. Take a moment of complete silence and then begin to play. As you listen,

Figure 48 Singing bowls are created from pure crystal (left) or metal - either brass (a Zen bowl, shown right), or in Tibetan bowls, from an alloy of seven sacred metals. Singing bowls are profound healing tools that provide healing sounds when played consciously.

feel the sounds embrace you. Listen to your body, and where the sound touches you. Feel it touch you deeply and from that place in your body, discover what sounds are hidden there. Let those sounds rise up to your throat and collect there until you can express them. It could be a gentle hum or the roar of a lion. Let the whole sound come out: do not keep back any of it. This is your healing. Then listen again: do the played notes touch another part of you? Continue releasing your inner sounds until you are complete. Afterwards, remain in silent meditation.

Effects: You may feel comfortable in your own silence and in your own conscious sounding. You may also experience the practice as directly bypassing your thinking mind with its words. The benefit of this is the regained control of your authentic self. The practice also feels incredibly good.

Maintenance: Make a commitment to practice daily for at least five days. The best, however, is to do an entire moon cycle, starting on the new moon.

Crystal Care: Place crystal bowls on a mat or firm pillow before playing. Keep them dust free and clean in an appropriate space. Tibetan metal bowls or the Japanese Zen bowls are also excellent. Treat all your instruments like sacred objects.

I'd like to conclude with a testimonial from a friend who is an artist and familiar with crystals:

Personal story: "I remember an experience when others used crystals to assist my healing: In 1995 I listened to a crystal bowl used in a concert by a wonderful Tibetan-style musician who lives in San Francisco. When he played the bowl in a small concert in his apartment, I felt blocks clearing in my solar plexus. There were involuntary tremblings going on. Eventually, I decided to slide off the couch and on to the floor. When I closed my eyes I saw a double spiral of white light going into the distance ahead of me. After the concert I thanked him and told him about the spiral. He said that it had worked and that I had received the healing. He was working to clarify our DNA! He also shared with me that he did not understand why there was not a line-up around the block for his concerts. "The effects are so strong. Perhaps people don't grasp what is going on". Love you, Andrew O.

Perhaps I can attempt an answer to his question. Unless asked, people do not like to work on their issues. Most assume that their view is the correct one. They have not had the experience of connection to a greater whole. They might think that they are separate, and do not need to be changed in any way. Such persons will have great difficulty interacting with challenges at first, but life itself will teach them. Even if we see what is wrong, that does not give us licence to bombard them with what we think they should do. Only if asked should we attempt to answer them. I can relate to this, as I was once one of those people who believe that all problems are external.

Summary

Intimate communication can be challenging in relationships, when words are used with emotional undertones. Words are created by our inner thought-feeling processes in accordance with our existing beliefs or programs. Our style of communicating depends usually on our family background. Loud and emotional words can intimidate someone from a quiet and rational family-style of communication. Benefit lies in bridging these styles and allows for change, thereby bringing more understanding for the other person in a relationship. Mantras are sacred sounds that are linked to creation and are used by many spiritual traditions. Affirmations are similar to mantras in that one might work on changing personal beliefs to open up a new way of being. Certain sounds are healing and may open blocked areas in the body. By playing a crystal singing bowl, the sounds may generate a range of tones for healing purposes. The practitioner listens to the body's inner resonance and then voice that energy. The sounds expressed, releases the blocked energy.

Practices:
Aquamarine Gem Water - to address communication
Voiced and Written Affirmation - to change belief for healing
Playing Singing Bowls - to hear and express your authentic self

The Mystery of Energy

I feel it but see it not
Invisibly powerful yet gentle

There is much talk about 'energy' when it comes to healing and in therapeutic situations. One may hear such things as: "I am working with energy. I am an energy worker," etc. What does this mean? The dictionary definitions for "energy" refer to: the ability, capacity, or power to work, liveliness and vigour, forceful effect, power supply and an usually positive spiritual force. Other words relating to healing and living systems include: prana, vital energy, chi, ki, Qi, elemental energy, mental energy, physical energy, life force and earth energy. It is clear that energy is not a single phenomena but a range of something that is measurable but invisible, has no weight and can travel through things.

Gross energy is stored in gas, as fuel for motors, or in a battery used by electrical devices. Energy (measured in calories) can be stored in the physical body in the form of fat. When we need

Figure 49 Energy and matter are two of the three components that constitute our being. It is energy, in its multitude of forms, that makes us alive. The third part is consciousness (mind), which allows for choice on how matter and energy will manifest.

more energy, the fat is digested and energy is released. Energy of subtler nature is called "vital energy" and permeates our body. It is the invisible nourishment that we need to stay alive. This life-force energy is present in our environment and we can access that energy though our subtle energy organs.

What does energy do? Energy's essential ability is to move, and will always move, unless it is contained in some form. Compare it to a balloon: when pushed under the water it pops right up again unless it is held down firmly. When energy is not processed well, it "dumps itself into something." A person told me that many years ago his hair turned grey overnight from experiencing acute fear: he said he got frightened to death by an apparition. His hair probable would be grey for the rest of his life, but the emotional shock might be dealt with. Compare it to a runaway train wedged into a hill. It takes considerable effort to dig it out, and it may be wrecked and as well leave a big hole in the hill. In the body it works in the same way. If energy is processed poorly, it can cause a heart attack or emotional crash. To repair such damage one has literally to excavate it. Once released as energy again, there is the possibility of processing it without harm. Upon release, such energy acts like a 'live' wire, and must be dealt with immediately.

How is energy moved? The process of releasing and dealing with blocked energy in our body is called "healing." It includes tracing a symptom to its cause and then dissolving the cause. It is through our symptoms that we can begin this detective work. The physical location can be easily identified by words like: *stiff, painful, hurting, aching, not working, diseased, irritated, wounded, injured, swollen, bloated, infected, inflamed, cancerous* or *simply hated.* Our entire life and actions are mapped out perfectly in our body. A clairvoyant may see a person not as a body with symptoms, but as a hologram of experienced events. Blocked energies could be used to our advantage if we realize that. Taking our power back literally means to free energy we have stored. The journey of discovering ourselves is an effective method to locate such energy. Forgiving and letting go releases the energy completely. Consider a situation such as when someone has hurt us. We have trouble forgiving him or her at first because of some reason we have, like 'He should not get away with doing such a bad thing!' By having thoughts like this we keep our hurt alive, and actually feed it energy. The initial hurt, however small it was from the beginning, might become a mountain. To forgive is to remove the initial cause inside of us, but it is not to say that what the person did was ok. Another way to see it is: 'I was thrown a weed seed, but instead of discarding it, I am watering it, and I will not pull the growing weed out because this is my evidence of their sin against me'. Letting Go is the action we make to pull that weed out. We are actually setting our boundaries in a new place. Inside, we may feel something hard melting, tension softening, or wounds healing up to yield fresh new skin. Now we know something more about how our inner world relates to the outside world: this is Self-Discovery.

How are energy and crystals related? Crystals can be seen as a battery, containing energy that can be unleashed from them. This is called the "piezoelectric effect." Shamans and other individuals have used this ability of a crystal to create power surges or lightning flashes. Modern scientists have created technology using this capacity of crystals in watches and computers. Crystals also channel energy. Healers may amplify their energy by putting it through a suitable crystal. A scientist may use a light source and channel it through a crystal to create a powerful laser. The letting go process may be aided by the use of crystals which can hold space for us internally, thus aiding the blocked energies in their release. (See *Practice of Forgiveness - Dioptase Grid*).

Inner Energy Management

In any living being, energy is either flowing or blocked. Energy is indestructible according to Albert Einstein, and this is illustrated with his famous formula $E=MC^2$, where energy can be transformed back and forth with matter times the square of the speed of light. We may discern this in how we deal with the myriad of energies in daily life (refer to the comparison with the train above). On inner planes there are three ways of dealing with energy: taking it in, sending it out, or not moving it. Translated into our life, this can be described as:

➤ We feel we can't have enough of it, and constantly are looking for more. (Desire)
➤ We reject it, dislike it, and do not want it - we constantly push it away (Aversion)
➤ We are unaware of it, and nothing changes (Ignorance)

Compare the three states allegorically: as the monkey, who is going from thing to thing, wanting more and more; the rooster strutting around and make loud noises about everything; and lastly the pig, not aspiring to anything, but just staying put in the mud[1].

How to increase energy? Like the ocean when the tide goes in and out, our capacity to retain energy varies as well. An athlete prepares for a race carefully by using conscious training and diet so that his peak performance can fall within the time of the race. We may learn how to do this in daily life by paying attention to where our energy goes. Energy zappers include: coffee, refined sugars, processed food, certain drugs, negative conversations and people, negative thinking, mindless activities, stress and joyless existence. Certain foods build our energy. Eating fruit gives an extra boost as the sugars in the fruits can directly be used in the body. Slow-burning carbohydrates, like grains, help maintain a

Figure 50 Wanting, Aversion and Ignorance: the three states of being that hinder complete freedom and happiness.

grounded presence and endurance. Also physical activity - like yoga postures, walking and stretching - makes the body limber and the circulation healthy. The crystal savvy may build up inner energy levels by yang (active) crystal practices such as: *Building Strength with Tiger-eye*, or using Yin (receptive) practices, which include: *Sacred Body using Red Garnet Oil* or *Self-Love with Rose Quartz Medicine*.

Special stones for working with the three energy states:

Aversion/Anger:
Aragonite - the Anger Remedy Stone, to absorb aggressive energies, therby gaining some space to deal with one's issues.

Petrified Wood – the Stone of Patience, to accept what is.

Eudialyte – the Anger Management Stone, to assit us to transform inner aggressive energy and feeling states.

Desire:
Rose Quartz - the Self-Love Stone, to release attachment to external objects, people and situations, therby dissolving the desire.

Imperial Golden Topaz - the Abundance Stone, to attract that which one wants, thereby fulfilling the desire

Ignorance:
Garnet – the Sacred Body Stone, to stimulate an interest and awareness of what supports and nurishes us.

Rutillated Quartz – the Energy Booster Stone, to put emphasis on regaining energy, therby learning how to increase vitality.

Blue Kyanite – the Mental Fog Remedy Stone, to bring into focus what distracts us, therby assiting us to clear it, and open up.

Clear Quartz – the Meditation and Attunement Stone, to help us to become more aware in general.

How to use our energy? Most people know how to spend money, which is a token of energy. We also know how to eat, and food delivers energy to us. But what normally is forgotten is how we use our energy field, the subtle body of energy patterns extending outside our physical form, called "the aura." We may violate other people by loud behaviour. We may take over other people's personal space by littering our possessions in their way. We may steal others' energy by demanding their attention, or take delight in humiliating others with cruel words. Usually the Bully, the Motor-mouth and the Power-hungry person have no idea how they affect others. Also, by allowing ourselves to be victimized, we subconsciously encourage others to take advantage of us and use our energy. Crystal practices related to our use of energy are: Obsidian Bubble (neutral) to create a protective barrier against invasive energy, to not be swayed by other people's forceful energy or negativity, Black Tourmaline Warrior Stance (Yang) to safely anchor our roots in the earth whilst being present, and the Hematite Grid (Yin) as a way of stating and creating personal boundaries.

Subtle Energy Organs

Energy in many forms, both gross and subtle, is available almost everywhere: one need just collect and assimilate it appropriately. Food energies, both solid and liquid, are assimilated through the digestive system, stomach and intestine; air energy (oxygen) is harvested through our lungs to be used in cellular metabolism via red blood cells. Subtle energies (life-force) are absorbed through our chakras, and transported via invisible tubular pathways all through the body. Traces of such ductile pathways have been detected[2] by modern researchers. Chakras[3] are found wherever two or more energy channels overlap, like two roads that meet at an intersection. Each chakra is tuned to integrate specific ranges of the energies that it can use. The lower chakras are related to physicality: survival, procreating, individual power and intellect. The central chakra, the heart, is the portal to feelings and the power of love. The upper chakras relate to expression, vision and spiritual aspects.

Ancient sages knew about the subtle bodies. Their teaching remains in spiritual traditions that describe varying uses and numbers of energy centres. Most commonly known are the seven major chakras: Crown, Third Eye (or Brow), Throat, Heart, Solar Plexus, Sacral and Root (or Base). Other chakras include: Navel, Spleen, Causal, Earth Star and the Soul Star[4].

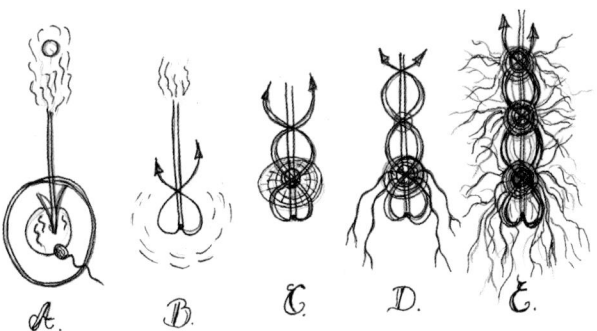

Our Beginnings. Perhaps our very first physical beginnings looked like this: in the pre-birth dimension as the impulse to incarnate is evident, a soul is attracted to its parents in sexual union (A). The conditioning blueprint of the new person is already available and the subtle central channel extends within the fertilized cell, and then it divides into two side channels (B), which curve back and forth upwards, knotting themselves along the central channel (C), thereby creating the major chakras within the growing foetus. From each nexus, smaller channels grow like root threads from a seedling (D). Then physical matter is attracted to the subtle form (E) which eventually produces a baby at birth. At death, or when someone attains enlightenment, the knots begin to dissolve forcing the vital energy back up the central channel. Most do not stay conscious at death but fall into the cycle of rebirth again. What was attained in the past lifetime comes with the soul as the conditioning blueprint. This blueprint governs the lessons to be experienced in the new lifetime. If your belief does not accept the idea of rebirth and incarnation, you might view this discussion as a metaphor for an inherited pattern from your parents. This might explain 'inherited sins' from a healing perspective. In everyday life we may not need to bother with the technicalities of various chakras, but the more we learn about the inner planes, the more we benefit from the proper terms in order to describe what is happening.

Energy, Channels & Energy Centres

In Hopi myths it is told that beings were created from a central vertical axis where the Creator placed five forces together, around which their life rotates. The placement of these forces was: top of the head, the brain, throat, heart and navel. The soft spot on top of the head was seen as "the open door through which each individual receives his life and communication with the Creator." On my visit to Zuni Pueblo in the American south-west, I saw a painting of the origins of the Zunis at their heritage museum. It portrayed a cave, a world under the Earth. People were climbing up a big tree that reached towards a small opening way

Figure 51 The Love Tree of grounded and connected balance of male and female energy expressed in this painting by Misun.

up in the ceiling of the cave. Crows were seen watching over the scene. Some people were going though the opening, up to the surface of the Earth. This painting, I thought, was an example of how our inner subtle anatomy and conscious evolution could be taught beautifully.

Some propose that Qi (a Daoist concept) could be perceived as being closer to the physical dimension than Prana (Hindu concept). At least 30 kinds of subtle energy are described, like qi of the elements, and the five pranas. 'Breath of life' (Judeo-Christian concept) does not distinguish gradations to my knowledge. Qi is described as ever present and not dependent on whether we are born or not. 'Breath of life' is what G-d used to create man from inert matter. It depends on the cultural conditioning and one's faith, as to how these concepts are to be integrated. Personal experience would be the best way to find out.

Most agree that meridians and nadis are pathways for subtle energy. Meridians are linked to the vital organs and populated with qi. When one of the more than 12 meridians approaches the skin, one can identify an acupuncture point. The microcosmic orbits are two major meridians forming a circular orbit around the front and back of the body, including the tip of the tailbone, perineum and the top of the head. We may use this orbit in circular breathing exercises. Nadis are channels transporting various pranas between chakras that are connected to the major glands. The locations of the 7 or 8 major chakras are along the central channels, located in front of the spine. On the surface of the body they are found along the central vertical line at the front and back of the body. Minor chakras are found everywhere else where minor channels intersect. Some similarities between nadis and meridians exist. It is possible that orbits, meridians and nadis may exist on different dimensions, overlapping each other.

Chakras are said to be a wheel, funnel or even a spherical organ

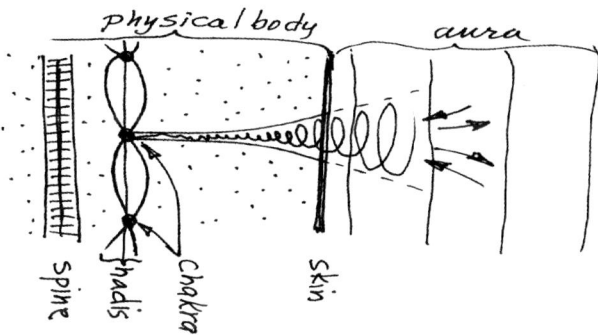

Figure 52 Schematic model of a chakra, at the crossing of the subtle channels (nadis) in front of the spine and its outer parts funnelling out outside the body, assimilating subtle energies from the environment. Some also consider a funnel towards the back of the body (to the left in this drawing).

assimilating various energies and vibrations. They manage levels of life from survival, intimate relations, power management, processing feelings, expression and self-responsibility, intuition, extra-sensory perception, miraculous powers and consciousness. It is said that there are up to 72 000, or even as many as 144 000 chakras in the body, and each chakra holds one small part of the total body of realization that a person would need to achieve to be fully liberated. How true this particular fact is would be impossible to ascertain, unless one were enlightened. The three dantiens, on the other hand, are mentioned in connection with a different cultural system, and should be developed by practice whereas we are born with chakras. Perhaps the dantiens could be seen as fused chakras - for example; the root, sacral and navel chakras joined into a fused centre when all issues in those centres have been integrated. One might see them as dimensional bodies. My teacher Katrina Raphaell taught[7] that there are five "high" bodies: High Body, High Heart, High Mind, and the bodies at the Knees and Feet. The access points for the first three are marked on the image on page 593.

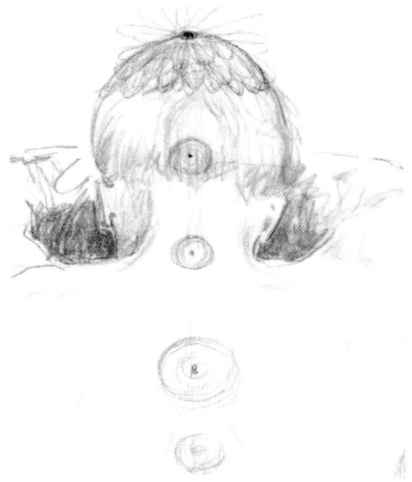

Figure 53 The chakra positions at the back of the body are important as well. I have the feeling that the chakras are funneling out towards the front and to the back meeting in the centre as a small point or in a developed or overextended chakra as a sphere, perhaps as big as an orange to the size of a large spherical field extending outside of the body.

No description of subtle energy organs would be complete without mentioning Barbara Brennan's work. She sees four dimensional levels[5] of our being: physical, auric, haric and core star. The auric level includes the complex system of seven chakras, along a central channel. The haric level is comprised of a vertical channel reaching into the core of the Earth, with three locations: ID point (above the head), soul seat (at the thymus), and the hara or tantien (below the navel). The subtlest level is a point, the core star (just above the navel), where our localised divinity resides.

I think it is crucial to realize that it does not matter what label we put on subtle centres and channels, but they are useful for communication and learning about what to look for in a process of awakening. Ancient traditions have approached the human subtle anatomy from different points of view, and their needs. If a system can be used for practical purposes, and yield practical results, then it is helpful for an individual with a problem. This is important to keep in mind. In my experience, the subtle pathways are affected by how we place our attention. Whatever path we are applying ourselves to for our energy, that path becomes stronger, wider and more accessible, comparable to the narrow walkway in the forest which, when many travel upon it, becomes a road.

Dual Flow Breath - Creating a Pillar of Light

How to utilize energy for healing? To facilitate healing one must have enough energy, and be connected to the source of it. If we are not connected, depletion and fatigue will result sooner or later. We can learn how to connect ourselves, by engaging the basic pillar of light along the spine, in the practice of the *Dual Flow Breath*. This practice, I feel, is central to any healing modality. It connects us to our energy source in the heavens and in the Earth. To train in circulating our subtle energies we may use this method to rejuvenate ourselves. You can prepare by standing in the Mountain Pose (a yoga posture where the spine is straight, arms at the sides, feet parallel, knees soft, pelvis gently tucked forward, head resting balanced on the shoulders, and eyes relaxed).

Why: If we are not connected with our source of energy, it is very difficult to perform healing on ourselves and others. The two flows help us to be more grounded and at the same time they expand us, thus helping us to perceive what is going on in a healing situation.

How to begin: 1) Visualize the top of your immediate aura, about a foot above your head. This is the Soul Star Chakra. See it as a radiant sun always brimming with energy from the Source. This energy can never be turned off. We can close our intake of this energy, but the energy source itself is always there. Inhale this radiant energy; bring it into your body. Your body will absorb as much as it needs of this nutritious vital energy, and then continue to exhale downwards. Let the energy sink down into the centre of the Earth before you inhale again. Repeat many times. This continuous down-flow of energy grounds you and refills your energy reservoirs. Notice how you feel.

2) Visualize the bottom of your aura, the Earth Star Chakra, located about 6" below your feet. It is the portal for upward-moving energies originating at the core of the Earth. Inhale this energy up from the Earth Star portal into your body, and then exhale it up through your Soul Star all the way to the Source. The upward-moving energy stimulates your being to evolve and develop your gifts. It also brings you closer to the Source, which is very useful in the process of your ascension. Inhaling brings energy into your body, and exhaling releases the energy outside of you. Continue breathing for several minutes. Notice if you get light-headed or spaced-out.

3) Combining the two breaths. In the next two breaths, do one complete inhale and exhale downwards and then one complete inhale and exhale upwards. By combining the two flows you get both grounded and expanded at the same time. Continue until you strongly feel the two flows along your central vertical line. This is your personal *Pillar of Light*. Continue for several minutes. Notice how the combined breaths affect you.

Maintenance: Practice the Dual Flow Breath anytime, several times a day, especially if you get distracted and ungrounded.

Effects: This practice helps you remedy distraction, confusion and lack of focus. You have a better opportunity to be present to what is happening inside and outside yourself. Others will have more difficulty manipulating you, and you are able to be better in command of your own power.

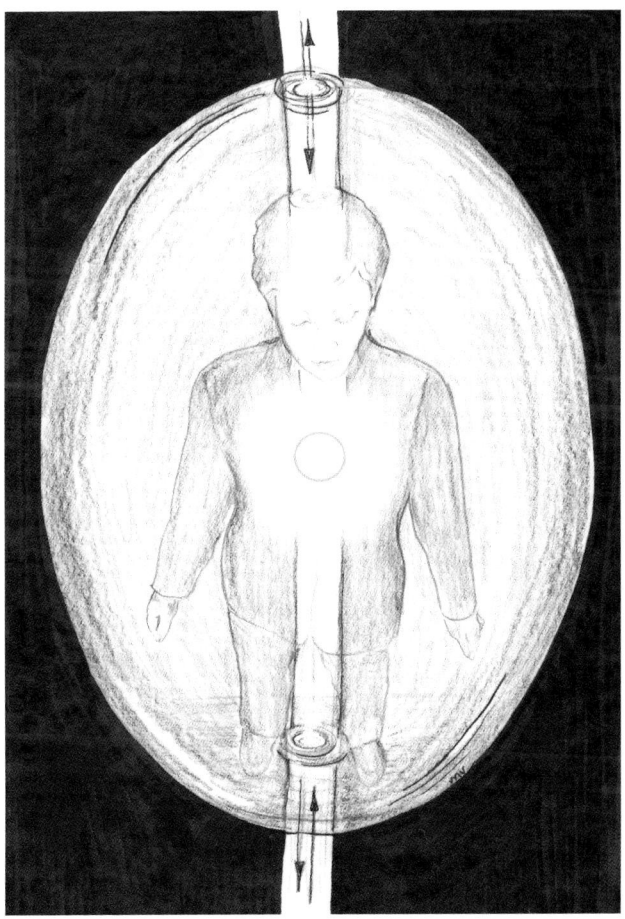

Figure 54 Creating a Pillar of Light within, using the Dual Flow Breath. The drawing shows the outer auric bubble, the central channel connecting the Soul Star chakra at the top and the Earth Star chakra at the bottom of the aura. The arrows show the two directions of the energy flow. At the centre, our heart, which begins radiating healing energy when we are aligned to our Source.

Accessing Chakras - Chakra Clean Layout

Prerequisite: *Attune to Guidance, Hematite Grid, Dual Flow Breath, Breathing the Stone.*

In the modality of Crystal Acupressure[6], tiny minerals are taped onto acupuncture points. The minerals both apply pressure to the points as well as energetically reflect and amplify to affect balance in the acu-point. We can be apprized of this therapy to understand the basis for 'Laying on of Stones.' The stones are placed within the field of each of the major 8 chakras (the navel is added in these layouts). By exposing a chakra to a crystal we may affect it in certain ways, especially if one is actively applying breath-visualization during the period of contact with the stone.

Why: Using this practice you may become aware of your energy centres and which state they are in. The intention for the Chakra Clean layout is to ready the chakras and deal with energies you already have brought forward. It can be used before or after other layouts. This layout is relaxing and refreshing. It literally dusts your chakras as well as grounds you, preparing you for greater energetic flow. It can be seen as taking care of energies that you already have released but which still hang around you. Hematite is highly absorbing and Pyrite may assist to ground and stabilize mental energies (this I learnt from Katrina Raphaell). Put the clean and cleared stones on a small tray, and set a Hematite Grid with four stones around the healing area. For any crystal work set your intent for what you would like to see, perceive, release or balance. Always include in this a request that the intent be for the highest good for all concerned.

How to begin: Attune to your inner guidance and set the intent to become aware of your chakras and their locations. Breathe in deeply from the top of your head and exhale down to your feet. Then breathe up from your feet and let the breath go through you out the top of your head (*Dual Flow Breath*). Lie down comfortably in the Hematite Grid, and starting at the root centre, place the stones one by one on your body. This layout is simply eight Hematites placed on your eight places: root, pelvis, navel, solar plexus, heart, throat, third eye and at the top of the head. In addition, place a Pyrite cube at your hairline, which is the lower edge of the crown chakra.

When all the stones are placed on your body, begin to '*Breathe*' each stone, one at the time. This means to inhale above the stone and visualize the vital air going though the stone bringing its vibration into the chakra down into your body, and then exhale into the earth. As you breathe, you may become aware

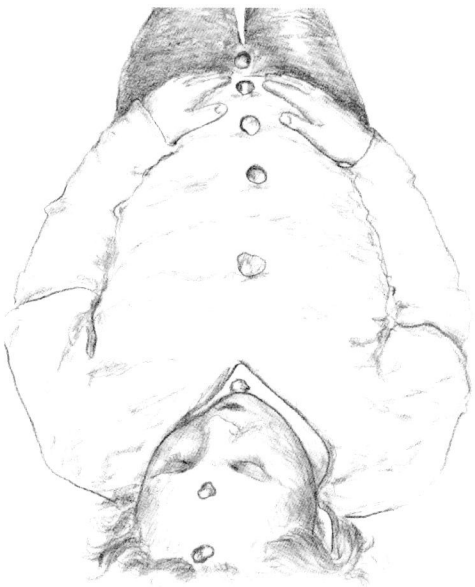

Figure 55 Chakra Layout. Crystals are placed on the body to affect the chakras in beneficial ways. The Chakra Clean Layout is shown, in which Hematite is used on all chakras, and as well a Pyrite placed at the hairline.

of sensations in your body. Observe any sensations and locate where they originate. Once you have located the area, breathe into it. Sensation may include momentary feelings of heat or cold, emotions, pain, discomfort, unease and impatience. Observe what is going on without analysing and continue breathing. Then continue to do the same at the next stone in the order in which you placed them. When you are complete (after about 15 minutes) remove the stones. With some practice you will know how much time you will need. Sometimes it is great to leave the stones on longer.

Maintenance: After the session, list the areas in which you detected sensations and discern which chakra it is closest to. Put some attention to it. Learn all you can about it, its function and its state. Discover if you can feel changes happen as you focus on it.

Effects: This layout is deeply relaxing and refreshing, and a starting point of discovering what is happening in the body, much like looking into a glass tank with tropical fish (the tank as the body and the fish being the energies moving). This exercise is the starting point to let you back into the "ocean" of life energies (where you metaphorically become the fish in your living ocean of life).

Crystal Care: Hematites can be cleaned and cleared by placing them in pure water overnight. Pyrite should not be put in water to be cleaned. Use smudge, singing bowl or place it in the sun for a few minutes.

Figure 56 Next page: Chakra Positions seen from a facliltator's perspective at a treatment table: At the top (below the feet) is the Earth Star followed by the Root, Sacral, Navel, Solar Plexus, Heart, Throat, Brow, Crown chakras and then the Soul Star above the head. Notice the three tiny dots indicating the Hip Points and the High Heart point. Auric layers are indicated around the body.

Chakra Balancing Layout with Quartz

Prerequisite: Chakra Clean Layout

Why: Balance in the chakra system yields balance to the rest of you. It is a starting point for a personal healing journey and a preparation for gaining confidence in your ability to affect your inner life. This layout uses eight varieties of Quartz. It is intended to balance and synchronize your chakras with each other. Katrina Raphaell first taught the Chakra Balancing layout. She emphasized the importance of placing crystals on all eight chakras to achieve the best effect.

How to begin: Simply set the intent to become aware of your chakras and to balance them. Breathe in deeply from the top of your head and exhale down to your feet. Then breathe up from your feet and let the breath go through you out the top of your head (*Dual Flow Breath*). Lie down comfortably in a Hematite Grid and place the stones one by one on your body. This layout is a group of eight varieties of Quartz minerals placed on your eight chakras: root, pelvis, navel, solar plexus, heart, throat, third eye and at the crown (top of the head). At each location place the stone and *Breathe the Stone*, which means to inhale above the stone and visualize the vital air going though the stone bringing its vibration into the chakra underneath, to balance it. As you breathe you may become aware of sensations in your body. Observe the sensations and locate where they originate. Once you have located the area, breathe into it. Sensations may include momentary

Chakra Balancing Layout with Quartz:

Placement:	Stone:	Stone Colour:
Crown	Clear Quartz	Clear
Third Eye	Amethyst	Purple
Throat	Blue Lace Agate	Light Blue
Heart	Rose Quartz	Pink
Solar Plexus	Aventurine	Green
Navel	Citrine	Gold/Yellow
Pelvis	Carnelian	Orange
Root	Smokey Quartz	Smokey

feelings of heat or cold, emotions, pain, discomfort, unease or impatience. Observe what is going on without analysing and continue breathing. After about 10 to 15 minutes, remove the stones, when you feel you are complete.

To finish and also put extra focus on particular chakras, see your source of energy like a sun above you. Inhale its light in through the stone and into the body. Pause before exhaling stale energy out and down. (You may also visualize this energy going into a garbage receptacle beside you. For more detail see *How to Use the Incinerator Orb*, in the chapter *The Crystal Orb*.)

Maintenance: The balancing layout can be used in conjunction with the *Body Scan* (see chapter *Pendulum Basics*). Then one would test the chakras before the layout and after to discover how the chakras have responded to the crystal placement.

Effects: If applied correctly, this layout is very rejuvenating, and it lets you know more about yourself and where in your body a particular issue resides. One may feel cleansed and rejuvenated afterwards. It is training you to breathe properly and to use your breath as the means of focusing your attention on something (for example a location in your body). As you connect with the crystals you may feel tingles or energy running throughout your body. In this way energy is brought to ailing areas and the overall circulation of energy is improved.

Crystal Care: All the crystals in this layout can be washed (washing with mild detergent and rinsing in water) and cleared by smudging or sounding of a singing bowl. Tumbled stones can be stored together.

Summary

This chapter explores the concept and reality of energy and how it is used within healing. Energy is occurring on an immense level for powering machines and on subtler levels in a living system, as vital energy that keeps us alive. Energy can be stored, measured and moved. By moving stagnant or blocked energy in the body we achieve healing and freely flowing energy. Internally, energy can be dealt with in thee ways: taking it in, rejecting it, or ignoring it. This relates to the states of desire, aversion and ignorance. By observing how we deal with energy we may learn to be in control of our life-force and energy field, and how we interact with others. On a subtle level the various kinds of vital energy, qi, chi, prana or life force are processed in our body by the various subtle energy organs, including chakras and dantiens, and then transported by complex subtle channel systems. Such channels include the central channel with its two side channels and the system of the meridian. By applying breath-visualizations together with crystal healing layouts, we may balance our chakras and energy levels.

Practices:
Dual Flow Breath
Chakra Clean Layout
Chakra Balancing Layout

Figure 57 Drusy Amethyst (geode). Amethyst is a stone for Mastering Change. Drusy means a cluster of tiny points. It is ideal for working with changing all the little things that may be bothersome. Amethyst resonates especially to the third eye and crown chakras. The crystal shown here is also perfect for 'Crystal Gazing' meditations, and as well for creating beneficial atmosphere in a room.

The All-Seeing Eye

Seeing is believing,
Believing is not always reality

Using one's mental faculty proves difficult at times. Distractions, stress and confusion may obscure clarity. The cause of it resides in our environment, our everyday life, and our conditioning. Toxic food and lifestyle do not make it better. It is said that we do not see things as they are, but as we are. When thinking is clear it serves as an instrument to carry out rational thought processes and make appropriate decisions. The resulting actions then become rational and clear. A clear mind becomes unengaged in emotional and automatic response patterns. The ultimate result is seeing one's true nature without the cover of social programming. It is not unattainable to begin to learn this.

To understand the mental faculty, let me digress into a discussion about the element of air. Its essence is closely linked with our internal winds and our physical breathing, but also to our intellect, with its movement of thought. From a cosmological perspective, the air element manifests out of the ethers of space. The physical aspect of air, as a mixture of oxygen and other gases, provides a model for what is occurring within us. Air moves quickly, is virtually invisible and has very little weight compared to other denser elements: fire, water and earth. The air qualities of a particular crystal include: inspiring, expanding, focussing, and blending. The energy organ linked to the air element is considered to be the heart chakra in the centre of our chest where we inhale air into our lungs. However, it is the third eye centre: the all-seeing eye, or mind's eye, that connects us to the faculty of inner seeing, and the ability to have intuition. Training in clear seeing may begin with the practice of engaged visualization and breathing. To have control of one's eyes, one also influences one's internal winds or prana, which in turn directly affect the stream of thoughts. Keeping our eyes still, keeps our mind still.

We begin with a practice in *Crystal Gazing* that clearly trains us in keeping our eyes still, without straining, and conclude with a breath-visualization practice: a *Crystal Installation*. The stones used are Elestial and Lepidolite. Elestial is a formation that occurs in several minerals: Quartz, Ruby, Kunzite and Fluorite. Lepidolite is a type of mica that is found as cleavage or in botryoidal form.

Gazing Meditation with Elestial

Why: Engaging in a gazing practice introduces meditation with an object to focus on, and in addition you are bathed in the crystal's resonance field. It is fairly easy to do. It is a perfect way to still an active mind and ideal to do at night, before retiring. Any crystal can be used, but here we propose using an Elestial. Prepare to spend about 20 minutes in each session.

How to begin gazing as a daily practice: Sit comfortably in a space conducive to meditation. Create this space for yourself in a way that you can relax and be undisturbed. Let yourself breathe gently for a few breaths with closed eyes. Then as you begin, open the eyes to about half to a quarter-open. The crystal should be placed or held in such a way that gazing is comfortable. Use a stand or crystal pillow to adjust the position of the crystal in

Figure 58 A gazing practice can be done with a smaller crystal. By keeping the eyes relaxed, and with unmoving focus on an object, the thought process have a chance to relax.

the most harmonious way for you. Let the Crystal take up your entire focus. Adjust your eyes so that they hold a soft focus. Look into the crystal as if you were looking through a camera, adjusting focus, and let your eyes zoom in and out. Your eyes should be relaxed and willing to let go of staring. Keeping your eyes unmoving and gazing onto an object, your mind becomes unmoving and still also. Thinking is directly connected with the visual stimuli outside of you that your eyes detect. Breathe into your eyes, as if the air is actually going into your eyes and into your head and down into the lungs. Visualize the energy of the crystal flowing into you. If thoughts come, let them, but let go of them also, at the same speed as you exhale. Watch the thoughts you have as a visitor to an art museum would look at the paintings exhibited there. The pictures do not belong to you, and as you pass by they are left behind. Continue to hold the eyes singly focussed on the crystal for the entire session.

Maintenance: As you become more familiar with this meditation, you can begin to look forward to this special time that is only for you. If feelings emerge, view them in the same way as you view your thoughts, just like the wind moving the leaves in a tree. The wind is not the tree, and the emotions are not you. You, as the observer, are not affected by the emotions. Notice as each feeling rises and subsides, leaving you unattached. What remains is a calm abiding presence. Continue in that state afterwards as the drama of life is played out.

Effects: This practice calms the mind and you may notice how pleasant it is to be still, without racing thoughts running all over the brain. Some do this meditation morning and evening: in the

Figure 59 Before installation with botryoidal Lepidolite. When we find ourselves ungrounded, or experience nervous energies, we may use this practice to regain mental balance.

morning to allow unprocessed thoughts and dreams from the night to settle, and in the evening to release all the events from the day. You will notice a more restful sleep and reduced stress when meditating daily.

Crystal Installation with Lepidolite (air)

Lepidolite is a type of lavender or purple Mica that occurs in flat cleavage as plates stacked in thin layers, or as a botryoidally formed mass resembling a brain. It was used in thin transparent plates as glass in fireplaces because of its resistance to heat. It acts as a filter to harmonize surrounding energies. Its properties relate to linking together energy forms along planes that do not necessarily need to be linear. This provides mental balance and the opportunity to expand awareness. Katrina Raphaell first introduced me to the method of installation within a crystal grid. Here is presented a variation based on visualization without a grid.

Visualization is a mental process, and by allowing its energy to be felt, we may access our emotional intelligence. The installation of a crystal is the process of embodying that crystal's energy signature and then visualizing it placed in a target area. This results in a possible balancing of discordant thought forms, such as traumatic memories. The entire body, its organs and tissues, is a storehouse of memories and patterns we operate from. These do not register in our normal conscious awareness, but nonetheless govern how we respond. A crystal installation may take up to an hour to complete.

Why: By using Lepidolite in this practice, we may begin to harmonize stored memories, and take command of our being. Decide beforehand upon the installation area, which is an area of the body or in the auric field that needs to be balanced, adjusted or aligned. Usually an area of pain is a target for installation practice. One may also install a crystal in a chakra which most closely relates to a problem that is occurring. Here, we describe a complete body installation.

How to begin: Sit comfortably, with the spine straight. Use a *Hematite Grid* with four pieces of hematite around you, or if you prefer, visualize them. Find your centre and ground yourself with a few Dual Flow Breaths, (inhaling above you and exhaling downward into the earth below, then inhale from beneath you and exhale upwards to the sky). Place a piece of botryoidal Lepidolite in front of you, or alternatively hold it in your hands. You can also hold it above your head for a while, to better tune in with its energy.

Visualization: Begin by gazing at the crystal until you are able to see it in your mind's eye. Feel its vibrational signature. The 'visualization image' is not only a flat picture, it is also a dimensional composite of vibrant colours, including texture, temperature,

Figure 60 Lepidolite - the Stone of Mental Balance, used in the breath-visualization practice 'Crystal Installation.'

Figure 61 Holding the stone near the crown for awhile may facilitate feeling its energy radiance in order to create a composite visualization image.

size and even possibly scent, in a radiating energy field. Close your eyes, become receptive to your visualization of the crystal. Intensify the image. Make it the most prominent item in your mind until all other thoughts and ideas fade away. Let it pulse with energy and let its lavender light radiate out in all directions.

Installation: Start to install the visualized crystal image at the top of the head, and then 'inhale' this composite image inside the crown. On the exhale, let its energy gently sink into the scalp and softly penetrate the skull. Sense the lavender colour seeping though the upper part of the brain until it reaches the centre of the head and the pineal gland, and then further down to the pituitary. Let the energy lubricate the brain and the nerves. Let the Lepidolite arrange your thoughts in the same way that the crystal structure is formed, in smooth curved layers neatly stacked and in perfect order. Let any worrying or anxious tendencies relax, and place them inside the crystal layers. As your thoughts become relaxed, let the entire head become a lavender cocoon with clean and relaxed thoughts, one after another, in an orderly fashion. See the Crown and the Third Eye centre become lavender to purple. You may notice that the colour sometimes begins to pulse, like a heart beat. Continue the installation of the crystal in the throat centre. Fill your voice with lavender calm and aligned energy. The pulsing can become even more pronounced now, as we enter the heart area. Breathe into the throat and down into the heart itself at the centre of the chest. Fill the lungs with lavender light. You have now completed the upper part of the body. Let the entire upper part of the body pulse in the same calm rhythm. Feel the unifying energy resonate and begin to flow down into your belly and hips. Let the energy flow like fine smoke would move in air over a smouldering fire. Lepidolite accesses the dimension of air, the mental realm. Allow this very delicate Lepidolite 'smoke' to circle each of the lower chakras in turn, with your breath, and finally emerge below your feet at the bottom of the auric field, at the Earth Star Chakra, which is the subtle centre where you may anchor your being into the Earth. From this under-most point of yourself, let the energy smoke rise up around you, in your immediate auric field. Let the smoke fill you from the bottom up, with each new exhale, until your whole field is filled with beautiful, clean transparent lavender and purple 'smoke'. The essence of the Lepidolite crystal, being in this way embodied, is now flowing through you, inside and out. Make the transparent quality more pronounced until it remains as a slight shimmer in your aura and inner being.

Reprogramming: During the installation, notice how your body responds. Listen carefully to these responses. Messages or sensations occurring may come to your conscious awareness. Breathing into each area facilitates a release of discordant energy. When these processes have come to completion, rest a while with your

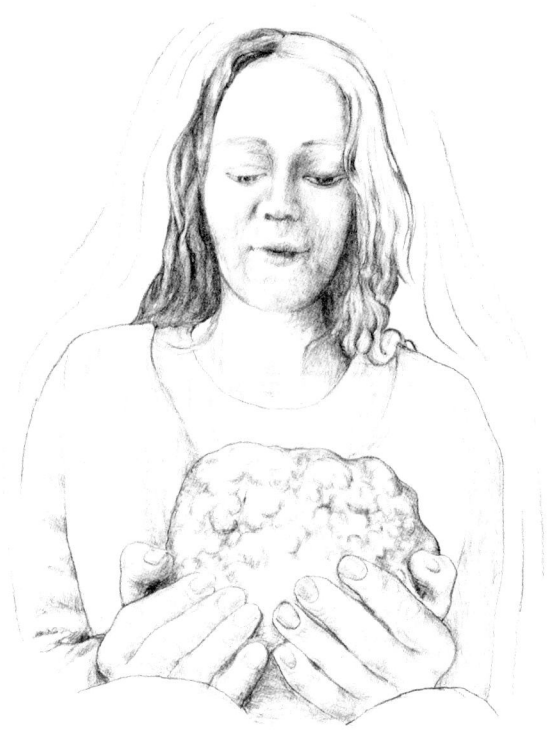

Figure 62 After the installation with Lepidolite: the energy field appears smoother, the breathing is notably more relaxed.

new levels of awareness until you are ready for the last step.

Scan yourself from the bottom of your feet and upwards for smooth balanced areas and areas needing your attention. In case of pain or areas of discomfort, begin reprogramming that area now to embrace balance, joy and health as your new default setting. One may simply say: *I am now filled by joyful balance and health.* Remain in the same body position until the energy imprint has settled into the new places. Notice the new levels of balance, calmness, acuity, clarity and resonance.

Maintenance: Practice this meditation several times, with a day or two in-between to ensure that you have a more effective installation, after which you can access the crystal more accurately. This is particularly helpful in a healing practice when you may not have access to an actual physical specimen of a required crystal. One can also do a Crystal Installation as a personal practice to alleviate a particular situation or problem as a part of a daily routine. Journaling your experiences in a special Crystal Practice Journal is a great way to record your progress.

Effects: As a direct result of this practice, one may experience clarity, peace and internal balance. Permanently installed crystals provide continuous support for your healing process. It may be similar to a vaccination, except there are no adverse side effects.

I can attest to the fact that installations work because of my own experience of such support. It is like a gentle continuous reminder of the new 'program' of balance. It has proven helpful for me in situations where there were tremendous emotional charges being released in my presence. In spite of those, I was able to remain fairly calm. I feel that I have Lepidolite to thank for that.

Crystal Care: If you are working within a Lepidolite grid (placement of many pieces of the same stone around you) to assist the installation, it may be helpful to provide a special container, tray or box to store the stones for easy access. The more times you do it, the easier it becomes, as the stones work together and amplify the effect. Storing or placing Lepidolite in sunlight will clear and energize it.

Summary

Functioning mental faculties are essential for a fulfilling life. Disturbing thoughts and confusion cover our real selves like a thick blanket; the result is that we fail to see ourselves clearly in the world around us. Anyone may begin his or her journey to seek such clarity and discard illusory screens, to become ever more masterful. Breath and the mental processes relate to the quickly moving air element. The eyes are our outward sensor providing us with images that in turn produce thoughts, so by stilling the eyes, one may control the creation of thought (*Gazing Meditation*). Engaged visualisation is a process where a composite image is used with breathing to remove, or affect mental-emotional energy blocks. To train 'clear' seeing, unaffected by inherent conditioning, one may engage in the described *Crystal Installation* that uses such breath-visualization.

Practices:
Gazing Meditation with Elestial
Crystal Installation with Lepidolite

Figure 63   A Crystal Talisman is an object empowered by intention. Its construction allows for creative space and reconnection to the natural forces around us. In this sense it is not a decorative piece of jewellery but an external object for our meditation and practice.

Crystal Talisman

*Magic is revealed as
Awareness of our true potential!*

She saw the dark shadow approach her. In the past she would have run for her life. Now she took a deep breath and turned around to face what had haunted her for so long. She finally had the courage to face her worst nightmare...

I propose this is the essence of what can be learnt from engaging in a crystal talisman practice. A talisman is an object empowered by intention such as: protection, abundance, fertility or health. It is usually fashioned from one or more components into a necklace or worn in a medicine pouch. Though the ages, people have been fascinated by gems and precious stones, and worn these on their bodies. What motivated them to do this? Prehistoric people are believed to have used stones as talismans for protection against seen and unseen forces. The word 'talisman' means an object producing apparently magical or miraculous effects. Early on, people learned to carve precious stones into shapes and symbols, as can be seen in Egyptian artefacts, which were used in ceremonial jewellery for various purposes including: protection of the wearer from harm, for life after death, for the safe and successful journey of the soul. These gem objects represented a variety of spiritual concepts. On the African continent, we see similar art expressed in carvings of wood, bone and stone. The medicine men, who were often the carvers, consecrated each piece of art with strong ritual elements involving its keeper, who would then use it for prescribed purposes. Traditionally their belief was that the 'spirit' of what the object depicted came to abide within it. This has been called Animism. Its relative, Shamanism, originating in North-Eastern Asia, operates with similar ideas. The concept is that the world is governed by unseen forces or 'spirits' and they must be appeased or influenced, for the good of the user. The native Zuni tribe, in the American southwest, to this day carve what are called "fetishes," a type of talisman which usually depicts different animals. By using a bear fetish, for example, a person would connect with the bear totem, and in this way establish a strong mystic bond with it. In this way the totem could protect and guide the person. Another fetish carved is the "corn maiden," used for fertility and abundance. You might compare this image, with other iconographic usages of female saints and deities/goddesses, including the madonna.

In modern times, where science and technology rule, the conscious connection with the natural world and its forces seems more or less eradicated, doesn't it? Traditional ritual objects appear to have been replaced by an abundance of personal high tech objects, such as cell phones that can do almost everything for you (except go to the bathroom). And notice their symbolic designs and colours. Where ritual objects were formerly made with the intention to appease evil forces for the survival of the tribe, does this modern phenomena contribute to misalignment within the divine order? Instead of connecting with true guidance, people are now communicating at isolated distances instead of face to face with their neighbours. Whereas indigenous peoples used their beliefs to sustain themselves and care for their tribe, we seem to have shown few such tendencies. Instead, we see violence, economic slavery and addiction. Arguably, the fear-based causes (such as greed, abdication of responsibility, denial, unfulfilled desires, lack of sustainability etc.), emphasizes the current misalignment and jeopardizes happiness and health. All these issues culminate in the present search for who we are, what we are, love, the ideal relationship, and the list goes on and on.

We try very hard to find new ways to stay connected with our natural world. Rituals within a spiritual framework have satisfied this need for millennia, the modern world is no exception. Only the tools may have changed. Crystal Talismans, I propose, are one of these ways where we may reconnect ourselves with what really matters - to discover and recover who we are.

Finding Intention

If you do not know where you'd like to go, the place where you are now is the perfect place. Begin with where you are now! Ask yourself if you are perfectly happy or are there things you'd like to change about your situation. An intention is a statement of what you strongly desire to manifest. The clearer your goal is, the stronger you hold it in your heart, and the faster it has a chance of appearing. And do not limit yourself. Make outrageous requests and be prepared to receive them! Test any proposed intent with the question: Is this intent for the highest good of everyone concerned? You may select a weakness you may have as a starting point for your intention, and then turn that into strength. For example: I feared essay writing in school so much that I got paralysed after two sentences, and was never able to write more than half a page, so I got bad marks in writing. However, I took hold of this weakness I had, and I decided to write a book, the very book you are now reading! I set the goal to do it, acted on it, put in effort and resources and continued in my conviction that it would be manifested, no matter what. Now it is a fact. I thank the crystals and my talismans for assisting me.

Inspiration and creating are two phases that we are equipped with. Inspiration is inhaling, taking in and listening. Creating is exhaling, out-pouring and producing (for example, works of art). Imagination is the faculty with which we can be inspired. Inspiration is part of our inner divine guidance - the divine works through inspiration and symbols, sometimes in spite of our desires or aversions that arise as a result of detrimental conditioning. The divine is that part of you, still connected to the Unified Field, or expressed in other words, G-d. The link there is through our Higher Self. The faculty for creativity is in our physical body that will carry out the work. Inspiration is received though our crown, creativity manifest though our sacral centre. When our intended manifestation is truly benefiting us and others, it is also confirmed in our heart.

State your intentions clearly, and write them down. Stay in touch with them often. For me it was to be heard (expressed as the idea to write a book). That idea kept on prompting me since I was a teenager. Contemplate on your difficulties and you might get an idea of what you like to select as a project. Here are some ideas: balance your body, improve your eyesight, heal an illness, repair a relationship, find a partner, create abundance, remove a debt, start a business, have more fun, fund an orphanage in India, have more time, buy a boat to sail around the globe, etc.

How Does a Talisman Work?

Jewels and stones hold vibration; they may act as amplifiers, radiators, anchors, magnets, recorders, filters, transformers, transmitters, and reflectors of the energy of our intentions. Each stone has a signature vibration, which is seen in the reference name given to some of the stones. The talisman acts as a lens and an amplifier for intentions connected with its creation, as well as the signature of the individual components. Together they form an orchestra that resonates in unison whatever intent is placed within it. The more specific the intent, the more precisely one may receive that which one asks for. Healing Jewellery such as simple *Crystal Talismans*, *Crystal Colour Life Spirals* and *Mandala Necklaces* (see chapter *Crystal Mandala*) may assist us in solving a problem or serving as an object for meditation, and the creation process helps us formulate our intention. This proc-

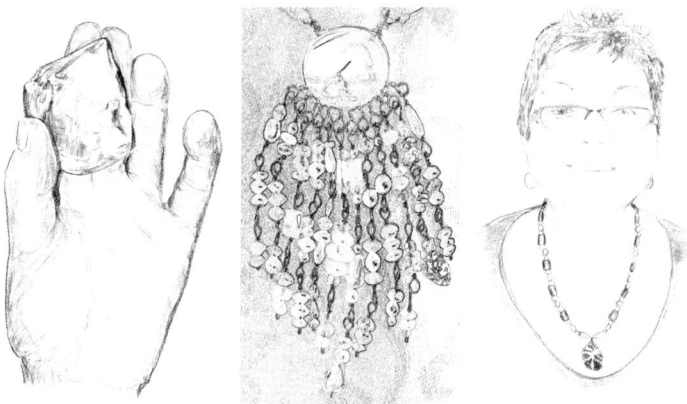

Figure 64 Left: Elestial Fluorite. Fluorite is the Mental Clarity Stone. In its elestial form it is ideal to assist in altering and resolving core beliefs to your benefit. Middle: A 12-Ray Talisman with crystals of twelve different colours on a cabochon of Quartz (multi-looped setting). Right: Crystal Mandala Talisman with blue Kyanite.

ess gives us the space to integrate and know what is really going on. Talismans created with intention have been demonstrated to profoundly affect and enhance the self-healing process. By personally taking responsibility for your intentions you will also empower your own healing.

Empowering your work: By wearing the talisman consciously and remembering your intent, you are doing the simplest kind of practice. To empower means to invest energy into it. It is also a consecration of your intentions, a solemn personal commitment to work on the intentions you set. Also, it is a blessing, in that it is your act of approval on all levels to contribute to your own happiness, well-being or prosperity. It is the means by which you can become more involved in solving your own problems. Practice can include a cleansing/smudging ritual, daily meditation, daily walking meditations, and yoga sessions with intent in the mind or in any other way that keeps your intent at the forefront during waking hours. Before bed consciously ask for dreams and messages relating to your intent.

Core Issues - Elestial Talisman

Elestials are a particular kind of formation that can be recognized by their many terminations on the surface. Most Elestials are Quartz, but one can find elestialized Kunzite, Fluorite and Ruby, to name three other minerals. The general action is that Elestials inspire us to go inside to uncover the roots of challenges and harmful thought patterns. This is why these master crystals are so important in healing work. A Crystal Healing Graduate reports:

"Elestialization! I first began working with Elestials about 6 years ago. I did not know at the time that these crystals would become very dear friends indeed. At that point in my journey, I needed to acknowledge and understand the emotional baggage that I had been carrying around. The emotional trauma dramas from my past veiled my entire existence. When the Elestials arrived, the long process of excavation began. My intention was then, and continues to be, to become aware of the absolute truth of my nature as a spiritual being living in this world. The Elestials supported that process and held me accountable when I "forgot" to take responsibility for my reality. They were not subtle about it either. On one occasion the Elestials I was using took a hold of my brain and literally rewired it.

I began wearing earrings and a large pendant made with Elestial crystals that at first left me with a migraine and brain 'fog' for several hours. I could feel the dismantling of the baggage, and for about 6 weeks, 24 hours a day, I allowed the process to unfold. Among other things, they were instrumental in delving into the root causes of my smoking addiction. Once those causes came to light, the release of the pattern was complete. In the last 3 years nearly every major shift into a deeper understanding of the 'cosmos' that I have experienced (for which there are no words, as yet), has been preceded by spending time in meditation with Elestials. The support and motivation they have provided me have been tremendous. When an Elestial presents itself to me now, I know that a new and deeper level of self-awareness and 'cosmic clarity' is about to arrive, and I get set to enjoy the journey once again.

Susan Kern

Make a Crystal Talisman

Lack of technique is not lack of creativity, but lack of creativity indicates an internal blockage that may be removed. Skills can be learned. Being creative and using creativity are the means by which the divine communicates through us. Technique and skill, as well as discovering our intentions, are necessary components in creating healing jewellery. This is a sensitive process where you are opening yourself to what your heart needs. Look for the place of flow. Allow yourself to adopt an attitude of trust for your excellent capacity to do the work. Acknowledge that practice makes perfect. Give yourself some slack. Take support from others to encourage you, avoid people with negative attitudes.

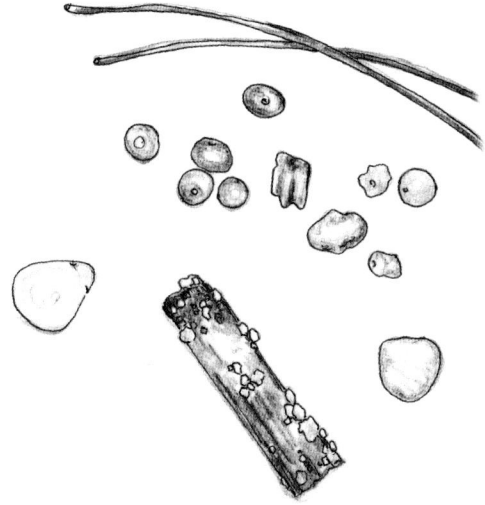

Figure 65 Materials for Simple Talisman. Gathered here are a main stone and some beads, as well as silver wire. It is an easy process, and in the beginning one does not need to be too concerned about how it is going to turn out. What is necessary, however, is to hold a sincere intention and try your best. Your Talisman holds that intent for you, so your intent can come true for you. Good Luck!

Don't take things personally, but listen to healthy advice. Work on yourself first! To create a real talisman for other people you must have their permission, so it is better to work on yourself first, rather than trying to change another. That way you may act as an example of how to be.

Why: Talismans are easy to use and wear. Usually a Talisman is in the form of a pendant, so that is the format we will make here. Talismans are very helpful for personal and intimate intentions

Figure 66 Simple Talisman completed. Watermelon Tourmaline with drusy Lepidolite was chosen as the main stone, and a small pearl and a freely hanging moonstone drop was added. Notice how the wire flows around the stone to hold it. Energy signature of the stones: connecting the heart and the head, staying true to yourself in spite of harsh environments and accepting any emotions that one may have. In sum: This talisman may assists me to "Hold my centre without waver in spite of what my environment pushes on me." Added to that is the personal intention, which is held in the silver setting and the way the stones have come together.

as they are in close proximity to your heart. Also, the dimension of beauty is added.

How to begin: First you assemble your materials: a variety of beads, some smaller crystals and something to hold the stones together with - it could be silver wire or cord of some kind like silk or leather. Then lay the crystals out randomly on a small tray or on a table in front of you, and cover all the materials with a cloth. To learn how to do the intricate Gem Weaving, one may have to practice for quite a while, but here we give you a very simple version.

Secondly, you will have to still your mind, to find out what ails you. The clearer you set your intent the clearer the result. That is why we always ask our clients what their intentions are. To just say 'I want to be happy' may not be as specific as 'I want to be free of my migraines." Write down what you want to have happen. Commit to work with the situation until it is resolved, for at least 21 days. Best is to do a three-month practice. This practice time should not be underestimated because it puts the power back in your court.

Thirdly, with your intent clearly in mind, look at your assembled stones and beads with fresh eyes and select at least one stone. Wrap your stone with wire or the cord in any way you are able to, and include a loop to hang it from. Just make sure any wire ends are securely tucked away so you won't hurt yourself wearing the stone. If an additional stone needs to be there, add it in any way that works. I have seen people do beautiful work just by using their hands with no tools. It is not necessary to aspire to have your talisman look like the crown jewels. What is important is that it will work with you, reflecting back to you how your problem can be solved or dealt with. If you are unsure which stone to choose, consult the list of stones in the crystal list or look up a word in the index that describes your situation.

Lastly, don't show your talisman to others, since you will miss your opportunity to look inward and actually deal with the situation within yourself. Talking to others dissipates energy, precious energy you may need for dealing with your situation. The only exception is, of course, if you work together with a qualified therapist or friend, who can assist you in your process.

Maintenance: When your talisman is completed, put it on and know you have begun manifesting your intentions. Each morning or evening, ask yourself these two questions:

> *What gifts and lessons have I received today?*
> *How have I been of service to others today?*

Some find it useful to keep a journal and write the answers to the two questions each day. It is fun afterwards to read the journal, perhaps 6 months later, and discover how trivial some problems may have been or how they covered up the underlying, real issues.

Effects: You will discover how easy it is to accomplish things when you set a clear intention. Most often one feels heard, as it is a way of expressing unvoiced concerns in a beneficial way. I have personally found working with talismans one of the most accessible ways of self-healing.

Crystal care: Depending on the size and the stones, you should be able to wear your talisman all the time. Wear the talisman in the shower, to clear it. During sleep, at least keep the talisman within your aura close to your bed. Some stones like Pyrite, Angelite and Selenite should not be exposed to contact with water. If your talisman breaks or gets lost, it may be a sign that you are finished with the process. If you are unsure, open a pendulum session to find out. (See chapter: *Pendulum Basics.*)

Summary

Talismans are objects empowered by intention that can be used for self-healing purposes. People of early civilisations used talismans made from various components, including crystals, to provide protection, fertility and abundance. Animistic beliefs considered a talismanic object to inhabit the spirit it was fashioned into. Even though we are in the modern era of technological innovation, humanity seems to have lost its real connection to the natural forces, and we yearn for meaning in our turbulent times by searching for authenticity. Working with this situation, as the ancients did, you may find that a talisman practice gives an opportunity for healing.

Practice:
Make a simple Crystal Talisman.

Figure 67 May the 'Crystal Wizard' be brought forward, he is a wonderful being who may shares some of his special stones and minerals with us.

New Horizons

Beyond the veils of illusion,
What awaits?

By application and effort alone will the serious seeker approach the horizon of known reality. The novice may begin with great enthusiasm and some beginner's luck, just to stop short of success because it was too far from his or her comfort zone. Yogis and Shamans of the past have used crystals, sacred plants, strenuous disciplined practice and purification rituals in order to enlighten themselves and be of service for those in need. The by-products of certain such practices include ability for clairvoyant visions, lucid dreams and attainment of extraordinary powers. Such powers were used to aid their people and to deal with life and its misfortunes. They were intermediaries between this world and the unseen realms, appeasing the spirits of their local area and invoking the divine for support. Still today if one is fortunate, one may find such living masters.

Extraordinary visions, such as seeing what lies behind a wall of concrete, and wild trips being an animal or flying in space, have been experienced as a result of taking certain drugs[1]. But what is the use of visions, if people do not use them to benefit themselves or others with conscious action? Would you want to develop your own innate powers that make it possible to do so? I propose to explore the use of two ancient methods: inner journeying (*Inter-dimensional Travel*) that is creating an opening for the seeker to explore what is going on, and the use of a medicine bundle (*Crystal Mesa*), which is a portable altar to our latent divine nature that we have the potential to recover.

Before addressing these methods, I'd like to go to the other extreme, and share a story of how a Quartz crystal helped remedy a drug overdose:

Personal Story: "Having seen crystals in a display, earlier in life, and aware they were from the earth, I really had no idea about their nature, properties or 'essence,' nor what they were capable of manifesting in the hands of people. In February of 1995, whilst assisting friends who were establishing a whole foods bakery in our rural community, I was travelling home in the wee hours of the morning when my car, on ice-covered winding roads, ceased to follow the laws of the Highway Traffic Act. Rather, it chose to obey the laws of physics, going airborne over an embankment, and into a very ancient rock cut . . . (my second encounter with crystals)! I was later informed that the car had to be towed away in two separate pieces, by two tow trucks. Needless to say, I was in a couple or more pieces myself, ending up in the hospital, with a broken neck, broken spine, and a broken leg and foot, amongst other various and sundry injuries. To make matters worse, I foolishly chose to accept numerous pharmaceutical drugs, offered to mediate the pain, and while I still consider the morphine to have been a blessing, the synthesized pharmaceuticals which I accepted over the next little while put me into a mental hell of a dream state and sleep apnea, which in retrospect, seems a worse trauma than the accident itself! Keep in mind, I had been a vegetarian and yogi meditator since the early 1970's, developing fairly attuned sensitivity, devoid of alcohol, tobacco, recreational drugs, caffeine, and was mostly sugar-free for all of those years, not even taking aspirin. On top of all this, my ever-wanting-to-be-helpful doctors prescribed, (and I trusted to accept), a new and experimental drug (I learned that later) in a dosage of 8 mg every 4 hours. I began taking the drug faithfully as directed, but within a couple of days I was having an LSD-type experience, without a

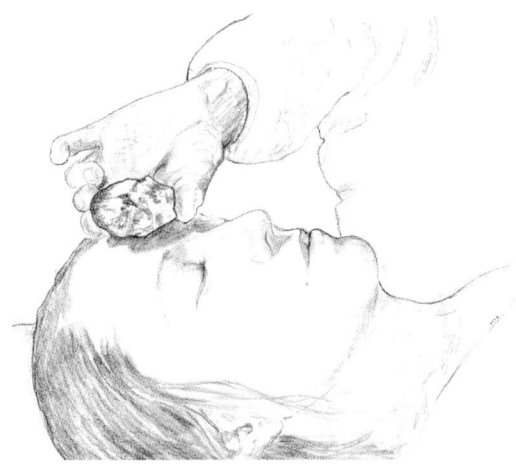

Figure 68 Placing a crystal on the Third Eye chakra.

wink of sleep each night, leading to a continuous, insane quality of dream state. I later discovered that the doctor had made an error in the prescription dosage, which should have been 4 mg every 8 hours, or about 1/4 the dosage I was administered. By the third night, the compounding effect of the drug, in combination with the other pharmaceuticals, culminated in severe tremors, great difficulty in breathing and severe arrhythmia of the heart. About 4 in the morning, it kept stopping and starting again and I thought at one point that it was going to jump right out of my chest. Now, I'm usually one to stay calm and collected through any crisis, but at this point I began to become a little concerned that death was imminent.

A friend had left a moderately-sized clear quartz crystal (about the size of a large man's thumb) upon the window sill, and to this day, I don't know why I intuited to do so, not knowing or having learned anything about crystals, but something compelled me to place that crystal squarely on my forehead above my nose and between my closed eyes, after which I lay there on my back, for hours, upon hours, upon hours balancing, that crystal in its place . . . ahhh . . . what a soothing relief from the craziness of that out of control, out of body experience, and the accompanying seething ... teeming ... boiling ... kettle of worms my brain seemed to have become during those days. I felt as if I had been transported to lie under the finest, coolest, clearest and most soothing Amazonian waterfall, on a hot hot day. I could literally see the streaming energies, in my mind's eye, spilling and swirling over my body's complete length, sort of like those steamy rainforest calendar pictures, shot with time lapse photography with the water flowing so smoothly over the cool, and mossy green smooth rocks. What a GOD-sent blessing! Somehow . . . miraculously, this harmonized my energies and organ functions, as well as neutralized all that crazy mental and nervous activity . . . and it wasn't long before my normal calm and clarity returned. I felt like I had been washed up upon the shore of love, after a great typhoon. Love IS in the Earth!

Karish

Inner Journeys with Apophyllite

At distressed points in life, when it almost seems too late, and when you have stretched yourself so thin that you almost break, guidance comes if you are willing to heed it. If you do not, the breaking point will be reached and the proverbial "spiritual two by four" is there - smack right on your head! Painful as that is, you'll eventually get to your destination sooner or later. A way to bypass the obviously painful way of learning the life lessons is to look for a solution right away, either externally by reaching out to others, or going inside; ultimately, all answers lie in the deepest part of our hearts. Inner journey meditation can be one of those ways. When profoundly relaxing and letting go of trying to control how it is done, one may enter a state of conscious dreaming. In that state, our inner wisdom leads us to previously unchartered territories. One may travel into emotional as well as purely mental dimensions, accessible beyond time and space.

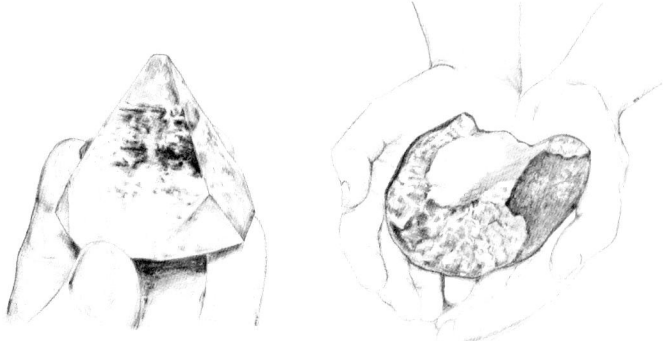

Figure 69 Apophyllite pyramid and within a geode. Apophyllite - the Inner Journey Stone, may facilitate an expaned mind and a deepening understanding of what is happening in your life.

I remember one crystal healing student who desired to find out about Van Gogh[2] and his art. Not only did she appear in his studio, but he also showed her how he painted in detail. As she described what her experience had been, one could really feel that she had actually been there in the flesh, even though he lived in another era of time and geographical location. As she described the scene, something seemed to have melted in her, perhaps blocked inspiration, because she looked absolutely radiant. I do not know how she has used this experience, but it showed all of us in this class how this method can work.

Why: This practice may assist in discovering parts, hidden from the conscious mind. It develops the natural ability of finding creative solutions to difficult problems, impossible to solve by reason. Crystal practice does not have to always be so serious. In addition, research work can be done this way as well. For example if one is researching the Mayas and requiring details about particular artefacts or life situations, why not travel there and find out in person? Some scientists may not approve of this particular line of investigation, but nevertheless it is worth trying.

Etherials are stones with affinity to the upper chakras: Apophyllite, Petalite, Angelite, Danburite and Prehnite. They assist in loosening the bond and attachment to the physical, and lets a person feel comfortable in his or her dream body. The main crystal, Apophyllite, the Inner Journey Stone, is a clear crystal that looks like a small pyramid. If we let the senses and thinking totally relax, the process of reconnecting and remembering may take place.

Prerequisite: Study *Connecting with Guidance, Hematite Grid, Obsidian Bubble* and *Black Tourmaline Warrior Stance* practice before you begin.

How to begin: Attune to your guidance and state the intent for your journey, as if you would look in a catalogue from a travel agency depicting various destinations. If you have a picture of or an actual artefact related to your destination, include it in your meditation. Set your meditation space up with a Hematite Grid by placing four Hematites around it, and make sure you are undisturbed. Place yourself in an Obsidian Bubble which will allow you to move in your experience more easefully and more joyfully while being clear and conscious of what is going on. This is your travel vehicle. The importance of Obsidian cannot be understated. Black Obsidian, preferably the gold-sheen variety, can be used. If you decide to invite a friend to facilitate for you, keeping time and recording your experience, then he or she will hold the Obsidian sphere. Make sure you are comfortable and have a blanket available if you need it. State your intention as clearly as you can. Set a timer for the length of the meditation, for example 30 minutes, and then place the supporting crystals and, lastly, a natural Apophyllite pyramid upon your third eye.

Breathe going out: Begin breathing by directing the breath outwards and up-wards. The Apophyllite acts as a reversed lightning rod, letting your conscious mind leap out of the confining physical body through the third eye. This is similar to what the

Inter Dimensional Travel Layout

Crown	Angelite
Third Eye	Apophyllite
Throat	DT Quartz
Heart	Danburite
Solar Plexus	Prehnite
Navel	Yellow Jasper
Sacral	DT Quartz
Root	Black Obsidian

Engage a Hematite Grid and your Obsidian Bubble.
DT means double-terminated.

dreamer does while sleeping. The difference here is that it is done from a waking meditative state. Ask that you will travel to the destination you have chosen (that is, fulfilling your intention). Continue to breathe and let yourself follow the breath up and out. Relax deeply into your breath, letting yourself feel the safe bubble of Obsidian surround you as the journey begins. Be the journey. Observe what is shown to you and ask yourself to remember supported by Prehnite. Do not let yourself get engaged or entangled in what is occurring. It is most often your own unconscious and undigested patterns that are revealed by this process. Knowing this, it is easier to just observe and take notes along the way. If you fall asleep without any conscious memory, this is good, too; you may have really needed to rest. Play and let yourself enjoy the journey. When you hear the timer, see yourself coming back into your third eye or through the top of your head. If you have a friend with you, he or she can help guide you to come back gently. Bring yourself to move and stretch. Sit up, take your time. Do the *Black Tourmaline Warrior Stance*, or light physical exercise of some sort, to integrate and ground the experience.

Maintenance: Did you find your answer? Journal your experience, and let go of it. Do you need to return to your destination, to fetch more pieces of your puzzle? Do the Inner Journey Meditation several times every other day until your intention has been completely fulfilled.

Effects: This practice assists in stabilizing one's control of being present, and being aware even in sleeping-like states. Subconscious dilemmas may be solved, as the journeyer visits them in a more detached state. Insights and resolution may occur.

Crystal Care: Apophyllite is a soft mineral and should be stored individually. Wash in water, clear with smudge or with sound of tingshas[3] or singing bowl. Apophyllite and the other Etherials can be energized by moonlight. Angelite should not be used with water, as it will dull the surface.

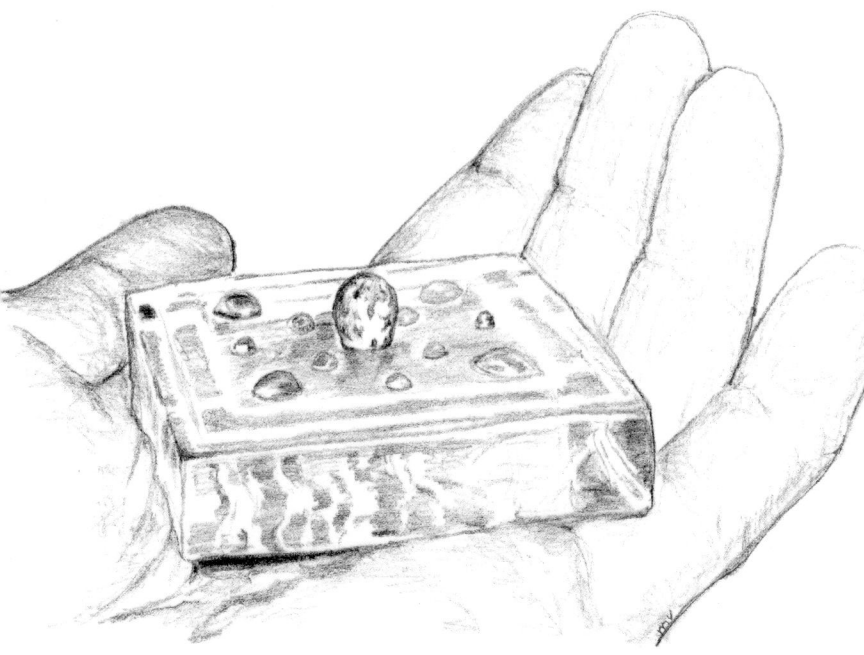

Figure 70 A totemic creation: the Crystal Dream Sculpture, was inspired by the Shamanic tradition of the Power Blanket.

Crystal Dream Sculptures

On a recent visit in Tucson, Arizona, I found an exquisite example of what is called a "crystal dream sculpture," obviously made with serious effort and lapidary skill by artist Eloise Bono. With strong resonance, I observed in her art the essence of what I myself had been exploring. What I dabbled with in wire, beads and stones to create talismans and bundles, she fashioned from solid crystal. I am grateful for having experienced it. I quote from her literature (which I have permission to use):

The inspiration for these totemic creations is the ancient Shamanic tradition of the power blanket. The most commonly known such tradition is the Sufi carpet, and its use for various metaphysical exercises... The most commonly known example is revealed in the story of the "Flying Carpet," which may be understood on multiple levels. A common practice is exemplified by the usage of a "Prayer Carpet" for the seven daily prayers. A revealing and lesser known example is the story of the prisoner whose wife wove him a prayer blanket, the pattern of which revealed the inner mechanism of the lock on the cell door. The prisoner then fashioned a key from the design and successfully escaped the prison. Another lesser known tradition is the Peruvian Dream Blanket. When an adept completed his training with a master Shaman, in some Peruvian traditions, the Master commissioned a special woven blanket incorporating the design elements of Water and Vegetation. This unique Blanket was presented to the adept upon completion of training and initiation. The Dream Blanket served a multitude of functions integral to the adept's shamanic practice. It was both mundane and transcendent. It served as an outer protective coat/cloak in inclement weather, as a pillow/bedroll for sleeping and even a wrap/container for carrying personal belongings and sacred tools. In his practice, the spread out blanket was his "office" for treating patients; the suspended blanket served as a sweat lodge/tent, and served as a sacred space for meditation for those who seated themselves on the blanket. An important function of the Blanket, hence the name, is to facilitate lucid dreaming, while sleeping rolled in the Blanket, for acquisition of personal power. Both totemic plants and animals are obtained as well as rituals, songs and formulae for healing/curing, maintenance of physical, social and environmental equilibria, and personal and social protection.

Assemble Your Crystal Medicine Bundle

Many indigenous people gather sacred items to wear and use in ceremony and ritual. A medicine bundle or mesa[4] is usually a small bag of collected items that hold precious meaning or power to the mesa keeper. These bundles are literally portable altars. With them the keeper may build inner virtues and consciousness. The practitioners of the Andean tradition[5] use a mesa as a sacred tool to serve the divine and their people. By engaging with the natural world around them, they return energies to nature as well, and honour and respect that which sustains them with food and shelter. This aspect is in part lost in the modern world view where nature is seen just as a resource to be exploited. Nature is abused instead of being served and honoured. If you are among those who see the world we live in as precious, and wish to work with the natural world, you can support it by creating a mesa. It can reflect to you how you place your energies in life, and you may discover how to offer up inner

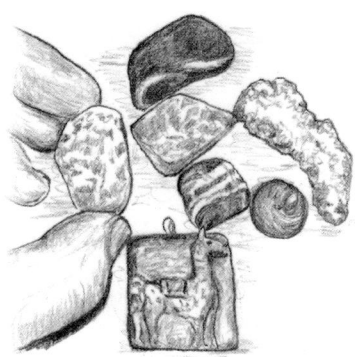

Figure 71 A simple Crystal Mesa can be assembled with items meaningful to the mesa keeper: a beach stone, a pendant and some crystals. From left: Lepidolite. Middle row: Lemurian Jade (top), below beach stone, Tigereye and Carnelian. Far right: Azurite-Chrysocolla natural nodule.

discords and non-beneficial behaviour. I have used the mesa as a healing tool and way of discovering where I personally had to adjust my way and become more aware of the energies in nature that are ever present.

Why: Practice with a simple crystal medicine bundle may engage all the senses and help us to see the world in terms of energies rather than from solid permanent matter. The practitioner may come to realize that his or her actual powers are already present, and only need to be brought to the conscious mind's awareness. It may be understood that one has to rise above one's material world to be able to affect it, and then come back there to live in better harmony and integration.

How to begin: Bring a variety of stones that you have and place them in front of you. Contemplate how you might be of service; choose an intention for creating your crystal medicine bundle, or mesa. Perhaps it can relate to finding your particular mission in life, or as a healing tool for an illness. The mesa could be seen as a kaleidoscope or lens with which you can affect your situation. Also, a planetary or a non-personal goal can be established. State your intention and select a centre stone. It should resonate strongly with you. It represents your own centre at this time. For a small bundle fitting in the palm of your hand the size could be as small a ¾ inches. With the centre stone as an anchor, pick the outer stones that you feel give you a sense of connection with your stated intent. There can be as many pieces that you see fit. Select a mesa cloth from natural material. Cut it into an approximate size of 6 x 11 inches. Your mesa is completed when your have cleansed and fed your stones. You might sprinkle sun-infused rose water to feed your stones, then wrap them lovingly in the mesa cloth, and tie it with the cord as an intention-setting ritual.

Mesa session: State your intent and open your mesa bundle. Place the stones how you see fit, and then gaze into the geometries

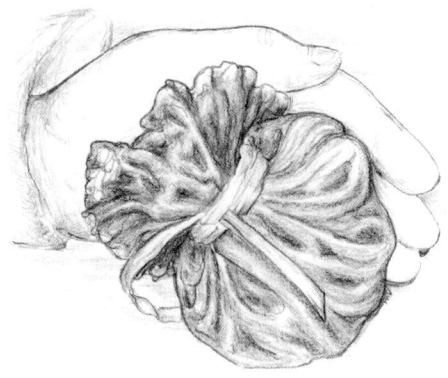

you have created. Allow your mind to relax into contemplation, as you move the stones in tactile ways into new patterns. Notice how energies are shifted and moved within you as well. It is your personal spiritual playtime. The stones in your mesa are tangible symbols of energies within. Each time you work with them, the mesa gathers energy and holds it for you, until you are ready to move. This is not engaging in worship of stone; rather, it is a practice that may foster deep inter-connectedness with yourself and other beings.

Maintenance: Practice with your mesa daily until you have come to the conclusion of your intent. The next step might be working with an elemental mesa.

Effects: Mesa practice in this way may help alleviate stress, tension and other conditions where the mind is overly engaged in a negative way.

Crystal Care: Treat your Crystal Mesa Bundle as a sacred object. Honour your Mesa by 'feeding' it with each of the elements: flowers (earth element), sprinkling water (water element), smudging (air element), lighting a candle (fire element), and chanting or sounding a singing bowl (space element). Give thanks for what you learn from using it.

Medicine Bundle for Elemental Practice

Why: The elements are the basis for our well-being, and refer here to elemental aspects within us: Earth to bones and tissues (our physicality), Water to our blood and watery flows (our emotions), Fire to our energy and metabolic fires (our digestion, or transformation from one element into another), Air to our breathing and mental winds (our thinking), and Space to sound and creation (our conscious voice). Elemental practice is beneficial for integrating and balancing our elements.

Prerequisite: Study the practices *Connecting with Guidance* and *Crystal Installation* before you start.

Creating the Elemental Bundle: Smudge and centre yourself before selecting your stones. Make a prayer that your chosen stones, will guide and help you to learn more about yourself, and the elements connecting you to all life.

Select four stones to represent each of the elements (earth, water, fire, air), and one for the fifth element (space). In the list of Crystal Keys elemental effect is indicated, and that can be used in conjunction with colour to assist your selection. When you have made the selection of the five stones, feed your stones and wrap them up, as described earlier.

How to begin: Centre and smudge yourself. Open your Elemental Medicine Bundle. Pick up each stone and listen closely to it. Where does its energy want to go? Let its energy flow into you where it is needed. Install it in that area of your body. Take as long as 20 minutes or longer with each stone. Notice how the elements within you are being balanced as you work with each stone. Perhaps the water element is out of balance. This can happen when one is feeling emotional (too much water). Activity or fire stones may assist you to go beyond the emotion. To much stimulation on the other hand needs cooling water.

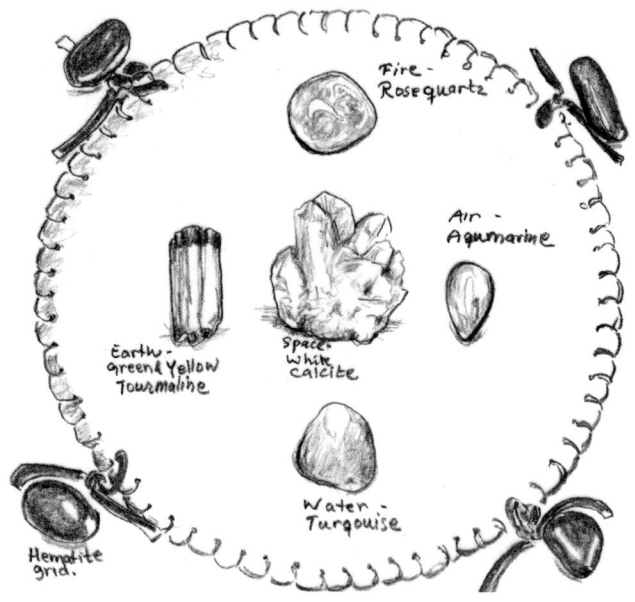

Figure 72 Elemental practice. A selection of a woman's personal stones to represent an inner situation. For her, the yellow & green Tourmaline connects to her stomach, Rose Quartz to her chest, Turquoise to her face (tears & lymph) and so forth.

Racing thoughts, are a sign of too much air or mental energy. In this case let your earth stone assist you be more grounded and to access a calmer state of mind. Too much earth (inactivity) needs some inspiration (air).

Maintenance: When your selection is made, do not change your stones. Continue the elemental practice daily for at least one month for best outcome. Notice how your bundle picks up energy as you work and feed with it.

Effects: One may discover the interrelatedness between our elements: thought with emotion, our physical body with sounds, and all of the combinations in-between.

Crystal Care: Wrap your bundle up, or leave the placement displayed in a private place until you have completed the practice of one month. Smudge after each session or sound cymbals or bell to clear the space.

The Master Mesa

The Master Mesa[6] includes the complete set of 33 energies, represented by the selected stones. (A colour image of the Master Mesa laid out as a Moon Mandala Journey, can be found on page 263). Roger Calverley writes:

"The work of the soul is to mediate Source, through its archetypes, and achieve expression of Spirit in Matter... We all possess a mystical inner world, from whence primal archetypes beckon us to taste the fullness of our inherent potential. The 33 crystals of the archetypal Crystal Mesa are keys to access a fullness of consciousness that lies within. Drawing from Lemurian and ancient Mystery School sources, this experiential journey moves through a series of crystal attunements which activate the jewel in the lotus of the spiritual heart and open the way towards alignment with the soul."

Why: You as the journeyer have this jewel, or soul seed, in your heart. To find it one may have to excavate it, and break though the barriers of conditioning. Practice is such excavation.

Opening a Crystal Mesa Session: The crystal medicine bundle, described earlier in this chapter, can be a starting point of gathering all the 33 stones in the master mesa. The cloth is the altar upon which the stones are laid, and will also become their container. Present the stones one by one in a layout, as circle, a cross or any other shape that you might create. The Master Mesa can be used in several ways, including problem-solving and the heart meditation described below:

1) *Mesa Session for problem-solving*: If you have a question to be resolved, write it on a card. Select one stone to represent your present situation. Place it closest to you. Now contemplate possible solutions. Find a still place within, close your eyes, breathe deeply and slowly and for each alternative pick a stone and place it adjacent to the first stone. Then for each alternative project the scenario, and what will happen, and choose stones to illustrate. Sit back, look at the stones, and let them tell you what you already know about the situation. Look in the Crystal Keys list for their messages, and select the alternative that fits your situation best.

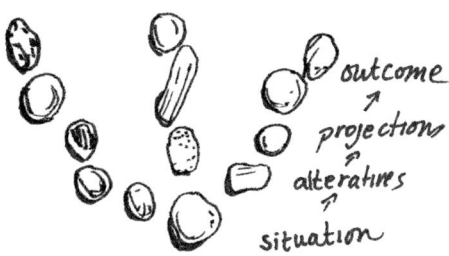

2) *Mesa Heart Meditation*: Make sure you are undisturbed, and sit with your spine straight in a comfortable position. Bring the entire bundle, with all stones, to your heart. Hold it there until you feel connected with the stones. Now close your eye and relax. Let yourself come in tune with your inner self. Release all thoughts and concepts and let the mesa embrace you with its energy field. Remain detached from any idea or thought or feeling. Become the seer of who you are. Continue with effortless breathing, slowly and deeply, until there is hardly any movement. Continue in this way until you are complete. Open your eyes. Remain seated for a minute or two before moving.

Archetypal Mesa Session

Source	the Centre	Clear Quartz
Water	the Child	Rhodochrosite
Earth	the Mother	Lemurian Jade
Fire	the Hero	Rutillated Quartz
Air	the Sage	Lapis Lazuli

3) *Meditation of my true self in the world of archetypes*. Gather the archetypal stones. Place the source stone and the four archetype-stones on the Mesa cloth and visualize yourself at the centre as you place the source stone, a small sphere of Clear Quartz, in the middle of the cloth. Bring attention to your heart. See this small sphere at your heart's centre as well. By this, you may be shining a light into your source, a very tiny point in the middle of your being. Now place your water archetype stone at the far side of the sphere. When you are visualizing, this stone is now in front of you. Rhodochrosite is the inner child stone. A small child is within you: it is your innocent nature, your water being who is related to feelings rather than rational thoughts. Bring yourself to feel how this child feels now. See him or her in front of you and then bring this child within your heart. Is there a message for you? Now look to your sides and you will find the Mother and the Hero. Place the corresponding stones at each side of the sphere. See yourself as a young impatient and fiery person hungry for adventure, breaking the ties with your parents to go out into the world. Bring your youth within your heart. Are you able to contain the impatience and develop patience and timing? Now see the mother: first your own physical mother and you as her child, then as the universal mother creating new life. Be her love and loving care. Eventually these images fade away to be replaced by your sage, your timeless wise elder,

who is standing behind you with ancient hands above your head to share attained wisdom. Relax into your new insights and give thanks for what you received.

Maintenance: Engage in a mesa session daily and before a major decision or before an important event.

Effects: A mesa session may transform negativity within, and be calming. In the process of handing the stones our mind may be able to relax and attain new focus. Touching stones assist us to be more grounded. If you are working through difficulties, these problems may sort themselves out and you may find answers to deal with complex situations. The connection to nature's gifts are strengthened, and attachments can be viewed and released.

Crystal Care: Treat your stones as the most valuable treasure, and then they mirror that in turn to you.

Figure 73 The Master Mesa, laid out in a cross formation. Notice the additional four grounding stone for each of the elements.

Summary

The practices of yogis and shamans manifesting extraordinary powers may not be available or possible to do; however stones can be used in preparation to cultivate our inner powers by looking inside ourselves and clearing inner obstacles (*Inner Journey meditations*) and then to progress by using stones to train our mind, and reflect on who is making the choices (*Crystal Medicine Bundle* or *Crystal Mesa*).

Practices:
Inner Journeys with Apophyllite
Crystal Medicine Bundle
Elemental Medicine Bundle
Master Mesa Practices:
> Problem-solving session
> Heart Meditation
> Archetypal session

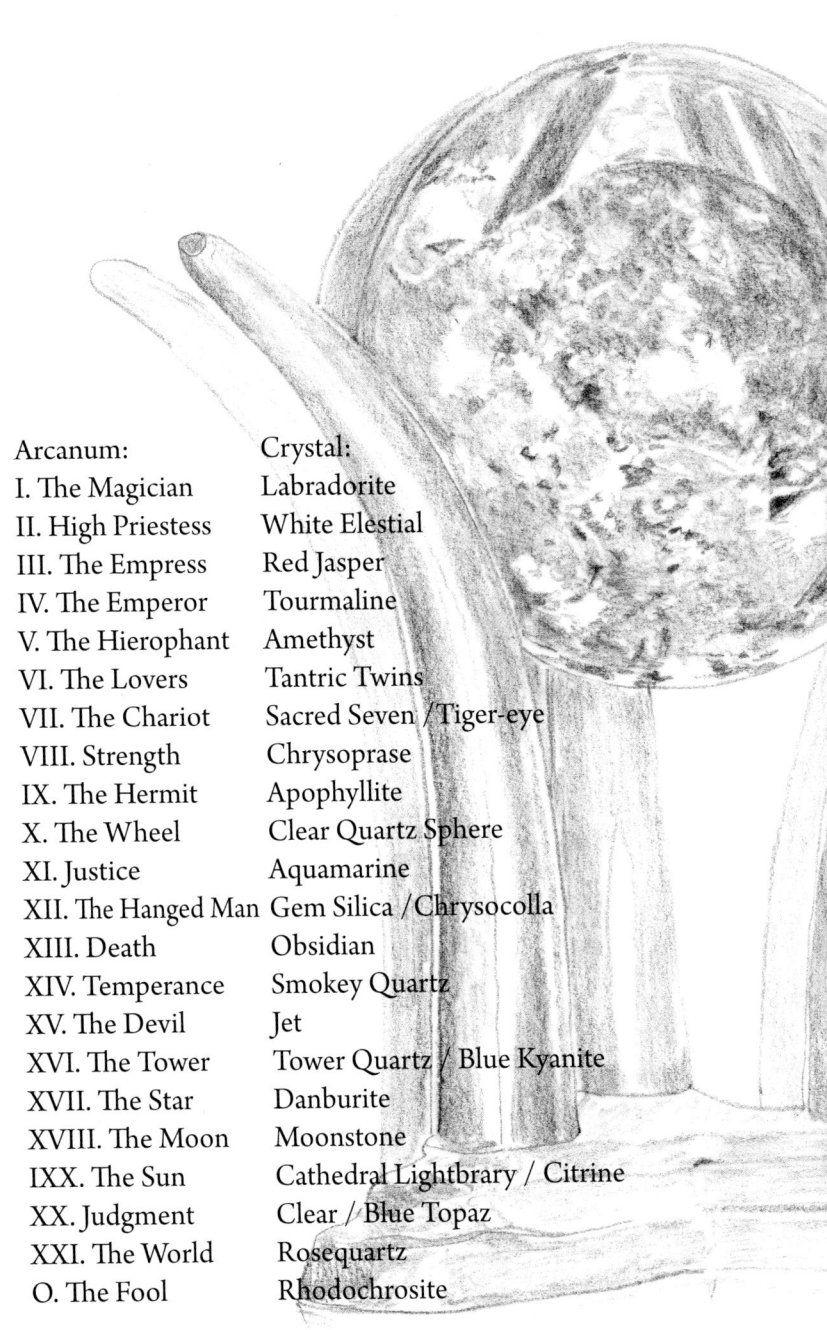

Arcanum:	Crystal:
I. The Magician	Labradorite
II. High Priestess	White Elestial
III. The Empress	Red Jasper
IV. The Emperor	Tourmaline
V. The Hierophant	Amethyst
VI. The Lovers	Tantric Twins
VII. The Chariot	Sacred Seven / Tiger-eye
VIII. Strength	Chrysoprase
IX. The Hermit	Apophyllite
X. The Wheel	Clear Quartz Sphere
XI. Justice	Aquamarine
XII. The Hanged Man	Gem Silica / Chrysocolla
XIII. Death	Obsidian
XIV. Temperance	Smokey Quartz
XV. The Devil	Jet
XVI. The Tower	Tower Quartz / Blue Kyanite
XVII. The Star	Danburite
XVIII. The Moon	Moonstone
IXX. The Sun	Cathedral Lightbrary / Citrine
XX. Judgment	Clear / Blue Topaz
XXI. The World	Rosequartz
O. The Fool	Rhodochrosite

Crystal Tarot

Ancient wisdom revealed by symbols
Obvious only to the true seekers

Tarot archetypes have always fascinated me. My mother gave me a deck of tarot when I first came to live in Canada. It had beautiful images inspired by Japanese art. I found them interesting to look at, but had no idea what they meant symbolically, but later there was an event that made them come alive literally. I made the connection with the images and the symbolic language they spoke. I realized this was a way for the ancient mystery schools to teach how we are, and live out our life. Specially in the 22 Major Arcana, I felt a strong resonance to how I believed I was and what I did, linked to the patterns depicted in the archetypes displayed in the cards. This breakthrough made me very interested to make also the connection with crystals and tarot. The following pages shows the major arcana journey through the lens of crystals. Intuitive healer, Jarmila, writes about the images in the Crystal Tarot:

I am witnessing, in these images, a magnitude of information encoded of the travelling consciousness. It is the expressed work, the perceptions, of the experiences of the journeyer.

With each image I offer a description and an affirmation. Please enjoy your journey through them.

How To Use the Crystal Tarot

Why: The goal of our work is to bring into focus mental and emotional patterns, or the motivating forces behind the various actions and habits that we may have. By attuning to each of the archetypes, we may gain valuable insight into our own condition, and be in a position to make appropriate changes for ourselves.

How to start: Find a private and peaceful space and relax for a moment. You may have a question in mind, for which you need an answer. This is helpful to begin with. State your question, and then select one of the archetypal images you feel most drawn to, it might also be the image you have the most aversion to, as well. Select that image and ask yourself what would the answer be if you were that archetype. Place the book in front of you and look deeply into the image. Let the symbols and crystals vibrate through the image and reach your centre, where all your personal answers are to be found.

Maintenance: You may enjoy a few minutes each day to tune in with your self, using the crystal images. Perhaps stating the same question each time: What archetypal pattern am I facing today? or What gifts does my inner journey provide today?

Crystal Care: Usually tarot cards are wrapped in a silk scarf, and you might follow this custom and treating the images (and this book) with respect.

Effects: Tarot work have always been an inner journey for me, and never a way of depending on outside forces, if you work with the images in this way, you may reap the rewards of knowing more about yourself.

Enter Here, to the mysteries within!

"I am manifesting anything that I believe is possible."

I. The Magician. Labradorite heart and beads, with dodecahedral Pyrite and Manifestation Quartz (top). Looking into the vast expanse of shimmering blue, green and magenta of Labradorite, inspired me to take the first step on the crystal journey. You may discover resources available beyond your imagination. Look beyond what you can imagine. Lesson: Accessing raw manifesting power.

"I am going to the core within, gaining the understanding to solve my issue."

II. The High Priestess. White Elestial Quartz with Clear and Smokey Torch Crystals at the sides. You are advised to go inwards for the answers you are seeking. The unknown may be scary but necessary to delve into. Your quest is to know yourself, but know you are guided on your way. Lesson: Using your intuition.

"I am nurturing myself. I am being lovingly embraced by mother Earth."

III. The Empress. Red Jasper, Mookite Jasper Talisman, and clay artefacts (Temple Stones) from an ancient ruin. Your search must begin within your hidden pool of emotions. Nurture yourself, and find comfort in your own skin. Your advice is to feel your way through a difficult situation. Lesson: Subconscious connection.

*" I am grounded in the world. I am a channel of loving energy
to the world around me, as I carry out my chosen work."*

IV. The Emperor. Black Tourmaline sphere, green Tourmaline (Verdite) and three golden Tourmaline (Dravite). You are advised to be strong, and work with the each task at hand. This is not the time to relax, but to act with clarity in the world. Lesson: Conscious leadership.

V. The Hierophant

"I surrender to the highest part of myself, letting Spirit touch me."

V. The Hierophant. Amethyst cluster and Amethyst Spirit Quartz at the top. You are advised to find a path toward the higher good for your Soul community. Listen to Spirit rather than to your ego self. This is not a time to do your own "thing."
Lesson: Working with tradition.

*"I chose balance in all my relations,
appreciating each for what I have learnt."*

VI. The Lovers. Tantric Twins (top and bottom) with indigo and green Fluorite (left & right), Ruby, Amazonite sphere and Sphalerite. You need to make a choice that serves you and others in the long run. End relationships of co-dependent or harmful nature. Lesson: Right choices.

" I am balanced in all things. I move toward my goal with grace."

VII. The Chariot. Sacred Seven Quartz (top) with Tiger-eye on botryoidal Hematite, a black stone and a white Zen stone. When you are facing an opportunity for transformation, maintain balance and stay present to your situation. Support yourself on solid foundations. Lesson: Learning from distractions.

" I am courage and balance. My life is harmony in midst of war."

VIII. Strength. Chrysoprase (top) with peach Heulandite (bottom), botryoidal Lepidolite (centre), Lemurian Jade (top left) and Tangerine Tantric Twin Quartz (bottom right). You are advised to be graceful, kind and strong even if you feel strong temptations. Embrace each challenge with courage. Lesson: Tempering urges.

*"I am seeing the true reality, and accept
responsibility for myself and my actions."*

IX. The Hermit. Apophyllite clusters with Lapis Lazuli, and Sandalwood carving and beads. Your question can only be answered by retreating, for a while, in solitude. By meditation, your spirit within will show where you need to look, in order to complete what you started. Lesson: Release attachment.

*"I am the master of my own being.
I am learning and evolving by serving Spirit."*

X. The Wheel. Clear Quartz Sphere with Staurolite on a mirror and a lotus carved in Gabbro rock. You are facing the same situation again in new "clothing." Your advice is to discover what you missed the last time it happened. Lesson: What you sow, you will reap.

XI. Justice

*'I am living in truth, free and
unbound in joy. Spirit is my light."*

XI. Justice. Aquamarine cabochons on top of a raw Aquamarine crystal. You are advised
to look carefully at your situation, to find where the real truth is. Any façade of lies is
bound to dissolve sooner or later. Lesson: Real truth, not relative truth.

"I see the wonder of my existence with clear eyes."

XII. The Hanged Man. Gem Silica and Chrysocolla (below) with double terminated Quartz (top) and Azur-Malachite sphere (very bottom). You are advised to put your problem down, move it around, and view it from a new angle. A fresh new attitude will bring results. Lesson: Changing perspective.

*"I am surrendering. I am Joy and Happiness.
I feel divinely protected and safe anywhere."*

XIII. Death. Black (gold-sheen) Obsidian sphere with clear rhomboid Calcite (centre), grey stellar beam Calcite with Marcasite (top) and Yellow Tiger-eye (bottom). You are advised to take a step outside of your comfort zone. What you are looking for is outside of what you know. Lesson: Letting go.

*"I breathe in the life force of Spirit within my body. I am patient.
I am in harmony and gentle with myself."*

XIV. Temperance. Smokey Quartz: a sphere, a wand and a tabular crystal. You are advised to wait for the right time and stay balanced. Lesson: Timing.

*" I am facing my fears, which are the source of
my addictions and cravings, this allows me to be free."*

XV. The Devil. Jet with Malachite beads. You are advised to approach you painful emotions and feel your desires fully. Now is the time to dare to be yourself. Lesson: Breaking limitations.

"I am in the present, and empowered to act."

XVI. The Tower. Blue Kyanite (centre), a Tower of Bent Quartz (bottom) and a Smokey Elestial (top). All what is misaligned must fall sooner or later. You are advised to wipe your slate clean now, it is the only remaining option. Lesson: Jump now, or you will be kicked out.

XVII. The Star

*"I reach out to my celestial guides and know that
I am connected to the Heart of Spirit."*

XVII. The Star. Danburite on a Selenite cluster. Life can be distracting and lead you to places, which do not serve your journey. You are advised to follow your heart and inner guidance. Trust yourself to act wisely. Lesson: Living your mission.

"I am exploring my shadows with a light heart. I am completing and ending projects. I am attuned to the hidden realms of my being."

XVIII. The Moon. Moonstone sphere, Selenite wand and sea shell. You are advised to approach your deepest shadows to dissolve the source of worries or despair. Then you are safe in the dark. Listen to your emotional messages. Lesson: Illusions revealed.

"I am cleared and balanced. I am new beginnings.
I am refreshed in the light."

XIX. The Sun. Citrine Cathedral Lightbrary (top), clear and opaque Citrine (left, bottom left) with Sunstone (bottom right), Rutillated Quartz (centre right), Ouro Verd Quartz (right) and a Gold Calcite sphere. You are advised to start anew, with the light a your guide. The past is now completed. Lesson: New beginnings.

XX. Judgment

*"I am letting go of control and judgment.
I am humbly awakening to my true self."*

XX. Judgment. Blue Topaz, Silver Elestial Quartz (middle), clear Topaz (below) and Hiddenite points (top and bottom). If you find yourself judging another, let go. You are advised to awake to a new world of consciousness, where you are free of limiting thoughts. Lesson: Humbly awake!

*"I am committed to love myself and others.
I value who I am, and present my worth to the world."*

XXI. The World. Rose Quartz Elestial and Rose Quartz Heart surrounded with Turquoise. You are advised to approach your situation with love for yourself, do what you advice others to do. You are the solution. Lesson: Healing.

*"I am inviting the innocence and
the adventure of my inner child."*

O. The Fool. Rhodochrosite (top) with Leaverite. Trust that you may accomplish what you set out to do. You are advised to see your situation through the eyes of an innocent child. Follow your star. Lesson: Total Trust.

Natural Elements

All the elements can be seen in nature, as illustrated in the following pages. Use these images to explore each of the five elements: Earth, Water, Fire, Air and Space. Let them inspire you in your practice of the Crystal Mandala. Life is the ultimate mystery, and it is yours to discover.

The element of earth is our physicality, the living form of all life inhabiting our planet. The main attribute of earth is to be solid. The essence of the water element is fluidity and it informs our emotions. The fire element is energy or heat which keeps us alive. The Air element is movement and is expressed in our subtle mental processes. The element of space is all encompassing, wherein the sound of creation continuously manifests. Our ultimate Source is beyond these five elements, and may only be known by direct experience.

Space

Air

Fire

Water

Earth

A natural mandala of rocks made by moving glaciers.

Principal stones in the Moon Mandala Journey. The first stone is green Jade, at the very bottom, then the journey continues counter-clockwise. Notice the central clear Quartz surrounded with the archetypal stones: Lemurian Jade below (south), followed by Rutillated Quartz (east), Lapis Lazuli (north) and Rhodochrosite (west). Left: Crystal Mesa Talisman on a traditional Peruvian mesa cloth.

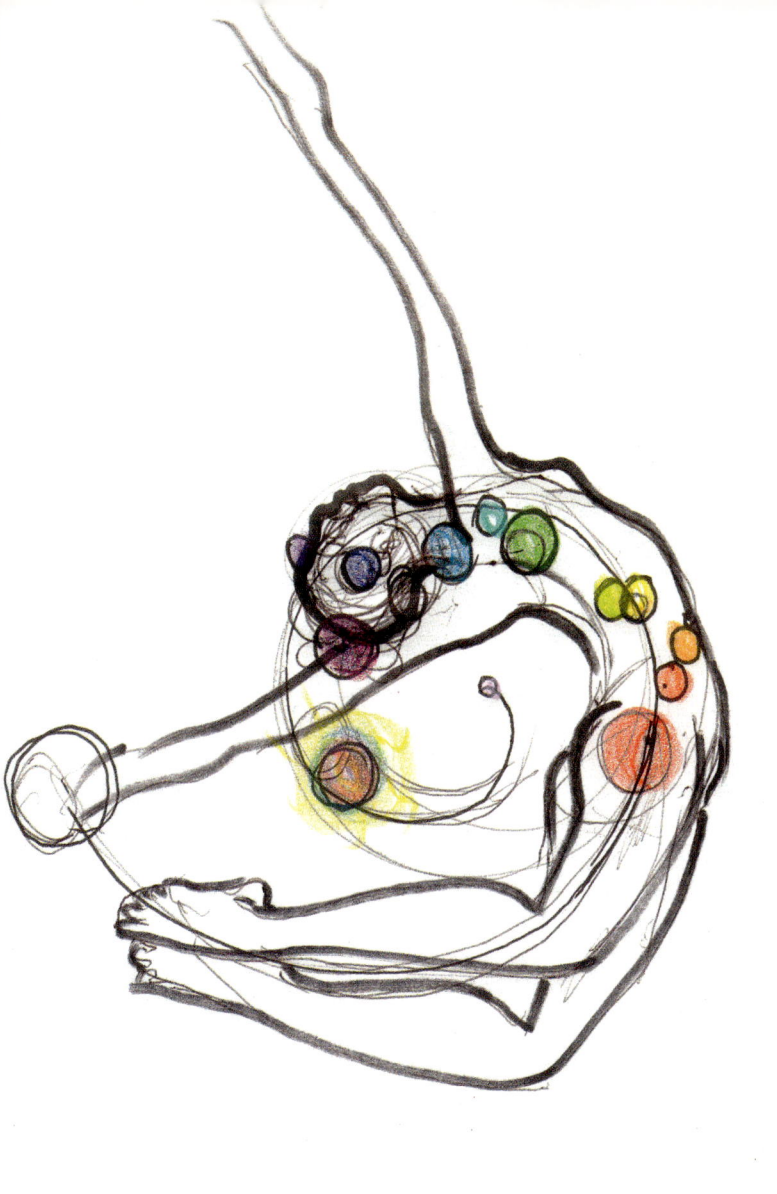

Images of Crystal

Our multidimensional body is a kaleidoscope of colours and energies. The spiral body attempts to illustrate the various subtle energy centres, like gems glowing within our being, and the journey to our inner source. Follow the spiral from below the feet, though the body along the middle and curving inward, out from the top of the head into a small circle. This show one complete turn around a cental axis. This small point begins the next leg of the journey into the next dimension. The figure is almost flying, arching back to fully open the heart, and experience life first hand without shields or limitations.

The following display of colour images shows healing jewellery and crystal images used in some of the practices in this book. These tools are intended to assist a crystal practitioner along his or her journey to be free.

Crystal Talismans - tools for healing. At the centre: Labradorite Crystal
Colour Life Spiral, followed clockwise from the top: four gem weaved
pendants, Petalite with Pietersite beads, 12 Colour Ray multi-looped setting with Quartz and gem-beads, Quartz upon a mandala of Amethyst and
Tourmaline, Ruby crystal, Quartz pendulum with Rhodochrosite bead.

Courage is Chrysoprase, shown here in Gunilla's lovely *Mandala Talisman* necklace with Peridot (humor and joy), Citrine (clearing) and Pearls (turning a challenge into beauty). These stones may assist a mandala keeper to maintain a happy and courageous outlook, in spite of difficulties, and to make the life journey beautiful.

Emerald: *My Divine Lover is within.*

Emerald sphere - the heart and love stone with the key of beauty. It is placed on a green silk cloth. Silk is a beneficial material to keep crystals in, or on, as it is keeping the crystals energetically clear. Next page shows a Moonstone Mandala with pearls.

Moonstone: *I am blessed on my journey into the unknown.*

From Top left: Epidote, Moldavite above a Black Kyanite, middle: crystallized and polished Hematites above a specular Hematite. Bottom: Black Tourmaline wand.

Sky-Blue Ray Stones

Left: Anhydrite wands (Angelite). **Middle:** Celestite, Angelite cabochon, raw Blue Calcite, Blue Topaz, and Tourmaline. **Right:** Blue Kyanite.

Top left: Elestial Rose Quartz, then Morganite, Pink Kunzite and Rose Quartz cabochon below. Lower triad: Apophyllite pyramid, Danburite with Pyrite on Quartz below.

I am a channel of Divine Light.

"Dancing Atlantis" Manifestation Quartz, and Devic Temple, embedded with several tiny crystals. A stone like this, can be used for crystal
gazing, for manifestation, or to connect with inner guidance.

Magenta Ray Stones

Top: Record Keeper Rubies, and Star Ruby cabochon, Sugilite below.
Lower triad: Drusy Kammererite, Garnet crystal and Madagascar Rho-
donite cabochon below.

Forgiveness Grid with Dioptase clusters

Pink , Clear and Lavender Stones

Top: Quartz cabochon, Rose Quartz on Tantric Twin. Middle: Sugilite/ Bustamite and Pink Opal. Bottom: Lepidiolite and Smithsonites below.

Emotional Balance
Green Ray Stones

Top: Fuchsite and Malachite. Four stones: Kabamba Jasper, Grossular Garnet, Chrysoprase and Zoisite-Ruby. Below: Raw Green Aventurine.

Top: Phenacite followed by tumbled White Chalcedony, Moonstone cabochon, and a raw Moonstone placed on a clear Topaz.

Gold and Yellow Ray Stones

Top: Polished Citrine. **Centre:** Citrine spheres and Gold Stellar-Beam Calcite. **Next row:** Libyan Gold Tektite, Gold Calcite sphere, Citrine point and raw Heliodor. **Bottom:** Polished Rutillated Quartz.

Elestial Power: *I am present to my true self.*

Smokey Elestial Sceptre and White Elestial Teacher Crystal.

Calcite: *I am present each moment.*

Wind polished Calcite vein and an ancient tree, from the White Desert in Egypt.
Right bottom: Heulandite cluster with Hematite beads.

Crystal Fun, Courses, Travels and Shows...

Thanks to all Crystal Friends!

Ten Gems for Elixirs

Sixteen Crystal Colour Rays

Crystals are here for us to experience and understand. As a result, we have every opportunity to align with the Divine, whereby we become truly happy.

The colour box shows the *Beginning Ten Gems* for elixir making (see page 402), a mini copper wand with quartz and central Peridot, used for energy work (see page 102). At the bottom, stones modelling each of the *16 Crystal Colour Rays* , (see page 310).

Figure 74 After lightning comes thunder and then rain. Light travel fastest, then sound, then matter. After the rain we may see colourful rainbows shimmering over the sky.

Light & Crystal Colour

Rainbows are afoot
Look for them appearing

Lightning is a tremendous force that balances conflicting energies. The instantaneously released energy displays sound, heat and light, and within its intensity we may perceive a glimpse of the creation process. The fiery thunderbolt may be seen as an active manifestation out of thin air, out of space, or an unknown source itself beyond conflict.

When white light falls on a surface, we see it reflected as colour. An Emerald is green because it absorbs all visible frequencies except green. The colour of something is what makes it stand out and easy to distinguish. Together with shape, colour makes up the world we perceive with our sense of sight. Colour is important as a sign language: bees, for example, focus their whole life on the search for particular colours. The receptors in their eyes are tuned to colours of flowers that give them food. Colour makes significant mental and emotional imprints on us. We stop at a red light and generally feel calm being in a blue room. A soft red dining area stimulates our appetite. A dark blue suit looks professional. The study of light and colour really affects several sciences and levels of our being. In Physics we can take advantage of knowing about radiation and optics, in chemistry how minerals and pigment are made, in physiology about the function of the eye, in psychology how we react to colour, and in cosmology the study of Spirit[1].

Colour Basics

If you have the three primary colours in light (red blue and yellow) you can mix them to produce all the colours in the visible spectrum. White is the sum of all colours and black is the absence of light. Rainbows appearing after a rainstorm exhibit the spectral colours. The moisture in the atmosphere refracts the light like a massive airborne crystal. If one looks at a rainbow in detail, one may see it as a graduated band that includes all visible colours, even though only seven spectral colours are normally mentioned. This can be clearly seen in greater clarity if one makes up a colour wheel. An artist is keen to know this and blends colours on demand. Pigments and dyes were originally made from minerals and organic materials locally available to people. The secret to preparing some of the pigments was kept well hidden from outsiders, since colour pigments and dyes were considered tremendously valuable.

SOURCE
△
High End
Cosmic Photons
Gamma Rays
X-rays
Ultraviolet
Visible Light
Infrared
Far Infrared
Microwaves
Radio/TV waves
Ultrasound
Audible Sounds
Infrasound
Low End
▽
AUM

What we see as colour is light particles (photons) or waves, vibrating at various frequencies measured in cycles per second. Red has a lower frequency than violet, which means that violet vibrates faster than red. A coloured object is all but the colour displayed to us. When light shines though a transparent colour gel (for example, a thin Lepidolite plate) all other colours are filtered out and we see only lavender, and thin slices of Hematite and Ruby appear red. A clear quartz prism does not absorb colour, but instead separates sun light into visible rainbow patterns. When Quartz is placed in the sun, however, it will absorb and radiate some warmth. Glowing red-hot coals radiate heat, which is within the infrared part of the light spectrum.

Octaves of Light

One may visualize the light spectrum as a keyboard of several octaves. In the lower end we have sounds, in the middle, visible light, and towards the high end, X-rays. In a spiral form the octaves would be seen as stacked above each other. If they are presented in this way, we might realize how higher dimensions work: they are literally stacked on top, or rather, within the third dimension. In effect, they are occupying the same space. Looking from the other extreme, we might realize that the highest vibrations, when stepped down, become physical matter.

Figure 75 Cross-section of a fossilized shell (Ammonite). The spiral is really a one-pointed energy source, a tiny dot growing into a circle that continually is enlarging itself. Nature is brilliant. We might learn from nature about ourselves.

Psychology of Colours

The receptors in the eyes detect patterns of light and shape; the brain interprets data input from the eyes into meaningful images. The human eye is tuned into the colours of the visible spectrum. Other beings may perceive light outside of the human range. We may train to discern variation in colour and see thousands of shades. A person conveyed to me that he had learned to match precious high-end gems in absolute perfect colour graduation for wealthy jewellery clients. He said he could detect the slightest distortion. I could see what he meant in his display. His clients would pay astronomical sums for such a necklace, but he said this was their second-best, since normally when they went out they would not wear their diamonds.

Colour is often associated with the emotions. The seven mortal sins: Envy, Pride, Gluttony, Lust, Avarice, Wrath and Sloth are associated with colour. For example, we speak of being "green with envy." Intense red colour displays more energy than dark grey, in which nothing much moves. The 'sins' mentioned are, in fact, mental-emotional states held within. They rob us of energy because it takes so much energy to support them. However, it takes more energy to change than to maintain the status quo. Consequently, people will not address their negative situation sooner. In contrast, a positive state of peace is usually seen as white, the full spectrum of colour balanced.

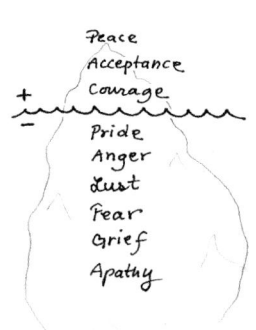

Figure 76 Emotional Iceberg[2]. The higher up, the less energy is held. At the bottom almost all available energy is tied up in the emotions. At the top, energy is flowing without being held at all. Notice the water level marking the line between negative and positive emotion.

Reaction and Transfer

Colour and shapes impact us immediately and we have learned to react to colour either with pleasure or disgust. There are combinations of colours that clash with each other, but the sensitivity is set to a varying tolerance, in the same way that some people cannot hear a note that is slightly off.

We react to colour along learnt patterns. This factor is used in advertising to connect something nice and lovely (like a rosy baby smiling), with a company's product. The colours and the image content make a positive emotional connection for the viewer, who then desires to buy the product. The colour and the baby really had nothing to do with the product but the connection was subconsciously made because of the emotional response in the viewer. This is widely used by authorities and institutions to lead people to learn what they want to promote, faster and more permanently.

Healing with Crystal Colour

Colour rays have been described as held by gems of various colours. For example, the red ray is carried in red or pink crystals, such as Ruby, Rhodochrosite or Rose Quartz. Each ray would carry its characteristics and challenges/lessons.

Colour affects one's mood. Warm sunny colours have a mood-lifting effect. Cool colours in the blue-green part of the spectrum are calming. Red and orange are stimulating. The seasons are connected with colours, too. Spring has bright warm colours, summer exhibits muted cool colours, fall shows muted warm colours and winter has bright cool colours. Our complexion also demarcates these characteristics, depending on race and climate. Colour may be used to remedy colour deficiencies in the aura. A person with all levels balanced is a happy person (white for peace). The colours that one assimilates help to balance one's system. Like the bumblebee, a human needs to receive all of the colours that are sustaining him or her. Training ourselves to discern life-force energy, as can be seen in the colours, leads to health in the body, mind and soul. A talisman can be made to match a person's need. The crystals used should either stimulate a deficiency or balance excess. This method used in my work with *Crystal Colour Life Spiral Talismans* proved helpful for people who have used them, as can be seen in these two reports:

Talisman to Remedy Migraine

Help with Migraine. For many years, I had been experiencing excruciating migraines. It was an intense piercing pain that went thru the side of my head and would be accompanied by nausea and vomiting. These episodes would last for 2–3 days and occur at least every one to two weeks. During those times, my head would either be under a bed sheet where it was completely dark and quiet or in the toilet bowl. This would of course leave me incapacitated and unable to work during those periods. For years and years I tried everything to solve this problem. It was extremely frustrating, especially as a yoga teacher. My migraines were finally cured with a talisman that Margherita made for me. We were working on a talisman to deal with some issues I had with my mother. And while Margherita was weaving the talisman, I relayed a story of a past life regression I had in which I was drowned by a group of hired men on orders from my mistress (who happens to be my mother in this lifetime). She was very angry with me. It was in that moment that Margherita became intensely aware of a strike to my head that I had received from those men before they drowned me, in precisely the same spot where I had been experiencing my severe migraines. She even described in perfect detail how my migraine felt!! Imagine that! So, what was happening in this lifetime was that every time someone got angry with me, that angry energy was able to pierce thru the hole in my auric field (which was made in that past life) and I would get hit

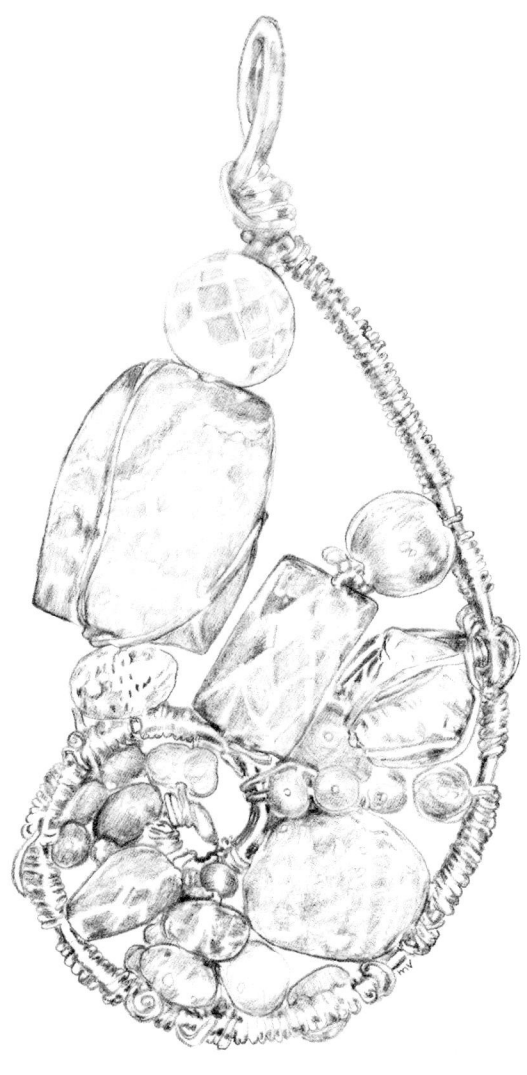

Figure 77 Crystal Colour Life Spiral Talisman created by Margherita. This type of gem woven amulet is created from the intention of
the person requesting it, and the skill of the gem weaver. Each stone
is meditated on and reflects a balancing or stimulating intention as
a result of a prior test of the person's field.

with a migraine. I have been migraine-free for five months now (in the past I would have had at least 15 episodes by now). I am so grateful to Margherita for not only identifying the problem after so many years of searching, but also for healing the wound, sealing the auric field and thus releasing me from the pain of those migraines. Thank you, Talisman. Thank you, Margherita. Savitri.

Talisman for Life Changes

I have received two Crystal Talismans to help me on my journey. The first one that Margherita made for me helped me through a major life change. I felt that the vibration of the Crystals helped me stay focused and grounded through my process of discernment. It helped me to embrace the moments of change as I moved into a place of knowing what I wanted to do next. I felt more in touch with what was my call of Spirit at this time in my life, and a deep peace. I amazed myself at how gently I was able to move on. I received the next Crystal Talisman, as I began to live my new way of being. This crystal Talisman has an energy of opening me up to the abundance of life and allows my Mind, Body and Spirit to open in an expansive way and let them be as big and as generous as they want to be. Since wearing this crystal Talisman I have truly felt and experienced abundance in all forms coming into my life, recreating my life in new and exciting ways. I have felt more able to receive and in so doing, have been able to give more in service to others. I am truly grateful for having met Margherita. She is a living Crystal Talisman of the highest good to empower one to align with who one truly is, through the beautiful crystal Talismans she creates. With blessings in abundance to you. Joanne.

Figure 78 Comparison of Colour Rays, first the challenge in each colour ray according to Stuber from "Gems of the 7 Color Rays" and then a description of the 7 Rays of Life, channelled by Alice Bailey.

Colour as Symbol

Colour Rays There is perhaps a connection in our discussion here to Alice Bailey's channelling of the 7 Rays of Life. As the question has been asked, I have included a comparison in the following table. A ray in this sense is said to embody a certain vibration sent to Earth, or into our dimension, for the purpose of our evolution. A person can receive this ray or be it, if he or she develops the ability to receive it. Maybe every ray is sent from the source, but we simply cannot receive it yet. The colour of this ray has really nothing to do with colour. It is just used to easily identify with that teaching[3]. Depending on the teaching, a ray transmits different knowledge and wisdom. Each body of knowledge is valid in the context it is given (its audience, the era of time it is given, etc.).

The Rainbow & Chakras. The seven rainbow or spectral colours are assigned to the system of chakras. The 7 colours model is helpful for relating to an esoteric science. It is important to

Colour Ray	Challenge	7 Rays of Life
Red	Anger, Impatience	Will, Power
Orange	Impulsiveness	Science
Yellow	Business Pride	Active Intelligence
Green	Need to Control	Harmony, Beauty, Art
Blue	Vanity	Love - Wisdom
Indigo	To Trust	Devotion, Idealism
Violet	Balance Integrity	Ceremonial Order, Magic
White	Judgement	

note that the actual colour of the essence of a chakra is different from the spectral colours of the rainbow. What is actually seen by yogis is the colour of the element in the chakra. The rainbow is only a model used to teach about these subtle energy organs.

The Medicine Wheel in the west and the **Mandala** originating in the east, are examples of the 'circled cross' symbol. Such symbols are used by all spiritual traditions to convey sacred teachings. Similarities are striking between them: their shape, division into four quarters, and representation of elements and use of colour. The circle might be seen as the sun, the source and the cosmos and from its centre appear the elements along the four spokes, resulting in the manifest Earth, our place of existence. The prime cause, or divine vibration (G-d's word, or sound) manifesting into matter, is thus illustrated as a symbol.

Figure 79 Medicine wheel. A layout using a mesa bundle. Stones used are Gold Labradorite at the centre and the remaining stones are Rutillated Quartz. Its purpose was to work with the fire archetype (spiritual warrior) and unity.

Mount Kaïlash - A Sacred Mountain

Small crystals are gifts to us as individuals, but great mountains are gifts to all of humanity. As this is a book on crystals, the sacred mountain cannot be ignored. My friends and fellow crystal keepers, Marc and Nicki, have had the privilege to visit the sacred pilgrim site of Mount Kaïlash, and they prepared the following:

This sacred and spiritual mountain is known to 4 different religions and considered to be Mount Meru, the centre of the cosmic Buddhist world. Tibet is the host of an impressive iconography of religious symbols and energies represented by images of various deities. They represent different qualities of the unique Buddha, the energy of perfection inside all of us. Kaïlash is thus considered a Buddha. When the great teacher Padmasambhava first came to Tibet to reform Buddhism, he decided to construct temples in a style that would represent Mount Meru, with its continents and satellite islands. He created mandala temples. In a mandala, everything radiates from the centre to the exterior. Four doorways or gates lead to the inner heart of a mandala, each with a different colour and meaning, each connected to one of the major ways we tie ourselves to suffering (samsara). These gates represent the cardinal directions. The western gate is connected with passion and negative senses (Water): a co-dependent relationship in which you become so attached to another person that there is no boundary between yourself and the other person. The eastern gate symbolizes aggression (Fire). For example, you are in war against yourself, allowing no kind of frivolity or softening. The northern gate represents the habit of crazed or paranoid comparison (Air). Others always seem better or more capable than you and in order to survive, you strive to become superior so that you can crush or overthrow them and emerge triumphant. The southern gate embodies the arrogant pride of the privileged (Earth). Being smugly confident you need nothing. The main reason for these 4 gates is to transmute these unskilled energies into something active and healthy.

What I am saying is that Meru or Mount Kaïlash should also be depicted as a Mandala with the energy of Adibuddha, Mount Kaïlash being the centre of the mandala. The pilgrim circumambulates, starting and finishing by the south gate: "you need nothing" energy, represented by Ratansambhava surrounded by a yellow colour and the earth element. You study equanimity and equality, developing your own sensations. You are into communication. Then you process west into the valley where the Divine river (Lha-chu) flows. Amitabha, representing infinite light, meditation, inner vision, the perfection of the lotus flower and the red fire element, is the energy that you walk through. This is introspection. You are into perception. You must pass over your inner uncontrolled destructive passion, learn discriminative vision. Approximately 10 km further we reach the northern gate, Amoghasiddhi, representing the air element, the infallible energy. Back into communication, we are in the green colour. Tara is protecting us. This is the blessing of fearlessness. Your ego, your over-confidence, may destroy you. From the active fire energy you are now into total action, esoterically and physically. You already walked more than 20 km (4 hours in a Tibetan one day kora) and you are going to Drolma-la, the 5650 metre pass, to reach the east side of mount Kaïlash. This is over 1000 metres climbing up in the snow, only to descend over slippery rocks to reach the blue side, the mirror of wisdom. This is the watery universe of Akshohya, blue and introspection again, the eastern side. Back to the basic level and introspection, Akshohya is unshakable. On this side of Mount Kailash the greatest of the yogis, Milarepa meditated for years. Then we go back to Ratansambhava to start again. Only after 13 koras can the pilgrim proceed to the inner kora, Vairochana, the brilliant white light, pure knowledge, the one who turns the wheel of law (teaching). This is ether, the cosmic gas, the superior level, the coordinate consciousness. Woar! I did not walk 13 koras and never reached the inner circuit. Whatever millions of levels we need to achieve in other to understand perfectly that kora (the samsara), the pilgrim will certainly make a small step reaching another level of consciousness[4].

By Marc Sheriff

Figure 80 A sacred mountain, contained within this Shadow Quartz, in the palm of my hand. A person circling a sacred mountain may approach it around the left side, around up the far back, to emerge to the right side and then to the front again, travelling in this way through the four elements[5]. Shadow Quartz may help us discover in what area we need to mend our ways.

We can see how the elements manifest naturally for the journeyers in this story. Having visited other sacred mountains, I am not surprised that past masters placed form for spiritual practice in connection with this precious and powerful form of nature.

16 Colour Rays - Breathing the Stone II

Why: Crystal Colour is a way to engage and manage the senses, and in particular the sense of sight. The colour you select may correspond to one of the elements and one of the emotional states that you feel is not balanced.

Prerequisite: Hematite Grid, Crystal Installation.

How to begin: Select a crystal you are drawn to, or if you are unsure, pick a red crystal. Place it in front of you, perhaps on an altar, or on a neutral surface in front of you. It is best if this could be done in a place of privacy suited for meditation. Set a Hematite Grid around you. Now watch the colour of your crystal. Let it be the colour that you are looking at rather than the shape of the crystal. Observe what will happen in front of you and inside you. Visualize the air in front of you, completely saturated with the crystal colour. Breathe in this coloured air though your eyes. Let it vitalize each part your body, and renew the flowing of energy.

Element	Direction	Colours used
Earth	South	Yellow, Black, Green
Fire	East, West	Red, Black, Gold
Air	North	Green, White
Water	West, East	Blue, White
Space	Space	White, Blue

Figure 81 The medicine wheel and its use of colours from various traditions. Note that the colour varies: it is not the same. The colour is a symbol, not an absolute representation.

These are some experiences I'd like to share. You may experience them differently but it will give you an idea what this practice is all about.

Turquoise. My selection was a small polished piece of turquoise. As soon as I started to observe the colour of the crystal, I became aware that it had a sort of spherical force field around itself that projected outwards in all directions. This field touched me very gently on the front of my body. I noticed several places of discomfort and old injuries. I thought that I really needed to tend to them. Then I was relaxing into the experience, letting the field of the crystal flow through me. Afterwards I felt uplifted and happy.

Clear and white Calcite cluster. As I viewed the crystal I noticed a really clear part that was sort of glowing. It was late at night; perhaps it was the reflection of the ceiling light. The top of my head began to tingle and the upper part of my ear lobes heated up. Something like a curved ray of glittering opaque light poured into my head, almost to the point of getting a headache. In response I began exhaling upwards into my head, visualizing any excess energy releasing out through my crown. I realized that I wasn't paying attention to my body's need for regular hours and enough sleep. I needed sleep to allow more dreams, as it is the dreams that give me the best feedback on my directions in life. I had not really been present to notice. The next day I realized I slept through the night in a really restful way. I felt refreshed and ready to care for myself better. I proceeded to do the dishes and make some bread in a way that I learnt from my sister. I felt joyful.

Gold Rutile in Quartz. I looked deep within the stone and felt as if rays of sunshine were touching the front of my body. All of a sudden I was like the crystal, with many rays of gold connecting within. I felt activated and energized. Very lovely. I liked this and I wanted more of it.

Dark Red Calcite. I felt as if there were slow soft flames caressing my belly. I became aware of my digestion and that last cup of coffee I had after my late lunch with a friend. I should not really have had that, I thought, it will keep me up all night. It tasted so good and now I will pay for it later. I let the dark soft red colour sweep my insides, to harmonize the effects of the coffee. I thank Calcite for my being able to fall asleep almost right away when I went to bed later.

Indigo Fluorite. Immediately upon gazing into this crystal I felt the tightness in my throat and was reminded how I am used to speaking. It is sad in a way not to just speak gently and say what is needed. Somehow I have to guard my speech and hold back, and that saddens me. I didn't know this before. I will let this tightness go. I let go of it now... I inhaled the indigo colour and let it circle around my throat and vocal cords. It felt nourishing and removed the previous dryness. I will remind myself to do this every day and whenever I am speaking.

Maintenance: Work with the same stone over several days. Then select a new colour until you are complete. It may happen that a few colours are predominantly chosen. Continue as a daily meditation over several months. Attempt to trace the colours selected to your circumstance and your present interaction with life. Perfect happiness is possible.

Effects: You may become aware of the subtle messages your body has for you, and be able to direct the healing energies of the crystal colour right away. The effect is not only on a physical level but in all parts of you. Let the colour clean you and align your subtle energy. The result is your awareness and subsequent actions that will make a difference in your life.

Crystal Care: Treat all stones as valuable tools. Clear your stones by smudge or by bathing them in the sun for a few minutes.

Rainbow Spine Bath

Why: The Rainbow Spine bath is a peaceful practice to harmonize your spinal energies at night. You may also engage children in this meditation. Any child would want to be a rainbow. When children understand how to do this, it can become a restful practice before bedtime. Engaging their personal rainbow may assist them in feeling safe and protected during the night.

How to begin: Select at least one crystal of each of the 7 rainbow colours. Lay them out in order of a rainbow as red, orange, yellow, green, blue, indigo and violet. See the 7 crystals as a ribbon of light. Breathe into your spine, energize it and "install" (visualize) the whole layout placed along your spine. Feel yourself bathed in radiant colours. Exhale numerous rainbows from all your chakra points. Let the light of them swirl around you and bathe you. Let any negativity be dissolved in this rainbow light. Complete the exercise by gently wrapping yourself in a bubble of rainbow light. Continue until you fall asleep.

Figure 82 Sharing the Rainbow Bath practice with a child is a fun way to integrate crystals and practices to become our true selves.

Effects: Your sleep becomes more restful and clear dreams may be manifest.

Maintenance: After the initial installation you can visualize yourself in the Rainbow Bath at other times of the day, especially in stressful situations. Apply your personal rainbow at such times and notice how your energy field changes.

Crystal Care: Continually inspect your personal rainbow. Let the colours be vibrant and peaceful in long swirls of energy bands moving easefully in your aura.

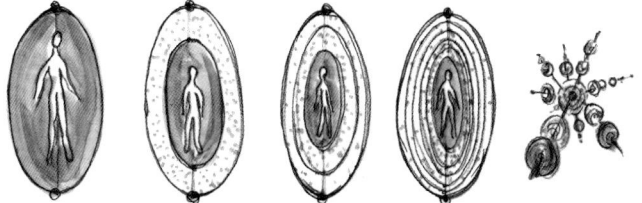

Figure 83 Five alternative models that can be used with the "Multi-dimensional Self" practice, from left tp right: 1) Physical & Aura. 2) Physical, Energy and Mind. 3) Four Bodies: Physical, Emotional, Mental & Spiritual. 4) Seven layers relating to the 7 main chakras and 5) Cosmic model of Oneness showing infinite spokes: each spoke (or ray) as an individual manifesting through all dimensions.

Multi-Dimensional Self

Why: We may see ourselves as multi-dimensional, and to exist as physical, emotional, mental and spiritual beings. The visualized aura then models these layers extending outside our physicality (see fig. 83). By tuning into each of these 'bodies' of ourselves we may begin to address subtle imbalances. Gaining control of our inner powers comes with conscious awareness of all parts of us in our world.

Prerequisite: Hematite Grid, Obsidian Bubble, Installation.

How to begin: Select stones to represent each of the 16 colours in the crystal colour list. Place the crystals on a picture or drawing of yourself in full figure (your body map). It is helpful to use a small tray underneath. Then place the tray close to you as you start your session. Place yourself comfortably, and tune in with each stone as you place it on your body map. Discover how that place in your body feels, then install the stone in that area. As each place on your body map is accessed, notice what is happening inside of you. Leave the layout in place for the next step. After placement, use each stone as a dial to turn on that colour inside of you. Let it shine through all layers of yourself. Do not worry if you only get to do one or two stones in each session.

Maintenance: Work though the whole selection over several days or even weeks. After each session, notice how each crystal colour begins to shimmer inside. Sometimes others can clearly see the colours that you have worked with in your field.

Effects: By linking together parts of our being we become more integrated. You may sense this as doing what you are really meant to do to increase self-discovery.

Crystal Care: Complete each session with sincere thanks to all the stone helpers.

	Colour Ray	Stone	Lesson (Key)
1	Green	Green Tourmaline Emerald Dioptase	Primal Power Beauty Forgiveness
2	Pink-Peach	Rose Quartz Heulandite	Self Love Graceful Love
3	Sky-Blue	Blue Lace Agate Angelite	Calmness Guardian Angel
4	Yellow	Citrine Sulphur	Clearing Digestion
5	Silver-White	Moonstone Petalite	Receptiveness Spirit Guidance
6	Blue-Green	Turquoise Chrysocolla	Healing Feminine Balance
7	Clear	Apophyllite Topaz	Inner Journey Judgement
8	Orange	Sunstone Carnelian	Solar Alignment Creativity
9	Black	Obsidian Black Tourmaline	Protection Personal Armour
10	Aqua	Aquamarine Blue Topaz	Truth Justice
11	Yellow-Green	Jade Prehnite	Heart Path Remembering
12	Deep-Blue	Lapis Lazuli Sodalite	Wisdom Understanding
13	Magenta-Red	Sugilite Ruby	Wrathful Love Passion
14	Violet	Amethyst Lepidolite	Change Mental Balance
15	Gold	Pyrite Gold Calcite	Manifestation Presence
16	Maroon-Red	Jasper Petrified Wood	Nurturing Patience

Summary

We see visible light as colour and hear audible sound. Both are part of the spectrum of energies permeating the universe. In studying light and colour we may have to involve several sciences including physics, chemistry, psychology, healing and cosmology to fully comprehend their effects upon us. A colour of a crystal shows what is not absorbed within its surface. We can use colour to affect our mood and emotion - it has a great impact on us, far more so than sound. This is used in advertising and spiritual traditions to control or facilitate learning. Colour can be used in healing to correct imbalances. Healing with the colour of crystals is utilized within the art of making *Crystal Colour Life Spiral Talismans* with the purpose of aligning unbalanced colours in the aura. Colour used as a symbol is seen in the tradition of the Native American 'Medicine Wheel' and in the Indian and Tibetan 'Mandala' of the East.

Practices:
Crystal Colour Meditation II - for controlling your senses
Rainbow Spine Bath - for harmonizing spinal energies
Multi-dimensional Self/16 Colour Rays - for self-integration

Figure 84 Colour Rays and example of Stones & their Lessons. Stones reflect/emit or absorb light frequencies, which we see as their colour (Ray). We may use the Crystal Colour Rays to gain total balance in our subtle bodies. This is necessary for complete health. Natural sunlight is a spectrum of frequencies, of which, we see only a small part. This visible part is here divided into sixteen Crystal Colour Rays. In addition to colour, a stone can be opaque or transparent to varying degree. The colours lavender, tan and gray are dilutions with white. For example, tan coloured Stilbite is a paler orange or peach. Brown minerals can be seen as dark (more absorbing) orange and maroon-red, or gold, which can be found in some specimens of Dravite. Note that some crystals also interact on a non-visible level, e.g. radioactive and ultraviolet.

Figure 85 It is through the heart that we can establish the connection to our true self and where we really belong. A crystal cluster held close to the heart may allow us the clarity to remove the heavy bars holding the heart door closed. By developing our heart we may open the connection to our source. Then we become selfless and in no need of others. This is the point of true love.

The Crystal Grid

*Spirit and Matter
Joined by Love*

The universe with its many galaxies and planetary systems is held in place inside space and time. Planets circumambulate their suns as our planet Earth does our Sun. We can surely feel the gravitational pull, but how is all this really held together? To answer this I ventured in my meditation to higher worlds of imagination, consisting of pure lights: a place of highly evolved beings with refined thoughts and subtle pure emotions. These beings were moving totally guided by the One, the very source of all existence. In fact, all creation seemed to be emanating out from this source as rays of light. These lights formed coherent patterns of indescribable beauty. Still visualizing this scenario, I was drawn to speculate on my own origins in this picture. Feelings of belonging sprang up within me and a sense of true home enveloped me. Perhaps I belong as a small speck of a holographic picture that has been torn into many tiny pieces. Each of these pieces shows a somewhat vague outline of what the bigger picture looks like. A hologram is created as a three-dimensional image that can be viewed from any angle. The smaller a fragment of the original image, the lower the resolution, and a soul incarnating might be just like such a small piece, but it has lost most or all memory of the larger image.

If such a model is true, our Source of being is everywhere, and in everything there is an ethereal Crystal Grid that embodies all planes of existence; consequently, I, as a part of the whole, have my own tiny place to fill. My personal grid or template exists in an unseen way right here and now, and I can act in accordance with it or against it, as I have been gifted with free will. In fact, such personal templates can be seen by a clairvoyant, as the aura. All forms of life have such templates, even large entities such as planets and galaxies, since they form and hold their place in the cosmos. It is in our mineral "crystals" that this template can be seen to manifest itself with the greatest clarity. If conditions are favourable, crystals form, but if disharmony pervades they don't. This is why crystals are such valuable tools for healing, since they show in form and vibration what alignment to the true Grid means. If you have a problem with this reasoning, read on. This is not in contradiction with anyone's beliefs. It is a model for how we can heal the things afflicting us in our realm. If this model does or doesn't work for you, it is up to you.

Source
Spirit
Mental
Emotional
Physical

Figure 86 Levels of our being as a pyramid (we may also see it as a section of a circle).

Let's first discuss the model of four levels or subtle bodies of our being. Later in this chapter I'll discuss how to create healing grids.

Physical and Etheric Body

The physical body is truly a miracle. The essence of living beings resides physically in the genetic code, our DNA. Just as the stars arrange themselves divinely into galaxies forming the universe, so is each cell placed perfectly in the body according to its individual grid. Our physicality includes our various tissues, bones and organs; this configuration is the earthly part of a vast multidimensional being, which in its Oneness manifests in a myriad of forms. Humans are just one such form. The underlying patterns make up our subtle bodies.

At conception a soul is propelled into the physical realm. Within a short time the etheric template of the future baby is formed from subtle non-physical matter empowered with vital energy. It is around this structure of energy pathways, called meridians, that cells organize themselves into organs and tissues of the growing foetus. We know this from research of meridians[1]. Where they are close to the skin they appear as acupuncture points. Such points can also be scientifically detected on the surface of the body[2]. Energy travels along these ductile pathways embedded in the fascia (our connective tissue). When blockage occurs along the meridians, problems or illness may manifest in the organs, in the same way as a plant, which gets little or no water, would wilt or die.

Emotional Body

It is clear that at death the physical and the etheric bodies dissolve. What remains are yet subtler strata of our being called:

astral, mental and causal bodies. As the astral plane houses emotional imprints it is also called the "emotional body." It is proposed that emotional imprints will carry over into the next lifetime. The phenomenon of ghosts is considered to be the astral bodies of diseased persons, who for some reason remain here. Fear, and strong attachment to their bodies are very likely the cause.

Emotional energy imprints are processed within the complex system of chakras and nadis, which create the field of the emotional body[3]. It extends beyond the physical/etheric body. How does this manifest in our life? To exemplify: The young lover sees his beloved and instantly thinks: "How beautiful she is." Inside he starts to feel incredible love welling up as a desire to be near her. In his aura the clairvoyant may see activity and the opening of his heart chakra, and that then starts to emanate a loving glow in conjunction with an arousal of the sexual energies at the root. He will have a hard time concentrating on a math problem at this point in time. In the following days he won't be able to stop thinking of her, day and night. He is "in love." If the love is consistently being supported and nurtured, it can mature into a deep friendship. When the two are together, their light bodies (aura) move together and many healthy connections are then established between them. Each of these bonds represents an interaction or challenge they have worked though and resolved, healthily. Other couples are perhaps not so skilled, and instead, affirm destructive bonds or cords between themselves. Perhaps they indulge in habitual arguing, nit-picking and fault-finding that hurt and damage. Such persons are, in fact, 'in-hate' with each other. The emotions of such interactions can also be perceived in the aura as negativity, greyness or heaviness. Healing or therapy can be applied here if the parties are willing. Our emotions are very 'sticky,' meaning that, when one is with a truly happy person, one feels uplifted and positive, whereas being with someone who is full of negativity might cause others to feel dragged down or zapped.

Mental Body

This is the location of our soul and our archetypal personas. When approaching a dense forest it is easier to walk where there is a path. However, if we search for our lost child, we don't hesitate to rush into the dense bush to retrieve her. On the way, we might discover a spring of potable water, and when we need water we may be strongly motivated to clear away the bush to get to it. If many people travel this small path, it becomes a bigger road. It is said: *When we think, we send out vibrations of a fine ethereal substance, which are as real as the vibrations manifesting light, heat, electricity and magnetism*[4]. This subtle substance is very real; when a particular thought is repeated often enough, it creates a habitual link between existing pathways in our neurological underbrush. This thought becomes easier to think of, every time it is repeated. For example: in a piano lesson a teacher instructs a student to practice a song over and over again, and eventually it becomes easier when the student doesn't have to think where to put the fingers for every note. In the end the student can play the song effortlessly by heart, and the brain has created a new path. Many such linked paths are created, in our life. Negative links (for example: if you do not do this ..., you will be punished) seem to be far more deeply imprinted and harder to change. Positive life affirming links (for example: if I breathe and stay present, I can deal with this danger better) add skill, wisdom and consciousness to the person. All programs or intentions are immediately obeyed when engaged. It is by conscious awareness of these processes that we may delete or change harmful behaviour patterns.

Spiritual Body

Our most subtle body, the Spiritual Body, could be explained as the blueprint for all greater bodies. This dimension or realm does not entertain mental concepts. It is the place where our individual spirit resides. This causal body manifests out of our very source. The universe is incredibly complex and beyond any normal comprehension, so how can we truly understand it all? The best we can do is to work with a model of understanding. We definitely exist on many dimensions. How many dimensions there really are might be irrelevant for our needs, and the spiritual body can perhaps be described on many other levels. Barbara Hand Clow mentions nine dimensions[5] in her channelled account from the Pleiadians. She gives the reader a concise framework in her study of how we may affect our lives by working with our intentions in various dimensional layers.

When Einstein died, his brain was removed and studied. He was a bona fide genius and his work showed that within the field of science. His brain was found to have an increased number of neurons packed into his cerebral cortex (grey matter) as compared with an average person, and unusual grooves existed in the part of his brain (the parietal lobe) which deals with mathematical reasoning[6]. He was perhaps already gifted as a young child, and had the nurturing and education he needed to develop his genius. His work definitely reformed and changed the paradigm about the world that came before him, and ended the Newtonian era. Isaac Newton, in his time, also changed the way people viewed the world and can be said to have contributed to the end of the dark age of ignorance. Both men clearly were using their intellect and mental clarity to explain the world. Einstein was, in addition, clearly beginning to tap into other levels of consciousness as well. The concept of Negative Space Time begins to explain realms beyond emotions, thoughts, and our tangible physical world. In more recent time, with the science of quantum mechanics,[7] other scientists have begun to explain further how the world is created or being created in each moment. In this new paradigm the dimensions begin to make sense and

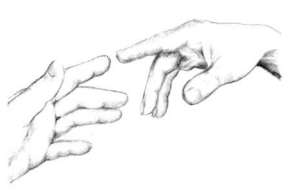

become closer to what ancient traditions have proposed for millennia. Looking at the very core of this science, the researcher would look directly into creation itself. I conclude that there "are" more to us than meets the eye.

Creating a Field

As discussed in the beginning of this chapter, we are living in a field of energies that is ever-changing. Its origination is often called the "Unified Field," which is available everywhere. In our life, we may detect any number of dimensional fields that we participate in. A field is created by how you feel and how you think. You (but not always your body) are always in the centre of your own personal field. In essence, any field always manifests from a source. To create a field we can look to this example:

As a child we threw pebbles to skip on the surface of a lake, and tried to have the stone touch the surface as many times as possible. With each contact, rings appeared: eventually the rings from two or three touch-downs met, 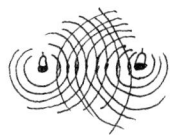 creating a sort of pattern that spread over a larger area. These patterns could be seen as the effect of our game. Now take a couple of buoys which are stationary and anchored in the water, moving up and down and creating the same effect as the pebbles. In the first example the effects pass after some time; in the second the rings continue until the buoys are removed. What is created is a pattern or field, within and around these items. Looking at any surface of water, one can usually see the combined effects of

Figure 87 An example of a grid with Lodestone, a grounding stone for the water element. The field set may assist the meditator to his or her own inner anchor of appearing emotions.

what has interacted with it, be it the moon, the wind, the beach or things inside it. If nothing else was there, the water would be perfectly still like a mirror. Water serves to illustrate how a field manifests visibly. This phenomenon could also be brought into other realms: gross and subtle energies, emotions, thoughts or Universal Love all existing within and around us.

Two questions may spring from this example:

How do we create intentional fields?
How do we disable harmful fields?

By the careful placement of special Crystals in a space, an energetic grid can be established. Such grids may bring harmony or havoc; it is up to you to decide which one it will be. Examples of grids of potential harm include those created by power lines and microwave towers.

When someone intends to create a sacred space in his or her home or office, it is recommended to tune in. This is a way of asking the intelligence of the land and building, and all material things included, to rectify obstacles of harmony. Placing sacred items, including crystals, in a grid sets up a field. In the case of the Hematite Grid described earlier, it resonates the state of being grounded and safe. The Earth (with her iron crystal core) absorbs ungrounded vibrations from outer space. It sets up a field where a specific vibrational pattern is maintained. Being inside a grid gives the impulse of aligning with its energy waves, and in the case of Hematite we then begin to feel more grounded and less spaced out.

Setting an intention also creates a field (a mind field or mine field, pun intended).

Personal Story: A Crystal Rose Garden. I felt the yearning for a space that was more private and intimate, with perennial flowers and herbs. I immediately thought of roses, as I always wanted a rose garden. So I acted on this intention and planted many very hardy roses in a circle, over a period of two years. I placed a foot-high Cathedral Lightbrary as its northern point. It forms a perfect circular grid with the roses and other stones I added, an emerald sphere in the midst of my Valerian patch and labradorite as well. The roses stand presently at about 3 feet tall, forming a perfect enclosure. Inside I have a garden bench shaded by a small apple tree towards the south and many herbs in their individual beds. A small oak is the centre of my rose garden. I love oaks. I leave this garden mostly to its own wise ways. It is quite a disorderly garden from a gardening point of view, but I love it. I go there to meditate and find calm. As I enter this garden, I feel tremendously supported. Even in the midst of winter it maintains a tranquil presence. Each season greets me there with joy and peace. Going though its imaginary gate transports me to a different reality closer to nature's source of the life force. Here, I, too, can receive its gifts first-hand. If something disturbs me, it leaves like a small breeze that slightly ruffles the flowers when I enter my garden. I never attempt to focus on the large crystal, as I am inside it already. It is not a mental thing - it is paradisiacal bliss.

Gwen, our garden helper, wrote this poem and said: "I'm so honoured to be part of your creation!"

> *Beneath traces of dusty feet*
> *Sun feeds light, wind stirs*
> *Fingers hang on a token of sand*
> *Stem pushes through the land*
> *Beginning or end clocks won't tell*
> *Falling rain, travelling wind, a mindful will*
> *Walking the path your heart has kept*
> *Reborn again this season's spent*

Practice Forgiveness - Green Dioptase Grid

Our state of mind creates a field that envelops us. If we indulge in negativity, resentment and out-right depression become a powerful negative field, draining us of our energy and also attracting more negativity. The remedy is to "let go." You may enjoy this practice with green Dioptase.

Why: Dioptase - The Stone of Forgiveness, vibrates to the heart in such a way that we may be able to open ourselves to feel, and let go. This practice is a powerful way of removing hurts, and we may in the end forgive ourselves, another person, or a situation. Spend up to one hour in this meditation.

Prerequisite: Study Connecting with Guidance.

How to begin: Ask your inner 'Divine Guide' to help you resolve your situation. Visualize clearly, when you are ready, the situation of injustice, hurt or pain; identify the person or situation you blame for it. Find something physical to represent it, like a photo of the person, personal item or written words of the event, and call it your "Mirror." Put a circular grid of Dioptase around it. Then place yourself comfortably, either sitting or resting on your back. Strongly tune in with the loving emerald green of Dioptase surrounding your "Mirror." Visualize the event or person, now separated with a strong green boundary. Let this green light penetrate into yourself, and especially in any part of you that is hurting. Surround it with green loving light. Let the pain and hurt melt away. Look at your "Mirror." How does it feel now? Discover how you feel different now, after the visualization.

Maintenance: Repeat this practice anytime you are reminded of the situation or person. Perform this practice at least 7 times, or until you have accomplished your intent of forgiveness.

Figure 88 A Dioptase Forgiveness Grid. In the centre, place a photo or an item related to that which or whom you want to forgive. This item is your personal "Mirror." See also page 275.

Effects: When I used this method, I had many pieces of the loveliest emerald green Dioptase on my altar; I placed my situation with a particular person, within its borders. Each time I performed this practice, my 'Mirror' looked friendlier and not so hateful anymore. I discovered in the face of this person my own hurt and anger, which really didn't have much to do with the event that I felt hurt by. In the end I was able to let go altogether. That was the moment I actually was in a state of 'Forgiveness' where I, and my blocked energy that I was harbouring, could move on.

Crystal Care: Dioptase is a soft and rather fragile stone. Store it carefully. To clean, place the crystals in a container with pure water. Add a few drops of rose water for extra support. Remove the stones after about 10 minutes and energize in the sun.

Grids - A grid is a formation of stones creating a resonant field.

Earth Grid - The Earth has her own grid that we are intimately linked to. It is made up of ley lines and power spots in her vast magnetic field that we may attune to. Listening to her needs, people have placed crystals at certain vital geographical points to embrace and support her and our evolution.

Standing Stones - Big installations of huge stones usually placed by earlier civilisations. Used as portals and in rituals.

Labyrinth - It is a pattern creating a walkable path (usually an installation of larger stones) that can be used as an interactive meditation tool.

Intentional Grid - This is a grid that is set up and applied around a geographical area (land grids, garden grids, house grids, bed grids), or on a grid board or altar, relating to a subtle body area (See: Abundance Grid, Forgiveness Grid, Four-Body Grid).

Healing Grid in Session - A specific energetic space is set up by the grid to do healing in (Hematite Grid, Extended Crystal Healing Grid, Infusion Grids or Crystal Spa Chamber).

Mind Grid - A visualized grid that can be practiced by setting up an actual grid with physical crystals. The benefit of mind grids is that one can apply them immediately when they are needed, (see Obsidian Bubble, Moon Mandala Grid, Black Tourmaline Warrior Stance).

Purging Layout - Accessing the Four Subtle Bodies

A layout is a set of crystals laid out on the body intended to act locally on the area it is placed over. In the Balancing Layout each of the eight crystals is placed directly on a chakra with the intention to balance it within a grid of Hematite that provides the energetic boundary for the session. We now move forward in the succession of the five layouts. We present the third, in which we aim to correct, cleanse and purge misaligned patterns and blocked energies in the subtle bodies. Each of the four subtle bodies in our model of human anatomy holds a part of our being: our physicality, our energy, our emotions, our beliefs, and our reason for existence.

Prerequisite: *Hematite Grid, Making a Crystal Mask, Dual Flow Breath, Breathing the Stone, Chakra Balancing Layout* and the *Crystal Orb Incinerator.*

Why: By intending to create a new baseline for our life, we may successfully achieve results with this practice. A new baseline means to set a different set of parameters in place that will give you a new set of tools to deal with the challenges in your life. Most students in my courses use this layout to release and integrate emotions, as many people have not been taught how to feel. Of course, everybody feels things, but do we normally put these feelings into an appropriate context? By 'appropriate context' I refer to the ability to experience deeply any emotion we generate, and then as the wind blows though the treetops letting these feelings leave us. When we realize that all our emotions are created by us, and not something outside, we can choose to take responsibility immediately for them. It is at this point that the Purging Layout is valuable. It is helpful for all of our subtle bodies, and offers a way to cleanse ourselves from the inside. You can do this by yourself, or ask a friend to assist you. We use four stones to address each of the four subtle bodies and several other supporting stones. In-between the main stones you can use small double-terminated Quartz (or DT Quartz) to facilitate any release.

How to start: Write down what your intentions are for the session, and have pen and paper nearby. Find an undisturbed place and prepare something comfortable to lie down on. Place your Hematite Grid around the area. You might smudge the whole area to clear the space. Put the stones in order on a small tray. This step helps you to place the stones more easily. Lie down and cover yourself with a blanket, if needed. Place the stones one by one carefully and prepare to engage the *Dual Flow Breath*.

1. Attune to your inner guidance and personal intentions. Breathe naturally in and out directing the flow downwards and upwards for a few minutes, and then focus your attention on the physical purger stone at your lower belly area. *Breathe the Stone* by inhaling from above it, and into your entire physical being. Visualize yourself in a cave deep in the Earth. You are comfortable here and safe. Use your sense of touch to find the areas of pain or congestion by placing your hands on them. Using your breath will assist these sensations to release. Continue until you are ready for the next step.

2. Then continue to the Emotional Purger, Malachite, at your Solar Plexus. Breathe the Stone from your safe cave; continue to visualize yourself entering a nearby cavern with a natural, softly-lit spring fed pool, to give you a comfortable start. Approach the pool area and dip your hand into the water. Can you taste the water? Is the water cold or hot? Would you like to go inside? Let yourself feel all the feelings you have avoided. Now is a safe time to express them. Cry or shout if you like. It might help you in this process. Continue to release until you are complete. As you release, engage your *Crystal Orb* to receive all your discordant energies, so as not to contaminate your space. You do not want to let it get back inside you again. At the end you'll receive new

Accessing the Four Subtle Bodies

Spiritual:	Copper Combo, or Charoite
Mental:	Azurite
Emotional:	Malachite
Physical:	Chrysocolla/Cuprite, or Red Pietersite

Layout as follows:

Crown:	Clear Quartz
Hairline:	Copper Combo/ Charoite
Brow:	Azurite
Throat:	Turquoise
Heart: Pink	Tourmaline (Rubillite) or Rose Quartz
Solar Plexus:	Malachite
Navel:	Yellow Tiger-eye
Lower Belly:	Chrysocolla/Cuprite or Red Pietersite
Root:	Smokey Quartz
Earth Star:	Black Tourmaline

fresh energy in return, cleansed from attachment and negativity. Now watch the pool of water. Has it changed in any way?

3. Access your mental body by focussing on the Azurite placed on your third eye. *Breathe the Stone* gently at first and then in a more concentrated manner, visualize your mental body perhaps as a large walk-in closet, brightly-lit with all your mental facades, beliefs and repetitive thoughts as though they are garments. Notice how it looks. Are there a lot of clothes? What stands out? Go to them and put them on. How does that feel? Is that really you, or can you let go of the layers? De-clutter this closet as you need to. Let each of the discarded items be disposed of in your *Crystal Orb*.

4. Enter your most subtle body via the Spiritual Purger Stone at the top of your head. *Breathe the Stone* delicately and involve

the entire aura in this breathing. Let it slightly expand and contract like a gossamer balloon. This is a realm of no concepts or thought, so let yourself exist here until something is tugging for your attention. Use your inner being, your higher self, as your guide. Expand and contract with the breath, and accept however you are. Fight nothing, and fill yourself with lightness. Any time you feel distracted return to the breath inhaling the stone again and again until it is filling you completely. Let go of anything that inhibits you from being with your guide. Let it evaporate until you and your higher self are one. Let this unity become your very centre. Rest in a state of unity until you are complete.

Maintenance: After the session, remove all stones and clean them carefully with the water method, over night. Journal your experience or just sit in contemplation for a while, before engaging in other activities. It is best to remain in a mode of observation for the rest of the day. Repeat this layout for one or two days, as needed.

Effects: Release on any level is freeing up your energy, and people report feeling great afterwards in spite of possible tears.

Crystal care: Azurite is a more fragile stone, so treat it with care. Cleanse your stones in water over night.

Summary

The cosmos in its entirety can be said to be an enormous holographic grid in which humanity inhabits a minuscule part. Still within that small part resides the grid for the whole. The journey of healing can be considered the joining with this ultimate grid. Our physicality is enclosed in subtle strata called the subtle bodies, which connect with the greater grid. Our model includes four such bodies: Etheric, Emotional, Mental and Causal/Spiritual. When they are purified, these bodies integrate and align our whole being. Grids create energetically subtle fields that influence our life deeply. Intentional grids can be created, by surrounding a space or area with crystals. The crystals vibrate and resonate with each other thereby generating a field of aligned energy that might be felt inside the grid. It is this capacity that makes crystals ideal to use with personal spaces as well as geographical areas, to harmonize or neutralize detrimental energies.

Practices:
Forgiveness with Dioptase Grid
Accessing the four subtle bodies with the Purging Layout

Figure 89 Kyanite (Yang Air) and Amethyst (Fiery Air) placed as a two-stone Mandala, with the message: "Transformation and change by active force of clearing." A Crystal Mandala is a circle of stones that we may use in the process of self-discovery and healing.

Crystal Mandala

The Journey makes us realize
the wisdom of the destination.

Amandala is a sacred circle of creative visualisation, a symbolic 'map' of the cosmos that includes several components. It is an ancient teaching tool that is intended to transmit a message to an audience in time and space. The Sanskrit word *mandala* comes from the root, *manda* (essence) and the suffix, *la* (container). A literal translation becomes thus "container of essence." The mandala pattern circling a centre comprises a visualized journey from the exterior into the intimate interior of one's psyche. Carl Jung considered mandalas to be "a representation of the unconscious self" and used them in therapy to identify emotional disorders. A mandala can be used to aid meditation, prayer, self-awakening and other spiritual practices to catalyze the potential oneness within.

A mandala may take many forms: circular diagrams, paintings in colour or sand, megalithic stone structures, labyrinths, medicine wheels, circular icons, circular church windows, and placements of stones and objects. Eastern mandalas are often depicted with a central deity, for example that of the well-known 'Kalachakra' (wheel of time). These assist practitioners to attain the attributes of that deity, through grasping its very essence and their own deepest intuitions. Mandala practice is thus a healing medium, a means to experience oneness and the merging of subtle inner aspects of our true potentiality. Such practice is capable of integrating opposing forces, or polarities, within the psyche. Ultimately the purpose of mandalas would be to resolve problems, remove illusions, find one's place in the world and rediscover the truth.

Walking the Labyrinth - A Journey To the Inside

 Labyrinths can be considered as walk-in mandalas. Walking a labyrinth with its characteristic single path allows a walker to access subtler brain states existing below the normal waking state. This normally occurs only during lucid dreaming while asleep or as a result of meditation practice. It is through these states of the mind that leaps of consciousness can occur that may result in extraordinary experiences. The image depicts the Chartres[1] design.

One can speculate on the past uses of the labyrinth, but meditation and devoted sacred prayer (to access the divine) seem to have been an important element of its use. Particularly beautiful and large labyrinths are now being constructed all over the world for peaceful activities, prayer and/or relaxation. Many people nowadays are very busy, leaving very little time to be contemplative and restful. That busyness can create stress. Labyrinth walking or building a labyrinth is a sacred ritual that is very calming. As a labyrinth builder myself, I can attest to its benefits. Connection with the Earth is one; another is the realization that without a healthy and living planet we are nothing and will vanish like any other endangered species. Often when walking in a labyrinth, one will find crystals placed within it, in the centre or along the path, to signify an offering, a request, or a new commitment. A labyrinth sets up an energetic grid over the land that harmoniously alters the energy in the area.

Personal Story: From experience, our labyrinth at Kyirong creates a dome-like effect, which can sometimes be perceived as an echo effect in its centre. In the summer when the bugs are out, one can use this effect. One simply attunes to the inner dome of peace, and in that state, the mosquitoes and other bugs have less chance of detecting you. As a proof that this is possible, I had the same experience while watering my garden (I was in the same state of peace as after labyrinth walking). Suddenly an event provoked anger within, and I literally fumed. Within a half-second, a dozen deer flies found the juiciest parts of my right leg. I suffered from those bites for quite a while. What had happened was that my normal, happy frequency of self was drastically lowered by the anger, and the bugs detected me much more easily. The labyrinth, especially when crystals are used, can assist in the process of improving one's healthy vibration.

Figure 90 Kyirong Labyrinth in eastern Ontario follows the Chartres design of eleven circuits. See design on previous page.

Crystal Moon Mandala Journey

The circular journey from new moon to the next new moon creates a wave and a cyclic existence. It can be directly experienced in areas that have strong tides, where the ocean moves in and out twice a day. By paying attention to the phases of the moon we may interact more wisely with our daily life. Farmers know this as they follow a planting and harvesting pattern, in order to create the most abundant crops. As the moon travels around the Earth, she is aspecting the sun, resulting in joined cooperation or opposition. At the new moon, the moon covers the sun and both of them are pulling in the same direction together. At the full moon they are in total opposition, creating maximum tension.

Thirteen times each solar year the moon guides us by her movements through her four-phased cycles of about 28 days (or 4x7 days). Each of these phases or quarters relates to an element. The Crystal Moon Mandala is a journey though the days of the lunar cycle. Each day is a combination of the predominant elemental energy at the four quarters.

●	New Moon	Earth
◐	Ascending	Fire
○	Full Moon	Air
◑	Descending	Water

Why: The crystal mandala positions provide a portal to deep awareness of our living world with all its manifestations and dimensions. Crystals may be seen as solid matter and as such many of them have been in physical form longer than any living being on this Earth. They contain in their chemistry all of the

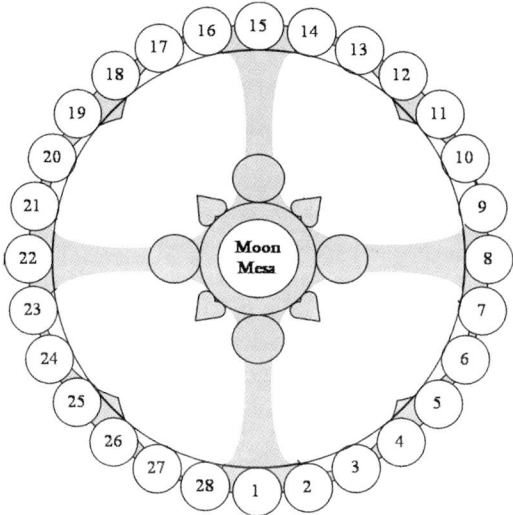

Figure 91 Master Mesa as the Moon Mandala. Notice the archetypal stones are placed at the inner circle close to the source position. The small "petals" demarcate transition to the next element.

elements of earth, water, fire, air, and space as the fifth element. Living beings are also created from these elements. The elements can be seen as the most basic components making up our very existence. Within ourselves the elements are representatives of the dimensional realms: our physical body as earth, our emotions as water, our energy as fire, our intellectual capacity as air, and our voice as space. The mind of creation, and the source that is permeating all, might be considered as the most subtle element beyond space.

By paying attention to the elemental qualities we can learn about ourselves. The Moon Mandala is a divine circle of gems containing 28 crystals, one for each day of the lunar cycle. In the centre of this mandala is our own source, represented by a sphere of clear Quartz.

How to begin: Look at the moon or consult a calendar to find

Figure 92 Personal Crystal Mandala. In the master mesa as a mandala shown here, we discover a journey in a counter clockwise fashion, congruent with the lunar journey. In it we start at the south position at the apex of the earth element on the New moon, then moving to the eastern position that of Fire, and then toward the top in the northern position of Air followed by water in the west. This is similar to the journey described in the pilgrimage to Kaïlash except that Journey was taken in a clockwise fashion, still the order of the elements is the same: Earth> Fire> Air> Water, etc. Notice the small double-terminated Quartz, your key stone, placed at the current day, here at Fluorite and as well a grounding stone for each element: Earth (Hematite), Fire (Obsidian as Apache Tear), Air (Black Tourmaline) and Water (Magnetite/ Loadstone).

when the new moon will appear. Gather all the stones or use the *Crystal Moon Mandala Cards*. Start on the new moon by placing the stones in a circle according to their moon day position. Bring attention to the 'stone of the day' and learn how that particular energy affects you.

Maintenance: Continue each day by tuning in with the stone of that day. You may choose to stay with a certain stone longer. In that case it is ideal to make a simple talisman with that particular stone.

Effects: You may notice that there is a natural attunement with the moon changes and a discovery of how you are affected, and an understanding of timing of things and when to complete them. Each of the crystals in this bejewelled necklace embodies a particular combination of elements. By attuning to this, one may attain awareness as to how the universe works its natural ways. Being part of that you may realize that you are not a separate being, but are included and can partake in living sacredness every day.

Crystal Care: Treat stones as sacred objects that are modelling your personal lessons. By being open and in a place of gratitude, you may integrate the wisdom they hold.

Lunar Days and Crystals

First Quarter - Earth archetype: the Mother - Lemurian Jade

●0	Source	Clear Quartz Sphere - Source
●1	New Moon	Spirit Earth: Jade - The Heart Path
●2	Yang Earth	Tiger's Eye - Physical Mastery / Green Tourmaline - Primal Power
●3	Airy Earth	Pyrite - Abundance
●4	Fiery Earth	Fire Agate - Transformation
●5	Earthy Fire	Obsidian - Protection
●6	Watery Fire	Gold Labradorite - Union / Blue Pietersite - Cohesion
●7	Yin Fire	Rose Quartz - Compassion

Second Quarter - Fire Archetype: the Hero - Rutillated Quartz

●8	Spirit Fire	Ruby - Passion
●9	Yang Fire	Sunstone - Solar Alignment
●10	Fiery Fire	Garnet - Sacred Body / Imperial Topaz - Alchemy
●11	Airy Fire	Citrine - Clarity
●12	Fiery Air	Amethyst - Aspiration / Lepidolite – Mental Harmony
●13	Airy Air	Fluorite - Mental Balance
○14	Yang Air	Kyanite - Clearing

Figure 93 Notice that some positions have more than one stone[2] - It was given that five stones would completely illustrate each element. This list shows the stones we have found so far.

Third Quarter - Air Archetype: the Sage - Lapis Lazuli

○15   Full Moon   Spirit Air:
                                Apophyllite - Inner Journey /
                                Celestite - Listening
○16   Yin Air   Blue Lace Agate - Peace
○17   Watery Air   Azurite - Freedom
○18   Earthy Air   Sodalite - Understanding /
                                Chrysoprase - Courage
○19   Airy Water   Aquamarine - Truth /
                                Amazonite - Honesty
◐20   Fiery Water   Labradorite - Magic
◐21   Yang Water   Blue Chalcedony - Perspective

Fourth Quarter Water - Archetype: the Child - Rhodochrosite

◐22   Spirit Water   Selenite - Light Activation /
                                Iolite - Dynamic Flow
◑23   Yin Water   Pink Chalcedony - Graceful Love /
                                Turquoise - Healer
●24   Watery Water   Moonstone - Attunement
●25   Earthy Water   Chrysocolla - Physical Temple
●26   Watery Earth   Malachite - Emotional Mastery /
                                Green Aventurine/Emotional Balance
●27   Earthy Earth   Jasper - Nurturing
●28   Yin Earth   Petrified Wood - Patience

  29   Key Crystal   Double-ended Quartz - Soul Seed
                                (representing You, as the journeyer)

Crystal Mandala Talisman - Practice Your Purpose

Why: A Crystal Mandala Talisman is a necklace which is tuned to your special circumstance. It may provide an aid to meditation and self-inquiry. The combination of stones and beads is based on an intuitive selection in a process of receiving your soul's message of healing.

Heart Map: To find your Mandala Intention, I'd like to introduce the process of the *Heart Map*[3], in which we go through eight categories of your life, first from the point of view of your obstacles as they are at present now, and then we look to the opportunities and lessons in each of these challenges. In the last step, we formulate an intention to best address your life goals.

> 1. *My Distractions*
> 2. *My Motivations*
> 3. *My Health*
> 4. *My Finances*
> 5. *My Relations*
> 6. *My Work/Vocation*
> 7. *My Skills*
> 8. *My Life Goals*

How to Begin: Draw out the map on a large piece of paper (or copy and enlarge the illustration). Mark the eight categories in the order they are drawn on the template. You find the reason for that later. Begin with your distractions. List them. What activities do you engage in automatically instead of going toward what you really want? Find at least 3-4 items, then go on to your motivations. What motivates you most? What makes you do things? Name 3-4 items. Next fill in any problems you might have in the categories of My Health, My Finances, My Relations and My Work/Vocation. Complete this step with making a list of your skills that you already have or skills you want to

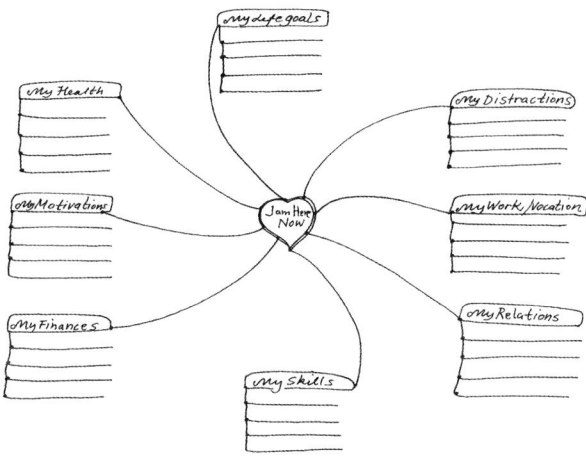

Figure 94 The Heart Map, which can be used in the process to discover our intentions /life goal for your Mandala Talisman practice.

learn. You should now have a framework of items to meditate on. Look at your map. Do some of the things you listed belong together? Can you turn a problem into an opportunity? Change to a different colour pencil and mark down Opportunities in each category.

Meditate on your purpose in this life. Are you following your purpose? Are you aligned with your personal mission? What is your mission? Look at your map again. Draw in the colours of the rainbow to each category; these are also your chakra levels. What does each part of you need? You might write keywords for what that can be. Your life goal/mission should include something from each category of opportunity.

Your eight categories on your Heart Map evolve into representations for the subtle energy centres and are thus incorporated in your work. If all levels are included, you are more likely to succeed in your endeavour.

My Health/Physical Body > Root
My Motivation/My Desires > Sacral
My Financial Power/Action > Navel
My Skills/Personal Attainments > Solar Plexus
My Relations/My Intimate Emotions > Heart
My Work/Vocation/Choices to Act > Throat
My Distraction/Mental Patterns Blocking Intuition > Brow
My Life Goal/Inspiration/Guidance > Crown

Obtaining a Mandala Talisman. You can have it made, or make it yourself. Best is to attend a course, or gather a group of friends and make them together. The full process takes two days to do in groups that I have taught so far. It is in the process of placing of stones and meditating on your heart map that the energies of your internal world are bound or woven into your mandala talisman. When you then wear your mandala, that energy imprint will help you to remember and actualize your goal. It may not be evident at first, but after some time you may discover smaller or larger shifts in your attitude and emotional landscape, and act immediately on your promptings to actualize a given opportunity. Expect to break your existing limitations of what and who you believed you could be and do.

Mandalas can be worn in the same way as talisman pendants; however it is also very helpful to use the mandala necklace only at special meditation sessions, where you focus solely on your intent. Engaging in daily sessions gives you the best results. If worn continuously, visualize your intent continuously. Repeat your affirmations, write them out, and put them up in your private space. See yourself as already having your intent fulfilled. Act as if you have already achieved it. Formulate a practice plan that you can accomplish. When you receive or attain your intention, or goal, your mandala becomes a sign of completion, success and celebration.

Summary

Mandalas are literally translated as containers of essence that are used as teaching tools for ancient wisdom. They are creative visualizations manifesting as circles surrounding a centre. The symbolic path to that centre is our life journey and practice. Mandala practice helps practitioners to realize their inner potential. Examples of mandalas include sand paintings, medicine wheels, megalithic stone circles, labyrinths and also circular placements of stones. A Labyrinth can be seen as a large walk-in mandala. Its single path will bring you into its centre if you continue your walk. Such walking meditation brings the walker into possible altered states. Looking outward we may observe how the lunar cycle models a natural way of being in tune with nature. We may follow the moon's journey with crystals created as a Crystal Moon Mandala. It is a daily observance of crystal energies, representing distinct daily combinations of elements. By attuning to each moon day in this way, we may harmonize ourselves to the natural harmony in nature and our own innate capacity to exercise our powers skillfully. For this we can also use a *Crystal Mandala Talisman*, a personally tuned necklace, used for the purpose of addressing life's major choices, our purpose and life mission. Working with a Crystal Mandala Talisman is an intuitively rewarding process that may reveal our true inner potential using the process of a *Heart Map*. It addresses the obstacles and opportunities in each of our chakra levels.

Practices:
Labyrinth Walking
Crystal Mandala Moon Journey
Crystal Mandala Talisman - Heart Map Process

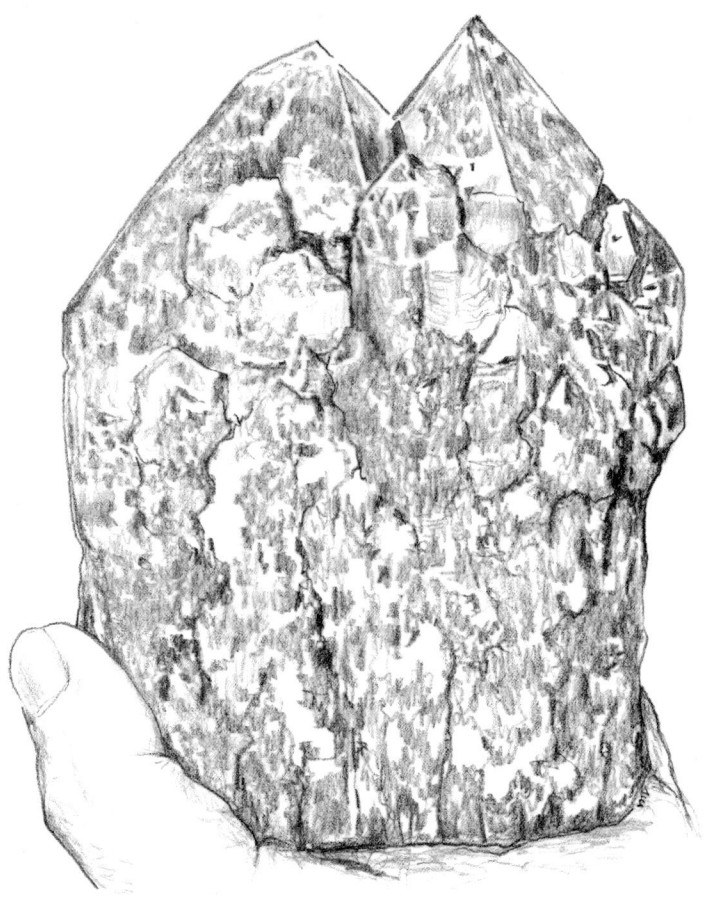

Figure 95 Amethyst Cathedral Lightbrary, a rare find. Amethyst, the stone for mastering change, is helpful particularly for the spiritual journeyer as changes can be gracefully embraced. The Cathedral aspect brings in the possibility to access the cosmic databases, the 'Akashic 'records.

Dropping the Drama

*The proof is in the pudding,
So taste yourself and share it with loved ones.*

While painting, I had a thought that the paint I put on the canvas becomes part of the future finished picture that I had envisioned. I select the colour and the texture as I apply each brush stroke. I am also influenced by my surroundings, and my skill in executing what I'd like it to look like. Distractions often interrupt my concentration, such as when my 'inner critic' tells me how bad my work is, or when the cat jumps on my palette making a mess of things. Painting is like life!

Fundamental to 'dropping the drama,' as I named this chapter, is the understanding that our thoughts create our reality. Before any action or feeling, there was always a thought. After the thought comes a feeling and a decision, consciously or unconsciously made. It is these decisions that create a person's life, eloquently expressed by Sakyamuni Buddha: "All that you are is a result of choices you have made in the past. All that you will become is a result of choices you make now."

A thought form is an established pattern of thinking that influences us to act and react in certain ways. The thinking of our parents and our cultural backgrounds created strong imprints (beliefs) in our minds. Everyone is conditioned by such imprints,

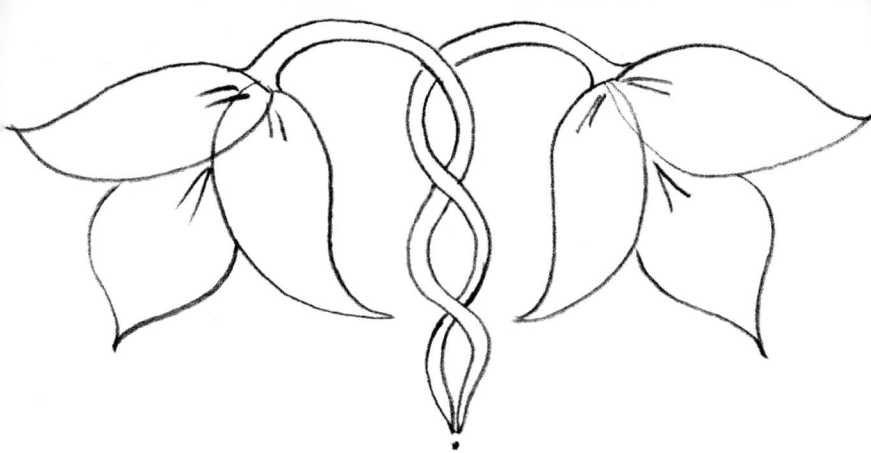

Figure 96 The male and female lotus, showing how two opposite expressions arise from a unity (the a dot below the stems).

and they strongly affect life. We act and live out our lives according to our early conditioning. Some of the ways we react are beneficial; others are decidedly destructive. Upon touching a heat source we automatically withdraw our hand. No careful evaluation took place because we already have an established inner program directing our precise action on an instinctive level, saying something like: "Danger, move!" We learn responses, which behavioural scientist Pavlov showed very well in his experiment with a dog. The dog was fed when a bell was sounded, the bell acting as a stimulus, something that could be perceived, seen, heard, sensed or felt, and which strongly became connected with the food that the dog wanted. After some time, the dog would salivate as soon as the bell rang, even though no food was present. In the same way, a person may connect particular stimuli with something less beneficial or even destructive. For example, in the program: "Shut down emotionally when criticised," a person with this learned program may have been criticised a great deal while growing up, making him or her feel worthless due to harsh words when attempting something. For a small child it is unbearable not to feel loved, so the child chooses a subconscious decision to shut down as a survival mechanism, in order not to feel those feelings of not being loved. The irony is that the child may have been very loved by the parents, but they had no idea that their behaviour (acts and words) would create this response in their child. Perhaps the parents just did what their parents in turn had done to them. If we can trace and identify the decisions that formed such imprints, we may heal trauma and subsequent dis-ease. To 'heal' means to rewrite a destructive program and turn it into a healthy one. The result can only be health and happiness.

Using Polarity Pairs

Without the shadows we cannot see the light. Our time on the Earth might have been created to gain experience and knowledge that each person (soul) brings back home. In order to come home, we have to dissolve the duality within. How can that be attained? If a person worries (thinking negative thoughts) about everything that could go wrong, he or she may feel anxious (harmful emotion). As a result of these thoughts, physical symptoms are produced such as stress, nervous stomach or an ulcer (dis-ease). The negative downward or descending pattern is thus:

Negative Thought > Harmful Emotion > Dis-ease

Such people may see themselves in one singular place, but they may not observe that they are, in fact, standing at one extreme end of a polarity pair. The opposite place is where they desire to be, which in this case could be to be calm.

Anxious <--------> Calm

It can be helpful to work with what is opposite to experience. By looking at the opposite state, one can shift the focus from a detrimental pattern to a more beneficial one. Then the thought process is geared in the opposite direction. Observing a challenging situation, one may begin to think differently: "In this challenge I see an opportunity to be calm. This opportunity gives me a chance to learn. This learning is great to have. I feel good about learning this. I feel calm in spite of this challenge. I am handling this challenge appropriately. I create well-being in myself by staying calm. Feeling calm is now part of my skill set." This person chooses to think differently about the situation, thereby changing any emotional response to the challenge. The ascending or upward pattern becomes:

Positive Thought > Beneficial Emotion > Health

Once such individuals reach the other side or desired state of calmness they may still not have what they believe they want. The suffering or dissatisfaction continues about another issue that appears on the scene (for example, being short of money). This new problem continues the progression of lessons to be dealt with. The new thoughts that occur as a result of the new issue fuel emotional responses, which fire another pattern off to be revealed. Looking at the opposite or desired state, individuals can become increasingly sensitive to where they are on their journey. In addition, focusing in a relaxed way on what is wanted, from a place of trust and gratitude, rather than what is unwanted, one can actually open up the energetic field that magnetically draws the intended to be manifest, and the desire to become a reality. It is most effective when the outcome is stated and one is released from any rigid expectation on how it is going to manifest. Continuing this work reveals that instead of one polarity line with two ends, we have several, forming a circle of many extremes. On close examination one can discover an increasing and decreasing length of the polarity lines, and as one progresses working with each pair, the result is smaller or bigger circles. Looking at it from a three-dimensional perspective, we detect a movement along a descending or ascending spiral that ascends into a singular point, or descends into a wider and wider spiral, much like the shape of a cone seashell. This is what is meant by ascension of the individual. When we reach into the tip of this spiral we have reached liberation, and are free to live without limiting patterns. In my work with crystals I have found that each crystal models the vibrational reality of specific polarity pairs, as they are specified in the list of *Crystal Keys*.

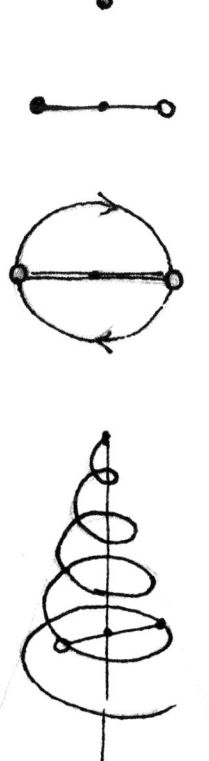

Figure 97 The four levels of understanding polarity in life: as a point, as a line, as a movement along a circle and ascending or descending along a spiral path.

Crystal Affirmation Practice

Why: By repeating a new program (affirmation) over and over, we learn it. When we have accepted the new program, we will behave according to that new pattern. The chosen stone helps us remember our new healthy program.

How to begin: One usually chooses an affirmation to remedy something. Look in the index of keywords and select the most appropriate one for you. As an example we choose "bodily cycles" and "stress." The corresponding crystal is Sulphur in Quartz. In the *Crystal Keys'* list we find the following:

> ### Sulphur in Quartz, yellow hue *The Digestive Wisdom Stone.* Sulphur in Quartz has been used to gain understanding of bodily cycles. Elemental Effect: Absorbing, Calming.
>
> Key 1: Buffering (Stressful Energies <> Calm Energies) I am bubble of calmness pausing before I respond. I am listening to my body's needs.

Select one of the affirmations and visualize the result for yourself. Write out the affirmation chosen on a small card like this:

I am listening to my body's needs.

Say it out loud until you can feel the words vibrate inside you, then repeat the affirmation silently. Alternatively do the re-programming in writing. Commit to a 21 or 40-day practice. Dedicate a particular time each day to saying and/or writing your affirmation: 21, 44 or 108 times each session, the more the better.

Effects: Sincere affirmation practice reinforces that which is said or written out. When practiced, the new program takes effect. In this case, the practitioner becomes a listener to what his or her body needs, and can take appropriate action to supply just that.

Maintenance: You can choose to journal after each sitting, as it may help you to release any emotions that may have come up. (See also: dealing with release, in chapter *The Crystal Orb*). Ask the question, "What do I feel now?" Refrain from analyzing, theorizing or blaming: just record your feelings. The benefit from journaling in this way is that it is akin to "emptying the waste basket." Do not read your journal until after your problems are solved. Stick with the routine, as that will give you the best results.

Crystal Care: Value the crystal you have chosen, and clean and sprinkle sun-infused water on the stone to clear it daily before your practice.

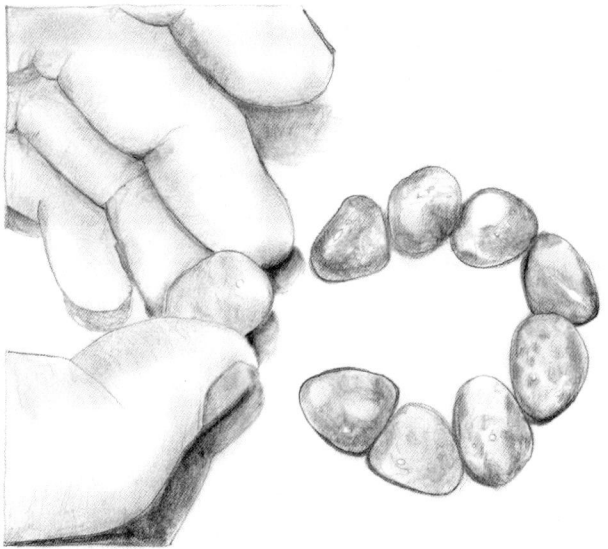

Figure 98 Sulphur in Quartz, shown as a medicine bundle.

Figure 99 Quartz Cluster of Laser Wands. Perhaps out of range for most people, a cluster of Laser Wands would be especially penetrating if used for clutter-busting. Notice how the crystal points fall into a perfect mesh with each other. If another crystal is in the way, they simply grow harmoniously within each other.

Opposite Practice

Why: Directing thoughts and feelings to the opposite of what bothers you changes the way you view your situation.

How to begin: From the Index list, find a symptom that corresponds to your situation. For example: dealing with 'clutter'. We find:

Quartz (cluster) *Sacred Space Stone.* Elemental Effect: Purifying, Elevating, Aligning.

Key 1: Meditation (Focus <> Distraction) I am present. I am aware of the eternal now.

Key 2: Sacred Space (Clutter <> Order) I release old patterns. I am clearing my inner and outer spaces. My space is clear and wonderful to be in. I love what surrounds me.

Select a Quartz cluster for your work. Look deeply into it. The opposite of your symptom is: order. Look for the order in the crystal. Even though the crystal points may go all over the place, discover its order. 'Dip' your hands into it and feel it inside your mind and body. Close your eyes and look inside your self. Let the energy of the crystal assist you to connect to your inner order, and what 'order' means to you. Relax. Breathe. Stay with it! Let things be as they are for the moment. How can you change to allow for the acceptance of this?

Maintenance: Repeat this meditation every evening before bed. When you are ready, you will change your clutter, perhaps seeing it as a resource to create order. Continue for at least 21 days.

Effects: This practice trains you to see the hidden resources in something you don't want. Then it becomes easier to remedy. In this case: instead of a 'pesky' clutterer, you might become a material resource person. You may find that your things are linked to emotional burdens and obligations. That is what makes clutter stay. On release of these connotations, the clutter goes, too. Note: You may not suffer from, or think that you have clutter, but others think so. Then it is their issue of perhaps judging you. They might, with benefit, choose to use Topaz to release their judgement.

Crystal Care: Thank your crystals and your guidance for your privilege to experience your symptom differently and its lessons.

My Crystal Key

Why: I have a crystal I really like, but what's its use? Here is a practice for you to discover the answer to that question.

How to start: Place your crystal in front of you. Find its Key in the list of crystals. As example, we pick:

Tourmaline (Watermelon) *The Heart of Heart's Stone.* Watermelon Tourmaline has been used as a Betrayal Remedy. Elemental Effect: Aligning, Purifying.

Key 1: Active Balance of Love Wisdom (Betrayal <> Feeling Loved)
I let go and trust. I flow with loving emotions, giving and receiving without resistance.

The Key says: "Active Balance of Love-Wisdom." Real love is not bound by needs, but by our pure and detached connection to the universe. This stone puts the focus on us to have the wisdom to see that. In my meditation with this stone, I let the Key words sink in, and I allow myself to feel my response. First I hold the stone in my right hand, and then in my left, to discover the difference. I may find that within I harbour both polarities, in this case: feeling loved and betrayed at the same time. Breathing continuously into my heart lets my stone show me where I can adjust my emotional controls and my mental settings that may have been causing me difficulties.

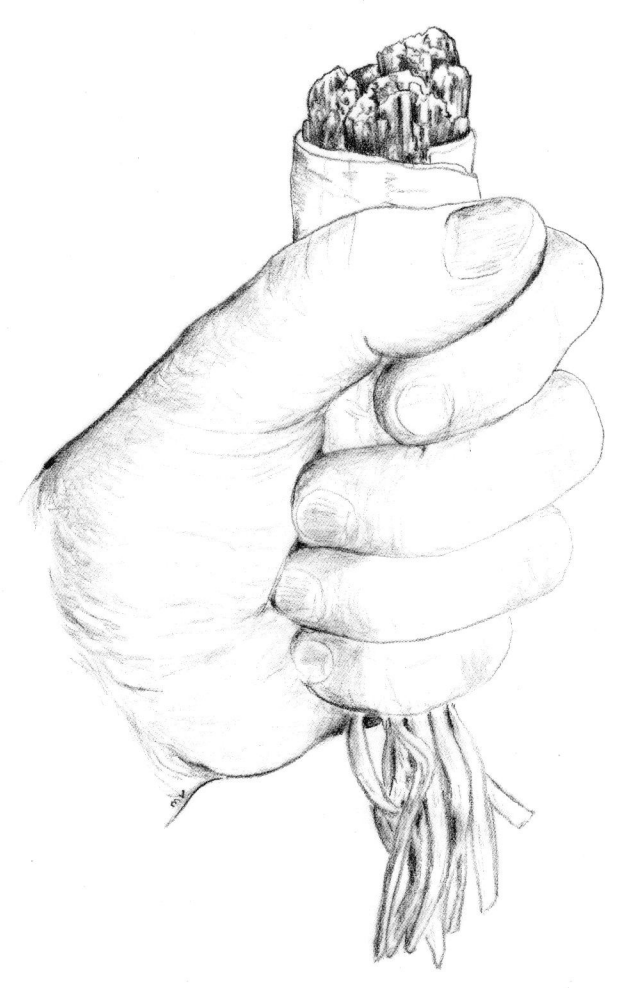

Figure 100 Watermelon Tourmaline - the Heart of Heart's stone. This specimen is wrapped with deerskin as a wand, and illustrates the practice: My Crystal Key.

Maintenance: It is advisable to continue to practice every day for at least a month, to reap the benefits.

Effects: The effect of concentrating on the heart in the way proposed is to discover the controls of your mental-emotional bio-computer.

Crystal Care: Your special crystal is literally the key to your heart. Keep it in the same way you would like to be treated.

Summary

Thoughts generate emotions and the decisions to take the actions, which create our life. Repeated thoughts make up thought forms, which become beliefs that condition our behaviour. Negative patterns create illness, pain and suffering. Positive thoughts create health, abundance and happiness. By recognizing the arrival at either extreme of a positive-negative continuum (polarity), one may transcend extreme states and come to a place of resolution and healing (key). Crystals provide the reality vibration of specific thought forms, expressed in words as *Polarity Pairs* and *Crystal Keys*. We can use this tool as a focus to heal by the three practices presented.

Practices:
Affirmation - to re-program ourselves
Opposite practice - to change our perspective
My Crystal Key - to command our mental-emotional responses

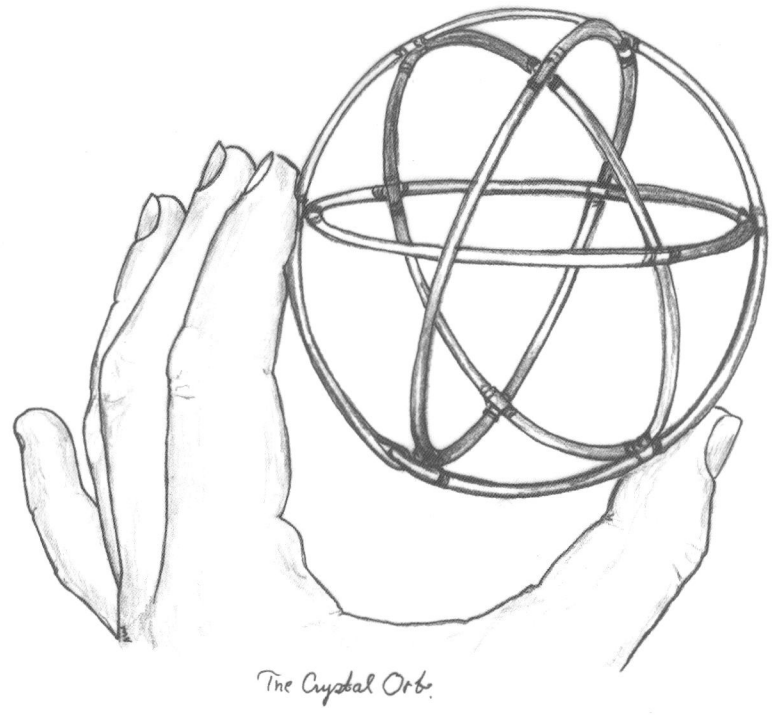

The Crystal Orb.

Figure 101 The Crystal Orb may be used for dealing with discordant energies. This shape is visualized and placed above yourself or
the person seeking healing. An actual Orb, like this one, is made
from copper, and can be hung above a treatment table or in a healing space.

The Crystal Orb

The Light transformed brings
Blessings again

Agood cry, and then one feels better. Expressed anger releases angry emotions that were stored within our being. But the question is: what happens to this energy? If one takes the analogy of compost, dead or discarded organic material falls to the ground and sits there until it is digested and transformed into soil. Worms and other organisms help make the process possible. Plants take root in the soil and can produce leaves and fruits that we or other animals may eat safely. In the case of toxic waste, this transformation into safe bio-available foods may take decades or even thousands of years.

A human being needs certain energies to live. Our subtle energy organs provide the right frequency by taking in energy from our food, our air, and other nutritious vibrations that surround us. If the energy is harmful to us, we may be harmed. In such a case, our system is not able to digest or assimilate it, as discussed in the previous chapter. Examples of toxic energies are the mental-emotional fields of: anger, grief, poverty, terror, deception, scarcity and greed. In my view this is pretty much exactly what the Bible calls 'sins,' the seven mortal sins included. After healing from such harm, we let go of these energies by means of releasing them. Instead of polluting our space with such noxious frequencies, I propose to recycle them in a Crystal Orb Incinerator right away.

Crystal Orb Visualization

A Crystal Orb is a visualization in our mind. To be able to do this activity effectively we should first build this sacred geometry structure, in a material that suits us. My favourite material is thick copper wire, which can be sourced at the local hardware store. At the end of this chapter you will find detailed instructions for making a Crystal Orb out of paper. You can use any material that holds the form sufficiently. My first Crystal Orb was made of paper towel and tape. I was participating in a friend's successful community project, manifesting something like 60000 dollars within a few months. The four rings symbolize each one of the elements: air, fire, water and earth. The inside of the orb represents the element of space. It is the very centre of the structure that provides a symbol for the Universal Mind, or Unified Field of all possibilities, and our Source. Manifestation goes both ways, in and out. By directing our released energy into the Crystal Orb, we allow it to be absorbed again into the greater energy field of the universal mind. It is like depositing it into our bank account, instead of throwing it to the wayside for someone else to deal with. Here we put congested, stored, unused or blocked energy back into potentiality by using visualisations. In the case of forgiving someone, you let go of and release the inner tensions between the two of you, placing them into the orb. The harmful tie between you is thus dissolved. Holding such shackles continuously drains our energy reserves. After release we always feel better and lighter. The beauty is that we can utilize this energy right away, in the same way as we may withdraw money from our bank account. The money we get in our hands is not the same amount as was deposited, but it comes in the denomination and currency you ask for.

Visualization: A small Crystal Orb is visualized above us. I call it a personal Crystal Orb Incinerator. Energy is taken in through the squares and the transformed energy goes out through the triangles. Instead of asking for certain energy, we use our own released energy and send it into the Orb. Inside the Orb, energies are transformed by our intention, and the energy field is created by the Orb. This detached energy is then poured outwards for our immediate use.

Angel Team: Clearly visualize your team of helpers, maybe a whole legion of angels. Possible areas of assistance are: protecting an opening in the aura, assistance with chakra functioning, cleaning of subtle tissues, directing energy flow, overseeing energy transformation (or incineration), dealing with released energy, or maintaining focus in the session. Ask to be assigned an *Angel of Protection*. An angel is a being who does not have, or has released the need to have, "free will." Their purpose is solely to serve. If we want to release our non-beneficial programs, energies or other beings trapped inside us, it is wise to have some help available; otherwise we may be taking them right back in again. For example, if we try to stop an addiction, we succeed for a while. Then we start the habit again with some excellent explanation or justification.

I remember one person who was a heavy smoker. She asked for assistance and in our session she understood clearly how the smoking was harmful for her and why she continued doing it. She made a sincere agreement with herself to stop. However, she started again because of high stress levels at the time, and in the aftermath she became very ill. In the transition of several weeks of her becoming well again, smoking was no longer part of her life. It is, of course noted that deep emotional patterns were affected as well, and not only the addiction, which was only the tip of the iceberg. Further levels of her issues came to light for her later, and consequently her smoking continued. We can see her process as steps towards wise victories, as she learned from

Figure 102 Illustration of the Incinerator Orb in use. Pure Soul Star energy is inhaled from above and directed to the affected area, in this case, the liver. On the exhale, discordant energy is directed into the Orb for transformation. This healing was a result of the botry-

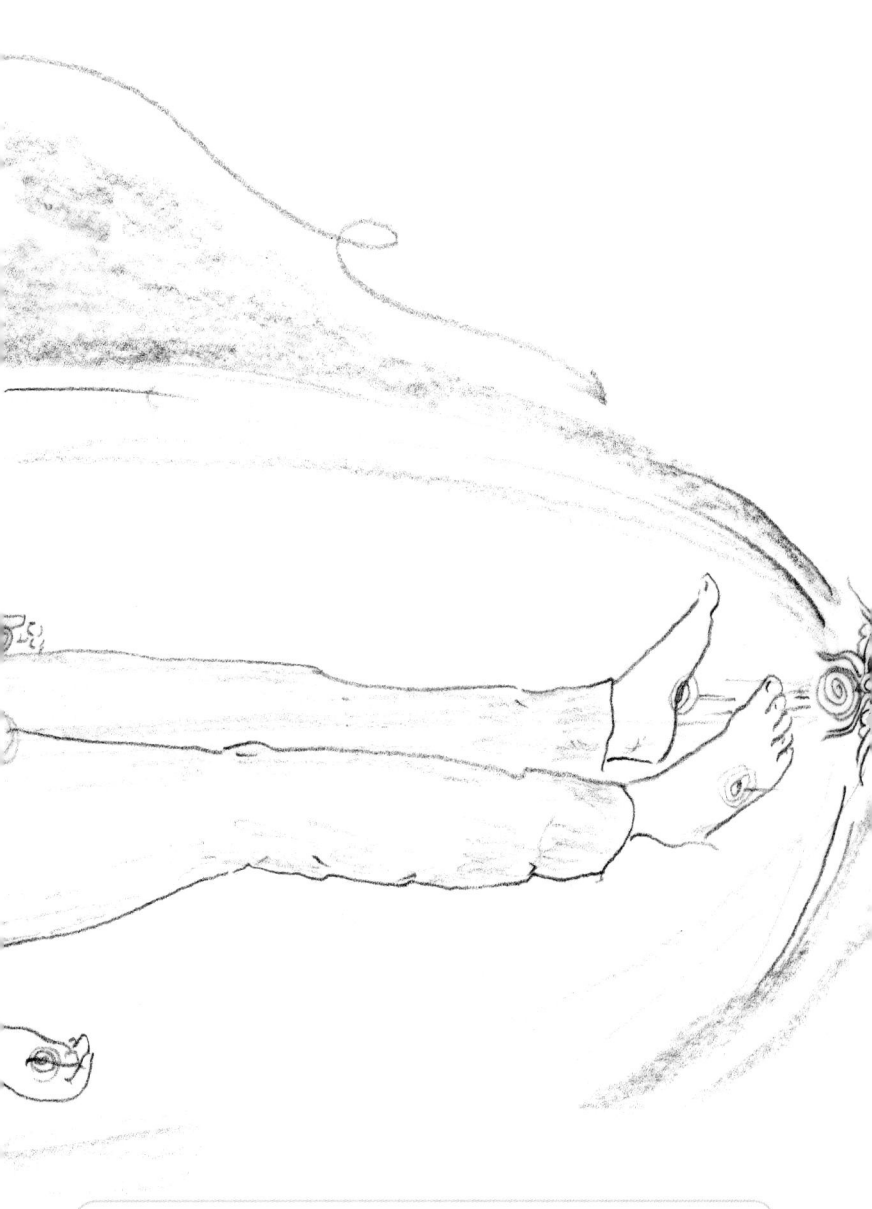

botryoidal Lepidolite installation described previously. We visualize being assisted by our team of angels, placed at the orb and at the affected organ and chakras. In the drawing are seen the Angel of Protection, the Soul Star Angel and the Earth Star Angel.

each part of the process. When she is done, she will not need to smoke again.

To use the Incinerator Orb in a healing session for ourselves, we inhale through our Soul Star into the place of discordance. In the picture we use the liver as the target area, and direct the released energy into the Orb above. At each end of our aura, we visualize the angels of the soul star and the earth star, assisting us in the release. The liver is a good place to start as it is the organ of detoxification, and we benefit greatly from assisting it. In the affected area (the liver and the closest chakra involved) we engage our helper team to deal with opening the area, cleaning it, letting go, repairing the subtle tissues, setting new programs, and dressing any subtle wounds. When this is done on the subtle levels, the physical cells and repair mechanisms follow suit.

Incinerator Orb Practice

Why: If we continue to pollute our space we will have to come back to clean it up sooner or later. By engaging in the Incinerator Orb practice we immediately recycle discharged energy. This is helpful in healing ourselves, as well as for being among people in our regular life. If we lose our calm, we can do this practice to return to our natural peaceful self.

How to begin: Visualize your personal Crystal Orb Incinerator above yourself outside your immediate aura, perhaps at arms-length. Make the orb a size of an orange to begin with. After that, choose any size you see fit. See the orb being activated by your Orb Angel. She turns it on; you may visualize it glowing like very hot coals. Your Angel holds the orb in place over your body to receive your release and transform it.

Now begin to inhale pure light from above your head into your belly, or the area of release. Make several inhalations into the area. Pause each time for a moment to collect any discordant energy, and then push it out with the force of the next exhalation. Visualize the energy going directly into the Orb. You may even hear a sizzling sound when the orb transmutes it. Then your angel will let the harmonized energy flow out in congruent waves, as being showered with bliss. Then start over from the beginning. Continue until you are complete.

Maintenance: When you are learning this breath, practice it several times a day, and whenever you need it.

Effects: This is particularly helpful when pain is experienced and during emotionally pressing circumstances, since pain and emotional suffering can be regarded as a build-up of harming energies begging to be released. This is particularly effective within a healing session, both for you and for prospective clients. You may benefit from teaching them this method as well.

Crystal Care: Visualize your Crystal Orb as perfect and sparkling and ready to use at a moment's notice. Always thank your angel team.

Building a Crystal Orb

Why: By actually building a Crystal Orb in paper, you may come to realize its perfection and the field it may generate.

How to begin: Draw a rectangle on a piece of paper, 6 1/4" by 2" wide. Draw three length-wise lines forming four parallel strips. Draw cross lines at each inch mark, and the 1/4" is used for joining the strip into a circle (1). Tape the joint and fold along one cross line (2) and cut the four joined strips (3). Open them into circles (4). Now join two circles at a 60-degree angle at top and bottom, and tape the joints (5). Add the third circle to form a triangle with the first two rings. Tape the four contact points (6).

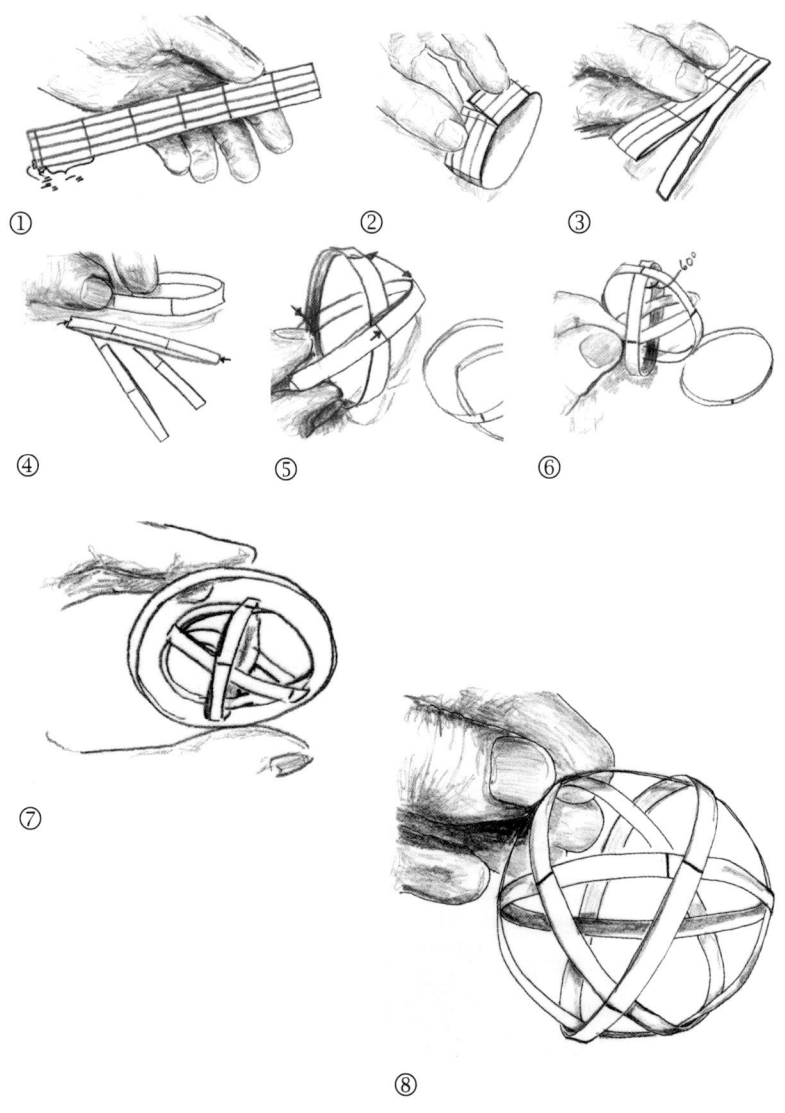

Figure 103 Making a Crystal Orb from paper. You might utilize this description to make a copper orb. In that case cut equal lengths of copper wire, and mark them as in step 1. Form circles, and continue to assemble from step 5. See also page 558.

Place your budding Orb on its triangle and add the last circle outside on the midriff. Join the six places (7). Finished Orb (8).

Summary

The Crystal Orb is a viable tool for anyone, as it may be used in several capacities. Here we show the use as a recycling incinerator for energy that is harmful to us. Engaging in a practice of learning how to dispose of our own released energies, we provide for an atmosphere of peace and harmony around us. The description on how to build a paper Orb is included. By building a Crystal Orb we can learn how it is constructed, and may have insights relating to its inner workings.

Practices:
Crystal Orb Visualization
Using the Incinerator Orb
Crystal Orb - building a paper model

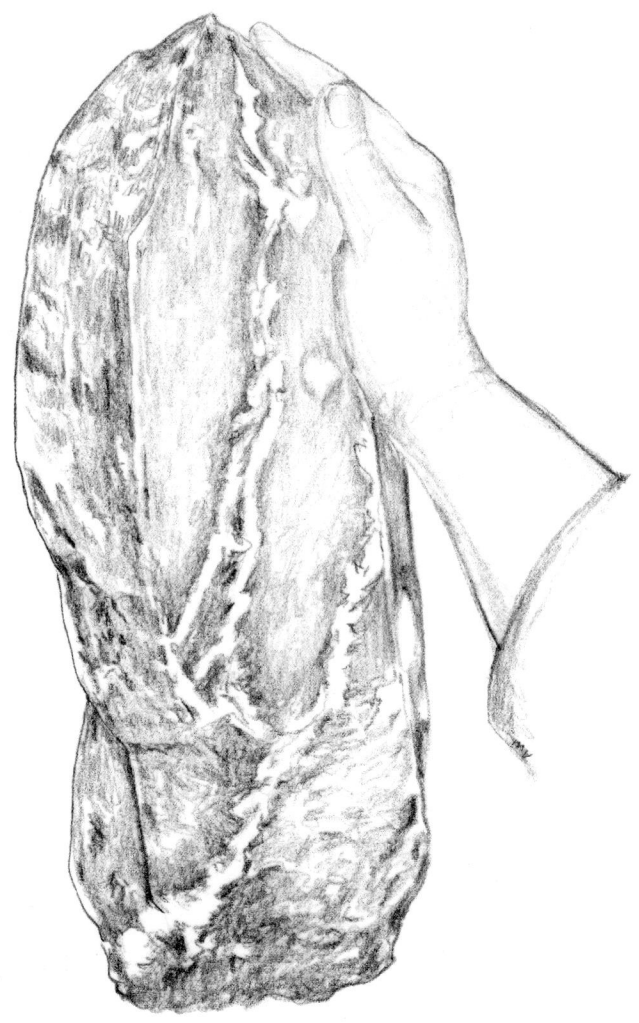

Figure 104 Lightning Crystal. One can clearly see the impact the lightning had on this crystal by several vertical transformation lines. When drastic shifts are happening, or need to happen, this is an ideal crystal to work with.

Crystal Yoga

*Awaken through
What is before you*

Awakening to our divinity for a split second has been reported, but to remain in this natural state that is available to
everyone is rarer. Carl Jung wrote:

> *"Man needs difficulties,
> they are necessary for health."*

When a baby is born, it is learning from its parents and from
society what acceptable behaviour is and how to think. Some
babies are born to caring and loving self-realized people; other
babies are born into abuse and severe challenges. In this way the
curriculum in the 'Earth School' is already begun even before
birth. To deal with life we may have chosen to put on rose-col-
oured glasses. We would then see everything through a screen of
rosy colour. Life will seem positive and happy perhaps, where it
is really not. That is called "denial." One may fail to see an im-
pending disaster, which all of a sudden rips this screen off. Many
have had an abrupt awakening after the event of a terminal illness or a serious accident. Likewise, if a person sees life though
a screen of fear, the world is experienced as hostile and unsafe.
That person may see and create dangers everywhere, where there

are none, making mountains out of molehills. In both cases the reality is distorted.

That which is experienced is preserved as memory fragments of inner mental emotional events in the subconscious, if we haven't dealt with them right away. Such undigested experiences may manifest as racing thoughts or worries, and at night some people cannot sleep because of these. The subconscious mind is attempting to process these fragments and make meaning of them, so rest is not peaceful. Compare it with a messy closet: things are hard to find, but in a well-organized office, data is filed with clear and distinct order. Our minds are mostly like disordered and over-packed closets, rather than a well-organized office. If no order is in effect, one finds things only with difficulty because the information is not sorted. Instead it lie embedded in layers and layers of unsorted and unprocessed files. The spiritual search to find oneself is really the cleaning up of such messy closets. However, it is through our challenges in life that we learn how to survive, and when we do, new skills are learnt and applied. With practice we may discover illusory screens and be present to what actually is going on. To be present is to accurately hear the 'song' that is playing. If one is distracted, there is no listening, and then reality in each moment is not truly experienced.

Past masters knew how to harmonize themselves and the environment around them. One single accomplished yogi could sit and meditate in a mountain cave above a village. By his or her doing this, peace and well-being to the entire valley and its people might be generated. Such energy could be felt by the people, and they would venerate the yogi, come for teachings and the blessing that the work was generating. Through practice these yogis became crystal-like, without dull screens clouding their sight. Meditation, prayer and chanting are proven methods or techniques that the trainee of consciousness might use. Initially, meditation is a process of looking inside and listening to what is really going on. Try sitting still. You might find that almost immediately thoughts comes pounding in like a heavy rain. We get distracted by our thoughts and the sensations in our body. That is why it is helpful to focus on an object like a crystal. Thoughts are coming and going, but the focus on the object remains. After some time we get less distracted and are able to truly meditate.

Traditional Tools and Methods

Meditation - A method common to all religions with the general purpose to calm the mind and heart, thereby discover who and what we are.

Object - An object for meditation can be an external physical object (e.g. a crystal placed before the eyes), or something intangible such as a visualized symbol or an emotional state (e.g. love or forgiveness).

Contemplation - A state in which one is joined with one's high self (or divine part), and un-distracted by thoughts.

Prayer - Informal or formal application to the Divine for the purpose of having one's intention fulfilled, or a ritual activity of devotion.

Mantra - Sacred words, given by a spiritual teacher to his or her students for use in practice.

Affirmation - A self-selected statement of intention, the selection based on a situation or condition one wants to remedy.

Chanting - Repeating intention (mantra, our prayer or affirmation) and thereby completely embrace it. It can be spoken, sung or silently repeated by our inner voice.

Visualization - A process of internally generating images, words, feeling or mental state using the intuitive faculty (our mind's eye or ear).

Breath - We may direct energy (or visualized object) to an area within, or outside of, our physical body by using our breath. Our inhale and exhale of vital energy makes it possible for directing it to a desired destination.

When fishing: the fisherman puts a worm on the hook in hope that the fish will bite and thereby be caught. Our ego self is such a fisherman by trying to have us and others bite on its bait (that means pushing our buttons). When we bite, we engage in a subconscious pattern usually by reacting in some way. Energy is released by this, and ego want to catch and absorb such energy for itself. Like the fisherman, it wants to bring its catch home to fry and eat it. Ego likes a lot of energy, the more the better. But when we start looking inside, we may catch ego doing its shady game. The integration of undigested thoughts and experiences is thus assisted, without engaging in the drama, and rises above inner obscurations. The meditator may discover what the motivating factors were for past choices, and the causes for unwanted situations or conditions. It is mostly fear that is the motivating factor. Fear helps us by alerting us to pending dangers, but most fears are fabrications in our mind, and have little to do with what is actually happening outside of us. If this is so with you, meditation may bring you to a place where you may shine a light onto your fears and dissolve them.

Chanting Mantras and singing has been practiced in the world for millennia. Gatherings of tribal people included music, drumming or clapping, while dancing and singing songs over and over for hours, sometimes for weeks. By engaging in such activity together, each individual aligns in harmony with the rest of the group. When the group has peaceful intentions, peaceful relations with self and others are fostered. Perhaps our modern youths are ahead of the older generation, by immersing themselves together with loud and strange sounds. Prayer on the other hand, can be more personal and asserts and clarifies our intentions. It is in the sincere asking that a communication with the inner Divine can be established. Being filled with reverent prayer can be a sacred experience. A person can choose to chant a prayer or affirmation to reprogram the mind for health and well-being. The affirmation is the 'New Program' he or she decides to embrace.

Personal story: As a child, I once saw a picture from a church. I recollect it appeared so still and peaceful and quiet. You could understand that being the oldest of five children, I was surrounded by noise often. In the one alcove of this church was a life-size wooden sculpture of a holy saint. I believe it was Saint Birgitta, a Swedish woman born in the year 1303AD. What struck me was the expression of total ecstasy. I did not know that word at the young age I was then, but that was how the sculptor had carved her. I could feel her, as if she was almost alive. What was she doing? She was praying, and in union with the Divine to such a degree that she had stopped to exist as a separate being.

Crystal Yoga

The gift of Yoga is a way whereby we can discover and maintain who we really are: divinely interconnected beings arising from the same source. Crystal Yoga, I propose, is defined as the crystal practice of awakening through challenges. Yoga postures can be added with benefit as well. If someone says: 'But I don't want to practice with any challenges,' well, that person is free to choose what to do. However, challenges are present in life anyway, so why not use them as a means to become happy? This quote by William Lonsdale expresses it in an alternate way:

> *"...if you use the very pressure bearing down on you to crack into your core, you'll free the rest of your life."*

The nature of Yoga is to practice. Why practice? Hearing a virtuoso pianist performing might bring a wonderful experience, but playing like the master can't happen without practice. Granted, some people have it easier than others. In the practice for life we try to stay healthy, keep our job, feed the kids and plan for retirement. Well, Crystal Yoga is a sort of 'retirement practice,' because the physical body deteriorates without exercise, the mind goes dull without challenge, and our love dries up without proper integration. The serious applicant may have to practice a little. The more aspects of yourself that is involved in your practice, the more effective it becomes. This is why, in any spiritual practice the teacher first asks us to hold a physical position, begin a cer-

Aspects of Personal Practice:

Body Position - for example: sitting, standing or moving.

Breath - inhalation, exhalation or holding of air and life force energy that can be directed to locations in the body.

Sensory Input - via sight, hearing, touch, pain, etc., which lets you engage with the surrounding environment. It provides information about a problem and its location, or contributes to distractions from practice.

Voice - our faculty of expression, consisting of energy and sounds (including words) in the release, or in the personal reprogramming practice of the mind.

Feeling State - a mental emotional state, which can guide you about what is going on in your body. Within practice one may learn how to generate a selected feeling state, e.g. forgiveness or love.

Mental Focus - a skill that can be trained, one thus becomes less in-attentive - study and meditation are then greatly facilitated.

Visualization - a process in which one may see an object or situation within the mind's eye. This capacity may be used in conscious dreaming. It is an aid to introduce new beneficial programs e.g. personal goals for health and wellbeing.

Hologram - a multi-dimensional image. A person is a minute part of a gigantic hologram called the Universe. It can be seen as a projection from our source into every dimension and reaches everywhere, (see chapter The Crystal Grid).

Blueprint - a schematic map that we are created after into the physical dimension. This blueprint is believed to survive physical death, and be updated each lifetime to include all accomplishments and spiritual debts (good and bad karma).

tain breathing pattern, and then other processes are added like visualizations to control the thinking mind. Then we are asked to move our body while meditating on one or more things, while at the same time chanting certain sounds. The reason for this process is to get the students to release their stubborn hold on existing thought patterns, and become free from ego identification. You can see it this way also; if a person is imprisoned he or she most likely want to be set free. However, if he or she does not know that they are in a prison, only unhappiness or challenges will create a momentum to realize what is going on. The practices discussed in this book are aimed at regaining mastery of our feelings, thinking and resultant actions. Yoga is the practice to become whole. Any practice aimed at this goal can be called yoga. It is a tremendously helpful term, as it embraces the very essence of how to become happy or, in other words, resolve all issues a person may have. There are numerous yogas involving one or more of our subtle anatomy aspects: physical, emotional, mental or spiritual (see chapter *The Crystal Grid* for more detail). If you have an issue or unsatisfactory situation in any of these layers of your being, using some kind of spiritual practice may remedy the situation if applied. See the following example:

Personal Crystal Yoga Practice

What is involved? Each crystal or crystal tool provides specific frequencies for potential healing. By using this property of crystals, we may attain the lessons they offer. In Crystal Healing, such frequencies are used to shift energy blockages held in the body. In yoga practice with crystals there are two components: personal aspects and the tools used. Personal aspects include: how we hold our body, how we breathe, how we feel, our capacity to generate certain feeling states, our ability to visualize, how we use our voice and our skill in maintaining focus. The tools are the crystals in their various forms and sizes. A complete list of all practices described, is displayed in the *List of Content*.

How to start: Most situations can be addressed with the following four-step approach to the practice:

1. Observe what is going on - meditation
2. Setting intention - prayer/affirmation
3. Practice - reprogramming our system
4. Receive result - become happy/fulfil intention

Observing what is going on: As a person we have to deal with our body. A seated position is ideal for meditation, but if you are performing a *Crystal Layout*, lying on the back is preferred. Standing, walking or a set of movement are also available to use. By keeping our eyes fixed on an object we may begin to control our level of distraction. The eyes and breathing are closely linked with generating thoughts. Using a breath pattern, with each crystal, anchors its energy and stabilizes our system. When the mind calms we are able to discern what is going on.

Setting Intention: An example: How to use Magic, the main Key for Labradorite? The left brain can interpret this word to include making miracles and inexplicable events to occur. If this key strongly resonates with your situation, perhaps a miracle really needs to happen in your life! If you work with this crystal, can you allow its quality to be part of your journey from now on? Just feel what the word means and breathe the energy of that inside yourself. Place the energy where it is needed. Where in your body does magic need to go? For some, placing the energy in their heart is most effectual. Crystals resonate stronger in some parts of the body than in other parts. The more you use the new words (your intention or new program) in the form of affirmations, the more profound is your inner and outer change.

Practice of invoking a mental-emotional state: Are there strong emotions involved in your situation needing to be resolved? The word "Magic" may inspire you to have a desirable feeling inside,

Figure 105 Crystals as the focus of meditation and visualization. A raw Rose Quartz (left) and a Smokey Quartz point (right).

perhaps that of positive outlook, optimism and enthusiasm. Allowing yourself to embrace that feeling will actually create it. The energy and colour of the crystal can be visualized in the Mind's Eye. By the process of visualization one is actually training the intuitive capability and the potential mastery there. Visualize Labradorite and its colours shimmering clearly, seeing the whole crystal on the inner screen, and then place it over the heart area. Let the image sink in and embrace the upper chest. Place the centre of this three-dimensional image in front of the spine. The image can be quite small at first: let it grow in size and then become smaller again until you have found the correct size. If this is your wish, install the crystal either permanently or temporarily at the High Heart. Later you may be surprised how easily you can access the crystal energy at a moment's notice, helping you to become less distracted and more centred. It is essential to practice such visualization often.

Receive the results: by understanding your Hologram. The idea of a Hologram and personal Blueprint of your self may inspire aspirants to regain their remembrance of who they are and to retrieve their inner, absolutely-perfected self to the surface. In this layer of practice we bring the crystal to it as a truth-mirror. Being still and going into a deep meditational place with assistance of the crystal can, at first, give you glimpses of the perfected state and then a solid foundation for maintaining this place of being. There, the surface mask provided by the ego-based persona may be removed. When the personality identification has served its purpose, it can be used without ego identification. The personas serve us by acting out the dramas and the issues needing to be worked out. You may choose to make it a joyous journey.

A Practice Plan

Any of the practices described in this book can be adapted for personal practice and thus be your personal Crystal Yoga. You are the designer of your own practice. If you are in doubt follow the four-step suggestion above. A daily practice may include:

Waking up: Taking a few moments to centre and ground with the *Dual Flow Breath*, and greet the crystal of the day, described in the *Crystal Moon Mandala Journey*. Attempt to embody its message/affirmation/vibration in anything you would undertake that day. During the Day: Place yourself in the position of learning from each challenge. Use some of the crystal tools or practices presented to address any issue, challenge or unfavourable interaction you may have had during the day. Seek to remedy any fault on your side immediately, but look to forgive others first, before expressing concerns to them. Cultivate the attitude of serving others by loving yourself first. Work out your issues before blaming others. Re-affirm your commitment to become conscious of your own non-beneficial conditioning and change patterns that do not work, or are harmful for yourself or others. Practice (silently repeat or write) selected affirmation or mantra.

In the evening: Practice Crystal Meditation or use the Crystal Spa Program (described in the chapter *Crystal Spas*). Clarify and reaffirm intentions and continuing commitments. The result of sincere practice is your own freedom and happiness.

List of Crystal Tools

Meditation Object - A single crystal point may be used to hold the focus in meditation. When the eyes are kept from moving, our thoughts are kept from moving as well.

Massage Crystal - A crystal ball or wand may be used in massage to alleviate pain or to move energy.

Layout - Placement of crystals on the body that are widely used in crystal healing to facilitate energetic shifts.

Installation - A type of visualization whereby a crystal (its image and energy) are installed at a location within or outside the body.

Crystal Grid - A particular placement of crystals that creates an energetic field. Within this field, healing or personal practice can be performed and accomplished.

Medicine Bundle - A group of crystals selected for their properties for a certain purpose. They are stored in a bag or bundle, hence the name.

Crystal Mesa - A specialized medicine bundle addressing elemental energies or conditions. Mesa stones are laid our on a cloth, that serves as the container.

Crystal Talisman - An intentional object composed of one or more crystals to deal with a personal intention.

Crystal Orb - A geometric structure used in processes of manifestation or de-manifestation (see 'Incinerator Orb').

Crystal Pendulum - A crystal instrument for finding answers.

Crystal Mandala - Sacred circular grids laid out to illustrate certain energies or elemental properties. This is used in the 'Moon Mandala Journey'.

Personal Practice Example:

Let's take Don as an example. He says he is: restless, unhappy and has feelings of being stuck right now and that he has no real clarity about what to do next. So far nothing has satisfied his real needs. He is attracted to the mineral Labradorite, and wants to give it a try. How to approach a practice with this stone? Identifying what is going on, we have:

1) Restlessness, unhappy feelings (emotions)
2) Feels being stuck (being unable to move forward or take initiative)
3) Does not know what to do (he does not have all the facts)
4) Has no clarity (inability to see options to choose from)
5) His real needs have not been met (he doesn't know what his exact needs are or how to satisfy them)

The first item is paramount, as it tells the experiencer that something is wrong. He has to deal with some unknown cause. 'Restlessness' is an emotion related to anger and aversion: he has too much energy and he wants to get rid of it. 'Unhappiness' tells us that he does not like what he already has, something is lacking. The second item lets him know that he cannot move forward before he knows the cause. Subconsciously he will not allow himself any energy to take the initiative. The third item lets him know that before he can find out what is wrong, there will not be any movement. He says with this statement, possibly, that he would like to know what options he has. The fourth item lets him know that it is clarity he seeks. And the last point lets him know he must find out what he really needs and must provide that.

Don decided to use a single, tumbled stone of Labradorite for his personal practice. From the *Crystal Keys List* he selected:

Key 1: Magic (Open-mindedness <> Narrow-mindedness) I invite magic into my life. <u>I am open to receive creative inspiration</u>. I receive clear creative inspiration from the divine.

Applying the four steps:

1) **Finding out what is going on**: Don set out to do: Crystal Meditation with Labradorite as an object. He decided to spend about 10 minutes each evening to meditate. After about a week doing this, he found out that at work he wasn't able to affect his situation. This left him dis-empowered and unhappy.

2) **New Intention:** He then decided to build up his strength to express his concerns. So in the morning before going to work he added the Tiger-eye practice, *Building Strength*. Even after 10 minutes of this practice he felt more rejuvenated and positive. When arriving at work he started to find himself more accepting. His next goal was to address his inability to speak up. He also used his affirmation: *"I am open to receive creative inspiration,"* whenever he felt stuck. It was a way for him to open up more and taking command of a new skill.

3) **His mental practice** was to notice how he was doing things, and what results that brought, rather than to give up and feel hopeless. In small and tiny steps he was persevering with the two stones Labradorite and Tiger-eye. Each session gave him confidence to believe he is able to make changes necessary for his symptom to ease up. He continues to practice and incorporate new stones as he goes. Stones are there to stay with Don. He feels grateful for having learnt about them.

4) **Receiving the results**. He decided to make a mental note every time he was not restless, when he was not stuck and when he did have some clarity. The result of his practice was that he began to take an interest in healing. He found that practice gave him clarity of what needed to be done. He got out of his rut.

Integrating Emotional Waters - Heulandite

The crystals in the *Moon Mandala Journey* can be used in practice as well. Installation of Lepidolite (fiery air) was described on page 183. Here I will bring in a water stone, Heulandite (yin water). A spontaneous healing occurred by letting Heulandite direct my healing: It was a great example of how to install a water stone. Yin Water is extremely accepting, but also has the capacity to transmute hurt feelings and make us take responsibility for our expectations.

Personal Story: Adversity seems to be the way we experience the world; few things go according to how we expect them to be. I pondered my situation about how much I missed the feeling of being truly loved by the person whom I wanted to receive love from. In the wake of Valentines Day one year (were none of my expectations was even acknowledged) I began again to work with Heulandite, a type of Zeolite from India. Tuning into my softly peach crystal that perfectly fit my hand, I felt enveloped by gentleness and sweet love. I call Heulandite the *Stone of Joyful Enchantment* for that reason. As I continued, my expectations

WATER STONES	BODY AREA INSTALLATION
Selenite	Light Body
Aquamarine	Throat, Central Channel
Amazonite	Neck. Vocal Cords
Rhodochrosite	High Heart (Inner Child)
Iolite	Kidneys
Moonstone	Lymph System, Lower Belly
Chrysocolla	Pelvis, Bones, Reproductive Organs
Lodestone	Earth Star
Heulandite	Diaphragm

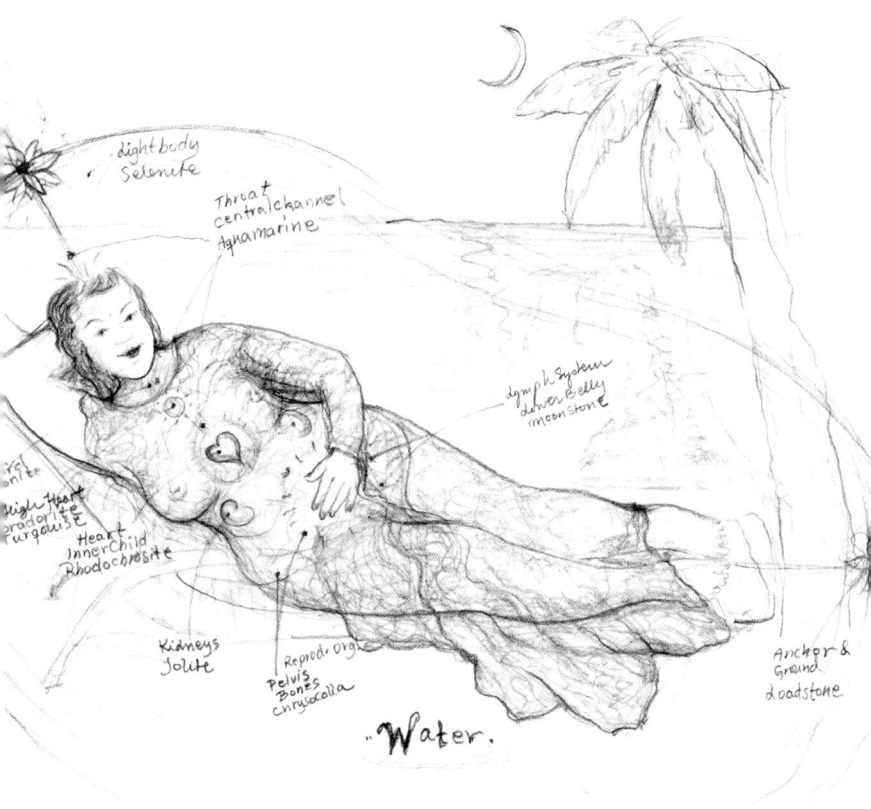

light body
Selenite

Throat
central channel
Aquamarine

lymph System
lower Belly
moonstone

Kunzite?

High Heart
Labradorite
Turquoise
Heart
InnerChild
Rhodochrosite

Kidneys
Iolite

Reprod. Orgs
Pelvis
Bones
Chrysocolla

Anchor &
Ground
Loadstone

"Water."

Figure 106 Places for Installation of water stones. The stones of the water elements in the master Mesa are indicated in the drawing.

softened, but my diaphragm felt so constricted that it was hard to breathe. The two opposing sensations touched in with each other like soft waves breaking on sharp rocks. It felt as if a soft warm sandy beach would be nearby, but not yet accessible. The sensation of warm water was moving over my tensions inside, in a soothing way. Holding the stone in my lap, I could imagine letting go of my inner attitude of tension as a response to everything. The soft moving Heulandite waves that I was feeling created a pleasant sound in my inner ear, like real water would. The sun rays broke through the clouds of tension on my inner beach, and I felt warmer and more relaxed. I discovered where my own roughness needed some more polish. I needed to expect

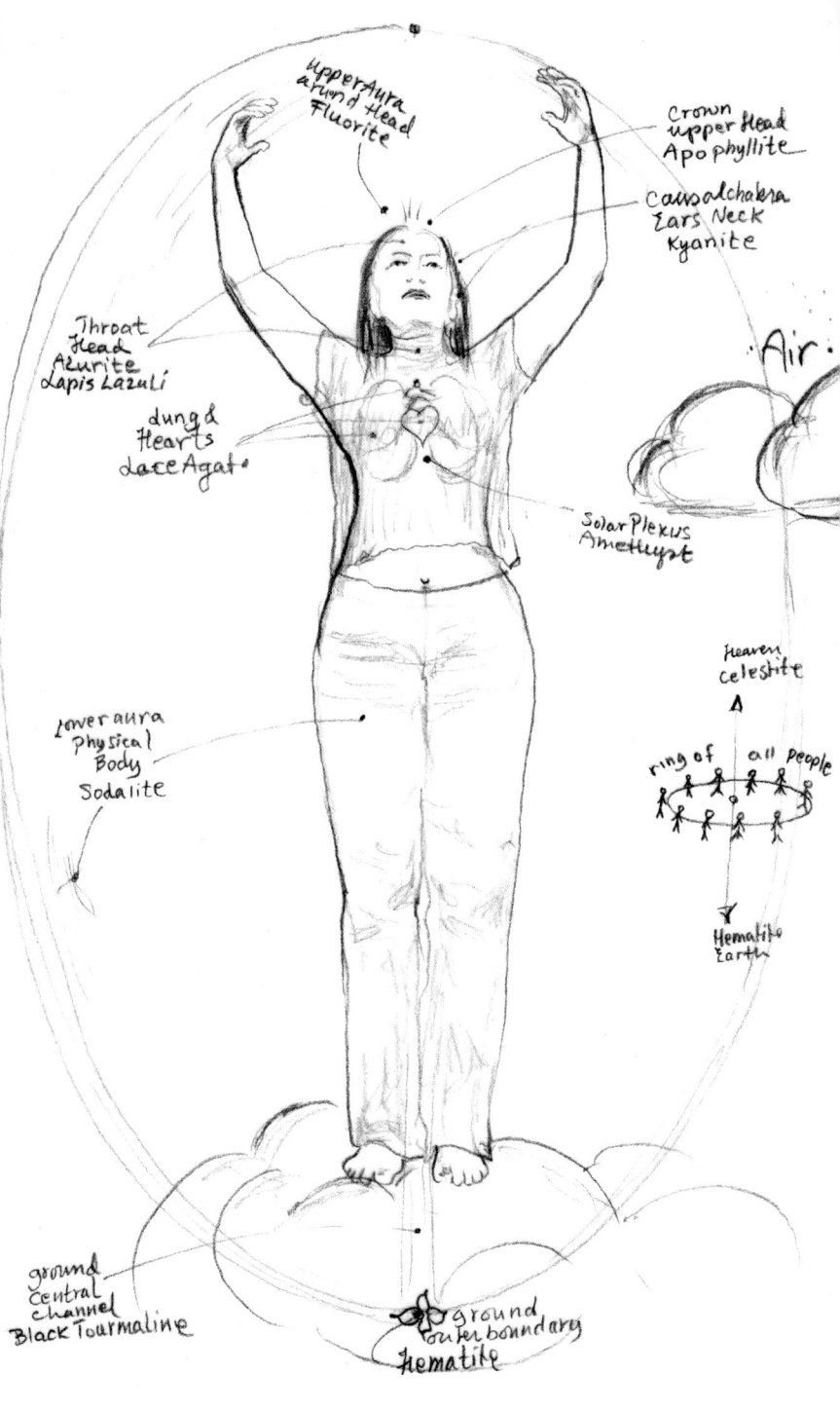

Upper Aura
around Head
Fluorite

Crown
upper Head
Apophyllite

causal chakra
Ears Neck
Kyanite

Air

Throat
Head
Azurite
Lapis Lazuli

dung &
Hearts
Lace Agate

Solar Plexus
Amethyst

Heaven
Celestite

ring of   all people

Lower aura
physical
Body
Sodalite

Hematite
Earth

ground
central
channel
Black Tourmaline

ground
outer boundary
Hematite

better, I thought, and create healthier expectations for myself without demands on others, and accept what is being presented to me from moment to moment. How would others know what we expected of them, if we didn't tell them? Maybe these were things that the other person involved had no idea about or how to provide. My constriction was caused by my own subconscious reaction. The energy from my stone never imposed on me, but surrounded me with the support I needed to realize what was happening. I treasure this stone as a helper, and an ally in my quest for inner harmony. As the saying goes, even drops of water may hollow out a stone, not by force, but by falling many times on its surface. Adversity seen in this way actually helps us to be happy.

AIR STONES	BODY AREA INSTALLATION
Fluorite	Upper Aura, Head
Apophyllite	Crown, Upper Head
Kyanite	Causal Chakra, Ears, Neck
Azurite	Throat, Head (mental body)
Lapis Lazuli	Throat, Head (spiritual body)
Blue Lace Agate	Lungs, Heart, High Heart
Amethyst	Solar Plexus and upper Chakras
Celestite	Heaven Earth Axis with all beings
Black Tourmaline	Central Channel - Ground
Hematite	Earth Star, Outer Boundary

Figure 107 Crystals resonate to organs in the body, and the Crystal Mandala is thus composed within. By mastering each crystal lesson, one may realize the union of the lower and the higher self (yoga). Here are shown the crystals pertaining to the dimensional realms of air. Notice the small drawing to the right for working with Celestite.

Recovering Fire of Passion - Ruby

Fire is the only element capable of transformation; it may take watery grief and rigid control (air) and convert it into something more beneficial. I asked which fire stone wanted to be in this example, and Ruby (spirit fire) volunteered.

Personal Story: What do you do when your passion has died? All though his life, William had a clear vision for who he was and what he had come to do in this lifetime, but life handed him only challenges - not once not twice but many times. I silently cried when he shared his fate the odd time, and I felt so utterly blessed to be born in a nice and supporting family without violence and serious injuries. He began a project in his thirties and invested his money and hard labour. But the universe would not support him, and would not provide what he thought he needed. Over the years he kept up his pace, but then at one point it was just too much. It was as if his heart broke and in that his passion died as well. He turned sad and angry; he was not even nice to his friends. How to assist the situation? I felt deeply that I should do anything that I could to help this man. I felt he was

FIRE STONES	BODY AREA INSTALLATION
Citrine	Mental Body, Head, Navel
Ruby	Mind (Centre of Chest)
Sunstone	Upper Chest, Shoulders
Rutillated Quartz	Aura, Solar Plexus
Blue Pietersite	Field of Balance at Navel (horizontal)
Red Garnet	Vital Energy Body, Belly
Imperial Topaz	Navel
Rose Quartz	Fetus in Utero
Black Obsidian	Outer Auric Bubble

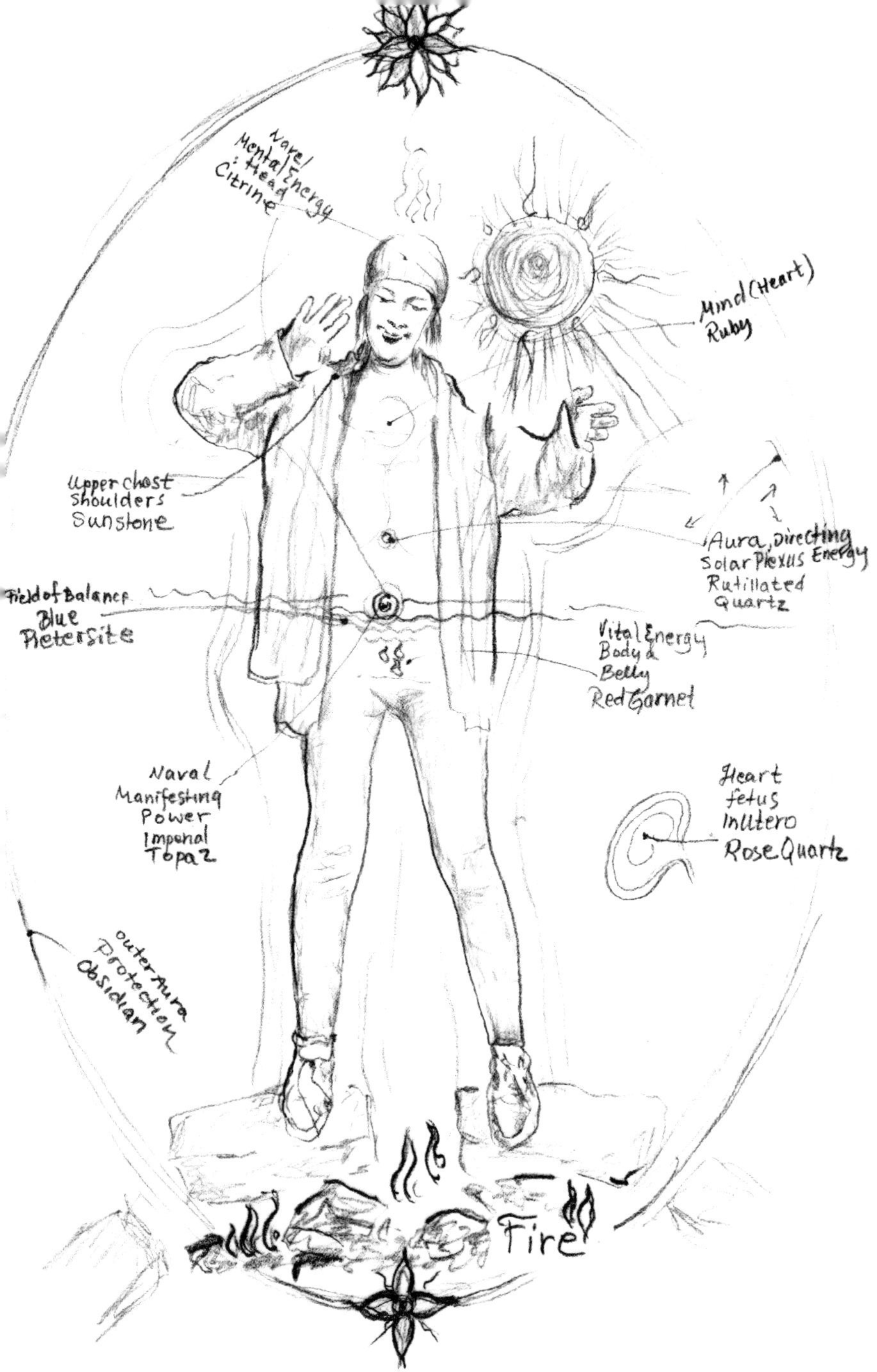

Naval
Mental Energy
: Head
Citrine

Mind (Heart)
Ruby

Upper chest
shoulders
Sunstone

Aura, directing
Solar Plexus Energy
Rutillated
Quartz

Field of Balance
Blue
Pietersite

Vital Energy
Body &
Belly
Red Garnet

Naval
Manifesting
Power
Imperial
Topaz

Heart
fetus
InUtero
Rose Quartz

outer Aura
Protection
Obsidian

Fire

very deserving. In the past I used a variety of stones to clear myself and my own patterns that related to him. When I realised what happened to him I felt I could be a proxy for him and use Ruby to assist. Here is how to proceed in a case like this:

How to start: I ask on the soul's level for permission to be a proxy. I ask also if I am able to help him in this way. Getting affirmative answers on both these questions I brought out a ruby crystal the size of a penny. It is covered with record keepers. My obvious location is my heart, but the installation had to begin at my feet. I visualized a small smouldering fire, which is almost dead. I visualize placing my ruby in its centre. The fire quickens and then burn with clear orange and red flames. In my visualization I step into the fire. It does not hurt me, and the flames feels like a warm caress. This ruby fire sends flames up my spine. I can feel my pelvis and my spinal cord awakening. I inhale and hold my breath for a moment so I can feel the action. There is a barrier in William's solar plexus that hurts. It is a burning feeling. I circle that burning feeling with the cooler subtle ruby flames. Like in a gas fire place I turn on a wide row of flames all across my diaphragm. My intention is to transmute the grief and the rigid control that is stored there. I stay in this meditation for a while, until symptoms relax. It will take a few sessions before I master this. I commit to do this for him until my guidance directs me elsewhere.

Maintenance: I ask how long I shall continue. I am directed to do two weeks monitoring and continued practice. After that time I'll share what happened.

Effects: This is written about three weeks later: The rigid control seems to soften at times and an energy of more inspiration and initiative did take place. He definitely has taken steps to empower himself greatly.

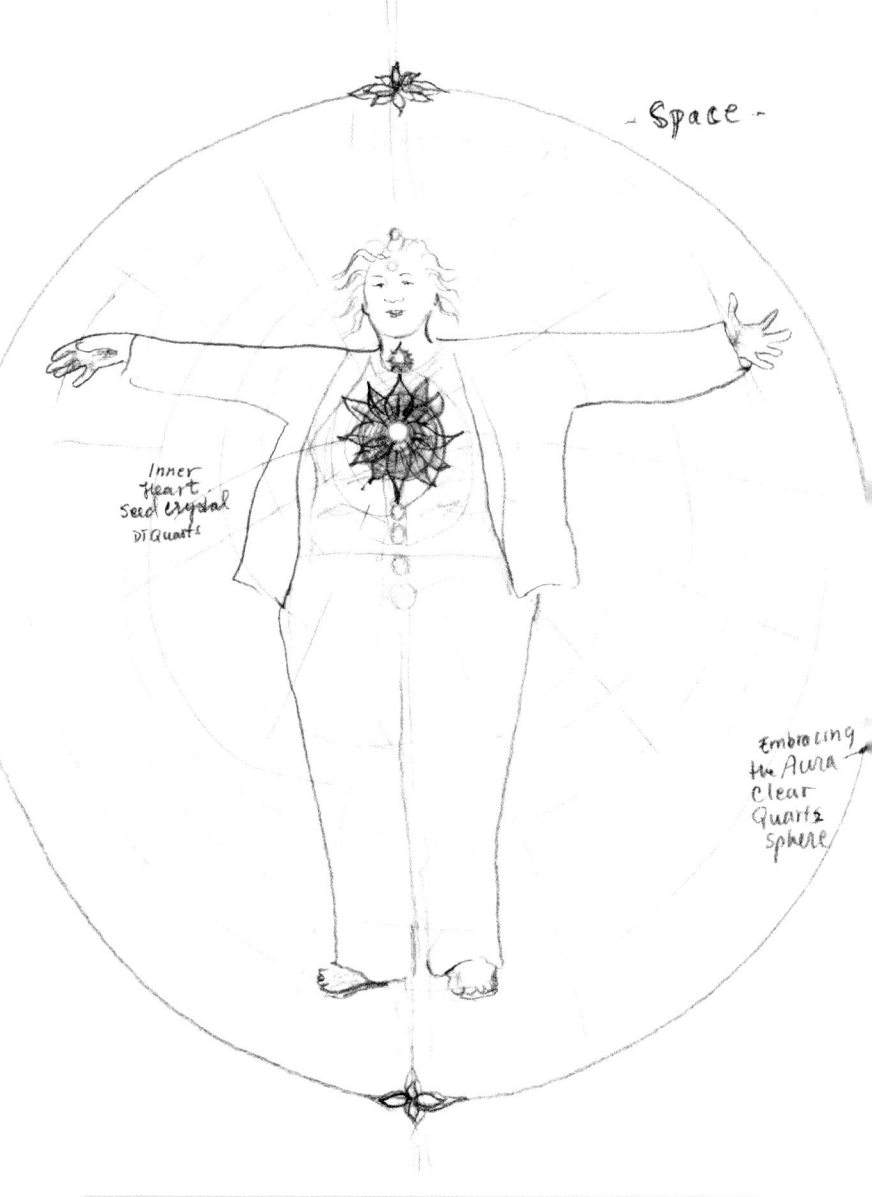

- Space -

Inner
Heart
Seed Crystal
DT Quartz

Embracing
the Aura
Clear
Quartz
Sphere

SPACE STONES	BODY AREA INSTALLATION
Clear Quartz	All Bodies beyond form
Key Crystal	Core of Being

Head. Nerves
Upper Aura
Pyrite

Heart Connection
Chest. Arms
Green Aventurine

Bones
Petrified
Wood

Heart
Path
Jade

Navel
Field of
Strength
Y. Tigerseye

Spine
Hips
Bone
Marrow
Gr. Tourmaline

Belly
Fire Agate

Lower
Body
legs Feet
Red Jasper

Ground
Outer
Boundary
Hematite

Earth

Earth Star
Lower Aura
Lemurian Jade

EARTH STONES	BODY AREA INSTALLATION
Pyrite	Upper Aura, Neck, Head
Green Aventurine	Heart Connection, Chest, Arms
Petrified Wood	Bones
Green Jade	Vertical Path (up to the heart)
Yellow Tiger-eye	Navel - Field of Strength
Green Tourmaline	Spine, Hips, Bone Marrow
Fire Agate	Belly
Red Jasper	Lower Body, Legs, Feet
Hematite	Ground, Outer Boundary
Lemurian Jade	Earth Star, Lower Aura

Earth - Green Tourmaline Forest

Why: This script may help you to visualize and experience the crystal vibration of Green Tourmaline.

How to start: Find a private space to tune in and feel comfortable, create a comfortable seated position (you might record the script for easy listening). Then close your eyes and begin the visualization. Green Tourmaline is displayed on page 229.

Script: Imagine yourself going into a forest. The summer is almost ending, and fall will soon be approaching. The noon sun is well past its mark and you may feel the remnant of its warmth still on the ground. Visualize your feet treading on this warmth; you soon notice that you have entered deep inside an old growth forest of pines and fir trees. The scent of pine rosin is penetrating your senses. In the distance you see a deep green glowing light meeting you, your eyes are slowly adjusting to the potent stillness that is impressed here. It is that of Green Tourmaline. The pine needles under your feet are crunching as you move closer to the centre of a small clearing from which the glowing green light emanates. A small Green Tourmaline crystal is the source of this light. Next to the crystal is a green presence, radiating strength and security. It is the spirit Deva of Green Tourmaline standing behind the crystal. He is slowly picking up the crystal and placing it into your hands.

Notice the sensations inside of you. Breathe deeply, let yourself relax. Observe how the energies move and affect you. The potency of the primal presence is surrounding you; your body is being engulfed in the safe and strong emanations of this crystal. Breathe in the green presence even deeper and slower to absorb all of its gifts into yourself. Your legs and hips are filled with the powerful green energy of Tourmaline; the very centre of your support system is being filled and rejuvenated by the primal power of this crystal and the forest. You will notice the strength being placed inside, deep within your being. It copies into your bones, into your hips and into the centre of your bones. The bone marrow is being replenished and vitalized. Breathe the strength and life force all through you, then exhale your troubles and your distractions - you are now part of this forest. You become aware of the trees near you; they are all made of Tourmaline. All the deeper shades of greens are present in this forest of Primal Power. Now it is yours to accept and to actively energize your physical body. You are becoming taller and stronger, like one of the grandfather pines. And you recognize your own ability to master your physical self and your life. Relax into this state of present alertness. It is solid, strong and stable, you become the green Tourmaline essence. Remain here for a while more...

Begin to move the crystal in your hands towards your crown. Allow this energy to be placed in your crown and filling your entire head. Let it imprint and fill you as a loving channel of potent love. Move the crystal towards the earth, fill each chakra one by one and all your limbs with this potent love of Green Tourmaline, the third eye, in the throat, deep inside your heart, inside your lungs and your diaphragm, into your solar plexus, your belly and hips, your back, and into your legs and feet, filling you with the strength of primal power. Say the affirming:

> *I am grounded.*
> *I am potent love.*
> *I am energized.*
> *I am a channel of loving energy.*
> *I am balance and harmony.*
> *I am balanced action.*
> *I am primal power.*
> *I am here to serve all sentient beings.*

The green presence is gently approaching you. You meet your guide's loving eyes; thank him for the gift of Tourmaline in its brilliant green aspect and return the crystal to its place in the opening. Rest here as long as you like...

When you are ready let yourself find the path where you entered. As you are moving back out of the forest the green glow is slowly subsiding, leaving a sense of deep wellbeing inside of your core. Returning into your private space once again, feel the potency of the love force that now is instilled within, and with the knowing that you can access it whenever you need it. Rest quietly here until you are complete.

Maintenance: Listen to this script as a way to relax and to recover (perhaps from an illness or period of stress), and return to your healthy radiant self.

Effects: The Bone Marrow replenishes your body with healthy cells and by communicating with them in this way, you may establish a link with this part of you. You may begin to feel stronger and healthier the longer you practice this meditation.

An insight

On my desk is a small grid of some stones including a white elestial teacher and a smokey elestial (see pages 280-281). As I ponder my question how to end this chapter, a strong light lit up inside the smokey elestial, in the same way as if someone turned on the light inside. It pointed out to me that my body is the earthly part of me that is to be enjoyed and celebrated. It is a precious gift to have, and engaging in Yoga of any kind, is really to remember to not waste this opportunity to celebrate and enjoy our body.

As we unwind the strong hold of attachments, we may truly experience this as joy filled freedom inside. The earth stones emphasize our strengths to do the work to get there. You may take advantage of the practices, and look to the drawings for each of the elements. Explore your body and your entire being with fresh crystal imprints that moves you towards your centre.

Summary

It is through challenging the stronghold of layers of condition-ing that the sincere practitioner may awaken to his or her inher-ent divine nature. Performing Yoga practices, one may become open to discover and stabilize this state of being. Crystal Yoga is defined here as the practice of awakening through challenges, assisted by crystals. A crystal yoga practice includes personal as-pects like: various body positions, breath-patterns, visualizations and using the voice, and the use of crystal tools and techniques. Each crystal in the Crystal Keys list propose three practice com-ponents (key, polarity and affirmations) that might be used as a bridge to attain the solution to a challenge or issue, and also to build a solid foundation for practice. A daily practice of Crystal Yoga may include the attitude of learning from all challenges and consciously applying self-love and forgiveness for others in using crystal tools and practices. Crystal Yoga also details instal-lations of air, water, fire or earth stones visualized within specific location in the body. The effect is awareness of our energy flow and increase of vital energy.

Practices:
Personal Crystal Yoga Practice
Water: Installation with Heulandite
Fire: Installation with Ruby
Earth: Green Tourmaline - Pine Forest Meditation

Figure 108 Water or another medium like oil can be used to make Gem Elixirs. Elixirs are valuable remedies that we can use to assist our healing process.

Gem Elixirs

Water's vibration
Bring life and rejuvenation

Water is the medium within which we were created and born. Without it we would shrivel up and age prematurely. As the human body consists predominantly of water, anything water-based is effectively absorbed. Infusing water with crystal energy is a profoundly refreshing and safe home remedy. Most crystals can be used to make simple Gem Waters or Gem Elixirs. Gem Elixirs are vibrational in nature and act via energy or vibrational transfer. No physical aspects of the gems are present in the Gem Elixir after it is made. In other words, by infusing the medium used with the gems, the energy or vibration is copied into it. Gem Elixirs are made by submersing gems into a medium such as water or oil, with a protocol of intention. Gem Water, on the other hand, is done without other intention than the gem vibration itself, and a gem in this context is a vibrationally pure mineral. In contrast, Herbal Remedies, Flower Essences and Homeopathic Medicines are made from the actual material in various dilutions.

Gem Elixirs are safe, as they do not exhibit such toxic side effects as have been found with some traditional medicines designed to alter physical biochemical processes in the body. Vibrational remedies act not on the physical biochemical processes in the body, but on the subtle energies and thought patterns, if ac-

Dimension	Field	Modality
Mind	Consciousness Talk Therapies	Intent, Prayer, Meditation Psychoanalysis, NLP Spiritual Counselling Hypnotherapy
Subtle Energies	Energy Therapies Vibrational Remedies	Acupuncture, Reiki Therapeutic Touch Crystal Healing Homeopathy Flower Essences Gem Elixirs
Physical	Allopathic Medicine Alternative Care Hands-on Body Work	Pharmaceuticals, Surgery Food, Herbal Remedies Chiropractic, Massage Reflexology

cepted by the user. They may access the causes for the conditions or situation for which the remedy is being used, therefore empowering the individual to begin the natural healing process from within. If a person creates such remedies without proper intentional protocol, little or no effect will take place. For one to begin a Gem Elixir practice, very little prerequisite knowledge is required other than a clearly defined intent, coupled with the discipline to carry out the practice. Any circumstance or condition a person may have can begin to be addressed, when so chosen by the practitioner. See above table: it puts Gem Elixirs in an appropriate context with examples of other modalities.

How To Make a Gem Elixir

The two main methods for making Gem Elixirs are Direct Infusion and Indirect Infusion. In the first method the well-cleaned and cleared crystal is placed in pure spring water for a length of time. Sun is usually used to energize the elixir. In the Indirect method the crystals used are placed in close proximity to the water container, but not in contact with the liquid.

Intention: Meditate on what you'd like to accomplish with your elixir. What condition or situation do you want to remedy? Then select your crystal. A crystal combination may be used when you have gained some practice, but it is wise to start with one particular crystal first. Write down your intent on a small card. The *Gem Elixir Session* chart might prove useful as a guide (see Appendix page 556).

How to begin: Clean your crystal in water with a mild detergent and rinse well to remove any impurities, then clear your crystal with one of the following ways: intention for clearing, smudging

Figure 109 Gem Elixir Charging Station. Gems are placed inside a glass container and filled with pure water to charge inside a Crystal Orb on a Gem Elixir Board. The station can be placed inside, close to a window, or outside in nature. Cover the container with a glass.

or using Reiki. You may find that tuning in with the crystal helps you to tune in with yourself.

Affirm the 'General Healing Intent' or your own personal intent, by speaking it sincerely and, in addition, placing a card with it written under the container.

> *May we call and acknowledge*
> *The One Supreme Source of all creation and*
> *Accept our Divine Team to guide us.*
>
> *May this Process and this Elixir yield results,*
> *which assist the process of healing,*
> *for the highest good of all beings concerned.*
> *In Gratitude, So Be It!*

Immersion. Then the crystal is placed in a clean glass container. Pour in clean spring water to cover the stone.

Note: If you are making a Malachite Elixir, use the vibrational method, which follows the same procedure as the direct method with the following exception: Place a smaller bowl with the Malachite into a larger bowl. Then pour pure spring water into the larger bowl in such a way that the water surrounds the smaller bowl but does not come in contact with the stone.

Cover the receptacles with a clear glass plate to stop dust or insects from contaminating the water. Place in the sun, either outdoors or in a window. If you know how to do the activation breath, do it at this point.

Note: If you are doing general Gem Elixirs with the stone vibration only, you still benefit from adding your own intent here. For example: "*May this Gem Elixir be of benefit to use in my practice with clients.*" For indications of the stone vibration itself, consult the *Crystal Keys List*.

Figure 110 Gems used in Gem Elixir Practice. Notice that we may use very small specimens (1/4") to make Gem Elixirs.

Infusion time: Let the crystal infuse the water for at least 11 minutes, to a maximum of 8 hours. One would need to dowse the correct length of time for the infusion. The length of time depends on the purpose, the person to be using it, and the circumstance to be remedied.

If the Elixir is to be used topically, pure carrier oil is advisable; in this way excellent massage mediums can be created; edible oils can be used in salad dressings or other food preparation. If you have any concern about the crystal you want to use being in contact with water or oil, always use the indirect method.

Completing: The medium is retrieved at the end of the infusion time and put in a sealable container, preferably of glass. This is called the 'Mother Solution,' and can be used as is.

Dilutions: To further empower your elixir, you may require dilu-

The Beginning Ten Gem Elixirs

1. Vital Health — Red Garnet
2. Self-Empowerment — Tiger-Eye
3. Grounding & Protection — Black Tourmaline
4. Abundance — Pyrite* (or Golden Topaz)
5. Joy Blend — Coral Calcite (or Peridot)
6. Focus & Concentration — Clear Quartz (or Flourite)
7. Emotional Balance — Aventurine
8. Mental Balance — Lepidolite
9. Meditation & Serenity — Blue Calcite
10. Clearing — Kyanite (or Citrine)

*) Use vibrational method

tions. Compare this with the strength of homeopathic remedies: the more dilutions you make, the more powerful it is. Powerful here means the remedy will reach more subtle levels. When the remedy reaches the level in the subtle bodies where the 'root cause' resides, it can be dealt with proficiently. The dilutions have to be made prior to preserving your Gem Elixir.

Tincture: If you are making elixirs to be stored for a longer period, alcohol or vinegar must be used to preserve your elixir. It is then called a Gem Elixir Tincture. The preservative needs to be of high quality and to be cleared, dowsed for the type and brand that would best be used for your Gem Elixir. Tinctures can be stored for long periods of time, preferably in a cool place, and away from light.

How To Make Garnet Anointing Oil

Follow the instructions above and consult the section for *Sacred Body Practice* on page 130, when setting your intent. Select 4 small tumbled pieces of red Garnet - four stones are used in this case to represent the physical aspect that is to be worked on.

Wash and clear the stones carefully. This oil is going to be used on the skin. Select a carrier-oil that is suitable. I have found that refracted pure coconut oil is very versatile for this purpose, as it is compatible with many people and does not have any scent. Grape Seed and Jojoba oil are other alternatives. Inquire at a health food store near you for other suitable oils. Put the Garnets in a small glass bowl; pour the oil to cover the stones. Let them remain in the oil at least 16 hours. Remove the stones and put the oil in a suitable container that allows for small amounts of oil to be dispensed.

Beginning Ten Gem Elixirs

To begin practicing with Gem Elixirs it is beneficial to first learn to make the beginning Ten Gem Elixirs. The reason for this is that unless you have direct experience with individual gems first, you would be less able to discern specific effects accurately. For example: in using the Self-Empowerment Elixir, you would first look at the effects inside you and learn how that feels. In addition, we might feel Self-Empowered, but discover we are missing some other areas that we need to learn more about, to relieve ourselves of illusion about ourselves.

Complex Gem Elixirs with the Vibrational Method

There is a time for complexity and there is a time for simple solutions. When a situation to be dealt with becomes filled with a number of variables that all have importance, a step-by-step approach may not work. In this case we place the whole situation on the table. And this is done literally on a Gem Elixir Board. This 1/2" thick wooden board is stained and naturally oiled or painted. One can really be elaborate when creating it. By preparing a functional place to work on, we are also creating a sacred space where the vibrational 'climate' is conducive to a successful process. Activate the board with prayer or chant.

How to make a complex Gem Elixir? There are two ways: the Intuitive way and the Rational Way, both work, and it depends on what the practitioner is most comfortable with. We begin with the Intuitive Way. First jot down some details about the situation in general, perhaps add images/photographs/personal items that fit the situation, then ask for guidance on what is the best way to approach the scenario. Let your mind be free to explore options rather than trying to pinpoint exactly what you'd like to accomplish with the Elixir. Then move to the stone selection. One may choose stones that 'call out' to be picked for the process, or alternatively, open a Pendulum Session. When all the stones required are selected, position each of them on the board. You may discover that certain patterns are forming and you might feel really good about this development. What is happening is that the stone energies begin to act together like a vortex. This is vital to reach because it will affect the water most potently. At this point you might have come to a conclusion about the specifics, which is: the name of the elixir, and its intended use.

In the Rational Way we make a flowing list of the facts on hand for the situation we intend to remedy. Then organize this list in categories and open a *Pendulum Session* (see pages 417 and 557). Carefully test each of the choices until you can make a decision about the name of the elixir, and what it is intended to address for the person who is going to use it. To select the crystals look up each of the qualities and the things you see as desired results in the List of Crystal Keys. Now you should have a shorter or longer list of stones you can use. Now gather the stones you have selected. If by chance you do not have a particular stone, proceed to acquire it or alternatively write the attributes and the name of the crystal on a small card and place it on the board. By doing this you are, in fact, calling to those energies to be present.

Figure 111 Gem Elixir Board, an ideal portable altar for making simple or complex Gem Elixirs. When searching to remedy something where a large number of variables is involved, a large number of gems may be needed to embrace the whole scenario. A Gem Elixir Board is then indispensable for effective work.

Then simply lay the gems out around the central place where the water container is going to be placed. You may place them in groups or simply in a circle. By engaging in a process like this, one can better sort out where the real problem lies and how best to address it.

A client asked me to prepare two gem oils for her situation. One was to be used at the computer as she was frequently experiencing tiredness and eye strain. I followed the Intuitive Way and prepared the Gem Elixir Board with a number of crystals. She reported:

Case Story. "The 'Computer Eyes Gem Elixir' helped ease my eyes significantly. I felt more comfortable in front of the computer screen and a lot less stress and strain - thank you Margherita, your intuitive work has a very real impact. I also engaged Margherita's input to create a gem elixir for my "Inner Goddess Playshop," I was working with "stillness" and asked hr to provide me with a product I could give out to all the women as a gift, which they would use at the Playshop and then take home and continue to be inspired by. 'Stillness' worked immediately! It was very deep and when applied to the body - especially on the wrists - there was an immediate feeling of peace and stillness. My awareness was drawn to a deep place inside my centre, I was inspired to take many deep breaths, and felt at ease. This was the same feeling experienced by the other women at the Inner Goddess Playshop - we used it to facilitate a deeper state of meditation and focus, and inner calm and love. The combination of the oils with the gems is very profound."

By darinka blagaj

Example of Healing Protocol

Any organ or part of the body can be chosen. In this example we have chosen the eyes and the faculty of vision to describe organ healing with Gem Elixir. Note! Be sure to have your medical professional aware of the process if you are under treatment or require medical attention. The proposed questions and suggestions are for the purpose of learning more about yourself and any situation you are in, but they do not replace qualified medical attention or diagnose any condition you may have.

1) Explore Symptoms/Problems:
Vision problems: blurred vision, trouble focussing, needing glasses
Physical problems with eyes: dryness, puffiness, itchiness, tiredness, dis-ease, other..

2) Sample of questions about care and use of selected organ:
How are you caring for your eyes?
Are you taking your eyes for granted?
Are you overusing your eyes?
Are you nurturing your eyes?
Are you feeding your eyes (giving them what they need to
  function)?
Are you storing energy or emotion in your eyes?
How are you depending on your eyes?
Is there computer-screen overload on your eyes?

3) What are your intentions, such as improved functioning,
  comfort/pain relief, etc.?

4) What are you prepared to do? Do you want to establish a
  daily practice to improve the afflicted organ and its functioning as far as: Rest, Nutrition, Exercise, Treatment,
  Meditation

5) Possible options for practice:
Daily Meditation
Eye breathing see practice of *Breathing the Stone I & II*
Eye movement in the 8 directions (visualize a large octagon
  in front of yourself and follow its perimeter - look at each
  corner in turn, first clockwise, then counter-clockwise)
Eye focussing on 2 depths (far and near)
Eye pattern Release; figure ∞ movement
Meditation with closed resting eyes
Eye Baths
Restricted use (at computer, etc.)

6) Understanding the sense of sight.
The eyes are connected to the faculty of sight. Sight is connected to mental activity and the element of air.
If a person is having trouble focusing or is confused, his
  or her eyes will move all over the place. Relaxing the eye

movements will relax the thinking processes.
The eyes are related to the air element.

Possible Eye Elixirs:
  Youthening formula: Ruby in Zoisite
  Strengthening formula: Garnet and Yellow Tiger-eye
  Relaxed Eyes: Blue Calcite (alternatively Larimar)
  Improved vision: Gem Silica/Chrysocolla and Amethyst
  Increase spiritual vision I: Apophyllite and Petalite
  Spiritual vision II: Moldavite and Phenacite

Media:
  A. Third Eye oil (applied to the third eye chakra, not inside physical eyes).
  B. Water-based Elixir, for Eye Baths - add one drop in pure water or as Gem Baths (entire body). Add 7 drops to bath water. (Dowse the correct dosage for you).
  C. Tincture (preserved Elixir), for internal use

Take care of your body by listening to what your body tells you. Take action on the things that make sense to you. Persevering with selected treatment programs until the end of the decided time frame of practice makes a difference. Note! Using an elixir correctly can never harm you, or any of your organs. Follow inner guidance closely; see also the chapter 'Pendulum Basics' for testing procedures.

Ethical Considerations with Gem Elixir Practice

Any qualified practitioners may use Gem Elixirs in their practices. You can use commercially available elixirs or create personalized elixirs yourself. The use of Gem Elixirs should be seen as an ongoing practice program for any individual using it, and not a quick fix. Gem Elixirs are vibrational remedies and access the subtle layers within, so that a person can be supported on his or her self-discovery journey. Persons accepting the use of a Gem Elixir do so because they have chosen to take responsibility for their own healing. It is important that if you propose or prepare your Gem Elixirs for others, you should ascertain that he or she understands and accepts this.

Summary

Gem Elixirs and Gem waters are easy to make using the direct method or the indirect or vibrational method. Water and oil are the most common mediums for Gem Elixirs. Gem Elixirs are made with the specific intention to remedy a situation. Simple Gem Waters have no other intention than the vibration itself. A preserved Gem Elixir is called a Tincture. Preservatives used are alcohol or vinegar. Gem Elixirs belong to the category of vibrational remedies and are safe to use and provide valuable insight into the self-discovery process. It is beneficial to understand the nature and root causes of a problem, as that is the essential key to remedying it. Detrimental imprints in various locations can cause us to engage in more or less harmful actions, when those locations are triggered. The solution is to locate the imprints/programs and change them, and then those problems will also be changed or removed. Gem Elixirs work through intention and vibration, to change or remove harmful imprints. Organ healing with Gem Elixirs is exemplified with a sample protocol of healing the eyes and vision.

Practices:
How To Make a Gem Elixir
How To Make a Garnet Anointing Oil
The Ten Beginning Gem Elixirs
Complex Gem Elixirs with the Vibrational Method

Figure 112 A personal crystal pendulum. By attuning to the movement of your pendulum, vital questions can be answered concerning your personal situation. This tool can be made from a number of crystals. The pendulum is widely used as a tool to assist in healing.

Pendulum Basics

Though a looking glass
Wisdom revealed

A Pendulum is any object attached to a string in such a way that it can swing freely. Granny might have used a ring or needle, and a piece of yarn to create a simple pendulum and swing it over the daughter-in-law's pregnant belly to find out the gender of the baby. It is true that one might find out answers to questions like that. A more practical example would be to find out what options are available in a difficult situation or how to find a lost item. In healing we can use a pendulum to direct us to where we should focus our work. The activity of dowsing for water is one of many techniques still in practice. A dowser may use a tool such as a pendulum or an L-rod. These can contain selected crystals which may enhance their effectiveness. The crystal will amplify any effect so that the user will feel it more clearly. More important is how the connections with the desired object of the dowsing can be done. Inner guiding is a strong component in the ability to dowse.

To divine is to discern the will of the Divine: it has been done in various ways, including scrying, tarot or administering herbs and other more obscure ways. Everyone has the potential to access his or her inner guidance system, but it is only with conscious effort and diligence that one can create a clear channel through which that guidance can be received. Crystals may assist the serious applicant in this process. Using tools like cards or pendulums can be a way to begin the journey; eventually these are not needed when clear access is opened.

One may see Dowsing as a process of accessing the fields of knowledge that are unknown to the conscious mind. The field of all knowledge available can be seen as a vast database reaching over time and space. This database has been called the *Akashic Records*[1]. It is assumed to contain all records or imprints ever made. In history records have been stored on clay tablets, carved in stone, documented on papyrus, and scratched on copper plates. In more modern times, written records were stored on pergament, leather or paper. In crystal lore it is known that data can be imprinted within a crystal. This has now come to be widely used in the age of computers, which use that particular capacity for data storage. Imagine now that a different medium is used, one that is not of three-dimensional matter. Instead, the record is imprinted on a subtle matter: that of ether or space, which is the source for the other four elements (air, fire, water and earth) known on our planet. How those records are made is beyond the scope of this book, but a small clue lies in our mental-emotional output.

A person may access this database by tapping into its resonance and asking skilful questions. By using a tool like the pendulum, it will show this resonance in its movement. Therefore questions requiring a yes/no answer should be used. Before asking for the answers needed, the dowser first establishes how the movements should be interpreted, by asking test questions. The further use of a test chart can be helpful to establish gradations, like percentages.

When a person loosens the grip of early conditioning by practice or by spontaneous awakening, he or she may become aware of things that were not so obvious on the surface. Such a person might be called a psychic or clairvoyant, but one does not have to be a psychic to be able to dowse. One needs only a little bit of trust and some practice. It could be said that dowsing is a lifestyle, because once you start looking at the real meaning and deeper answers, it is hard not to want to know, after experiencing such knowledge. Joey Korn[2] stated: "We are energy beings. We live in a sea of consciousness. Dowsing is an extension of Consciousness. It is Consciousness Itself."

To divine the truth, in my opinion, is to bypass the contriving lower ego-guided mind. That is why tools such as crystal pendulums are helpful to ascertain certain questions in healing. The use of such tools is for the purpose of training ourselves to be more open to see, hear, and intuit what is right in front of us. This is beautifully expressed by Chögyam Trungpa[3]:

"Divination is generally used when you are somewhat trapped in a situation. You really have no alternative but you are too cowardly to commit yourself to your actual intuition of the straightforwardness. So you turn to the pretence of divination. And what happens in divination is that, even though you may be highly biased in your view of the situation, you pretend not to be. You step back from the situation altogether and then you open your mind and allow yourself to make a decision in accordance with the divination practice. Or, more precisely, once you are there in no man's land, the answer is there already. Then you come back to your own territory and make a decision."

Methodology for Questioning

Every answer has the right question. The correct question gives you the correct answer. The dowser observes the movements of the pendulum, in relation to a specific question. Depending on this movement, questions may be answered. It is of vital importance to understand how to ask the right question. You will receive the answer to the question you are asking! Most people do not like the answers they are getting, so the questions have to be asked skilfully. There are three areas of answers to a question:

> *The Known*
> *The Unknown*
> *The Unknowable*

Known answers are readily available information. We can learn such information from the internet, text books and from teachers who know it. The Unknown is not readily available; you can probably not find out the status of your chakras by googling it. It is, however, available. This is the area where dowsing is indispensable. The Unknowable cannot be known, but one can ascertain if a question can be answered. The first step is to select the area of questioning. Look at the list of dowsing subjects and note your areas of interest. Pin down the information by stating some test questions. State at least three questions. Meditate on each question to see what you really need to find out.

Personal example of a dowsing process: I wanted to find out what was happening in my solar plexus as I had a burning sensation and a strong tension at the bottom part of my frontal ribs. It felt like my diaphragm was having trouble. I use the word *tension*, but I could also have used: *block, pain, discomfort*, etc. I felt that it had to do with discordant energy of some kind. I decided to find out what it was and how to deal with it by using my pendulum. I named the process: *Diaphragm Tension*. First I made a list of words

Health Assessment:
Auric Scanning
Chakra Evaluation
Colour Diagnostic
Organ Status
Meridian Tracing
Moving Energy
Repairing Auric Tears
Locating Thought-forms
Entity Mapping
Allergy Testing

External Objects/Spaces:
Testing Food
Locating Lost Items
Mapping of Energy
Locating Ley Lines
Locating Water
Identifying Locations
Geographic Directions

Personal Issues:
Finding Best Choices
Clearing Space
Infusing Energy

Figure 113 List of Areas for Dowsing.

and ideas of causes I came to think of in no particular order, a flowing list of *Diaphragm Tension - causes: Nervous tension? Outside influence? Attacked from somewhere? Need a break? Tired? Weather change? Radiation? Got a Bug? Change in organ rhythm? Someone's hostile feelings? My worry? Ate something bad?* Then, I organized the flowing list a bit like this:

Internal: (worry, tiredness, got a bug, change in organ
   rhythm, bad food, need food/water.
External: (someone hostile, weather, radiation, hostile
   entity).

Verify: For each entry I asked with the pendulum: Is it internal? No. Is it external? Yes. Is it someone's hostile feelings? No. Is it Radiation? Yes. Is it a hostile entity? Yes. Is it a radiation from this entity? Yes. Is it directed to me personally? No. Is there anything else causing this tension as well? No.

I was now in a position to decide what to do to remedy my situation. Back to a flowing list again of possible things I could do: *lie down, ingest something, breathe, set up protection, clear radiation, ask the radiation to stop, ask angel for help, do practice, other.* Organizing my list:

> Physical action internal (position, ingest something, breathing, do practice)
> Action externally: (clear radiation, set up protection).
> Communicate: (ask for help, ask it to stop).
> Other:

Verify: I ask with the help of the pendulum. Internal action? No. External action? Yes. Communicate? No. Clear radiation? Yes. Set up protection? No. Other? No. Ok! Next is how to clear the radiation. Flowing list: *Smudge, Chant Clearing Prayer, Use drum, Use other sound, Cut radiation with crystal, other method.* Organize:

> Smudge: (sage, incense, tobacco, other)
> Sound: (chant, drum, other)
> Cut with crystal: (Laser Wand, Kyanite, Selenite, other).
> Other:

Verify with the pendulum: smudge-no, sound-yes, chant-yes, drum-yes, other-no, crystal-yes, laser-yes, other crystal-no. Other? No. In conclusion: I will now do a clearing of the radiation with a laser wand, chant a clearing prayer and use my drum. The last details: In what order? Is it chant, drum and crystal? Yes. Is there more I can do? No. So now I go to do this and we'll see how my tension responds. During the whole procedure the tension has not changed, although the burning sensation ceased almost right away. I did the three actions and was waiting to see what would happen. I asked how long it would take for the tension to subside. The answer was: between 2-3 hours. About 4 hours later there was still a tiny sensation left but after the next meal, I felt the radiation was fully cleared. I discovered in the hours after this clearing another tension covering the middle part of my ribs, or, more precisely, in front of my physical heart. To complete I asked: Is this process (*Diaphragm Tension*) complete? - Yes.

The radiation from the hostile entity was cleared but revealed to me another layer of work. Note that one doesn't need to understand what all the details mean to affect the problem. Later I opened another session to get insight about what to do with the *Tension over Heart,* as I called the new session. I found the process highly effective as it involved an analysis of my problem and provided me with precise things I could do to remedy it - and it worked! Personally I feel that the process helped me to identify and deal with surrounding energies and their effect on me.

Open a Pendulum Session

Why: It is an effective method to discover answers to pertinent questions we may have. This procedure may also be applied with other dowsing tools, including kinesiology.

How to begin: Open a session by stating that your work will be for the highest good for all concerned. If other people are involved, always ask for their permission[4]. Create a *Name of session.* If the area is not identified clearly, the process will be less likely to work, or be too vague to be useful. Next, make a *Flowing List* of words you feel relate to the particulars/causes/options of your query. Let your mind loose, and jot down anything that comes to you. After the flowing list is complete, organize it into categories. Always add the option: 'other' to make sure you have all the variables covered. Use your pendulum and mark the answers. As in the example above, summarize your findings and verify the statements. Then open a flowing list again for possible actions relating to your findings. Verify each option and summarize what you need to do. There can be quite a number of options to choose from, so if you organize your work from the beginning it is quite easy. You might use a copy of the *Pendulum Query Template* in the Appendix see page 557.

In your flowing list you might add things like: look at a map, search for more detail, look in dictionary, search the web, ask a doctor, is it ethical, ask a teacher, etc. You don't have to come up with everything yourself.

Effects: The benefit of being organized like this is that you can find our exactly what is going on in an objective manner and then use the answers to deal with it.

Maintenance: Always commit to doing the actions required by your process, but the caveat is if you get actions you know would be harmful to you or others, you should investigate the cause of this by asking about it. We should in no way harm ourselves nor others by using this process. It should be done as a way to help ourselves heal[5].

Crystal Care: Store your pendulum safely and treat it with respect as it is a tool just for you. As a surgeon's tools are kept sterile and clean before surgery, you must treat your tools in appropriate ways. Your tools do not replace your common sense, but they are there for you to use, to expand your own conscious awareness.

"Dowsing is one of the most important things anyone can learn because you can be self-sufficient. When you learn to Dowse correctly and accurately you have a tool that will be with you for the rest of your life, and, it can save your life." ~ Sandee Mac[6]

How To Use a Pendulum

Here is the fun part of your pendulum work. Hold your pendulum in your dominant hand[7] and make sure your middle finger is touching the string or chain. The middle finger is believed to connect to the subconscious, so I was taught to always connect with that finger. At first one can begin the movement with a small swing. After a while some can feel an energy moving through the hand and fingers, directing the movement of the pendulum. Let this happen and see what results you might receive. Spend several minutes sensing this energy until you feel comfortable to proceed. It is important to be relaxed and have a sense of joyfulness.

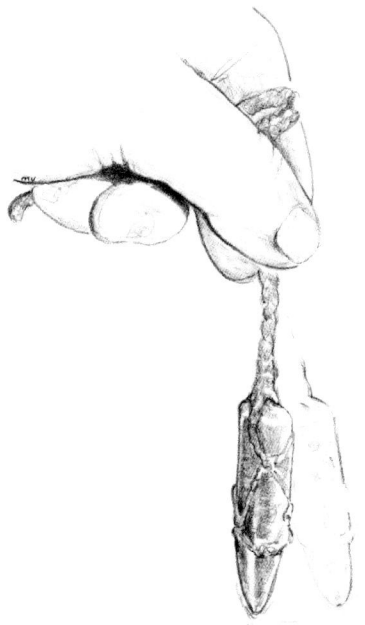

Figure 114 Watch the movement of the Pendulum to discover the answer of your question. (Quartz point wrapped in silk yarn).

If you let yourself doubt or allow stress, it will hinder the process. Remember to give yourself and your pendulum a chance to feel the vibration coming; it may take a few moments. The energy felt here is the beginning for tuning in with the akasha. The pendulum is the outer extension of your own non-personal antenna to the subconscious. Ask for the pendulum to show you what a 'Yes' answer looks like. Record the movement pattern. Usually it is circular, either clockwise or anti-clockwise. Other responses are ovals and side to side or no movement. Now ask to be shown a 'No' answer. Record the movement. Also ask to be shown the third option: the 'not available now' answer. There are several more options one can include but these three will work for most situations. Some practitioners prefer to 'program' their pendulum with preset responses as follows.

Yes: Clockwise
No: Counter-Clockwise
Not Available Now: Up-Down

Now you are ready to ask your first question. Test yourself with a question you know the answer to. Do this, until you feel comfortable with the process.

Make a Personal Pendulum

Although a pendulum can be made from almost any material, using a crystal pendulum has added benefits. Depending on the crystal, a variety of energy work can be performed in addition. The most-used crystal is clear Quartz, which amplifies the answer, in my experience. A simple pendulum can be made with the stone of your choice and a piece of silk yarn, as was done to create the pendulum on the previous page. In what area is your pendulum to work? Select the crystal for the active side (bottom), as well as the crystal for the stationary side, the side you hold on to while dowsing.

The Crystal Kingdom plays a vital role in amplifying and mirroring what is going on. The variety of crystals is like the strings on a harp - when played they produce a specific note. To make music we might need a selection of notes to be used to achieve balance and harmony. The table below shows some crystal families, and the primary area of use with relation to crystal pendulums.

CRYSTAL FAMILY	GENERAL AREA OF USE
Clear Quartz	Amplification, Extracting & Aligning
Colored Quartz	Balancing on specific chakra level
Beryls	Truth and Expressions of truth
Corundums	The Mind and Conscious awareness
Feldspars	Emotional development and flow
Coppers	Mental-Emotional purification
Etherials	Expansion of awareness, Guidance and Inner journeys
Calcites	Acceptance of the present, the Now
Tourmalines	Physical-Mental link (grounding & expansion)
Garnets	Connection with Life-force and Health
Obsidians	Boundary and Protection
Irons	Earth connection and Protective grids (grounding)

Figure 115 Table of minerals and their suggested general use in a personal pendulum. Etherials includes: Apophyllite, Angelite and Petalite. Irons are primarily Hematite but the group also includes: Pyrite, Pyrotite, Marcasite, Magnetite, Lodestone and Tiger-iron. Coppers are minerals containing copper such as: Azurite, Malachite, Turquoise and Chrysocolla.

Pendulum Applications

Awareness of chakras. In a healing session we may ask which chakra areas need our attention. An open healthy chakra usually shows a nice open movement, showing a 'Yes=Open'. It becomes natural to 'ask' when engaged in the process of dowsing. By asking questions related to healing we are actually paying the present issues some attention. The benefit is that we can be apprised of our options and make informed decisions. When asking chakra status we either hold the pendulum directly above the chakra in question, or use a schematic picture of the body to assist us (see *Body Scan Template* page 555).

Crystal Colour Balance. The pendulum can also be used to check your colour status, meaning the overall balance of your system on a subtle energy level. The benefit is that what is tested is something that one can relate to easily, without complexity. In the art of Talisman making, crystal colour is used as a model to remedy discordant energies; this science can be used to work directly on the body by applying the crystal colour a person may require in a talisman or in a layout of crystals. In my own work I test for accumulation or depletion over a time frame of 3 months. This makes sure that day-to-day energy variations are not interfering with long-range solutions. The result is displayed in a graph for easy reading.

Moving energy with a pendulum. In order to move energy, practice with the pendulum as a query tool first. Then, when sensing the energies are available, one may be able to define and move them:

Personal Story: I experienced shoulder pain while sitting at the computer for too long. I became acutely aware of it and tried to stretch and breathe but to not much effect. So I asked my pendulum to assist me for the highest good for all concerned, to simply move the pain out. First, I wrote on a piece of paper 'shoulder pain' and made a rudimentary sketch of head and shoulder, marking the area, and then I proceeded to swing my clear quartz pendulum clockwise relatively fast (about 3 turns per second) over the sketch. After about 90 seconds I began to feel a shift from pain to tension. I knew that I would have to go back and sort it out more later, for all the tension to be dissolved, but for now, I could continue to do my work. Thank you!

Opening a chakra may be done in the same way by asking the chakra in question to open safely using slower and then faster clockwise rotations. One might hold the pendulum with shorter string to get the right speed (from 2 to 5 turns per second).

Detecting an energy line. To follow an energy line like a ley line, program the pendulum to swing one way when on the line and a different way when off the line. For example, I have detected a ley line on my property and I want to find out where it goes. I might program my pendulum in the following way:

I am on the line - show forward/backward swing
I am left of the line - show anti-clockwise swing
I am right of the line - show clockwise swing

You can go out on the land itself, or use a detailed map. With detailed recording work one may get quite a precise picture of where the ley line is. I suggest using a Tourmaline pendulum here, since it will strengthen the connection to the earth-bound energy, thus giving a clearer picture.

Summary

A pendulum is an item attached to a string that may connect you to your own inner antenna in the process of dowsing. To dowse or divine is to find knowable answers that are hidden. When a connection can be made to the divine-knowing part of us, we may see what is present right in front of our eyes. This information is proposed to exist in the vast database imprinted in the ethers called the *Akashic Records*, which stores all data ever created. To find information you need for healing, locating things, or solving any issue you may have, the success of a pendulum session is in formulating skilful questions. This procedure follows: opening a session, stating the area of query, making a free-flowing list that is organized so that each option can easily be verified by a yes/no answer and then summarized into causes/particulars of the query and possible actions to apply. Applications described include testing chakras and colour balance of the human subtle energy field. A pendulum can also assist in moving energies or detecting energy lines.

Practices:
Methodology for questioning
Open a pendulum session
How to use a pendulum
Make a personal pendulum

Figure 116 Ruby Calcite - The Wrath Remedy Stone. A stone perfect for getting in touch with what truly makes us move.

Crystal Healing

Arrays of Crystals illumine the body
Wise ones use them consciously

Healing is like doing laundry. We place our dirty clothes (the issues in our subtle bodies) in a washer (the place of healing). Then we put in detergent (crystal modalities) and start the machine with a flow of water (the life-force channelled by ourselves, or our facilitator). When the soapy water touches the dirt, the dirt starts to dissolve, and the movement of water removes it. The life force channelled by the healer is received and flows through us, identifying areas of blocked energy and misalignments. Then the rinse cycle starts. Our healer may do auric sweeps to remove released energy forms. At the end the last remnants are removed in the spinning cycle. Our clothes are now clean, ready to hang out and dry (the process of recovery before we go back into regular life renewed). After the labour of laundry we may pay closer attention to dirt-producing activities (doing maintenance) and choose to act differently, whereupon healing has been accomplished and we are now 'cleaner' within.

What are the problems a person may experience? We can identify three categories of symptoms: behaviours, pain and dysfunction. Physical problems are usually the last place where a problem shows up. For example: it is well-known that long periods of stress can create nervous disorders, ulcers and heart attacks. Stress is the internal result of how a person responds to his or her environment.

Healing is the process in which someone or something becomes whole and complete: a broken leg restored, or a depression lifted. We are in health when our energy is flowing unimpeded within us. Constricted energy flow causes diminished well-being. Creating space for such energy to flow allows a person to restore balance and health. Conventional[1] treatments with drugs or surgery are effective methods to address emergencies, but may miss the multidimensional aspect of the patient, and rarely address deeply-embedded causes for troublesome symptoms. If we acknowledge the body's subtle energy systems, and view ourselves as complex beings of physical and non-physical substance layered within the physical, emotional, mental and spiritual dimensions, there might be more possibilities to find the real causes for experienced problems. Healing would then be the investigation and application of remedy or method that reach and affect the causes of those problems. When the cause is removed we may heal.

Health and Happiness - A State of Mind?

Our body is a composition of various tissues and organs in a delicate state of balance. Our body makes most of the components needed in cellular chemical factories. Some substances cannot be produced, like vitamins and minerals, and must be present within our food for us to remain healthy. Scientists have discovered that mental or emotional states are induced by biochemical processes in the body. When happy molecules (for example, endorphins) are released in the body, we feel really good, euphoric, and pain is reduced, but stress molecules (like adrenaline) are produced when we face danger or fear. Our body's emergency system releases stress hormones, such as adrenaline, as a response to perceived danger. It prepares us for immediate action.

Figure 117 A small raw piece of gemmy Prasiolite - the Cerebral Activator Stone. It is a green type of Amethyst helpful in the practice of gaining mastery of our brain function.

This is called "fight or flight response." Our normal reasoning mind is disengaged and emergency protocols overrule our behaviour. Researchers have also identified a spiritual molecule[2] (dimethyltryptamine). This psychoactive substance gives rise to extraordinary experiences and clairvoyance. This may be just a glimpse of what goes on within our body, but the question remains: how do we control our inner chemistry to reflect health and happiness? Can we affect our bodily production of certain critical substances?

By applying various subtle modalities in addition with training our body and mind, we may indeed affect an imbalance. Stimulating certain acupuncture points is known to influence the production of specific enzymes[3]. Ingesting Flower Remedies or Homeopathic medicines may address condition or mental-emotional states favourably. These remedies contain mostly the vibration of the medicine rather than physical components. Applying breath practices and yoga postures opens inner energy channels so the nutritious flow of energy can be restored. Internal negative reaction responses can be reversed with mind training. As a result, production of destructive stress molecules would not be engaged. An example of this occurs when we do not take a remark someone makes personally, and therefore do not react to it. We can stay present and happy instead. In the case where we can maintain such detachment we must by default be completely happy, at least in that area. Our immune system becomes strengthened and we are not so susceptible to foreign energies or entities such as toxins, viruses and other people's negativity. By studying our subtle anatomy we may discover where healing already is manifest:

Do we experience physical health? (Root centre)
Do we experience nurturing and fruitful relationships?
   (Sacral centre)
Do we experience abundance? (Navel centre)
Do we feel happy? (Solar Plexus)
Do we feel compassion for others? (Heart centre)
Do we feel joy? (Throat centre)
Do we have trust in ourself? (Brow centre)
Do we experience peace? (Crown centre)

Understanding Root Cause

Health, I propose, is an effect of balancing loss and accumulation of energies. When we lose energy we become depleted and weak. This may result in being un-grounded, confused or spaced out. When we have too much energy and cannot process it, we store it and thereby create pockets of energies in ourselves that sooner or later will erupt. This may create a short temper, uncontrollable rage, or bitterness. In the first case we let the energy be lost as parts of ourselves, such as soul fragments. To heal we

Figure 118 White Stellarbeam Calcite - The Alternative Realities Stone. The stellarbeam formation enhances its vibration and one may with its help transcend barriers to clear awareness.

must recover those parts. In the second case we must return to others (let go) what we took on, or in other words dispel the influence or parts of others. The source of an experienced problem resides either inside or outside of us. Inner causes include: our response patterns to real or imaginary events and our physical constitution. External causes include actions of others, the environment, and collective beliefs.

A problem (symptom, condition, or situation) might have several causes. For example: both dust and a cold can produce a stuffy nose. The body responds naturally to dust or infection by producing mucus to remove foreign material from the body. When a root cause for any problem is removed, the problem will "heal." For example, you awake from your afternoon picnic-blanket nap, to find that you are becoming wet. You discover that water is drizzling down on you. A sensible person would look around to see where the water was coming from (perhaps rain or someone's sprinkler system) and then move to a dry area. It takes a while to get dry again, but the problem is solved. To discover causes for things happening inside us follows a similar idea, but is ever so much harder to discern.

When certain 'stimuli' appear there are detrimental responses or reactions for some individuals only. Examples of stimuli are: smelling toxic dust, seeing an image, hearing emotionally-loaded words or being touched in certain ways. These activate previously imprinted patterns, which then produce problems (symptom, condition, or situation). Our conscious mind is usually not aware of this process. A remedy or action might work for one thing but not another, even though it was caused by the same thing. For example, a large open wound (physical symptom) must be dealt with differently than the feeling of being helpless (mental-emotional symptom). In the first case, the wound has to be cleaned, sewed up and dressed with adequate skill in order for it to heal. In the second case the person may have to learn to think and feel about himself or herself in a more constructive and empowered way, perhaps by engaging in therapy, spiritual practices or meditation. One wouldn't treat a wound by simply talking to it. To eliminate the cause we must find its location. In analyzing the above situation, we can propose that the wound and the feeling of helplessness may have been a result of a deeper pattern manifesting both physically and mental-emotionally, perhaps originating from a trauma. If this were the case, altering that deeper pattern could result in addressing both symptoms effectively, such that in the future, both are likely not to manifest again. The deepest-embedded imprint is the root cause. The person in this case might explore the decision to: *not trust my instinct* (because I was told this is not valid) > *therefore I do not need to pay attention* (because others will do it for me) + *take any initiative on my own* (as my decisions do not count). To change a response pattern we must trace the decision that created it. To do that we might need to go to the possible traumatic event that preceded our decision. When a person is ready to change such decisions, it literally changes his or her life. In our example above, both the physical wound and the emotional trauma still need time to integrate (heal). This person could perhaps work with a new program of: *"I trust myself to act."*

How Is Healing Accomplished?

Healing may manifest on one or more levels of our being. Healing of our deepest issues may be a complex process, but nevertheless attainable. Here, I like to propose some of the components involved. Obstacles are clearly doubt, blame, and denial, whereas the components of trust, love, forgiveness, letting-go, and trust make healing possible. Believing it is possible to heal is the starting point. If it were not so, we can only he helpless individuals waiting in suffering for death. Self-doubt is harmful to us. It sabotages our own ability to make decisions and act appropriately. Some believe that only a doctor can help them, then, only a doctor can help them. Other alternatives are then not possible. We can assist ourselves by embracing all forms of help available by trusting our decision to do so. Miracle healings are reported: cancers can go into remission and paralysed persons have walked again. Why not hold this option open? Healing becomes possible at the point when a person discovers his or her part in a problem. People, who focus on the mistakes and faults of others fail to recognize their own part of the equation. The fact may be that they see themselves mirrored in others. When people continually accuse others, they might be projecting their problem onto others. To blame others for our ills is hardly fruitful, as it puts us in a position of being a victim. Life then provides further challenges until the point when we have exhausted the possibility to blame others and outside phenomena for our problem.

If one were to look at a person's body, possessions and behaviour, what patterns are in effect would be revealed. A person's inner reality is manifesting outwardly as physical symptoms, clutter and behaviour. An emotionally-loaded letter is left unanswered; a childhood keepsake could not be given away. A person's present state is the result of what he or she has experienced[4]. Experiences dealt with appropriately are integrated in his or her being, and do not cause problems. Instead, they are the source of wisdom. Anything unresolved is stored somewhere embedded in the body; it may cause problems or issues experienced later in life. Such areas act as a magnet to others with the same or opposite issues. When one layer is complete, the next layer is ready to be addressed. When the mental-emotional baggage has been cleared the physical counterpart usually follows suit.

To forgive is really to let go of the ideas we had about how it is supposed to be, thus releasing reactions of disappointment and unhappiness[5]. A person who entertains harmful thoughts is clearly suffering. Why do this to ourselves? A person who understands this can forgive and heal sooner. We can see this in persons who suddenly lost a lot of weight and stayed healthy.

They simply let go of "extra baggage." Persons with a lot of clutter were able to clear it out as a result of inner clearing. Asking a friend about her healing (a writing project), she said: *As for life, it is proceeding, and I have no ability to define or label anything right now. I am writing and not writing, but I am feeling so much brewing in me - it is a great feeling, the pressure on the dam is growing each moment and I anticipate the burst very soon. I seem to be opening in new and profound ways, stepping outside 'my box' a bit more every day and feeling - on new and more expanded levels. All the while attempting to live my, quote, "regular" life, very odd indeed, I eagerly welcome the dissolution of it all, whatever that would look like. I suppose it looks like heaven on earth, huh?*

Wanting to 'understand why' may block healing. It is easier perhaps to 'let go', if there is understanding, but holding on to the idea of understanding may instead provide an obstacle to change. When the 'letting go' is complete, usually understanding comes naturally. It might be difficult to see a great challenge as something good at first, but afterwards we might see its gifts. Integrated experiences make us stronger, and we may have learnt a new skill.

A person, who loves deeply, creates a field from his or her heart that has the capacity to transform anyone in contact with it. We may experience this by holding a newborn baby. Love is an emotion, a type of vibrational energy. Being in love feels wonderful and inside the body happy molecules are released. As long as the object for the love meets our expectation, we remain in this state. However, this personal love is not permanent. A masterful person[6] can intentionally generate so-called 'non-personal' love, which is essential to healing. This is the particularly nutritious life-force that exists as the manifestation of divinity in everything. This force, I feel, is part of the 'glue' that brings physical matter into living form.

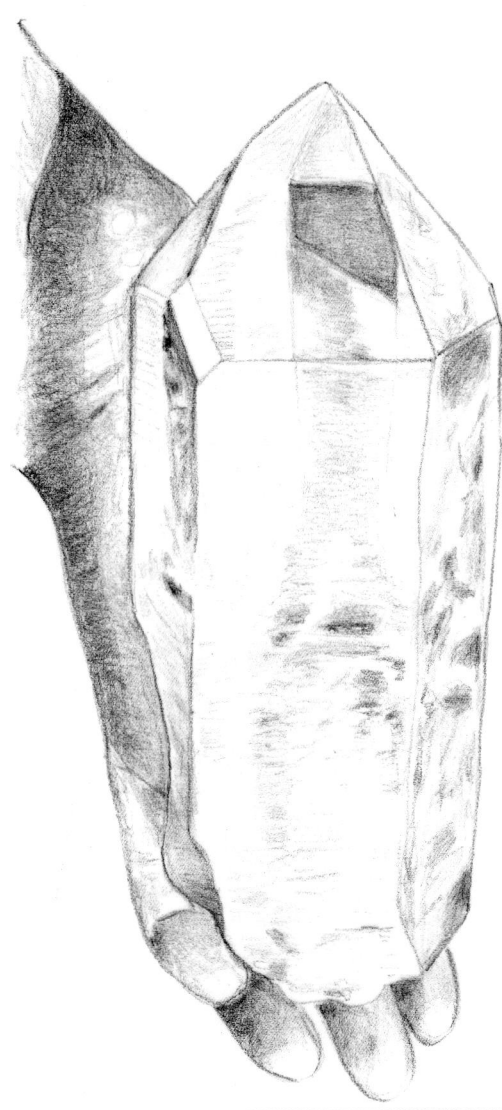

Figure 119 Time Link Crystal[7]. In meditation and healing, the hea-lee can gaze along the small ribbon-like face to the left of the main face at the top to travel to the past.

Accepting Healing

Being ready to begin with, is essential; otherwise, we would only do another's bidding and not our own. A Crystal Healing Graduate reports her experience with healing sessions for others:

Accepting Healing - People who agree to receive versus people who seek to receive. As a practicing crystal healing facilitator I have had the great opportunity to assist in the healing process of others. Through this experience, I have come to realize that the healing experience for both the receiver and the facilitator is different depending on the expectations of the "healee." With a desire to practice the crystal healing art, I have asked family members and friends to be participants. They are often unfamiliar with what the healing process involves, and after explanation seem to agree only as a favour to me, as it is not something they would seek to do for themselves. These are people who agree to receive healing energy. I have also been asked to facilitate a healing environment by others who are on a personal journey to self-discovery. They are often knowledgeable about vibrational healing and have a positive belief in the outcomes that can be produced. These are people who seek to receive healing energy.

People who agree to receive a crystal healing session comment on how relaxed they felt during and after the process, and because of this response they are often willing to be participants again if asked. When asked about their intentions for healing, they are vague and non-contributory, leaving me unsure sometimes on which crystal layout to do. It is during the healing process that I, as the facilitator, have become aware of the degree of energy exchange that occurs. The participant is often guarded in their responses to questions designed to motivate healing on a deeper level than a feeling of relaxation. They find questions regarding how their physical body is feeling irritating, because they just want to relax. The amount of energy exchange, though definitely present, is like a night light drawing energy from an electrical outlet – not very much. After the healing

Components of Healing

Client. A person who requests healing; another term is "healee." This is a person who takes responsibility for his or her life and requests personal services like healing in the progress of resolving existing challenges. (We do not use the term 'patient' as it refers to a person who is in the care of an authority, like a doctor or medical professional, who assume responsibility for his or her patient's diagnosis, treatment and the prescribing of pharmaceuticals, etc.)

Facilitator. This is a person who assists the client in his or her healing; another term is 'healer'. The facilitator holds space and focuses the work towards the client's intent. The facilitator needs to be centered and detached of outcome in an impersonal way. It is always the client who is 'doing' the healing. A person who assumes the role of facilitator, or healer assisting healing, must act impeccably so as not to create challenges for himself/herself and the client.

Symptom. This is what the client experiences and decides to address. Symptoms include: physical, emotional and mental conditions such as pain, illnesses, dysfunctions, accidents, relationship issues, depression, confusion, poverty, abuse, addiction, etc. or, in other words, anything that is perceived as harmful or unwanted in the client's view.

Cause. If the cause of any symptom is correctly addressed, the symptom should disappear. A cause is a thought pattern (program) that a person may have. Such patterns attract accidents, trauma, illness or invading energy forms. (From a cosmic perspective, it may be that individuals are writing such program themselves before birth, so that the lessons from it are achieved in the coming life-time).

Guidance. As described earlier, each person is equipped with non-physical guides (or guardian angels) as well as a High Self. When clients become aware of this connection, healing is easier as they can do more work for themselves without outside help.

Tools. Any remedy, technique or modality can be seen as a tool for healing. Crystals are seen as tools in this way.

session I have a sense that something of a healing nature has occurred but am not precisely sure what. In contrast, people who have asked me to facilitate a crystal healing session for them tend to be open to providing feedback about what their body is feeling, often unsolicited. They freely share their emotional experiences, both past and present and the energy exchange is like a huge marquis sign with hundreds of light bulbs illuminating a message that cannot be mistaken. I, as the facilitator, receive an intense confirmation of my abilities as a clairsentient in that I am able to intuit, more easily, energy fluctuations in the bodies and therefore focus more intently on healing that is most pertinent to the healing receiver.

These observations became evident to me when I facilitated a crystal healing session for a friend of mine named P. P is a person who has been on a healing journey to becoming breast cancer-free – twice. She has used alternative healing methods only and has been success-ful both times. She is knowledgeable about vibrational healing and has a tremendous belief in its power. Before the session, P made some comments about her intentions for healing that assisted me to eas-ily discern the type of crystal layout to use. During our 'balancing' healing session, P offered freely what her physical body was feeling, describing pulsating energy flow through her body from her heart down to just below her right great toe (which is the reflex that cor-responds to the heart). I was able to detect intense heat several feet from above her heart chakra. After the healing session, P relayed a very personal emotional experience that she had been avoiding pro-cessing for several years. She felt that the healing session had assisted her to let it go and to forgive the person involved. She was emotion-al, but felt a sense of needed catharsis. During the healing session, I felt overwhelmed yet joyful by the energy that was flowing through my body. After P and I parted, I felt like I was 'walking on air'.

I have learned that regardless of the person and their expectations, healing does occur. I believe that the healee can receive as much or as little healing energy as they are willing. And so it remains that as a healing facilitator, I am the electrical cord that healing receivers can plug into no matter how much energy they are willing to accept at the time.   *By Paula McClintok*

The Healing Session

Like an Agatha Christie novel, we can play a detective's game. The inner detective can find clues and hunches of what is going on. Find the scene of the crime, look at the victim, what has happened, look for evidence and clues, trace the 'guilty' parties, confront and arrest them, present the facts, solve the mystery, place the whole scenario in front of the judge, have a trial, issue judgment, hear the guilty repent and restore honour.

The crystals are like the detective's looking glass. They will amplify small treads of evidence for examination. The client is the detective and the facilitator is the detective's assistant who asks the right question, or brings the right tool at the appropriate time. The victim is the acting archetype ego played out. The guilty parties are the decisions/programs/response/behaviours rather than outside situations or people. Others may have acted on and attracted themselves to the client's thought forms, causing trauma, accidents or dis-ease. The trial is the hearing of the evidence, the sentence client's decision of new boundaries, retiring discordant beliefs and letting go. The term of 'imprisonment' is then over.

In a healing session clients may encounter fragments of traumatic memories that do not seem to pertain to the present life but to earlier lifetimes. The past may be accessed as in 'past life' experiences. The process may involve the following steps: tracing an issue back to its creation and integrating past events causing trauma. In the Appendix, I have included more details of what a healing session may include (see page 548).

I will now describe in more detail how the facilitator can assist a client in releasing blocked energy. Apart from applying Crystal Modalities, it is done with the *Dual Flow Breath* and training our *Healing Hands*.

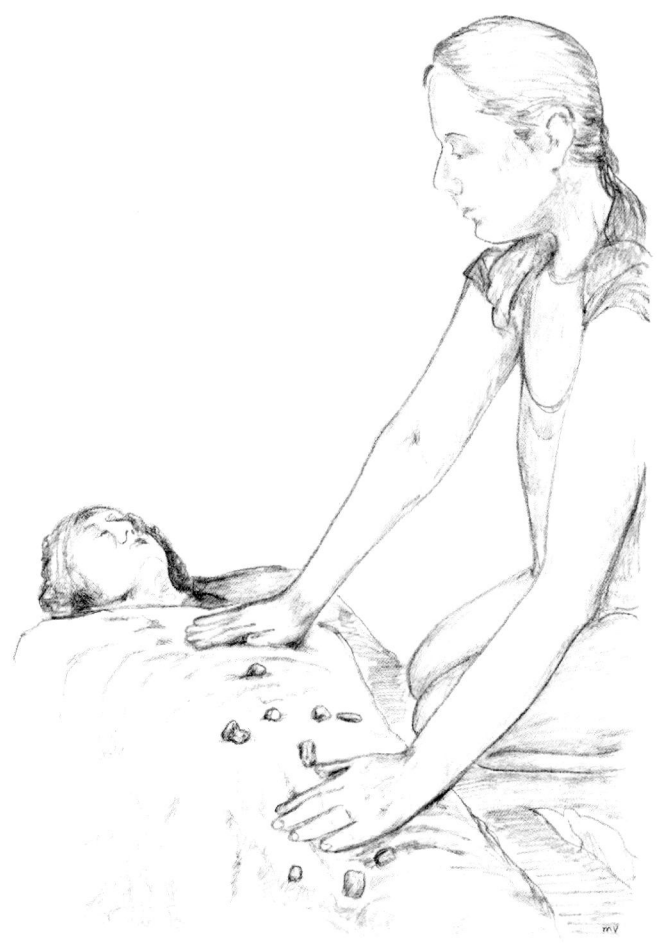

Figure 120 Laying on of Hands in a crystal healing session. Energy is directed through the hands with a special technique called the Dual Flow Breath. The Crystals act as lenses for this energy and may tune or draw out misaligned energies. It is by the recipient's intent, the capacity to receive and let go, that makes healing possible. The facilitator holds the space for healing and must maintain her loving focus during the entire session as the healee may access intimate and vulnerable spaces.

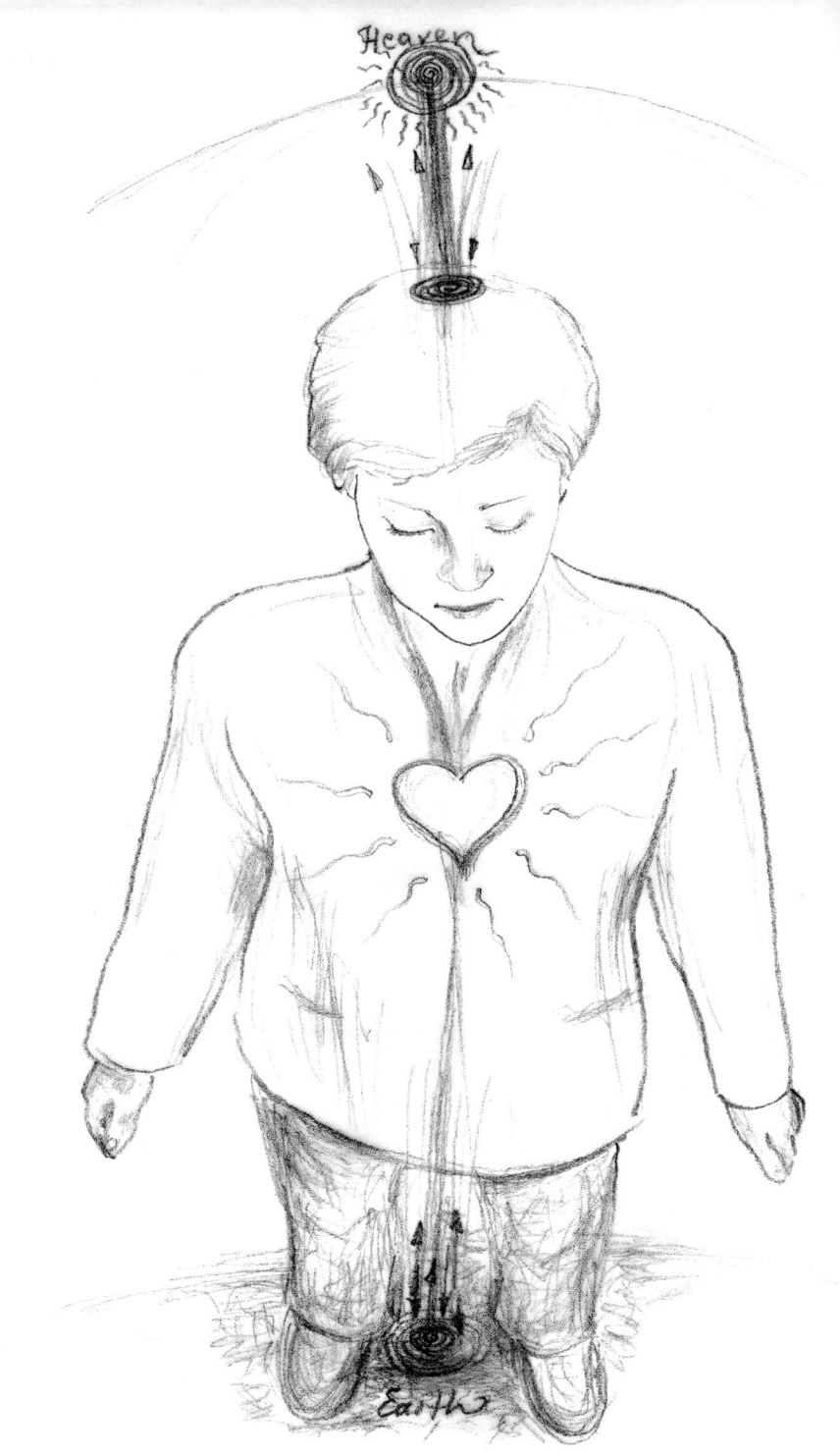

Healing Hands - Opening Our Energy Channels

To assist another person as a facilitator, we may channel energy to assist him or her. In the same way as we water and care for small seedlings until they have enough strength in themselves to grow, we may assist another seeking our help. He or she is doing the "growing," and we provide the juice to do so. It is best to have a teacher[7] to accurately show how this is done. This practice provides you with tools to prepare.

Why: In the wish to assist others, we are training to become compassionate. We are also learning how to give without selfish expectation. In return, we receive great healing each time we engage in the practice as it opens us up.

Prerequisite: Hematite Grid, Attune to Guidance, Dual Flow Breath.

How to begin: Place yourself in a Hematite Grid (visualized or actual). Practice your *Dual Flow Breath* several times until you feel completely centred. Attune to your heart and the connection with your guidance. Imagine you are a perfect and clear crystal that channels the pure heart energy given from source. No thinking is required as it does not occur on a mental level, but from the core of your being. In the physical body we can visualise our central channel and our heart.

Building a connection with our hands: When your heart connection is firmly established, rub your hands together rapidly until they heat up. Then separate your hands slowly and attempt to feel the built-up energy collected between your hands. Practice this until you feel the energy clearly, then move to the next step.

Create a small energy ball: Inhale into your heart and exhale from your heart out to the palms of your hands. Here visualize and feel the build-up of energy. You can hold an actual small crystal Quartz sphere between your palms for a moment to get an idea

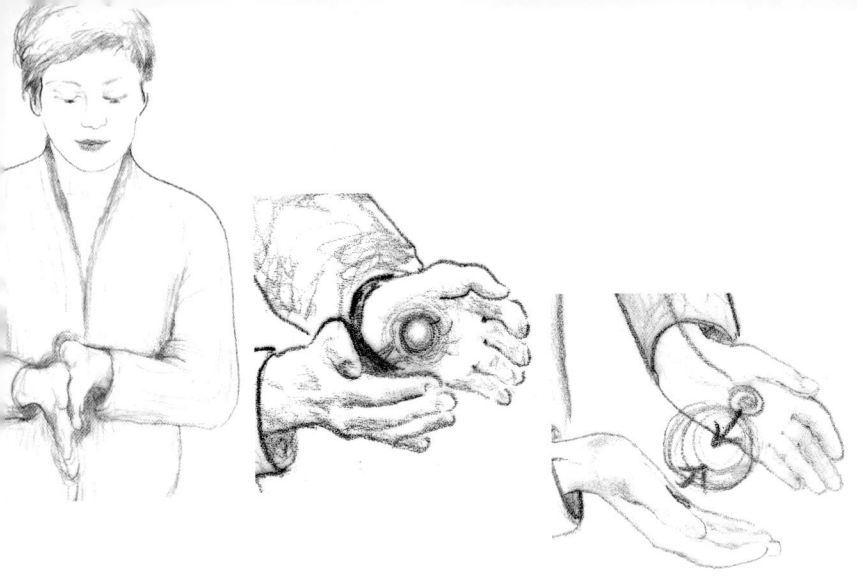

of how it feels. Then place your palms together again rubbing briskly, and then separate the palms. Each time feel the build-up of an energy ball. Inhale and exhale energy into this ball until it is brimming with energy. Then place your hands on your heart (or other area of your body) and let the energy release into you. Notice how that feels. Continue this practice until you can manage a large energy ball, compact the energy with your breath, and then release it into an area of pain or discomfort. Notice how that affects you. If you encounter problems to do this, I invite you to write to me about it.

Maintenance: Practice your *Dual Flow Breath* and *Healing Hands* every day and when you think of it. That attention will serve you when you are in an actual healing session. It is rather a life-style, as you then are connected more often with your own source.

Effects: By doing this practice, you learn how to manage and release energy[8].

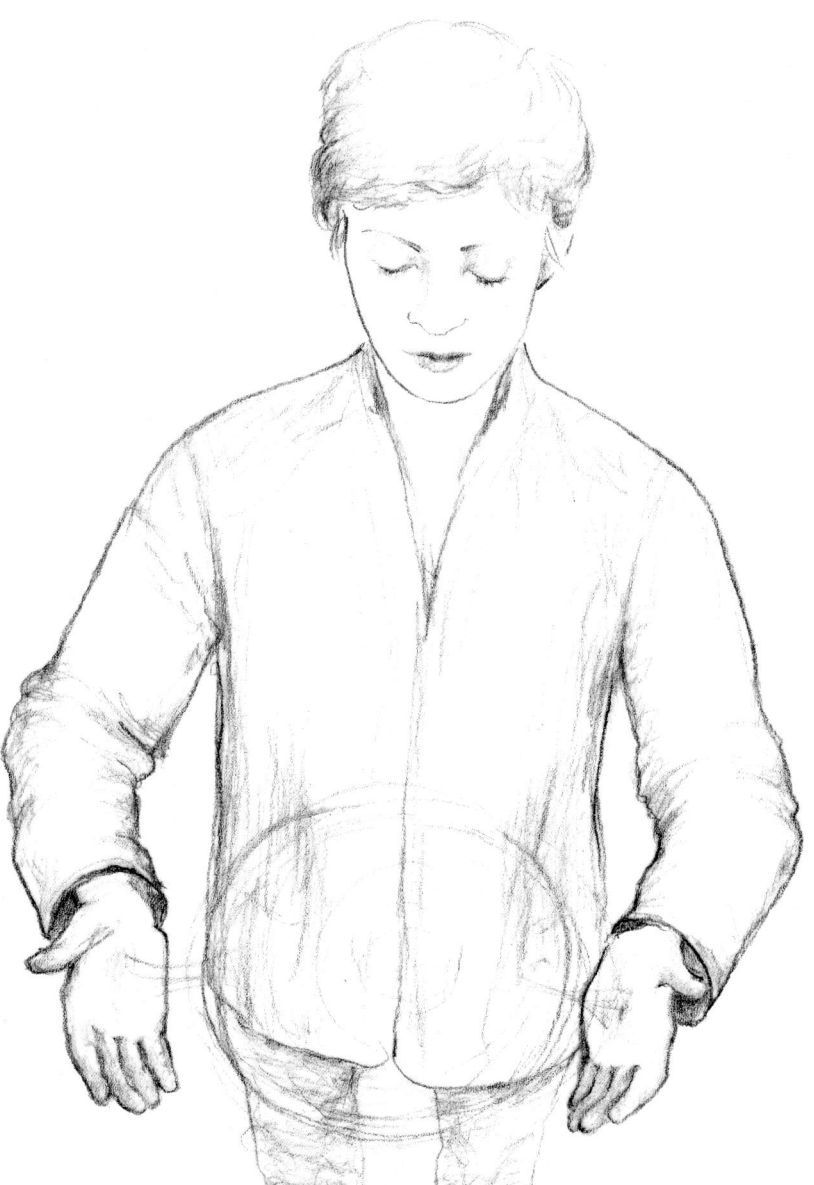

Figure 121 Healing Hands, the drawing shows how a healer can collect energy between the hands and use it for the purpose of assisting oneself or another person. The hands are in essence an extension of the heart chakra, and it is through the heart that life-force energy can be made to flow.

Remote Crystal Healing

Distance Healing works in the same way as when the client is present physically. The same steps and layouts are applied. For the facilitator it requires good focus and steady intention in order to be able to assist. The recipient must have given his or her consent either verbally or on the soul level. One may advise caution against 'sending' people energy without their permission. Distance healing is ideal when learning healing between students, as it is an excellent way to learn how to tune in with the healee. Afterwards one can communicate what had transpired and thus learn greatly about ones capability.

Distance healing for a dying person, a Crystal Healing Graduate shares her story: *I have been drawn to hospice care in the last days of a patient's life. Long-distance healing and crystal healing work with a client through this life to the next is a unique way of assisting that client to come to terms with his or her death. As a Registered Massage Therapist, I feel that it is a unique expression of hospice work. It is also a way for us as therapists to understand our very special relationship to the dying client. It is imperative, however, that I do my own inner work: that I learn to live consciously, learn to forgive myself and others, and to learn to love unconditionally before I can ask that of my clients.*

Sometimes my work brings me to a greater understanding of the human connection we all have one to another, and this was even more so in the case of Bonnie. I was called back into Bonnie's life shortly before her death. She had terminal cancer, was in immense pain, and afraid even to talk about death. In the few days that I had with Bonnie, we talked about the use of crystals and how they could help, about the end of life being like going through another door of the house and about her fear of the palliative care unit. We also discovered that we had gone to the same school and been in the same club at high school. The concepts of crystal healing, chakras, higher planes of consciousness and auras were all new ideas to Bonnie, but she was open and even eager to explore this new field of experience. I felt off-balance, recognizing as I did that Bonnie had been in my life briefly when we were teenagers, and that I had suddenly been called back into her life for the conclusion.

It was important for me to be very grounded and to make sure that I stayed neutral and in the Light before treating her. I came to understand that each meaningful relationship in our lives-- and perhaps all significant contacts -- have spiritual cord attachments from the past. Spiritual cords may be positive, but also may act as "hooks" we have in each other that create harmful co-dependencies and prevent us from releasing and forgiving old hurts. These cords are also the hooks we have between each other that connect us to past patterns. These are the same patterns that we strive to release during this lifetime in order to ascend to higher consciousness. The place where we have connected with another soul and need to repair the harm done (either real or perceived), forgive and accept and give unconditional love and release, is a roadblock on our spiritual path.

With Bonnie, who was reluctant to say the "D" word with reference to her own dying, I learned many things. One was that as a caregiver and therapist I had to resist my natural inclination to want to "fix things." I could not save her life and did not want to hasten her death. I had to deal with the conflicted feelings of her family and friends who wanted her suffering to end but her life to continue. I realized that we often want to find immediate solutions or rush through what we are doing, especially in this age where dealing with the dying makes so many people uncomfortable. For Bonnie (who was dying and in the palliative ward) I wrote down my intention to clear her chakras on all levels and for a long-distance healing.

Starting with meditation and prayer I asked for guidance in laying out the stones and in the meditation I used the Angelic Team Prayer for release of foreign energies/entities[9]:

"I call forth: my Angelic Team of True Protection and my Inner and Higher conscious Self. I ask that: all entities, harmful energy forms, destructive thought forms, soul fragments and any being harmful to me be removed from my body, auric field, personal space, property, dwellings and where I am in each moment, and be escorted to their rightful place in the Light. For the Highest Good of All, So Be It."

As well, I used song in prayer that was appropriate for assisting her spirit to move to the next plane. All crystals in the room were smudged and cleared.

After asking guidance to assist in the choosing of the crystals, I placed the crystals on the table and I sat in meditation with Danburite in each hand. There was a struggle within me, knowing that the sadness I felt and which I needed to acknowledge would not benefit Bonnie in any way – if anything it would prevent me from clear and conscious facilitation of her healing. This was truly an exercise in setting myself aside so that I could be a clear channel for her spirit healing. In an odd way, I knew that by doing the healing I would hasten her death by releasing the cords that were tying her to the earth plane, but that not facilitating the healing would have been worse on all levels.

I have now realized that my being brought back into Bonnie's life has meant that we had strong past Karmic connections and that they needed to be cleared. The first cord connected to my heart and I could feel it in the right atrium. I unwound it very slowly. Instead of severing the cord, an act which felt very aggressive to me, I felt that there needed to be a gentle pulling so that the whole cord could be removed and that there would not be any parts of it left. I saw the cord as a pink opal and garnet rope and I saw a vibrantly-coloured, pink-beaded spider. The cord felt like the spider's web that needed to be unwound and returned to Bonnie. Then I saw the beads as pink opal and pearl being sent back to Bonnie – waiting for

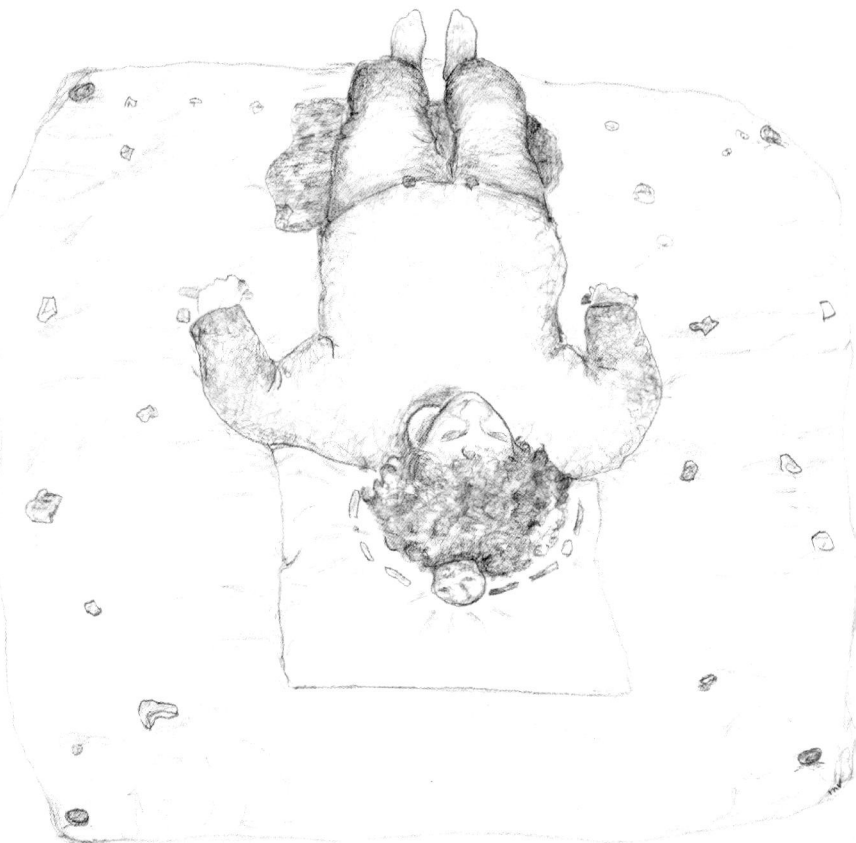

Figure 122 Extended Layout from the Intermediate Level Crystal Healing. The healee has selected all her stones pertaining the issue she wants resolved. The healer has then placed each stone in the pattern proscribed by the healee. Up to 1-200 stones or more can be used in an extended healing. The purpose for the extended layout is to place the emphasis on the healee and her own participation to resolve her current situation.

her to take up the slack in the rope and sending it along until at last I could feel no heart attachment – no hook.

After dowsing, I knew that there was another cord from my womb to her womb and I installed a mother Cathedral Lightbrary into my womb and began to unhook that cord. This cord was beaded with small clear quartz crystals. All through this process, both for two days, I repeated the prayer "Ho'oponopono," which translates to "I am sorry, please forgive me, I love you." This prayer[10], above all others, helps me explore the concept of unconditional love. It is a phrase that trips off the tongue lightly but is more difficult to feel, conceptualize and understand -- yet it is our truck and trade. I understood at a soul level that there had been a hurt between us at some point in the past. I could feel in my body and soul "I am sorry, please forgive me," but I had to sit back and think about what love really means, whether it was personal, or impersonal love without conditions. The original intention was to clear the chakras on all levels and release any ties that were binding Bonnie to this earth realm. I felt blockages in the solar plexus and heart areas and worked with double-terminated quartz crystals to clear those areas. The treatment was a success – the client let go and passed from earth realm to spirit shortly after the treatment was completed.

In summary, for myself, I understand that I do not need to be physically present to be there for another person. I had visited my client physically but also conducted crystal healing for her either through meditation and long-distance healing. There is in our culture the sense that we need to be physically present – to witness death- but the spirit has no such preconceived notion. There is no separation in spirit, so we can connect from one dimension to another as easily as reaching out a hand to our neighbour. So let us give thanks to Bonnie and wish her joyful ascension to spirit.

My work with assisting friends and clients with their physical deaths and ascension to spirit has shown me that crystal healing can be a positive healing experience for all involved: patient, family and healer. Crystal healing for the dying, however, must be predicated on a clear understanding of its necessary technical and spiritual components, a respect and sensitivity for patient, family, friends and healer, and above all, a sense of joy that transcends bereavement.

By Pamela Polley

Figure 123 Black Kyanite - The Boundary Stone - may help in putting an end to spiritual confusion and invasions of foreign energies by working with clear, personal intention.

Ethics of a Healing Facilitator

Before entering into a client-facilitator relationship any facilitator should evaluate[11] if, in fact, he or she is able to assist the healee, and has addressed what can be dealt with in a healing session. The facilitator should be attentive and act professionally. And to become a facilitator we must also do our own healing work first. Preparation practices can include: grounding, centring, protection, guidance, dual flow breath, installations, crystal orb breath & visualization.

What can be addressed in a crystal healing session? Basically one can address any problem or issue a person may seek a solution to. We may only work with situations regarding our client and not other persons involved. If someone is seriously ill under the care of another health care practitioner, he or she should be consulted. Not everything can be addressed in a session offered by a qualified healer. Some things cannot be healed in a session by you as a facilitator; it is not up to you, but to the client.

We should listen to the problem or situation that is sought to be remedied and help the client formulate an intention for the session. If a client is willing to commit to address a problem, the Crystal Healing Facilitator may provide helpful assistance in working to correct energy barriers and blocks. If a client asks about help in one area, but you can see there are a number of other things going on, in this case you have to abide with what the client is asking for. The other issues may reveal themselves in the healing process. Posing objective questions is better than informing someone about what we think. Begin to work with the obvious, such as: relieve the pain, improve a relationship or manifest abundance, etc. Sorting out the 'real' problem and its cause is part of the homework. In the process a healee can uncover layers and layers of undiscovered territory within, and as well states of happiness not felt before. The facilitator may help the client to trace and reprogram a particular belief relevant to the client's intent. By the active participation of the client he or she is in the director's seat and can take responsibility for his or her life in a better way. If clients resist looking at deeper causes for their suffering, beyond suggestion, there is not much point in attempting to convince them to adhere to a protocol you may feel effective. All one can ultimately do is model health and sanity for others and be generous with time and energy, when appreciated.

Do not generally share your own visions, images, messages or personal ideas about what the healing was about. Instead listen and ask questions relating to the experience of the healee, who is gaining skills to heal with your assistance. Do not interpret a clients' experiences or make a promise of certain results. You should under no circumstances prescribe or pronounce diagnosis. Do not offer your opinions on what happened to them in the past or pass judgement. Teach clients to do healing for themselves.

To assist another person the facilitator must have a sincere interest to serve and feel compassion. Healing should never be done primarily for money. Skills should include knowledge and experience of the modalities provided. He or she should provide benefit for the recipient, follow ethical behaviour and be honest to what his or her abilities are both verbally and in written material. Fees must be clearly stated and preferably be adjusted for 'low income' clients. It is of benefit to encourage clients to heal sooner rather than creating a dependency on your services. The facilitator should be transparent about what the provided modalities involve and what the client can expect.

A professional facilitator should keep clear personal boundaries with clients. Personal involvements will likely contaminate the healing process. It is ok to do some practices with friends or family with their consent when in training, but it is not advisable to facilitate deeper issues with loved family members, as one cannot easily stay objective. A centred person is less swayed by fear. He or she stays present to what actually is going on and can deal with the present circumstances better. An example of this was a refrigerator repair man coming to our home in the country; he completely ignored our dog, who always gives any visitor a big show of sound and teeth. What this man did was to stay completely outside of any reaction to the dog's protective behaviour; he didn't even look at the dog. The dog got tired of barking and lolled away without further bother. In this case this man removed himself from being a target of biting, so he could do what he came for: repairing our fridge.

Appropriate behaviour includes: showing respect, listening carefully to the client's situation and maintaining personal boundaries. The healer's appearance should be professional, clean and tidy (hair should be tied back so as not to interfere with session), and hold an open and clear mind.

Obstacles for facilitation are: distraction, tiredness, inappropriate personal relationship with client, aversion, doubt or fear. For a highly-realized person, it might be easy to simply intend something and then perhaps it would manifest. For 'conventional' individuals, our intentions may not be as focused, as distractions often afflicts us. Try going to the kitchen for a spoon to stir your coffee with. On the way, we might encounter other people, the laundry pile, demanding kids, a hungry dog, or a phone call, and then half an hour later we've totally forgotten about the spoon and our coffee is now cold.

Immersed in a constant battle of thought forms generated by oneself and others, one could say we are living in the midst of a thick mental-emotional soup, potentially obscuring our clarity as to the how and why of our condition.

Summary

Healing is a process of cleansing and repair in which one may become whole. By opening constricted pathways within our subtle bodies we can help our energy to flow again, this is the basis for health. Our being includes physical, emotional, mental and spiritual layers. Pain, illness and dysfunction are symptoms that might be addressed in a healing session. Health and happiness is proposed to be a state of mind and the result of a delicate biochemical balance that may be negatively influenced by internal stress levels. On the other hand, training our mind with support of vibrational modalities, can be used to promote health. To correctly address certain problems it is vital to have the correct understanding about their root causes. Locating a cause helps address the problem. Healing is accomplished when a person addresses his or her part in creating the problem. Doubt, denial and blame are detrimental to healing but love, forgiveness, letting go and trust facilitate healing. Acceptance plays a vital part in whether or not healing takes place. A Healing session can be seen as a detective investigation, where the symptoms are seen as clues to healing. Crystal Healing is a vibrational modality using crystals as lenses for intention of healing. By placing crystals on the body's energy centres, the chakras, a person can balance his or her energy and thus begin to correct misalignments. Within a healing session several components can be addressed: balancing of subtle energy organs, tracing the source of a problem and integration of lessons presented. In a remote healing session, the facilitator is working with the client at a separate location than the client. Two case stories are presented to illustrate how acceptance for healing gives far better healing results, and how a remote crystal healing for a dying person facilitated completion both for the healer and the healee. Ethical considerations for effective facilitation are also discussed.

Practice:
Healing Hands - for opening our channels to energy

Crystal Spas

Embraced by Wisdom-Love,
I see my true self

A 'Crystal Spa' is an energetic chamber of crystal vibration that can be created anywhere. Essentially it is an accessible intentional crystal grid. Sometimes treatment with a crystal locally on the body does not have the desired effect. It is within the practitioner's intention that we may find a solution.

To access the intention we need to integrate, and the whole body should be synchronized. To unify ourselves the Crystal Spa treatment offers a solution. Embracing the entire body within selected vibrations has been immensely valuable in the development of deepening knowledge, as well as for health. By creating a crystal spa, one may reap the benefits in the same way as if one were to immerse one's self in a pool or hot spring. It acts broadly on the entire body. My experience has been that of rejuvenation, relaxation and clarity, in times of unspecified challenge and stress. To work best, one has to approach it as a series of treatments or sessions. This is an inexpensive and joyful way of receiving treatment in your private space, which usually needs no outside facilitator. Use each spa in the order presented, before you move on to the next one, for best results.

Figure 124 Yin Fire Wave Spa. This is how the energies joined together and appeared while I was being inside the grid.

These are the four main Crystal Spas that have been given:

1) Yin-Fire Wave - restoration
2) Crystal Soul Cave - navel re-connection
3) Heart Tone - heart awakening
4) Mind Presence Spa - joining head and heart

Yin-Fire Wave Spa - Restoration

Why: To begin healing we may have no idea of where to start. This Spa appeared in response to my prayer for rejuvenation and release of mental stress. It helps to restore and rejuvenate the body and emotional system when one has been exposed to periods of stress.

Crystals: Raw Rosequartz and Selenite plus Pyritized Ammonite and a Haematoid Quartz Laser Wand. (A Pyrite, tumbled Hematite and a regular Laser Quartz Wand may be used as well.)

How to begin: Prepare space on the floor with a thick blanket and a sheet on top, with the stones placed in a wide oval that would enclose the person when lying down. Have a warm scarf to cover yourself if needed. The stones I was guided to use were: raw Rosequartz and Selenite wands (at least 12 pieces each) and in addition a Pyritized Ammonite at the top, and a Haematoid Quartz Laser at the feet. I visualized a Hematite grid with four Hematites around the entire space. Feeling immensely tired and aching all over, from carrying many boxes of rocks, I was dying to dive in. I had no idea what this arrangement would accomplish,

Figure 125 Stones for the Yin-Fire Wave Spa with a grid of raw Rose Quartz and Selenite wands for restoration and rejuvenation. Simply place the stones in an oval grid large enough for you to lie down within. Then breathe relaxed and let all your worries and troubles vanish from your being.

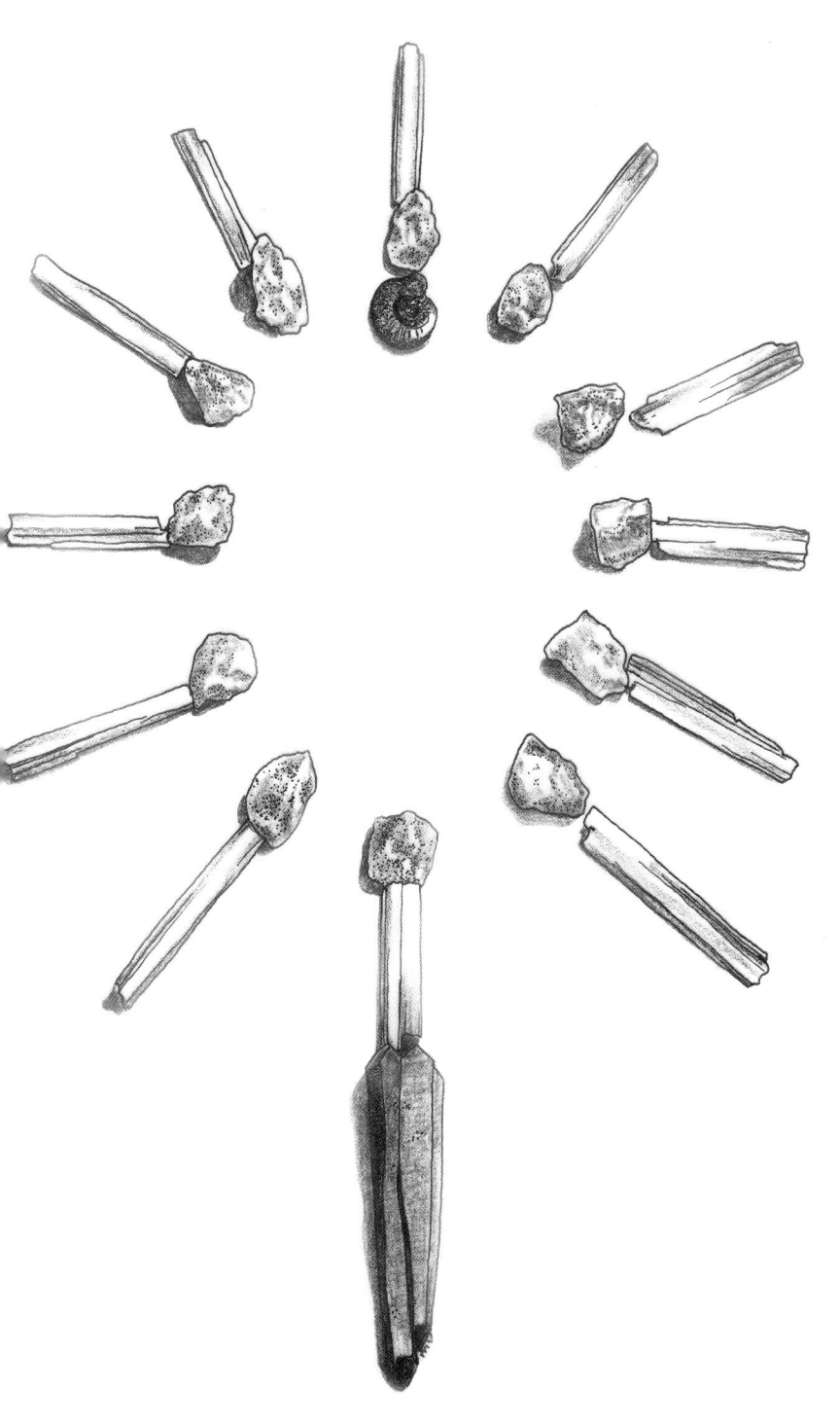

but I listened and prepared it as directed by my guidance.

Effects: I placed myself inside of the *Yin-Fire Spa* and discovered first a grounding sensation along the inside of my legs from big toe to perineum on both sides. Then I put my focus on the pyrite-ammonite above my crown, but moved it to my forehead for greater comfort. My system started to recharge and I felt better all over as my grounding improved and the energies began to move along my body. I then began to relax and found myself connecting with all of the Selenites placed as a starburst around me. Tuning with them made me expand and open up spaces inside. This occurred within the first minute or so of being in this Crystal Spa. Then without notice a soft wave of Rose energy welled up around me. All at once the stones sort of beamed at me, asking me to receive and relax. I was surprised and grateful for this gift. It felt like being immersed in a sea of gentle Yin-Fire. My aches and pains washed away as I stayed clear and present, just placing myself in the hands of the Spa Devas. I could have remained there forever, but I was prompted to complete the session after about 20 minutes. My whole being had become clearer and my tiredness had vanished.

Maintenance: I left the grid undisturbed on the floor, and continued to use this Crystal Spa every evening after work for about 2 1/2 weeks. It was my life-saver.

Crystal Care: I smudged the area and the crystals carefully before and after each session.

Crystal Soul Cave Spa - Navel Re-connection

Why: This is a way to connect to the navel centre and the intelligence we have there. When the navel centre is engaged we are better able to integrate with normal physical life.

Crystals: Tourmaline in its golden brown form is called *Dravite* (the ones I used here came from Nepal, but one may find great Dravite from Australia as well). Dravite is used in this Soul-Cave Spa together with Citrine and Black Tourmaline.

How to start: Prepare the Spa by surrounding it with a Hematite Grid (visualized) then add the 6 Black Tourmalines in the corners and above and below. Add the Dravites as a star burst in-between, emanating inwards and sideways. Then add the natural or tumbled Citrine to join the circle radiating outwards. I was curious why I had to use Dravite, but it became clear as I entered. I felt deeply grounded and safe within this Spa, cocooned in a way that stopped my brain from thinking. I just sort of floated downwards into a safe deep space. It was dark

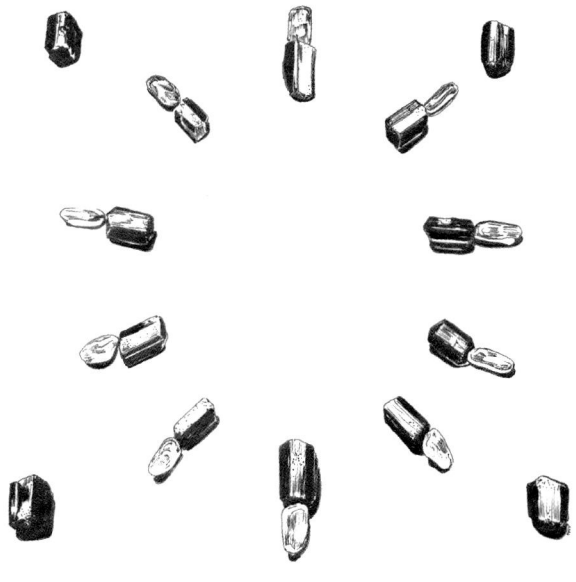

Figure 126 Crystal Soul Cave Spa for Navel re-connection. Crystals are: golden Dravite, black Tourmaline and gemmy Citrine.

but at the same time bright with subtle light. My navel area was distinctly worked on. I wasn't exactly sure how, but definitely the energy was shifting around my entire belly. I tried to figure it out afterwards because, as I mentioned, I couldn't think too much. An intelligence beam beyond me gave me an image of a cave where my soul retreated. There I sensed I might have continuing work to do. I visited my Soul Cave several times in the first week of practice.

Effects: The belly area held for me many imprints relating to self-worth, dignity and perhaps unconscious shame. What amazed me was that the process was not related to any thinking, but to energies moving very gently. There was no emotionality or release, as can happen frequently in crystal work. Instead, other levels of my being were accessed and tuned. Afterwards I thought that I had neglected my navel centre too long, and I wondered how that could be remedied. The answer came as a series of promptings about the use of energy. A person can use his or her energy and power in a variety of ways; some ways are more or less harmful or wasteful. Other people can be adversely affected by the energy we put out. Normally, we are not conscious of how we use our precious inner fire. Conscious use nurtures our organs and our bodily functions toward health. By giving attention to our navel and our 'Soul Cave' we may become aware of inner channels and healthy use of subtle energies.

The mystic and elusive navel is important for any spiritual attainment. Virochana Khalsa[1] states:

"Without vitality of the navel and what it commands, spiritual development of the physical body is only a fantasy."

Figure 127 Crystal Spa chamber laid out using the Crystal Soul Cave stones. If possible, let the stones remain for several days or weeks, until you are complete and ready for the next spa. It sets an energetic pattern to the space it is in, as well as supporting you.

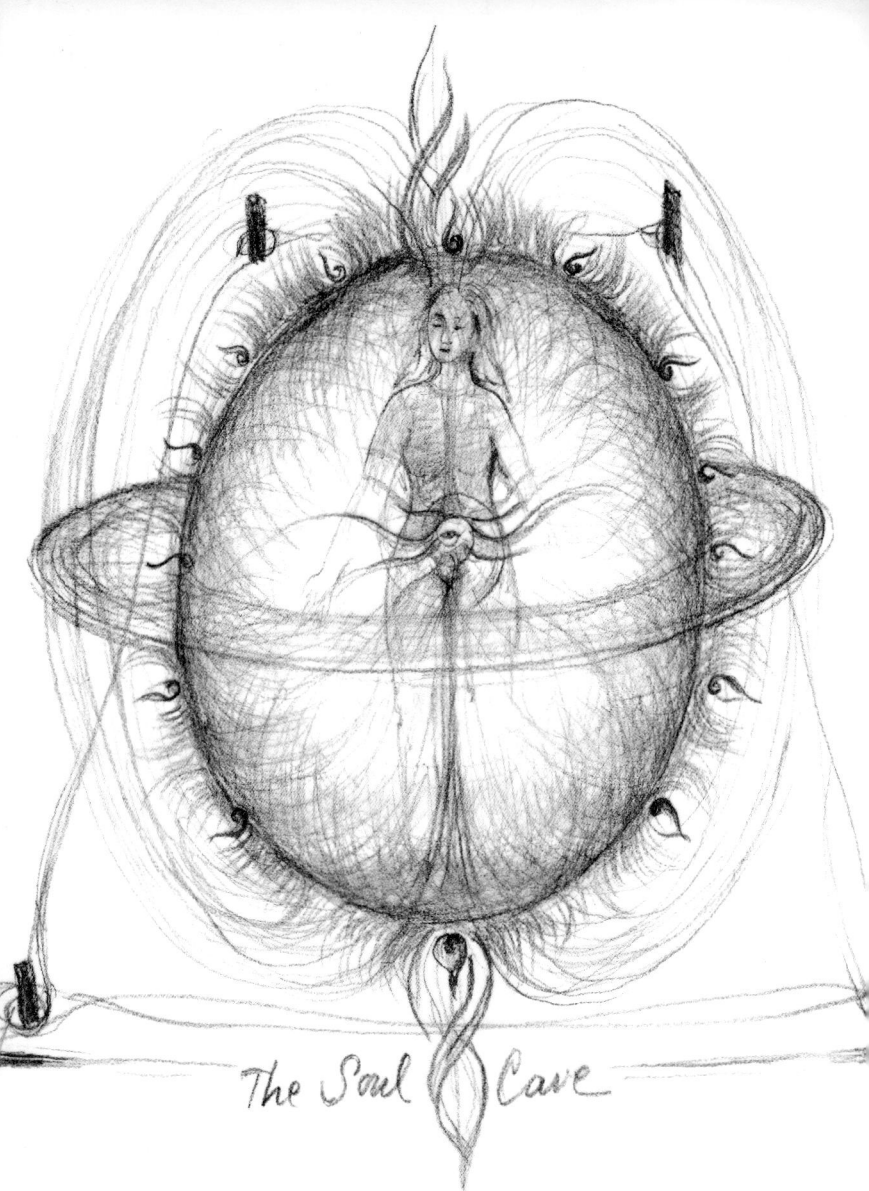

The Soul Cave

Figure 128 Soul Cave Spa energy pattern that I saw and felt during my sessions. The Navel Centre appeared foremost in my mind and the centre of my physical universe. Notice the field around the physical navel perpendicular to my vertical channel.

The entire belly area, or *Navel Centre*, encompasses several energy centres: the Tan Tien (2 inches below the belly button towards the front of the body), the Navel Chakra (at the level of the belly button but in the centre of the body close to the spine) and the solar plexus (at the level where the bottom front ribs meet, as part of the lower orb of the heart[2]). I see the *Navel Centre* as a large command centre with connectors radiating like a sun to various organs that it feeds with subtle energy. It may hold vast amounts of energy and it is a place where we normally put things we cannot digest. Blocked navel energy makes us less grounded and out of touch with our body and also, we might have difficulty relating to others properly. I have found that in some people who consider themselves 'spiritual' the navel is often out of balance. Symptoms include digestive tract problems, difficulties to relate socially and low vitality.

The Navel's Soul Cave as seen from an energy perspective: The Black Tourmaline grid placed on the four corners forms an interconnecting energy field to protect the work. The flames around the body are the Dravite/Citrine points that create the spherical/eliptical chamber (cave) together with our own navel energy. This Crystal Spa may provide users with the sense of connectedness to their inner fires and they can begin to integrate their energies into wholesomeness. Notice the energetic vortex forming an eye at the centre. (It looked to me as if it were an eyeball of the belly of consciousness - the navel fire stoker). The Saturnine rings manifesting around the belly horizontally (when standing up) are part of our own personal force field.

Maintenance: Practice this Spa whenever your personal energy is low or when the physical world (our normal reality) seems challenging. See also the Tiger-eye *Building Strength* practice where our personal force field is visualized and practiced.

Heart Tone Spa - Heart Awakening

Why: Without connection to the heart we really do not have proper direction in life, so then it is our senses that direct our every action. Cravings and aversions are our boss, and we have less ability to truly affect our life and our spiritual growth. The Heart Tone Spa is one way we may begin the journey into our precious heart.

Crystals: 12 pieces Nirvana Quartz, or if you do not have this crystal use 12 small Quartz points charged upon the *Nirvana Charging Mat*. You are free to make a personal copy, perhaps laminated, to create this Crystal Spa charger at home (see page 560).

How to begin: If you are fortunate enough to be in the possession of some of the soft pink Nirvana Quartz, you can easily apply them in this heart-connecting Spa. I often use this type of quartz, harvested in the high altitudes of the Himalayas, to connect clients to their hearts and to be laid out directly upon the heart area. As a spa chamber, they are laid out in a star tetrahedron around the body. See drawing on the right, which shows the pattern to use.

Effects: The effect is the sense of homecoming and connecting with the deeper mysteries of your inner being, quite different from Rosequartz, which relates more to the emotional levels of safety and nurturing for our child self. Imagine you could bring a small, safe rose garden to the top of a mountain where you could view the world from the perspective of an eagle. You might have a sense of being deeply protected and yet fearless at the same time. I found the result to give me a tremendous sense of the empowerment that I had available underneath my fears.

Maintenance: Use the spa daily until you feel reconnected with your heart.

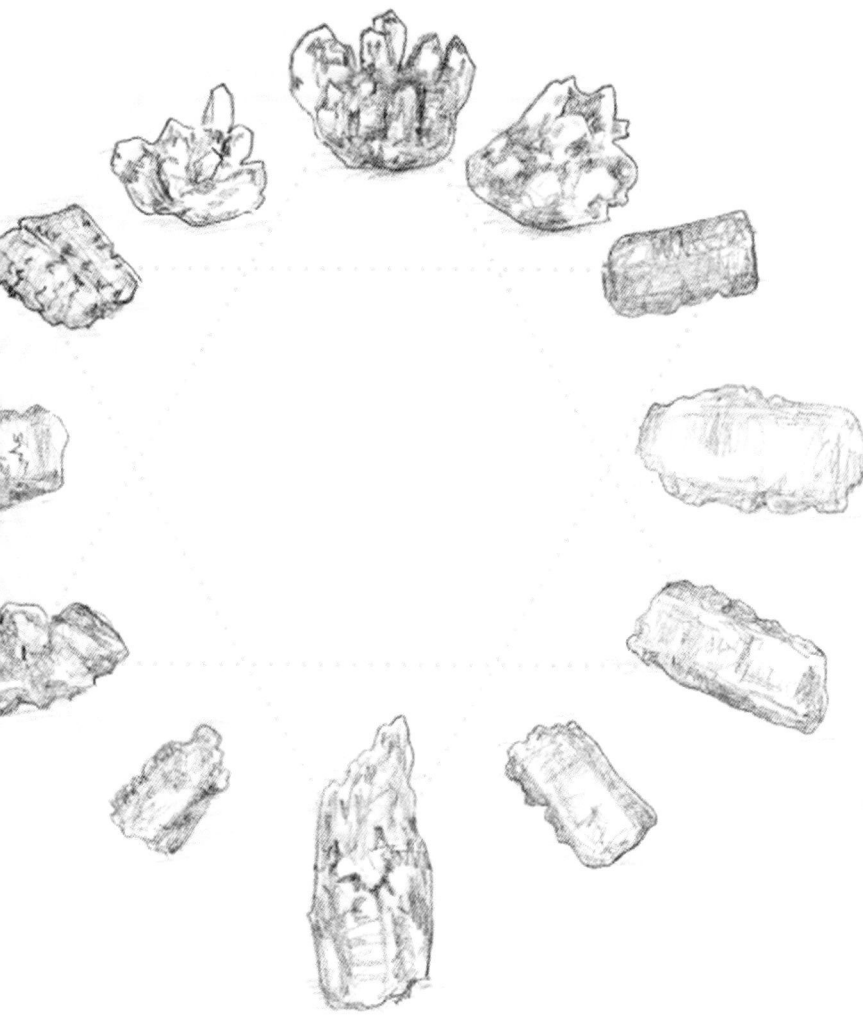

Figure 129 Charging Mat with added pinkish Nirvana Quartz from the Himalayas. You can use this pattern to charge regular quartz points with the vibration of Nirvana Quartz.

Crystal Care: If you are using the charging mat, clean the stones and place them on the mat whenever they are not in use. You can benefit from smudging the stones after use in the spa and place them in the sun for a short time to recharge.

Mind Presence Spa - Joining Head and Heart

Why: Our longest journey is that of travelling the 12 or so inches from the head to the heart. Here you have the possibility of actually doing this for yourself.

Crystals: Gather at least 9 pieces of Angel Green Fluorite and place them in an oval formation so that you fit inside it, either sitting or laying down. To the outside of each fluorite, place one or more gemmy Clear Calcite pieces. Then one Yellow Calcite is added to the Earth Star. (A clear Stellar-beam Calcite, seen in the picture, is optional at the Soul Star). The placements are similar to the previous spas on a carpet or soft blanket, with a simple Hematite Grid in the four corners.

How to begin: This spa was the most challenging to establish of the four Spas. I was guided earlier to have fluorite and calcite available. As it turns out, it was the angel green fluorite and gemmy clear calcite that were to be used. I tried to introduce the fluorite in the earlier Spas but that was rejected. I understand this now - it needed its own place. And each spa had to be explored in turn.

Maintenance: This Crystal Spa proves most valuable as a practice over a longer period of time, perhaps daily for the first week and then weekly over several months.

Crystal Care: Clean in water, and let the stones dry in the sun to charge them.

Effects: I was not prepared to encounter an old grief from 10 years ago, but there it was. Being inside the Mind Presence Spa

Figure 130 Stones for the Mind Presence Spa laid out with gemmy clear Calcite and angel green Fluorite. This Spa proved helpful to connect the head to the heart and to release old grief.

Figure 131 Here is how the energies of the Mind Presence Spa felt like, as far I can depict them. The forms congealed and blended together into a bejeweled mirror for me to look into.

for only a short while, I felt this grief suddenly appear (with tears and some thoughts). I watched it carefully, feeling the hurt, and then the pattern dissolved slowly. Recapping that old situation, I realized this was to be the last chapter of this book.

Calcite is said to have that ability to shift vision into other realms and other viewpoints, and to transport us into a new mind place. This is what happened to me. I am so grateful for all I have learned about crystals in the last decade and all the people who have helped assist me, and who have taught me to be who I really am. I wish your crystal journey to be at least as fruitful as mine has been for me. Blessings to All!

 Margherita

Summary

The technology of the Crystal Spas is only beginning to emerge. A Crystal Spa is an intentional grid acting like an energy chamber. They are easy to receive, and quite powerful to emerge from. A person may follow a series of sessions in each grid in order for the best results. Here is described the first four Crystal Spas that are to be used to re-store, re-connect, re-awaken, and rejuvenate our being. The first is the Yin Fire Wave (with raw Rose Quartz and Selenite), which is best used in a series of sessions after a long day at work to relax. It may be followed by the Crystal Soul Cave (with black Tourmaline and Citrine), in which the navel centre is in focus. This is a possibility to re-connect with the source of our power. Our heart must also be tended to and this might be accomplished with the Heart Tone Spa (with Nirvana Quartz). This formation follows the star tetrahedron that is vital for personal growth. Lastly, we may try the Mind Presence Spa (with angel green Fluorite and clear gemmy Calcite) for integrating our head and thinking with our heart. Our deepest patterns may be revealed by engaging here.

Practices:

Yin-Fire Wave - restoration
Crystal Soul Cave - navel re-connection
Heart Tone - heart awakening
Mind Presence Spa - joining head and heart

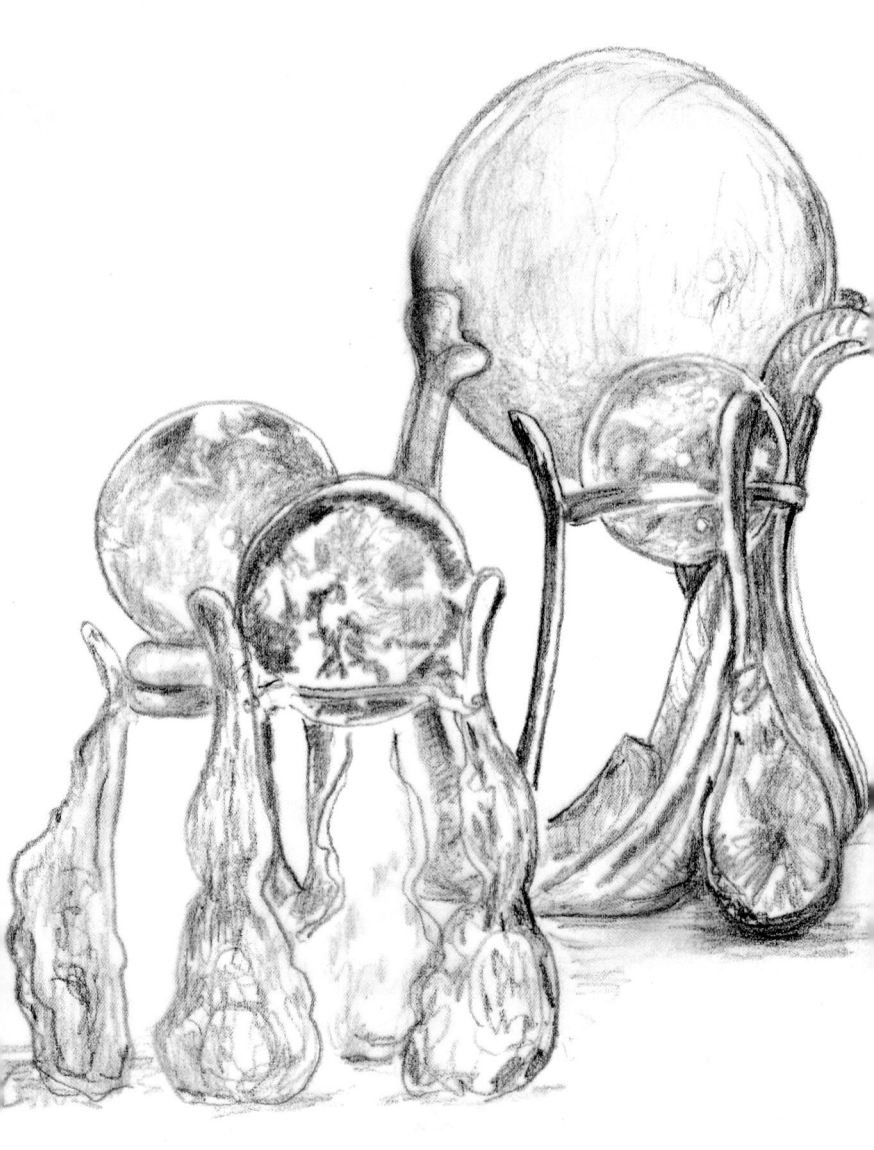

The Crystal Keys

She said, "How we can open this door?"
The rabbit said, "Use this key."

The Crystal Keys method is a unique approach to working with your self and crystals. Below you will find an extensive list of crystals and their corresponding keys.

As you examine the list you will find the mineral name (eg. Agate), its country or origin (eg. Botswana) and its energetic usage (eg. Aloneness Remedy Stone). This stone is especially effective in assisting with the release of the mental concept and resulting issues that surround feeling 'alone.' In some cases, a short description has been added further illustrate the nature of the stone.

The Crystal Key: The key is a quality or mental-emotional state that we may want to attain. The keys were discovered during meditations and attunements with each crystal, and they evolved from the perceived duality or polarity, or a Positive <> Negative pair. Each set of such contrasting extremes, which we often fluctuate between until this balanced state is mastered, evolves into a key.

It is important to emphasize that it is necessary to dissolve both of the extremes in the polarity in order to attain the resulting key. The key is the balance point, the healthy state we are seeking. In our example, Botswana Agate has the following keys:

Key 1: Support (Fearing <> Allowing)
Key 2: Harmony (Suppression <> Openness)
Key 3: Peace (Aloneness <> Solitude)

Feeling supported, being in harmony and being at peace, (the three keys) are the resolutions of the internal polarities or opposites (set in parenthesis) that may exist within. Each crystal may have additional keys; feel free to explore them, as well. Use the polarity and key that resonates strongly for you; then meditate on this quality in yourself and in others that are part of your life.

Choosing a Polarity: In the third key we see Peace (Aloneness <> Solitude). Rather than working with being alone versus being in a relationship, you may realize that accepting your present state is the best platform for attaining peace. From a place of peace, you have a much better possibility to manifest whatever you so intend, including a relationship. Through the use of the polarities, deeper insights on your specific issues may be illuminated. Then you can act effectively in your own life situation, and shift or release current issues completely.

I Am Affirmation: Within the Crystal Key you will also find affirmations for each key. Affirmations are statements that you may use to strongly affirm a new way of interacting within the world. They may be helpful for you in attaining and maintaining your balanced healthful state. After you complete a particular issue and thoroughly attained its wisdom, that problem will not confront you in the future. Great, isn't it? Imagine never to be upset about the same thing again!

Elemental Effect: The elemental effect is indicated: this entry may assist you to ascertain the suitable use of the crystal energy selected. For example, earthy energies are listed as: grounding, absorbing or strengthening. The elemental effect can with benefit be used in practice of the Crystal Mandala and the Moon Journey.

Personal Practice: The Crystal Keys are best approached as a practice. Work with your situation for a period of at least three weeks (21 days), and then rest for one week (which is, in total, one moon cycle) before any further issue is addressed. You can use the affirmation in front of a mirror, looking deeply at your image, saying sincerely the chosen affirmation. This sets the tone and feeling for your intention, embodied by the affirmation throughout the day. Stating affirmations correctly combined with clear intention and focused actions will change your life to your choosing. For particular practices with the Crystal Keys, consult the chapter: *Dropping the Drama* on page 345.

	Earth	Water	Fire	Air	Space
Earthy:	Grounding	Calming	Opening	Focussing	Aligning
Watery:	Absorbing	Penetrating	Purifying	Blending	Rarefying
Fiery:	Strengthening	Moving	Transforming	Inspiring	Illumining
Airy:	Stabilizing	Balancing	Stimulating	Expanding	Elevating

Figure 132 Table of Elemental Effects. For example: Angelite is described as being Balancing and Aligning, which means it firstly belongs to the airy aspect of the Water element, and then secondly to the earthy aspect of the Space element.

List of Crystals Keys: Bon Voyage! Here is the complete list of Crystals that have assisted me on my journey. May they serve you well also.

Agate (Botswana) grey-tan *Aloneness Remedy Stone.*
Agate is a type of quartz found with banding in nodules or geodes. Elemental Effect: Balancing, Grounding.

Key 1: Support (Allowing <> Fearing) I am supported in my feelings.

Key 2: Harmony (Openness <> Suppression) I am relating with openness to other people. I am in harmony with others. I am open to receive Spirit into my life

Key 3: Peace (Solitude <> Aloneness) I am peaceful in my solitude. I value my alone-time.

Agate (Fire) *Creative Fire Stone.* The vibration of Fire Agate resonates with opening chasms of fears held within. You can use this stone to connect with your inner vital fires, both destructive and healthful, and use them for what you would like to do. Elemental Effect: Grounding, Stimulating.

Key 1: Manifestation (Creating <> Living in Fear) I connect with my creative fire to manifest my wildest dreams. I face my deepest fears. I manifest my dreams. Through my creative fire I manifest my goals.

Agate (Gaia) reddish-brown tan *Earth Connection Stone.*
Elemental Effect: Grounding, Stimulating.

Key 1: Dance of the Goddess (Moving with Fire <> Thinking it is Fire) I am participating fully in my life. I use my life to fully experience myself and what I want to do.

Agate (Green Tree) *Nature Connection Stone.* Elemental Effect: Absorbing, Balancing.

Key 1: Nature (Harmony <> Destruction) I am a nature lover. Nature loves me and gives me all I need. I honour and respect Nature and the Earth. I see myself reflected in the trees and in the plants. I belong here. I feel peace.

Agate (Blue Lace) light blue *Calm Expression Stone.*
Blue Lace Agate is the first remedy for stress, agitation and rest-lessness. Let yourself relax sitting by a table. Put two pieces of Blue Lace Agate on the table before you, and then place your hands, palms down on them comfortably. Remain still for several min-utes breathing (use the Dual Flow Breath). Notice how you can affect your energy state. Elemental Effect: Balancing, Calming.

Key 1: Calm Expression (At Ease <> Stress) I release the need for stress. I am peacefully expressing myself. I am relaxing. I am calm.

Agate (Snake) tan, white *Worry Remedy Stone.* Elemental
Effect: Grounding, Blending, Calming.

Key 1: Fear (Relaxed <> Nervous) I am calm. I see myself clearly. I am rational. I face my fears.

Agate (Turitella) *Past Life Stone.* Turitella Agate is the
fossilized remains of sea creatures. Elemental Effect: Absorbing, Balancing.

Key 1: Life Lessons (The Past <> The Future) I am a result of my past, all of my past actions and experiences. I now accept myself and take responsibility for my future. I am fully present here and now.

Agate Red *Tribal Unity Stone.* Elemental Effect: Grounding,
Strengthening.

Key 1: Life Vitality (Joined <> Isolated) I am united with my family. I am home. I am healthy.

Ajoite in Chrysocolla *Divine Feminine Stone.* Ajoite in
Chrysocolla may assist in recovering your inner vision. Elemental effect: Blending, Inspiring.

Key 1: Receptive Power (Softness <> Toughness) I am able to see my feminine softness as my strength. I am co-creating my life with the divine.

Amazonite
blue-green *Stone of Personal Expression.* Amazonite is a type of Feldspar, effective to help us to use our voice skillfully. Elemental Effect: Opening, Balancing.

Key 1: Honesty (Skillful Self-Expression <> Not Speaking) I am perfecting my personal expression. I am listening to my body. I am the source of my own contentment.

Amazonite (Love-struck)
light blue-green with hint of pink *Stone of Loving Expression.* The Love-Struck Amazonite has inclusions of pink Feldspar. Elemental Effect: Opening, Stimulating.

Key 1: Communication (Loving Appreciation <> Criticism) I am choosing to express loving thoughts. I am the love I talk about.

Amber honey-gold
Stone of Love and Commitment. Amber is the fossilized remains of sap from prehistoric trees that grew almost fifty million years ago. Amber has been used as a sign of commitment in marriage ceremonies. Elemental Effect: Balancing, Aligning.

Key 1: Light (Confusion <> Aligned) I allow confusion to be my teacher. I am grounded and aligned in the light.

Key 2: Commitment (Decisive <> Uncertain) I honour my ancestors' wisdom. I am committed to serve my promises.

Amethyst
purple *Stone of Mastering Change.* Amethyst is the perfect stone for beginning our journey of self discovery. Elemental Effect: Inspiring, Balancing, Opening.

Key 1: Surrender (Controlling <> Submissive) I surrender my mind to accept the highest part of myself. I surrender to change. I change into my true self.

Key 2: Mastering Change (Allowing <> Fear) I allow myself to see my beliefs as guidelines under revision. I allow myself the privilege of being free to change.

Amethyst (Australia)
The Cultural Independence Stone. Elemental Effect: Inspiring, Balancing, Opening.

Key 1: Staying Present (Tradition <> New Thinking) I release Old World patterns and embrace new ways of thinking.

Amethyst (cluster) *Stone of Mastering Change.* An Amethyst cluster can be used as a charging bed for other crystals and personal items. Elemental Effect: Inspiring, Grounding.

Key 1: Staying Present (Tradition <> New Thinking) I let go of old ways of thinking. I open my mind for change. I clear myself.

Amethyst (Elestial) *Self-Realization Stone.* This stone is helpful for letting go, especially in regardes to your old home that you are trying to sell. It is truly the stone to use for tricky challenges without a hint of a cause. Elemental Effect: Purifying, Inspiring.

Key 1: Self-Realization (Supreme Mind <> Ignorant Mind) I am joining my higher self. I am surrendering to any change necessary for my inner growth.

Amethyst (Red-Cap) *Stone of Mastering Change.* Red-Cap Amethyst exhibits several quartz varieties: Smokey, Red, Citrine and Amethyst. It facilitates spinal awakening in practice. Elemental Effect: Inspiring, Balancing, Opening.

Key 1: Spinal Awakening (Flowing <> Controlling) I am opening myself to the world of energy.

Ametrine purple & gold *Stone of Clearing and Change.* Ametrine is a gift of the earth! Elemental Effect: Inspiring, Opening.

Key 1: Transformation (Taking Action <> In a rut/Bored) I have the guts to do what I choose. I am ready for change.

Key 2: Power (Taking Charge <> Avoiding Responsibility) I am taking responsibility for myself. I am facing my challenges.

Ammonite (fossilized shells) *Symbol of Life Stone.* Elemental Effect: Absorbing, Balancing.

Key 1: Life Purpose (The Now <> Distraction) I am a result of my past experiences. I accept myself and take responsibility for my future. I am here and now. I have the wisdom to be clear.

Andalusite (Chiastolite, cross-formation) brown-tan *Ego-Buster Stone.* Elemental Effect: Grounding, Inspiring, Expanding.

Key 1: Empowered (Victim <> Abuser) I am centred in my heart. I believe in myself. I am taking charge of my life. I love myself.

Key 2: Balance (Ego <> Spirit) I am a balanced spiritual being. I allow my present personality to be put in its proper place.

Andalusite (Chiastolite, gemmy) golden green *Spiritual Purpose Stone.* Elemental Effect: Inspiring, Expanding.

Key 1: Crossroad (Stay <> Act) I make up my mind now. I choose, therefore I move forward. By choosing I move toward my purpose faster.

Angelite powder blue *Angelic Guardian Stone.* Anhydrite is crystallized Angelite. Angelite is helpful to invoke a sense of safety and also to connect with our internal guidance system. Elemental Effect: Balancing, Aligning.

Key 1: Safety (Tension <> Relaxed Feelings) I relax my emotions and ask for what I need. I am safe. I am loved.

Key 2: Exploration (Adventure <> Holding on) I am supported and safe. I allow myself to experience other realms and dimensions.

Apatite blue *Stone of Service.* I feel that Apatite is an essential stone to all who desire to do healing work; it inspire us to do selfless service and being happy about it. Elemental Effect: Inspiring, Balancing.

Key 1: Humility (Service <> Controlling) I humbly serve a higher good. I use my voice softly. I do my work willingly.

Apatite brown-black *Stone of Service.* The darker varieties are helpful to us as a reminder that we are mortals and severely affected if we stay in patterns of selfishness. Elemental Effect: Strengthening, Balancing.

Key 1: Fulfilment (Flowing <> Rigidity) I am in emotional balance. I balance myself and increase my abundant flow. I am fulfilled and happy.

Apatite red *Stone of Service.* The red variety can be used where we really need to take action to help ourselves or others, including weight loss activity. Elemental Effect: Strengthening, Balancing.

Key 1: Body Care (Tender Attention <> Neglect) I serve a higher good, and still tend to my needs. I take action to help.

Apatite yellow *Stone of Service.* The nobler the motives we may have, the more we have to realize the basis for them. Yellow Apatite helps us to discover our deeper motivations. Elemental Effect: Inspiring, Balancing.

Key 1: Humility (Subservience <> Domination) I am serving a higher good. I am the servant of my Higher Self. I meditate on my deeper motives.

Apophyllite clear *Inner Journey Stone.* Apophyllite may prove vital to our ability to do dream work and command our subtle energy body. Elemental Effect: Elevating, Rarefying.

Key 1: Truth (Letting Go <> Fearing the Unknown) I allow myself to go to the unknown to experience the clarity of truth.

Key 2: Integration (Fresh Start <> Being in a Rut) I am discovering the whole truth to allow my Soul to heal.

Key 3: Vehicle (Open to the Unknown <> Escape) I am free to go to the end of the universe.

Apophyllite green *New Paradigm Stone.* To let go of social/cultural beliefs is not so easy unless you can experience the new realities possible for a harmonious world. Green Apophyllite is an ethereal stone and facilitator for just that. Elemental Effect: Elevating, Rarefying.

Key 1: New World Order (Resistance <> Letting Go) I allow myself new experiences that can create new foundations.

Key 2: Serenity & Meditation (Focus <> Disturbance) I allow myself the space to be myself. I am a sovereign being on the Earth.

Aquamarine blue *Stone of Truth*. Aquamarine is a blue Beryl that is effective on all chakras on the body, and especially at the throat where we may express who we really are. Elemental Effect: Aligning, Balancing.

Key 1: Universal Truth/Blueprint of Humanity (Manipulation <> Honesty) I am expressing Universal Truth. I am releasing ego-agendas.

Key 2: Trust (Wounded <> Vulnerable) I am healing my awakened soul by removing my shields.

Key 3: Peace (Order <> Turmoil) I choose to abide in internal and external peace now.

Aragonite tan & white *Anger Remedy Stone*. Aragonite is a highly absorbing stone for aggressive energies, and may be used to alleviate the results of anger in its expressions by pacifying hostility within. Elemental Effect: Absorbing, Balancing.

Key 1: Masterful Expression (Serenity <> Anger) I am releasing my anger peacefully. My thinking process becomes clearer. I am choosing to stay calm.

Astrophyllite black with multi-colour *Star Seed Stone*. Astrophyllite may assist us to connect with our original home. Elemental Effect: Elevating, Grounding.

Key 1: Bridge (Star Seed <> Human) I am connecting with my original home and purpose to love all. I am here to bring peace.

Aventurine green *Emotional Balancer Stone*. Green Aventurine is an essential stone to use for balancing our emotions. When in balance we are better able to deal with the causes for our emotional states. Elemental Effect: Balancing, Stabilizing.

Key 1: Balance (Fulfilled <> Emotional) My emotional needs are being fulfilled and balanced. I feel hope and optimism. I am emotionally stable.

Aventurine red *Choice to Love Stone.* Red Aventurine, also called Raspberry Quartz, may help us to make the choices we need to do to come to balance. Elemental Effect: Flowing, Inspiring.

Key 1: Choice to Love (Emotional Choice <> Fulfilled) I choose to feel all my feelings, in order to experience love.

Aventurine white *White-Hot Anger Remedy Stone.* When we are so angry we may burst, that is the point when something must change. You are the one to make that choice for you. White Aventurine may help you to make that choice. Elemental Effect: Balancing, Purifying.

Key 1: Access to Feelings (Peacefulness <> White-Hot Anger) I am experiencing my anger and I acknowledge it. I am letting go of my anger and rage peacefully. I am becoming emotionally stable.

Azurite royal blue *Mental Purger Stone.* Azurite is essential for learning about our ability to intuit without obstacles and be free in our mind. Elemental Effect: Inspiring, Purifying.

Key 1: Freedom (Free Mind <> Limitation) I let go and dare to live freely. I am a limitless being. My mind is free to explore all.

Key 2: Listening (Observing <> Reacting) I am listening without reacting. I hear and understand what is needed.

Azur-Malachite see: both Azurite and Malachite

Barite clear tan *Dream Realization Stone.* Barite helps to connect us to our dream. By tuning in where and what our dreams are, we can realize them. Elemental Effect: Inspiring, Stabilizing. Rarefying.

Key 1: Living my Dream (Fulfilment <> Fear of being Worthy) I follow my heart's dream. I choose to follow my star.

Beryl (Ocean) green *Emotional Truth Stone.* The Ocean Beryl is helpful in the process to rise above one's emotions. Elemental Effect: Balancing, Moving.

Key 1: Sea of Emotion (Emotions that heal <> Hostile emotions) I explore my feelings, and let them guide me. Experiencing my feelings brings me in contact with myself.

Beryl blue see: Aquamarine

Beryl green see: Emerald

Beryl peach *Divine Mother Stone.* Elemental Effect: Inspiring, Balancing.

Key 1: The Graceful Child (Rebellion <> Wrath) I am responsible for my life. I love my parents. I love myself.

Beryl silver-black Earth Star Connection Stone. Elemental Effect: Absorbing, Penetrating.

Key 1: Earth Connection (Happy <> Depressed) I love being here. I am feeling great. I am home here. I take delight in life.

Beryl white see: Goshenite

Beryl yellow see: Heliodor

Bloodstone (Heliotrope) green with red dots *Blood Energizer Stone.* Bloodstone, also called Heliotrope, helps us to vitalize our body. Use this stone when feeling weak and tired. Elemental Effect: Strengthening, Stimulating.

Key 1: Physical Strength (Energizing <> Stagnation) My physical body feels clear and energized. I stimulate the flow of vital energy and physical strength. I am active and strong.

Boji Stone™ *Co-Creation Stone.* Boji Stones™ have been used to affect headaches and ground both yin and yang energies within. Elemental Effect: Grounding, Stimulating.

Key 1: Co-Creator (Grounded <> Un-connected) I am a co-creator on the Earth, and I know her intimately. I am grounded and balanced.

Bornite *Grief Remedy Stone.* Grief hits hardest when we are the least aware. Grief is a challenging lesson to master, as we experience it in connection with what we most cherish. Meditating with this humble but wonderful stone may assist you in difficult times. Elemental Effect: Grounding, Balancing.

Key 1: Acceptance (Grieving <> Letting Go) I am allowing myself the time I need to let go. I am supported in my grieving. My grieving gives me the gift of acceptance.

Bronzite *Courtesy Stone.* How about learning to treat and be treated really well? Here is an opportunity to gain new confidence in relating to others in a new beneficial way. Elemental Effect: Inspiring, Grounding.

Key 1: Courtesy (Observing ritual <> Respecting others) I am mindful of the needs of others. I am respectful of the beliefs of others. I respect myself.

Bustamite/Sugilite *Conflict Cleanser Stone.* Elemental Effect: Penetrating, Blending, Purifying.

Key 1: Peace (Cause of Conflict <> Acting out the Conflict) I am peacefully letting go. I deal with all challenges from a point of compassionate understanding. I act from my higher self.

Bytownite see: Labradorite gold

Calcite (Mangano) pink *Heart-Ache Healing Stone.* Deeply troubled hearts are more closely shut. Allow a small opening to what ails you. Mangano Calcite brings a message of peace in troubled times. Elemental Effect: Aligning, Balancing, Absorbing.

Key 1: Messenger of Peace (Land of Peace <> Terror) I feel peace and trust to all loved ones on this planet.

Calcite clear *Being Present Stone.* Clear Calcite vibrates to a higher frequency of our being than Quartz. Use this capacity to become present. Elemental Effect: Elevating, Rarefying.

Key 1: Being (Clarity <> Clouded Vision) I master the art of being. I am present each moment.

Calcite blue *Stress Remedy Stone.* Stillness is a state of the mind greatly sought after in a stressful world. Blue Calcite may inspire you to stop the stress and become present to what is. Elemental Effect: Balancing, Inspiring, Rarefying.

Key 1: Peaceful Presence (Purpose <> Suffering) I bring Spirit into matter. I am present to guidance. I am remaining calm in any situation.

Calcite cluster with small Gyrotite balls.

Calcite coral *Joy Stone.* The energy of Joy is one of the most healthful ways of being, it heals our mind and picks up the spirit of others. Let Coral Calcite inspire you to do just that. Elemental Effect: Purifying, Stimulating, Elevating.

Key 1: Joy in friendship (Happiness <> Sadness) I am Joyful: it is my choice. I am my own best friend. I cheer myself up.

Calcite golden *Higher Awareness Stone.* Gemmy golden Calcite has been used to become aware of how abundance is created. Elemental Effect: Inspiring, Elevating.

Key 1: Presence (Abundance <> Poverty) I am present to what is available for me. I become aware of all my gifts.

Calcite green *Stone of Inspiration.* Connections with what has hurt us in the past can be made when we are ready. Green Calcite may assist you to become ready. Make the choice now. Elemental Effect: Inspiring, Balancing, Purifying.

Key 1: Conscious Connection (Healing <> Heartache) I am the connection of heart and mind. I am healing my soul.

Calcite honey *Manifesting "Now" Stone.* We desire so many things, but hardly move ourselves to act upon our desires. Let Honey Calcite bring some impetus to move, and take action about what is real around you. Elemental Effect: Stimulating, Inspiring, Grounding.

Key 1: Being in the Now (Believing in Poverty <> Healthy Well-being) I feel and think in the present. My body is nourished on all levels. I am conscious of my feelings and what my mind thinks.

Calcite orange *Creativity Booster Stone.* Orange Calcite has be used as a Sex and Play Stone. Well this is a risky statement but how many disregard natural urges within? By dealing with these impulses skillfully we may express them healthily and within accepted boundaries. Elemental Effect: Stimulating, Elevating, Stabilizing.

Key 1: Spontaneity (Rigid/Stern <> Playful) I am a joyful being. I allow myself time for play and fun.

Calcite orchid orange *Lucid Dream Stone.* This is a truly happy stone. Elemental Effect: Stimulating, Elevating, Grounding.

Key 1: Divine Manifestation (Reality <> Pipe Dreams) I am the reality that I dream. I am divinely inspired to love what I do.

Calcite pink/green *Loving Feeling Stone.* Transparent optical Calcite in pink or greens may assist you to be aware of the power of love. Love is an emotion that most find elusive, but tangible when present. Look on how you perceive your self-worth. This focus will guide you to learn how to love, from a non-personal level. Elemental Effect: Inspiring, Purifying.

Key 1: Presence of Love (Ability to love <> Unworthy) I allow myself to BE in the state of Love. I embody my soul's infinite love.

Calcite ruby *Wrath Remedy Stone.* This stone is perfect to get yourself in touch with what truly makes you move. Staying present while doing that is what Calcite resonates best. Elemental Effect: Stimulating, Blending.

Key 1: Movement (Stagnant <> Wrath) I am a mover. I do it now. I choose my action quickly and accurately.

Key 2: All-Seeing Eye (Hurricane <> Eye of the storm) I am present to any changes. I am the change I desire.

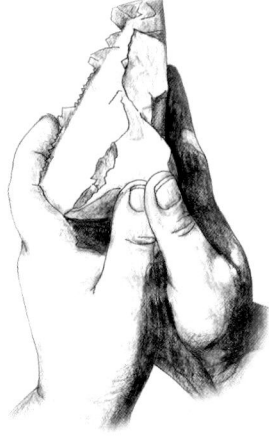

Elestialized Stellar-Beam Calcite.

Calcite (Stellar-Beam) clear, white or grey This formation further increases the Calcite vibration. Stellar-Beam Calcite would have to be described in a separate book. It has immense uses for humanity. Elemental effect: Elevating, Rarefying.

Key 1: Reaching the Stars (Presence <> Ignorance) I am a multidimensional being. I am present. I rise above my ignorance. I humbly accept what is.

Carnelian orange *Creativity Stone.* Carnelian is a staple on the spice shelf of stones. No collection is complete without Carnelian. It is helpful in all endeavours in life, whether we create something small, or on a global level, creativity is the solution to any of our problems. It keeps us trying again and again against bad odds. It is by true creation and expression of who we are that we can come fully alive. Carnelian is that stone to support us. Elemental Effect: Balancing, Stimulating.

Key 1: Creation (Free Energy <> Addiction) I balance my sexual and creative energy. I allow the flow of passion to create what I truly love. I am my own creation. I love myself, and what I create.

Cat's Eye (Cymophane, Chrysoberyl) *Discovery Stone.* Cat's Eye is an unusual stone, affecting us to explore the unknown. Elemental Effect: Penetrating, Purifying.

Key 1: Intellectual Depth (Facts <> Guessing) I am sure of myself. I am researching and building knowledge about where I am yearning to go. I walk my talk.

Cat's Eye Tourmaline light-green golden Cat's Eye Tourmaline is a sweet and soft energy to enhance any mandala talisman. Elemental Effect: Balancing, Rarefying.

Key 1: Balancing (Human <> Non-Human) I am a being of trust and light.

Cavansite deep blue *Stone of Penetrating Honesty.* Cavansite (a form of Pentagonite) has been used for relieving pent-up feelings without harming others, and to fully own one's own part in our drama. Elemental Effect: Penetrating, Purifying.

Key 1: Penetrating Honesty (Resolution <> Emotional Issue) I stand in my own truth. I take responsibility for myself. I am an emotionally honest person.

Celestite sky blue *Divine Listening Stone.* I do not hear because I haven't stopped to listen to the song that is playing. Celestite may show you how to stop the inner dialogue and start listening, not only to others but to your inner guidance as well. You may best help others by showing it with your own actions. Elemental Effect: Aligning, Opening, Elevating.

Key 1: Role Model (Angel <> Beast) I am a messenger of peace and trust. I become open to listen, and to know.

Key 2: Listening (Alive <> Numb) I truly listen to what is said.

Cerrusite clear-golden *Load-lightening Stone.* It was

discovered that the use of this stone in layouts could alert the recipient as to where the heaviest burdens were stored, and possibly assisting in losing weight by accessing the reasons for gaining it. Elemental Effect: Grounding, Stabilizing, Focussing.

Key 1: Release of Burdens (Light <> Heavy) I am ready to let go. I am lighter and lighter. I carry only the things I truly need.

Chalcedony blue *Effectivity Booster Stone.* Blue Chal-

cedony holds the yang water position in the crystal mandala, and the active force of emotional capacity. Blue Chalcedony is vital to include in a healing set because of its ability to inspire us to effectively deal with our emotional landscape. When our inner world is balanced and blended, we are more able to effectively deal with normal life. Elemental Effect: Penetrating, Inspiring.

Key 1: Easeful Expression (Being silenced <> Forced to speak) I am expressing myself with ease.

Key 2: Perspective (Flowing Action <> Resistance to change) I have an overview; therefore, I act with confidence.

Chalcedony white and pink *Stone of Gentle Love.*

White, or pink, Chalcedony provide a subtle loving force. Such force is emanating when we are in our essence; then we do not need to force anything, as all falls in place in total harmony. Let this state happen within. Elemental Effect: Balancing, Flowing.

Key 1: Gentleness (Forceful <> Weak) I am following the flow, allowing whatever is needed to happen. The more I allow the more I receive.

Key 2: Graceful Love (Fragile <> Impervious) I surrender to my natural blissful self. I am living in a field of Love.

Chalcopyrite *Vanity Remedy.* Chalcopyrite is also called the Peacock Stone and contains Sulphur. Elemental Effect: Purifying, Absorbing.

Key 1: Arrival (Affliction <> Addiction) I am here to learn. I purify myself by wanting to do so.

Charoite violet *Spiritual Purger Stone.* It is a stone for transforming our lower self into our perfect essence, which is already there underneath our conditioning. Elemental Effect: Transforming, Elevating, Purifying.

Key 1: Pure (Delusion <> Awake) My inner spiritual fire burns away the remaining obstacles to my complete freedom.

Key 2: Liberation (Personality <> Soul) I am allowing my true self to manifest.

Key 3: Devotion (Self-Worth <> Arrogance) I devote my life in service to the divine.

Chlorite Phantom see: Shadow Quartz

Chrysanthemum Stone black & white *Writers Block Remedy.* Ideal for the budding writer or artist who wants to express their art now. Let the inspiration gather force to action and perfect expression in your chosen art. Elemental Effect: Purifying, Stabilizing.

Key 1: Art (Inspiration <> Block) I am a vessel of divine inspiration and art. I am writing. I am doing my art now. My written words flow like angels' wings, light and inspiring. My art is being manifest before my eyes.

Chrysoberyl yellow, green to purple *Heart Purifier Stone.* Varieties of Chrysoberyl are: Alexandrite (exhibits colour change depending on viewing angle) and Cat's Eye (shows appearance of a cat's eye in a cabochon or tumbled stone). Elemental Effect: Purifying, Aligning.

Key 1: Purpose Bringer (Hitting the wall <> Breakthrough) I am letting the energy of my challenges move me to resolution. I am letting my true experiences erase my inhibitions.

Chrysocolla blue-green *Feminine Balance Stone.* The whole world in one stone, that is Chrysocolla, a miracle in a stone. Without the natural world we would just float endlessly in space. The Earth is truly magnificent if you care to look deeply. Enjoy your experience, even if it is a short one. Elemental Effect: Balancing, Absorbing, Inspiring.

Key 1: Feminine Balance (Lack <> Over-achieving) I nurture my truth. I am one with my inner feminine force. I take delight in the natural world, which sustains my every need.

Key 2: Physical Temple (Disease <> Health) I have a beautiful and sacred body. I am allowing my physical body to be completely cleansed and joyful. I love my body.

Chrysoprase *Stone of Courage.* This stone we can hardly forego. Without courage to assist us, there is not much hope to achieve any project. Learn to love your challenges. Elemental Effect: Strengthening, Inspiring.

Key 1: Courage to Love (Struggle <> Inner Balance) I am in perfect balance with my three inner aspects: male, female and child. I am instilled with courage here and now.

Cinnabar (Dragons-blood) *Detoxification Stone.* Use this stone as a talisman or in meditation if you are overburdened by toxins or toxic involvements. Elemental Effect: Purifying, Balancing.

Key 1: Self-Care (Cleansed <> Impure) I am allowing healthy vibrations to flow though me, and let go of all else. I care for my body. I choose health.

Citrine yellow *Clearing Stone.* Citrine is the ideal balancer for the navel chakra. Also keep a small piece of Citrine in your wallet, and then you will always have a piece of gold with you, and never be broke. You can use Citrine in a house clearing, and to purify an area of your life. Elemental Effect: Inspiring, Purifying.

Key 1: Empowerment (Light Forces <> Dark Forces) I am clear and balanced. I transmute my fears into light.

Key 2: Abundance (Material Lack <> Wealth) I am manifesting all I need with conscious awareness. I am happy.

Citrine Cathedral Lightbrary
yellow gold *Self-Empowerment Stone.* Citrine Cathedrals assist us to realize the wisdom of self-empowerment. Elemental Effect: Clearing, Purifying, Rarefying.

Key 1: Clarity (Purification <> Effort) I am the Love Wisdom I seek. I let go. I am clear to see my destiny. I discover who I am.

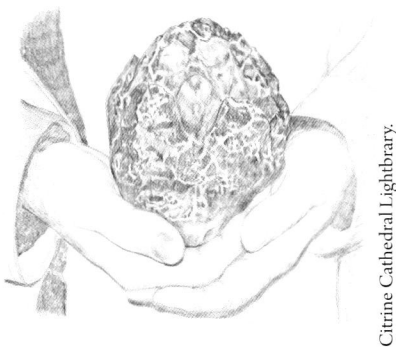

Citrine Cathedral Lightbrary.

Copper Combo Stone
blue-green black This stone contains a mixture of copper minerals, including Shattukite, Copper oxides, Chrysocolla & Gem Silica. It may assist in purging our mind of its source of negativity. Elemental Effect: Purifying, Balancing.

Key 1: Emotional Mastery (Observing Feelings <> Having Emotions) I am purified and free. I take responsibility for my own well-being. I allow my feelings freedom of flow.

Copper Native
metallic copper *Harmony Connection Stone.* Use this stone to make connections suitable to you, be it improving inner circulation, or networking in business. Elemental Effect: Inspiring, Flowing.

Key 1: Electric Connection (Flow <> Congestion) My energy channels are open and ready. I connect with others as a conduit for energy and beneficial thoughts.

Coral
(Fossilized) white, tan or red *Emotional Flow Stone.* Elemental Effect: Moving, Balancing.

Key 1: Flow (Patience <> Impatience) I am a drop of water in the emotional ocean. I let patience rule. I balance my emotions.

Corderite *Leadership Stone.* Corderite is Iolite Sunstone with Hematite. Elemental Effect: Transforming, Penetrating, Grounding.

Key 1: Vision (Too much to do <> Delegation) I am a leader in my field. I organize my work effectively.

Covellite dark blue metal sheen *Mind Detoxification Stone.* Covellite is a copper mineral and a well-needed stone in our age of accelerated mental activity. It is ideal to grid your computer with. Elemental Effect: Purifying, Expanding.

Key 1: Mind Detoxification (Conscious Thinking <> Toxic Thoughts) I am training my mind to think loving and pure thoughts.

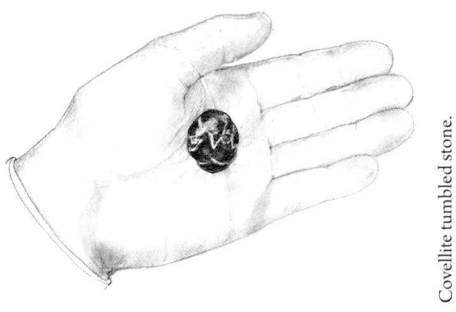

Covellite tumbled stone.

Crocoite orange *Relations Stone.* This stone has been used to improve marital happiness. Elemental Effect: Stimulating, Blending.

Key 1: Happiness (Collaboration <> Conflict) I am part of a team. I am joyful being in a group.

Cuprite red *Physical Purger.* Cuprite is a copper oxide and occur usually in Chrysocolla. Elemental Effect: Purification.

Key 1: Radiance (Pure <> Toxic) I am clear. I am healthy.

Danburite pink to clear *Spirit Heart Stone.* To access our spiritual heart is to come home from a very long trip. Danburite is a guiding light showing us the way along our arduous journey. Elemental Effect: Elevating, Inspiring, Aligning.

Key 1: Divine Connection (Hell <> Heaven) I am letting my heart expand to the inner realms of blissful divinity. I am connected with my celestial guides and teachers. I am One with all. I trust in my guidance.

Datolite light-green *Stone of Conscious Integration.* Datolite is a calcium borosilicate. Elemental Effect: Aligning, Calming, Stabilizing.

Key 1: Integration (Clarity <> Confusion) I am a multi-dimensional being capable of anything I set my mind to be. I am here to learn to be fully physical. I love my life.

Desert Rose tan *Tender Self Stone.* Desert Rose is gypsum sand-concretion (Selenite) found in the desert. Elemental Effect: Grounding, Rarefying, Transforming.

Key 1: Light Transformation (Energy form <> Physical form) I adapt to any circumstance. I create joy from my experiences, both good and bad ones.

Diamond *Oneness Stone* Not recommended in Healing at this time. When I visited the blue diamond (Hope Diamond) in the Smithsonian Natural History Museum, I thought that there would be a time when this rare gem could be utilized in healing. I was happy that there was public access to view it. When the level of greed, lust and anger on this planet is diminishing, diamond may again be used to serve humanity with its full capacity. Elemental Effect: Focussing, Aligning.

Key 1: Ascension (Evil <> Power of Love) I am carrying the hologram of divine perfection in my being.

Dioptase chrome green *Forgiveness Stone.* Dioptase provide a perfect tool for letting go of the past. See practice of Forgiveness.

Elemental Effect: Purifying, Stabilizing, Rarefying.

Key 1: Grace (Holding Grudges & Tension <> Forgiveness) I heal my heart. I am forgiving you. I am letting go of any grudges or tensions in my body.

Dumortierite   blue-black *Stubbornness Remedy.* A must-have for any stubborn person, perhaps even including yourself. Elemental Effect: Grounding, Absorbing.

Key 1: Humility (Stubbornness <> Service) I am now releasing stubbornness and choosing flexibility.

Key 2: Anger Release (Impatience <> Ease) I am developing patience and endurance.

Edenite   in Quartz green *Self-Destructive Behaviour Remedy.* Edenite energy may prove essential for those who engage in destructive behaviour. Use in a talisman or in meditation. If nothing else, breathe with it when you feel the need for support. Elemental Effect: Opening, Grounding.

Key 1: Empowered (Self-Abuse <> Self-Care) I am caring about my being. I am a source of joy and abundance. I create my paradise here and now. I am creating a transformed reality of love, now and forever.

Egypt Stone   *Anchor Stone,* also called Prophesy Stone, was found in the desert surrounded by white calcium deposits (fossils) from a past ocean. Minerology is unknown. Elemental Effect: Stabilizing, Aligning.

Key 1: Anchor (Centred <> Turbulent) I am in a physical body with a soul of an immortal being.

Emerald green   *Heart and Love Stone.* Emerald is a great symbol of love in all forms. Elemental Effect: Inspiring, Elevating.

Key 1: Beauty (Loved <> Un-Loved) I am love and beauty. My love creates beauty. My divine lover is within.

Emerald pink *Cosmic Heart Centre Stone.* Pink Emarald

(Morganite) is valuable to use in case of a broken heart. Our hurt may, in fact, open our heart. This may be a gift of learning. Our heart is capable of generating the strongest force in the universe: love unbound by conditions. Only a truly opened heart would be able to achieve this. Pink Emerald offers the key vibration to facilitate such true opening. Elemental Effect: Purifying, Elevating.

Key 1: Love (Heart-Broken <> Heart-Centred) I am opening my heart's capacity to love. I remember that I am part of Spirit, whose love unifies all.

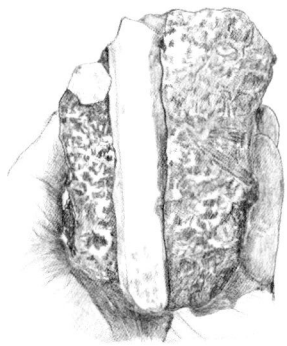

Emerald in matrix.

Epidote black or green *Destructive Behaviour Remedy.* Work-

ing with Epidote may bring you in contact with the darker side of yourself that hinders you from being happy. The idea is to access our heart by looking at the causes for addictions and behaviour harmful for us, and stay grounded and less swayed by distractions. Elemental Effect: Absorbing, Grounding.

Key 1: Self-Love (Pleasure <> Harm) I love myself. I learn to love slowly and surely.

Epidote in Prehnite dark-green inclusions *Personal Ra-*

diance Stone. Elemental Effect: Inspiring, Elevating.

Key 1: Personal Radiance (Remember Love <> Forgetting Source) I am instilling beauty and space in my heart. I love all of myself. I remember who I really am. I am unified within.

Eudialyte red, black & white *Anger Management Stone.* Eudialyte is a deep red complex silicate exhibiting black and white inclusions. It is an ideal stone for bringing anger and its related emotional states into proportion and resolution. Elemental Effect: Grounding, Purifying.

Key 1: Anger Management (Scolding Fire <> Healthy Passion) I integrate conflicting energies into creative blessings. I am patient and kind.

Flint grey to tan *Fire Spark Stone.* Flint is used to cast the spark on the fire to light it. My sister Nina always used to carry a piece in her purse for this reason. Elemental Effect: Transforming, Illumining.

Key 1: Self-Sufficiency (Light my Fire <> My own Light) I have all I need. I create all the components of my life that I need.

Fluorite clear *Mental Clarity Stone.* To act and integrate with life with a clear mind is essential for happiness. Clear Fluorite may inspire you to discover the difference between *struggle* and *observing doing the struggle*. A change of perspective changes a problem into a gift. Elemental Effect: Focussing, Inspiring, Elevating.

Key 1: Observing Mental Process (Creative Intuition <> Mental Struggle) I am thinking with ease and clarity. I use the tool of logic to help my thinking. My intuition guides my actions.

Fluorite purple *Mental Clarity Stone.* Purple Fluorite puts the emphasis on mastering the mental processes and also to go beyond the mental realm. Elemental Effect: Focussing, Inspiring, Elevating.

Key 1: Mastering Mental Processes (Brain fog <> Clarity) I am clearing my mind, revealing the causes of my condition. I become aware of how I think. My mind is clear and crisp.

Fluorite (Angel Green) *Air Element Stone.* Rejecting what harms us is difficult when we are addicted. For myself: I still want my coffee in the morning. The issue becomes if I am so attached to it that I will go out in a snowstorm to get it, then I will be the slave of it. To aspire to become free of such slavery, one might want to aspire to serve something more fruitful. When we are ready, Angel Green Fluorite lets us feel the vibration of what it could be like, to feel free of such slavery. Elemental Effect: Inspiring, Focussing, Elevating.

Key 1: Mental Balance (Highest Potential <> Unfulfilled) I am achieving my highest potential. I become aware of my conditioning.

Key 2: Detachment (Desire-less <> Deprived) I am content.

Fuchsite green *Emotional Guidance Stone.* Fuchsite is a form of Mica/Muscovite that includes Chromium. Our solar plexus gives us immediate responses to what we are experiencing on a gut level, but we do not always know what to do with such responses. Placing Fuchsite on the affected area may assist you to discover the message of any symptom you may experience. Elemental Effect: Opening, Balancing.

Key 1: Guidance (Being Lost <> Accepting Intuition) I am clearly listening to the guidance of my inner healer. I am opening to receive guidance.

Fulgurites.

Fulgurite *Transformation Stone.* Fulgurites are formed when lightning strikes sand to create hollow tubes. Elemental Effect: Transforming, Opening, Aligning.

Key 1: Transformation (Wealth <> Rubbish) I am transforming into the best form known to me. I learn to adapt to circumstances.

Gabbro black igneous rock Carved objects are often made from Gabbro. Elemental Effect: Grounding, Strengthening.

Key 1: Support (Helped <> Denied) I receive the support I need.

Galena grey metallic *Virus Alert Stone.* Working with Galena may direct your attention to, and make you aware of, mental programs that are not yours, i.e. "viruses." Elemental Effect: Absorbing, Grounding.

Key 1: Overview (Poverty Control Patterns <> Mind-Debugging) I am creating mental order. I allow myself to be flexible and think outside the box.

Garnet red *Vibrant Body Stone.* Red Garnet helps us appreciate and be in our body as well as move us toward action in areas we need to tend to. Use as a gem oil for personal practice or grid your workspace to get things done. Elemental Effect: Stimulating, Purifying.

Key 1: Sacred Body (Dis-ease <> Health) I care for my physical needs. My body is a sacred temple vibrating with joy. I have empathy for others' needs, as well as for myself. I love myself.

Key 2: Achievement (Get it Done <> Inactivity) I am acting where needed. I am acting to reach my goal.

Garnet (Grossular) green *Fair Banking Stone.* Green Grossular Garnet has been found to resonate with any type of activity relating to banking and management of money. If you suspect inefficiency in this area, you might benefit by doing crystal practices with this stone. Elemental Effect: Stabilizing, Stimulating, Blending.

Key 1: Money Management (Material Depletion <> Exploitation) I create well-being, both for myself and others.

Key 2: Rejuvenation (Physical-Emotional Depletion <> Letting Go) I energize my physical and emotional bodies. I am moving to a place of trust.

Garnet (Hessonite) orange-yellow *Relationship Stone.* Depending on others or having dependants is a choice we may make. If we don't know we are engaging in such patterns, problems arise sooner or later. Hessonite Garnet vibrates to the dissolution of co-dependency in any form. We may utilize this vibration in a meditation practice with Hessonite, perhaps as a talisman. Elemental Effect: Aligning, Stimulating.

Key 1: Divine Relationships (Co-dependency <> Self-Responsibility) I am a powerful manifestor. I know that I can create beauty and love. I am taking responsibility for my needs. I am aware of the needs of others and decide how I best can assist them to be themselves.

Red Gaarnet Crystal.

Garnet (Spessartine) orange-red *Project Completion Stone.* Spessartine Garnet vibrates to conservation of energy which we may use to complete things. The result of having unfinished projects or ideas costs us a lot of energy in the long run. Why not use Spessartine to assist you? Elemental Effect: Inspiring, Stimulating.

Key1: Joy (Unfinished <> Completed) I finish my projects with joy. I let go of old ideas about how things "should be done." I am now solving problems with new creative energy and joy.

Gem Silica blue-green *Feminine Wisdom Stone.* Gem Silica is formed by Chrysocolla and Quartz to create a beautiful blue stone. We may address our inner blindness by working with Gem Silica. Elemental Effect: Elevating, Balancing.

Key 1: Vision (Spiritual Blindness <> Seeing) I am letting my inner vision guide me on my path.

Key 2: Compassion (Alone / Separated <> Connected) I now empower the Divine Feminine Essence within myself. I am surrendering to the divine compassion within. I allow myself to love unconditionally.

Goethite in Aquamarine *Truth Awakener Stone.*
Elemental Effect: Stabilizing, Penetrating, Aligning.

Key 1: Awaken (My Truth <> Your Truth) I become aware of how each person sees the world differently. I accept my truth as my expression. I aspire to know the real truth.

Goethite in Amethyst *Wealth Acceptance Stone.* Elemental Effect: Inspiring, Strengthening.

Key 1: Acceptance (Wealth <> Material Possessions) I accept the wealth I have. I discover what my wealth is.

Goshenite white, clear *Water Clearing Stone.* Goshenite can be used to clear internal and external waters (emotions) by bringing light to them. Elemental Effect: Penetrating, Illumining.

Key 1: Clear Media (Emotional Clarity <> Emotional entanglement) I become a clear channel. I use my emotions to my benefit. My emotions are my outer antennae for knowing the world. I use my capacity to feel wisely.

Halite (Rock-salt) *Being Stuck Remedy Stone.* Use salt in the water purification method to clear other stones. Specimens can be placed in a grid to purify a space. This stone is water soluble. Elemental Effect: Absorbing.

Key 1: Freedom (Suffering <> Pleasure) I am dissolving my attachments, negativity and fear.

Hawk's-eye see: Tiger-eye blue

Heliodor yellow *Mastermind Stone.* Gemmy Heliodor (yellow Beryl) vibrates to affect key areas of our mind when we work with this stone. We may then rise above our limitations and expand outside our comfort zone. Elemental Effect: Inspiring, Purifying, Elevating.

Key 1: Mastery of Mind (Limitation <> Expansion of Mind) My intellectual mastery rests on how I use it. I am opening myself to my psychic abilities. I balance my ego-personality.

Hematite *Grounding Stone.* Hematite (in botryoidal, tabular crystals or massive form) is immensely helpful for bringing us down to earth, a place we need to be if we have a physical body, and act effectively in the world. Elemental Effect: Grounding, Absorbing.

Key 1: Boundaries (Invaded <> Protected) I am protected and safe. I honour my life force and my body.

Key 2: Grounded (Spaced Out <> In Sacred Space) I am grounded. I am fully present in my body. I am unified with Mother Earth and All Life.

Hemimorphite blue-green *Despair Remedy.* Hemimorphite is a hydrous zinc silicate formed at low temperatures. It is helpful to assist in integrating emotions. Elemental Effect: Balancing, Inspiring, Elevating.

Key: Serenity (Despair <> Calm) I flow with the emotions in my life. I feel at peace in the face of adversity.

Herkimer Diamond *Attunement Stone.* Herkimer Diamonds are perfectly clear double-ended Quartz, which may remind us of our perfect state of being. Elemental Effect: Stimulating, Purifying, Elevating.

Key 1: Attunement (Being Lost <> Feeling at Home) I attune to Spirit, connecting myself to the source of bliss. I am at home wherever I am.

Key 2: Illumination (Despair <> Bliss) I am aspiring to attain the highest goal of my journey. I humble myself to accepting all aspects of Spirit.

Heulandite pink *Stone of Joyful Enchantment.* Working with Heulandite may provide consolation, and bridge emotionally difficult times. Elemental Effect: Elevating, Inspiring, Absorbing.

Key 1: Graceful Flow (Opening to Love <> Holding Back/Tension) I am trusting others as well as myself. I embrace my being with loving-kindness. I am relaxing.

Hiddenite clear, green *Mental Power Stone*. Elemental Effect: Inspiring, Purifying.

Key 1: Mental Mastery (Choosing Thoughts <> Reactive Thinking) I am observing my thoughts without distraction. I listen to the wisdom of my inner guidance.

Hornblende *Addiction Remedy*. Elemental Effect: Absorbing, Grounding.

Key 1: Self-Responsibility (Co-dependency/Addiction <> Liberated) I am releasing self-destructive behaviours. I expect to rely on myself.

Howlite white-grey *Support Stone*. Howlite is mostly known as white Turquoise, and are often dyed to look like it. Elemental Effect: Absorbing.

Key 1: Solid Support (Anonymity <> Clear Identity) I show who I am. I am supported in my endeavours. I am firmly grounded.

Idocrase see: Vesuvianite

Iolite (Water-Sapphire) indigo *Dynamic Flow Stone*. Iolite can be used as a Bitchy (Beastly) Behaviour Remedy. Supportive of kidneys. Elemental Effect: Balancing, Elevating.

Key: Integration (Materialistic <> Intuitive) I am an intuitive being expanding my intuitive vision.

Key 2: Flexibility (Resistance <> Expression) I discover joy when feeling freely.

Jade blue *Dream-Maker Stone*. Blue Jade is lovely to use as a dream stone. Elemental Effect: Balancing, Elevating.

Key 1: Path of Truth (Path-Finder <> Path-Maker) I am safely finding the path to express my truth.

Key 2: Dream-Maker (Carrying Burdens <> Catching Dreams) I dream freely and express what I have learnt.

Jade green *Heart Path Stone.* Varieties of Jade from Peru is also called Inca Jade. Elemental Effect: Balancing, Penetrating.

Key 1: Path to the Heart (Aggressive Emotions <> Loving Feelings) I am the path way between my ego and my heart. I am a feeling being. I am calm.

Key 2: Subconscious Connection (Forgetfulness <> Good Memory) I am remembering my dreams clearly.

Jade lavender to clear *Path-Maker Stone.* Elemental Effect: Elevating, Inspiring.

Key 1: Path-Maker (Animal Aspect <> Soul) I am finding who I am. I remember my past dreams.

Jade (Lemurian) black *Mother Archetype Stone.* Lemurian Jade is black Jade from the Andes with inclusions of Pyrite. Elemental Effect: Inspiring, Grounding, Absorbing.

Key 1: Cycles of Life (Creation <> Destruction) I nurture all my relations. I honour the divine mother in all mothers. I pay respect to Mother Earth by my actions.

Jade (New Jade) See: Serpentine

Jasper red *Nurturing Stone.* Elemental Effect: Grounding, Absorbing.

Key 1: Nurturing (Divine Child <> Wounded child) I nurture myself. I feel supported. I listen to my needs.

Key 2: Safely Loved (Abandoned Child <> Embraced Child) I am embraced lovingly by Mother Earth. I am both a child and my parent merged. I am Loved.

Jasper red-yellow *Earth Changes Acceptance Stone.* Red and Yellow Jasper from Australia is called Mookite. Elemental Effects: Grounding, Absorbing.

Key 1: Flexibility (Safe <> Unsafe) I adapt to change. I accept the changes that come my way.

Jasper yellow *Acceptance Stone.* Elemental Effect: Grounding, Absorbing.

Key 1: Protected (Safe <> Fearful) I am grounded. I feel safe to experience the unknown.

Jasper (African Queen) *Equality Stone.* Elemental Effect: Balancing, Blending.

Key 1: Equality (Worthless <> Self-Worth) I am equal. I believe in myself. I have my work to do. I feel free.

Black Kyanite.

Jasper (Chocolate Cake) *Sugar Buster Stone.* Just now I am thinking of the Chocolate chip cookies I have in the cupboard. I want them now. Chocolate Cake Jasper helps me to recognize the folly of having 10 cookies instead of 4. Elemental Effect: Grounding, Calming.

Key 1: Compromise (Craving <> Overeating) I negotiate healthy behaviours. I watch my desires and fulfil them wisely.

Jasper (Kabamba) black-green *Spiritual Confidence Stone.* This stone comes from Africa and features orbicular patterns. Elemental Effect: Absorbing, Inspiring.

Key 1: Confidence (Worthy <> Not Good Enough) I am part of humanity. My place is here. I am confident. I am in tune with the mystery of being alive.

Jasper (Ocean) *Relaxation Stone.* Ocean Jasper is fossilized coral. Elemental Effect: Calming, Absorbing.

Key 1: Passage of time (Integration <> Trauma) I heal myself. I am emotionally stable. I am safe.

Jasper (Orbicular) *Taking Care of Business Stone.* Orbicular Jasper displays a pattern of small circular marks which we can utilize. Each mark is a sign of a project or detail we may need to attend to. Elemental Effect: Grounding, Strengthening.

Key 1: Management (Discipline <> Laziness) I am taking care of my business. I am a manager.

Jasper (Pinto Bean) orange *Food Choice Stone.* Effect: Grounding, Absorbing.

Key 1: Nourishment (Health <> Addiction) I am eating that which nourishes me.

Jet black *Addiction Remedy.* Black Jet is fossilized wood. Elemental Effect: Grounding, Absorbing.

Key 1: Freedom (Love <> Addiction/Fear) I am free to face my fears.

Kunzite pink *Stone of Emotional Commitment.* Elemental Effect: Inspiring, Elevating, Purifying.

Key 1: Emotional Commitment (Overwhelmed <> Emotional Balance) I commit to love and nurture myself. I take care of my own emotional balance. I am quiet and peaceful. I am connecting my thoughts to my feelings.

Kunzite (Elestial) *Core of Commitment Stone.* Elestial Kunzite helps us to see that our core is free from fear. Elemental Effect: Inspiring, Transforming, Aligning.

Key 1: Commitment (Cause of Fear <> Fear Pattern) I commit to uncover my true self. I am true to myself. I discover my joy by committing to self-awareness.

Kyanite black *Spiritual Boundary Stone.* Elemental Effect: Purifying, Elevating.

Key 1: Wisdom (Confusion <> Grounded) I am grounding spiritual energies into wisdom. I remember who I am. I know my boundaries.

Kyanite blue *Mental Fog Remedy.* Elemental Effect: Purifying, Inspiring.

Key 1: Clearing (Confusion <> Alignment) I am peeling away the layers of time, and release the past. I redefine my boundaries. I stand up for myself, empowered and clear.

Blue Kyanite.

Kyanite green *Stone of Right Action.* Elemental Effect: Purifying, Inspiring.

Key 1: Putting Love into Practice (Passive Confusion <> Right Action) I am unifying the left and right side of my body. I am clearing the path to the heart, and stay grounded. I act with integrity.

Kyanite orange *Sacred Relations Stone.* This stone has been used to remove obstacles between people in relationships. Elemental Effect: Purifying, Transforming.

Key 1: Cutting Ties (Letting Go <> Keeping Bonded) I am unattached to people and things. I am enjoying my friends as they are. I accept myself.

Labradorite grey, multi-colour *Magic Stone.* Elemental Effect: Transforming, Penetrating.

Key 1: Magic (Open-mindedness <> Narrow-mindedness) I invite magic into my life. I am open to receive creative inspiration. I receive clear creative inspiration from the divine.

Key 2: Mirror (Blocked Perception <> Seeing) I see a mirror of my inner light reflected in others.

Key 3: Potential (Self-Confidence <> Self-Worth) I am in charge of my own healing. I use my ability to create what my potential holds.

Labradorite golden Divine Connection Stone Elemental Effect: Elevating, Purifying, Rarefying.

Key 1: Union (Forgetfulness <> Divine connection) I remember the magical union with the golden light of Spirit. I remember where I belong. I am blissful.

Lapis Lazuli blue, gold *Stone of Wisdom.* Deep blue Lapis Lazuli from Afganistan is a silicate with calcite and pyrite. Andean Lapis Lazuli usually contains more calcite than other varieties, and allows one to stay in the present moment. Effect: Transforming, Inspiring, Elevating.

Key 1: Enlightenment (Ignorance <> Awareness) I am committing to release myself from ignorance.

Key 2: Wisdom (Illusion <> Knowledge & Understanding) I removing all obstacles for intuiting the Truth. I accept responsibility for my increasing awareness, as well as the freedom to choose.

Key 3: Present Moment (Ignorance <> Awareness) I am present to experience wisdom.

Larimar light blue *Dolphin Stone.* Elemental Effect: Balancing, Elevating.

Key 1: Emotional Wisdom / Balance (Upset <> Calm) I am remaining calm. I am riding with the dolphin energies of wisdom. I manage my emotions and stay balanced.

Key 2: Transition (Extreme Sensitivity <> Emotionally Numb) I shift perspective in order to heal.

Larvikite black multi-colour *Stone of the Magician.* Larvikite is a type of Labradorite. Elemental Effect: Grounding, Transforming.

Key 1: Magician (Impossible <> Magic Actions) I manifest anything that I need, including fun and joy.

Lazulite deep blue *The Seed of Wisdom*. Lazulite is a phosphate mineral, helpful for gaining understanding with clear perspective. Elemental Effect: Inspiring, Penetrating.

Key 1: Seed of Wisdom (Understanding <> Ignoring) I am open to understand. I learn to be wise.

Lazurite See Lapis Lazuli

Leaverite all colours *Stone of Non-Attachment.* Leaverite is any mineral left behind by others and is abundant in construction sites, near cities and at most mining localities. To get a good Leaverite, contact your local gem club. Most old rock hounds have lots of it, and it is usually free! Elemental Effect: Grounding, Inspiring.

Key 1: Non-attachment (Rejection <> Hoarding) I now release the need to own anything beyond what I truly need. I release all that I truly do not need.

Lepidolite lavender *Mental Balancer Stone*. Lepidolite is a purple mica and occurs in cleavage, as wands, and botryoidal (it looks like a brain). Lepidolite is heat resistant and have been used in old wood stoves as glass. Elemental Effect: Balancing, Elevating.

Key 1: Mental Reprogramming (Depression <> Joy) I am Letting Go. I choose Joy. I bridge the gap between my heart and my head. I am letting go of suffering.

Lingam *Sacred Body Stone*. Originally Lingams were birthed out of the Ganges River, and illustrate the union of the male and female. The shape resembles the male phallus and the female is illustrated by the red mark to the middle of the stone. Originally these red-brown stones were washed up on the river shore. Most Lingams available, are now manufactured from rocks near the holy Ganges. Devotees of Shiva use these special stones in sacred religious rituals. Lingams are also made from clear Quartz and other minerals. Elemental Effect: Grounding, Balancing.

Key 1: Divine Union (Frigidity/Impotence <> Ecstasy) I create sacred space inside my body. I honour my body. My body is my sacred temple here on Earth. I balance my male and female polarity. I nurture myself.

Lingam black *Earth Intimacy Stone* Black Lingams have

been used to grid points on the Earth similar to acupuncture treatment. Elemental Effect: Grounding, Transformation.

Key 1: Vulnerability (Defensive <> Needing no shields) I am safe to be vulnerable inside and outside my home.

Key 2: Earth Healing (Exploitation <> Abundance Gifts) I am attuning with Nature, my earthly home.

Lepidolite Cleavage.

Lingam clear Quartz Lingams can be used as a symbol for

the sacred essence in all things and in practice to realize our great gift of a living glorious planet as our home. Elemental Effect: Inspiring, Elevating.

Key 1: Spirit Within (Sacredness <> Ignorance) I am treating life with sacredness and honour. I am a model for others. I honour all life.

Lithium Quartz *Mental Aligner Stone.* Elemental Effect:

Inspiring, Focussing, Elevating.

Key 1: Alignment (Peace of Mind <> Terror) I am focussed and clear to take action in my life. I am a clear light and act rationally. I am balanced and clear. I am inspired to create.

Lodestone
blackish metal lustre *Stone of Grounded Direction.* Lodestone (Magnetite) was used by ancient seafarers to guide them on long journeys. Its magnetic properties allowed them to be used as a compass aligning with the magnetic north. We may use Lodestone to ground our emotions. Elemental Effect: Balancing, Grounding.

Key 1: Guidance (Lack of Direction <> Hyper Focus) I am allowing myself to be guided, finding my way without struggle. I am at home wherever I go. I am finding my way, even in the midst of chaos.

Magenta Stone
magenta *Love Unity Stone.* Magenta stone is a serpentine called purple Stichtite (hydrated magnesium chromium carbonate). Elemental Effect: Stabilizing, Elevating.

Key 1: Life Journey (Nature <> Spirit) My inner being is in the earth school to learn. I am more than my mind.

Magnesite
white *Toxicity Absorption Stone.* Elemental Effect: Absorbing, Stabilizing.

Key 1: Cleansing (Healthy Body <> Letting go) I am now ready to be free. I have health and I love myself.

Magnetite grey metallic see: Lodestone

Malachite
green *Emotional Purger Stone.* Malachite is a basic copper carbonate. Elemental Effect: Purifying, Penetrating, Moving.

Key 1: Emotional Mastery (Joy/Peace <> Frustration/Hate/Anger) I transcend trapped emotions, harmful to others and myself. I am a skilled sailor on my emotional ocean. I am an emotional master.

Key 2: Change Now (Feeling Trapped <> Feeling Free) I am challenging limitations, allowing change to come. I am healing my emotional body.

Meteor
Space Traveller Stone. Meteor is extraterrestrial material that is catapulted into the Earth's atmosphere. Meteors contain mostly metal, including iron and nickel. Shamans and sword makers valued this material for their masterworks. Excalibur, the sword in the Arthurian legend, is said to be made from meteor metal. Elemental Effect: Transforming, Penetrating, Grounding.

Key 1: Family of Origin (Lost Child <> At home) I am connecting to the stellar realm of my initial birth, where my seed consciousness still resides.

Key 2: Spiritual Warrior (Fight <> Surrender) I am following my conviction, letting my guidance lead me on my path. I am becoming a humble vessel, doing only what is needed for the benefit of all people.

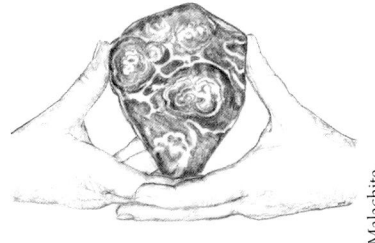

Malachite.

Mica
gold *Mirroring Stone.* Mica occurs in cleavages or thin hexagonal plates, fragile but heat resistant. Elemental Effect: Elevating, Opening.

Key 1: Process of Self-Awareness (Personal Flaws <> True Nature) I discard flaws and delusions that cover my true nature.

Mica green See: Fuchsite

Mica green-gold
Layers of Life Stone. Elemental Effect: Elevating, Opening.

Key 1: Divine Essence (Brute/Bitch <> Saint/Angel) My inner core is embraced in the loving light of G-d. I am aspiring to become the best I can be. I am patient in my search for myself.

Mica purple see: Lepidolite

Micalated Quartz *Past Life Review Stone.* Elemental Effect: Elevating, Opening.

Key 1: Lesson Review (Free <> Past Baggage) I learn from past mistakes and experiences. I am grateful for my lessons.

Moldavite green *Spirit Communication Stone.* Moldavite is formed from the earthly debris created by a meteor impact. Elemental Effect: Blending, Elevating, Illumining.

Key 1: Star Born (Foreigners <> One of Us) I am open to accept others, regardless of their origin. I accept wisdom from wherever it comes. I am present in this moment. I accept my inner mission.

Mookite see: Jasper red-yellow

Moonstone ivory or white *Feminine Stone.* Moonstone is a Feldspar mineral that exhibits a moon-like lustre. Elemental Effect: Balancing, Absorbing.

Key 1: Femininity (Strength <> Beauty) I am strong and beautiful. I am a caring human being. My femininity adds to my character.

Key 2: Benediction (Shadows of the Soul/Fear <> Knowing) I am exploring my shadow side. I expand into the realm of my inner senses. I am blessed on my journey into the unknown.

Moonstone (Rainbow) *Unknown Future Stone.* Transparent, or white Moonstone from Madagascar with bluish or rainbow luminescence, has been highly treasured in jewellery. Elemental Effect: Penetrating, Calming.

Key 1: Fearless (Emotional Peace <> Worry) I am at peace. My worries guide me to become fearless. I venture to unknown grounds with ease and joy.

Moonstone peach *Femininity & Rejuvenation Stone.* Peach is a colour of joy and happiness. Find your shade of perfect peach. Elemental Effect: Balancing, Absorbing, Elevating.

Key 1: Rejuvenation (Depleted <> Juicy) I am monitoring my emotions, letting them flow with grace. I travel gently on the river of my emotions.

Moonstone silver-sheen *Feminine Reflection Stone.*
The grey and black moonstones are beneficial for working with the Earth Star chakra below the feet and also to feel how the new embryo would have felt in the darkness of the womb before birth. Elemental Effect: Absorbing, Grounding.

Key 1: Earth Mother (Light of G-d <> Black Void) I am both yin and yang, I honour each side. I am integrating the wisdom of both the Earth and the Heaven. I am safe wherever I am.

Muscovite *white Stone of Reflection.* Muscovite occurs together-
er with Quartz. Elemental Effect: Absorbing, Elevating.

Key 1: Reflection (Seeing <> Denial) I look into the matrix that holds my beliefs. I am opening myself in relation to the whole.

Muscovite in Quartz *Trauma Remedy Stone.* Elemen-
tal Effect: Absorbing, Elevating, Expanding.

Key 1: Trauma Release (Free <> Hurt) I am open to feel joy. I am free to experience life fully. I am learning how to feel free.

Nuumite *Global Intuiter Stone.* Nuumite (from Greenland) has
been used to enhance psychic abilities and extra-sensory perception (ESP) and to find solutions to physical illnesses. Elemental Effect: Expanding Penetrating, Elevating.

Key 1: ESP Training (Psychic <> Intuitive) I am a being capable of knowing all I need to know. I may learn to grow by using my ESP.

Obsidian black *Self-Security Stone.* Obsidian is a volcanic
glass and is the result of volcanic activity. Elemental Effect: Stabilizing, Purifying, Elevating.

Key 1: Protection (Attacked <> Safe) I am protected and safe in all situations.

Obsidian gold-sheen *Stone of Psychic Protection.*
Gold-sheen Obsidian has been used as a violation remedy and is helpful to use in the practice of Inner Journeys. The gold sheen variety has a particular protecting quality in healing work, especially beneficial in the shape of a sphere. Elemental Effect: Stabilizing, Elevating.

Key 1: Protection (Violation <> Facing My Demons) I am safe. I am protected. I feel safe and in balance. I allow the heart of the matter to emerge. Feeling safe, I am able to look at my fears.

Obsidian mahogany *Pain Remedy Stone.* Elemental Effect: Absorbing, Stabilizing.

Key 1: Freedom/Gift of Learning (Pain <> Release) I am allowing my body to feel joy. I accept that pain is my teacher.

Obsidian rainbow *Journey Protection Stone.* This variety exhibits bands of rainbow colours. Elemental Effect: Absorbing, Inspiring.

Key 1: Angelic Protection (Abused/Needy/ Dependent <> Healing) I am divinely protected and safe. I am healing the most vulnerable parts of myself.

Obsidian silver-sheen *Stone of Protection.* Elemental Effect: Balancing, Grounding, Elevating.

Key 1: Belonging/Grounded (Confusion/Fear <> Facing Fear) I am connecting to the essence of my roots in the Earth. I belong here. I am safe.

Obsidian smokey *Boundary & Completion Stone.* Smokey Obsidian, also called Apache Tears, can be found in desert areas and is said to be the tears of the wives of fallen warriors that had died in battle. Elemental Effect: Stabilizing, Elevating.

Key 1: Released/Completion (Running from Fear <> Facing Fear) I dare to encounter the unknown on my spiritual journey. I release my attachment to grief and fear. I am complete.

Obsidian (Snowflake) *Serenity in Chaos Stone.* The essence of a snowflake is water irregardless of the surrounding temperature. Elemental Effect: Absorbing.

Key 1: Indestructible (Chaos <> Serenity) My essence remains the same irregardless of outer phenomena. I remain peaceful.

Onyx black *Grief & Loss Remedy.* Elemental Effect: Absorbing.

Key 1: Support (Grief/Denial <> Mourning) I allow my process of grieving. I accept my feelings and let go.

Opal blue *Emotional Integration Stone.* Andean blue Opal is helpful for remaining in peace. Elemental Effect: Expanding, Balancing.

Key 1: Emotional Peace (Relaxed Awareness <> Stress) I am in a state of relaxed awareness. I am peaceful. I love the feeling of being in command of my emotions.

Opal pink *Heart Journey Stone.* Pink Andean Opal helps us to stay kind. Elemental Effect: Stimulating, Balancing.

Key 1: Diplomacy of the Heart (Kindness <> Harshness) Kindness will reach the depths of the heart, where force cannot go. I act with kindness.

Opal white with fire *Emotional Observer Stone.* Elemental Effect: Moving, Balancing.

Key 1: Observing Emotion (Emotional Reaction <> Choosing to feel) I can choose how I feel. I choose to feel Love and Compassion. I am conscious of my emotional flow without engagement.

Opal yellow *Liver Detox Stone.* Elemental Effect: Purifying, Grounding.

Key 1: Unaffected (Toxic Contamination <> Detoxification Regime) I stay impervious to toxins in my emotions and in my mind. I am strengthening my physical body.

Opal Chalcedony see: Quartz (Girasol)

Opalite
mustard green *Digestive System Stone.* Elemental Effect: Blending, Moving, Absorbing.

Key 1: Digestion (Nurturing <> Being Fed) I am receiving the nurturing I am given. I am mindful of what I eat. I am respectful of all the nutrients I use (air, food, light, energy and love).

Opalite caves
Earth Mystery Stone. Opalite caves is a geode with chalcedony, opalite and other minerals. Elemental Effect: Absorbing, Elevating.

Key 1: Mystery (Source of Life <> Source of Death) I am initiated in the Earth's own Mystery school by being here. I am part of the mystery of life. I am conscious of the precious place I inhabit.

Pearl
Stone of Purity. The pearl (created by the oyster from an irritant) shows us the result of inner purification made perfect. Elemental Effect: Transforming, Calming.

Key 1: Process of Healing (Peaceful Solution <> Aggression) I affect my situation. I am capable of altering my fate. I am willing to do what it takes to heal.

Peridot
chartreuse *Humour Stone.* Elemental Effect: Transforming, Elevating.

Key 1: Humour (Illness/Addictive Habits <> Health) I am restoring my health on all levels. I invite humour and a light heart. I am a joyful being.

Petalite
clear white/pink *Spirit Guide Stone.* Petalite is essential for conscious connection with our guidance team. Elemental Effect: Elevating, Inspiring, Aligning.

Key 1: Guidance/Prayer (It's all about me <> The Bigger picture) I am inviting angelic vibration into my being. I have the galactic forces at my command; all I have to do is to ask.

Petrified Wood brown-red *Stone of Patience.* Fossil remnants of ancient trees. Elemental Effect: Grounding, Stabilizing.

Key 1: Patience (Restlessness <> Unhurried) I am patiently waiting for the correct timing. I act when the time is right.

Key 2: Immortality (Fear of Death <> Acceptance)I am an immortal being beyond death.

Phantom Quartz *Ignorance Remedy Stone.* Elemental Effect: Purifying, Elevating.

Key 1: Awareness (Ignorance <> Active Search) I am seeing through the veils of ignorance.

Key 2: Precious Gifts (Idiots/Difficulties <> Friends/Fortunes) I accept all experience as opportunity to grow.

Phantom Quartz white *Higher Self Guide.* White phantom quartz is also called Angel Phantom (Amphibole). Elemental Effect: Elevating, Aligning.

Key 1: Higher Self Guide (Contraction <> Expansion) I am embraced by Spirit. I am open. I abide in bliss.

Phenacite clear or white *Cosmic Connection Stone.* Elemental Effect: Elevating.

Key 1: Cosmic Connection (Smaller Self <> Higher Self). I am One, merged with all that is. I accept what is here and now.

Pietersite blue *Tempest Stone.* The blue Pietersite is usually from Africa. Elemental Effect: Transforming, Balancing.

Key 1: Transition (Emotional Storm <> Good Weather) I see the purpose of my inner storm. I transform the past into my present choice for the future.

Pietersite red *Physical Purger Stone.* Red Pietersite is found in China. Elemental Effect: Purifying, Balancing.

Key 1: Purge (Health <> Torment/Dis-ease) I purge my physical being. I am a vibrant being of the universe.

Prasiolite yellow-green *Cerebral Activation Stone*. Prasiolite is yellow-green Amethyst. Elemental Effect: Stimulating, Aligning.

Key 1: Brain Activation (Clarity <> Diffusion) I take care of my brain. I select thoughts that benefit sentient beings.

Pyrite Sphere.

Prehnite pale green *Shamanic Journey Stone*. Prehnite can be used as a 'substitution stone', meaning you can use Prehnite as proxy instead of a stone you do not have. Elemental Effect: Elevating, Aligning.

Key 1: Remembering (Learning <> Forgetting/Ignoring) I remember my dreams, and their messages. I create space within to remember.

Prehnite yellow *Last Resort Stone*. Elemental Effect: Transformative, Absorbing.

Key 1: Transformative Journey (Resourceful <> Dead Ends) I am discovering new resources as I journey forward.

Prehnite with Epidote pale green *Shamanic Journey Stone*. Elemental Effect: Elevating, Stabilizing.

Key 1: Transition (Addiction <> Self-Knowledge) I journey to my centre of love. I tend to my needs with loving care.

Pyrite metallic gold *Poverty Remedy Stone* Elemental Effect: Grounding, Inspiring.

Key 1: Abundance (I have <> I have not) I have the mental clarity to see and manifest abundance.

Key 2: Nurturing Trust (Poverty <> Prosperity) I trust myself to be nurtured. I see how my beliefs have created my situation.

Pyrite (cubic) *Mind Balancing Stone.* Elemental Effect: Grounding, Inspiring.

Key 1: Mental Acuity & Balance (Confusion <> Learning) I am strengthening my mental capacity. I am widening my mind.

Key 2: Timelessness (Not enough time <> Having Time) I am a timeless being, abundant by nature. I have infinite time available. I use my time for what I deem important.

Pyrite (dodecahedral cluster) *Stone of Love and Abundance.* How one feels about abundance and prosperity are only cultural or social beliefs. Elemental Effect: Balancing, Inspiring, Stabilizing.

Key 1: Group Consciousness (Poverty <> Material/Spiritual Prosperity) I am abundantly supported on all levels of my being. I am a prosperous spiritual being.

Pyrite (Isis-Osiris) *Mental Integration Stone.* Elemental Effect: Balancing, Inspiring, Grounding.

Key 1: Integration (Receptive/Passive <> Giving/Active) I am in balance between giving and receiving. I integrate my situations into balance.

Pyrotite golden metallic *Magnetism Stone.* Elemental Effect: Inspiring, Grounding, Aligning.

Key 1: Force Field (Being together <> Scattered) I am in harmony. I am part of the divine hologram held by magnetic forces. I am following the divine flow.

Quartz clear *Mastery Stone.* Elemental Effect: Inspiring, Elevating, Aligning.

Key 1: Mastery of Unity (Good <> Bad) I am the master of my own being. I am centred and aligned to my source of being.

Key 2: Self-awareness (Negativity <> Optimism) I am becoming aware of all I need to know. I am a beacon of Light, inspiring and uplifting others.

Quartz (Bent) *Life Changes Stone.* Bent Quartz is the result of changes within the earth where it is growing, may it be earthquakes or other changes. It broke the crystal completely or partially, but the action of growing ensued and healed the break starting in a new and different direction. Elemental Effect: Transforming, Stabilizing.

Key 1: Acceptance of what is (Rigid Thinking <> Freedom) I am already in the place I seek. I let go of trying to control my life.

Quartz (Beta) *Stone of Perspective.* If we realize that by changing perspective we will see more of the complete picture, Beta Quartz shows this by growing along a different axis than regular Quartz. Elemental Effect: Expanding, Aligning, Stabilizing.

Key 1: Vision & Trust (Fear Habits of Comfort <> Effort) I am seeing things from other perspectives, while letting go of control, and trusting my perception.

Quartz (Cathedral Lightbrary) *Temple of Knowledge.* A master of crystals that truly transmits the wisdom we seek, but only those who apply themselves will see and receive its treasures. This is the safety switch. It is up to you to turn it on. Start by assuming the responsibility for yourself now, and then you are free to go wherever you choose. Elemental Effect: Elevating, Inspiring, Expanding.

Key 1: Wisdom/Responsibility (Ignorant <> Knowledgeable) I enter the inner temple of my being. I take full responsibility for what I know. I am what I have been - I become what I do now.

Quartz (Channeller) *The Channelling Crystal* is one of the precious master crystals given to us. Use it to discover the wisdom you want to achieve and open up to the dimensions of life previously un-encountered. Elemental Effect: Elevating, Opening, Aligning.

Key 1: Consciousness (Foggy Mind <> Clear Mind) I am opening myself to become increasingly receptive. I am aligned to my inner guide who helps me to recover myself.

Quartz (Clarity) *Clarity Stone.* A variety of Clear Quartz
that occurs with Aluminium, which makes it very clear and gives it moon like lustre. Elemental Effect: Inspiring, Expanding.

Key 1: Meditation (Confusion/Dissociation <> Clarity) I am assisted to see with perfect clarity. I am looking deep within to find solutions.

Quartz (cluster) *Sacred Space Stone.* Elemental Effect:
Purifying, Elevating, Aligning.

Key 1: Meditation (Focus <> Distraction) I am present. I am aware of the eternal now.

Key 2: Sacred Space (Clutter <> Order) I release old patterns. I am clearing my inner and outer spaces. My space is clear and wonderful to be in. I love what surrounds me.

Quartz (Devic Temple) *Place many Devic Temples*
in your home, and many stone devas will come to live with you. They are delightful sparks of inspiration and gladness, as well as a source of a deep sense of joyfulness. Elemental Effect: Inspiring, Elevating, Rarefying.

Key 1: Self-Realization (Exclusion <> Inclusion) I create sacred space in myself, and in my home. I am guided on my path towards self-mastery. I honour sacredness. I move in service to Life.

Quartz (Double-terminated) *Life Force Stone.*
Elemental Effect: Stimulating, Expanding.

Key 1: Embracing Life Force (Depletion <> Energized) I am letting the Divine Flow of Energy guide me to Harmony, Perfection and Health.

Quartz (Dow Crystal) *Universal Consciousness Stone.*
A stone to come back to again, and again. Learn from its vast wis-

dom about the world and beyond. Elemental Effect: Aligning, Purifying, Elevating.

Key 1: Clear Consciousness (Imperfect <> Perfect) I let Spirit flow through me; this is my reality. I am inviting perfection on all levels, and realize the Great Perfection.

Quartz (Elestial) *Core Issue Remedy*. Elestial Quartz is an essential healing stone for healers. Elemental Effect: Purging, Stabilizing, Aligning.

Key 1: Healing (Treating Symptoms <> Treating the Cause) I am going within, to the core of my issue to heal. I am healing.

Quartz (Elestial) clear/silver *Ascension Stone*. A master to help break through our densest inner barriers. Elemental Effect: Elevating, Purifying, Rarefying.

Key 1: Healing (Higher Self <> Ascension) I am. I am purifying myself to the point of Ascension. I accept healing now.

Quartz (Elestial) smokey *True Self Stone*. A master to guide you slowly but very thoroughly. There is no point in hiding. Elemental Effect: Purifying, Grounding.

Key 2: Healing (Survival Mentality <> Grounding) I am grounded and centred. I am present to my true self.

Quartz (Elestial) white *Solar Plexus Healer*. If you are working though power issues with emotional undertones, then this is the stone for you. Elemental Effect: Purifying, Aligning.

Key 1: Healing (Higher Self <> Ego Self) I am embracing my inner divinity, accepting all changes with grace.

Quartz (Girasol) *Clutter Buster Stone*. Elemental Effect: Purifying, Aligning, Stabilizing.

Key 1: Wise Path (Observation <> Ignorance) I am releasing the obstacles on my road to freedom. I use my energy and actions efficiently.

Quartz (Generator) *Light Amplifier Stone.* Generator
Crystals are Quartz with symmetrical termination (six even triangles forming the apex). They are powerful stones to use in Crystal Grids, as they create a harmonized field for intention. Elemental Effect: Stimulating, Elevating.

Key 1: Ambassador (Darkness <> Light) I invite a force field of radiant light to become a beacon of light whereever I am.

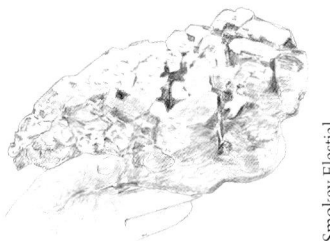

Smokey Elestial.

Quartz (Isis Crystal) *Crystal of Divine Balance.* The
Isis Crystal is a master exhibiting a pentagram on the main face of its termination. Elemental Effect: Inspiring, Elevating, Balancing.

Key 1: Balance in Change (Passive <> Active) I am constantly celebrating my inner male and female in union.

Key 2: Community (Separated <> Shared) I celebrate the life force available, I receive and give it freely.

Key 3: Conscious Journey (Direction <> Ignorance) I am attuning to the subtle energies behind worldly realities to become whole.

Quartz (Laser Wand) *Etherical Aligner Crystal.* Laser
wands are elongated points, which exhibit a tiny but very sharp tip and have an etched, ugly looking body. Do not confuse this crystal with what are regularly called lasers, with broader tips. To discern if it is a Laser Wand, feel the energy emanating from the tip. It should be very sharp and cutting energetically. Elemental Effect: Aligning, Opening, Purifying.

Key 1: Etheric Surgery (Dis-eased energy <> Clearing) I clear out my mental-emotional closet. I move, guided by Spirit.

Quartz (Lemurian Seed) *Ancient Wisdom Stone.*

Lemurian Seed Crystals are said to bear the preserved records of the early era of Lemuria. Elemental Effect: Illumining, Rarefying, Stabilizing.

Key 1: Ancient Wisdom (Healing <> Afflictions) I am a son/daughter of the ancients, and I remember what I have learnt. I act in accordance to the inner wisdom I trust.

Quartz (Manifestation) *A Manifestation Crystal* is

a clear Quartz crystal that has another tiny Quartz crystal completely enclosed within it. It is a very rare crystal to find. Elemental Effect: Inspiring, Transforming, Stabilizing.

Key 1: Intent (Lack <> Having) I create my dreams by surrendering to Spirit. I am a channel of Divine Light.

Quartz (Metamorphosis) clear opalescent *Metamorphosis Stone.* Upon radiation, this stone turns into golden green Ouro Verde Quartz. Elemental Effect: Transforming, Purging.

Key 1: Hidden Quality (Radiance <> Desolation) I am the source of my well-being. I have the knowledge to heal, with my body and spirit to guide me.

Quartz (Morion) black *Black Rider Stone.* Morion Quartz is created in the earth by irradiation. Elemental Effect: Absorbing, Stabilizing, Transforming.

Key 1: Hidden Treasure (Ultimate Strength <> Weakness) I have an untapped potential within. I access my inner strength when I need it. I have strength.

Quartz (Nirvana) peachy-rose *Heart Tuner Stone.* This variety seems to have grown in red earth that can be found in many sacred places. See the practice of Crystal Spas. Elemental Effect: Stabilizing, Purifying, Elevating.

Key 1: Attuned (Separation <> Together) I am part of the One. My heart brings me together with my source of being.

Quartz (Rainbow) *Inspiration Stone.* Has been used as a Disease Remedy and to inspire artists to start creating their art. Elemental Effect: Elevation, Inspiring, Aligning.

Key 1: Meditation (Pain/Dis-ease <> Bliss/Health) I am connecting to my Inner Divine Self on all levels. I am a rainbow bridge between Earth and Spirit.

Nirvana Quartz.

Quartz (Record Keeper) *Insight Stone.* The Record Keeper Crystal exhibits small raised triangles on the terminating faces. One can find record keepers on several crystals, including Quartz, Ruby, Dioptase, Kunzite and Hiddenite. See also entries for the individual minerals. Elemental Effect: Inspiring, Elevating.

Key 1: Meditation/Wisdom (Ignorance <> Knowledge) I open myself to all wisdom. I am listening and become more aware.

Quartz (Sceptre) *Stone of Spiritual Power.* Elemental Effect: Elevating, Stabilizing

Key 1: Spiritual Power (Lack of Power <> Earthly Power) I am filled with spiritual powers that I use with loving kindness.

Quartz (Singing) *Self-Expression Stone.* Quartz crystals that make audible sounds upon touching each other. Elemental Effect: Inspiring, Elevating.

Key 1: Celestial Sound (Suppression <> Expression) I attune to the sound of Creation. I reclaim my voice, expressing who I am.

Quartz Singing Bowls
Moulded bowls of Quartz that sing when played. Elemental Effect: Aligning, Elevating.

Key 1: Tone/Tuning (Harmony <> Discord) As I sound my bowl, I heal. My sounds create harmony in myself and in my home.

Quartz (Snow)
Lesson Learning Stone. Elemental Effect: Stabilizing, Blending.

Key 1: Learning (Achievements <> Desires) I open to new things. I am open to learn.

Quartz (Star Gate)
Inter-Planetary Travel Stone. The Star Gate Quartz features a hexagonal shape at the main terminating face that points sideways. Elemental Effect: Aligning, Expanding.

Key 1: Multi-dimensionality (Joined <> Isolated) I am part of the oneness of the universe.

Quartz (Star Gazer)
Star Gazer Crystal is distinguished by a tiny horizontal crystals attached to the very tip of the main crystal. Elemental Effect: Focussing, Elevating, Grounding.

Key 1: Infinity (Vision <> Rigidity) I am aware of the infinite possibilities in the universe.

Quartz (Star Wand)
Grid of Light Stone. These are slender Quartz points (I have seen only sizes up to 1-2 inches long) that exhibit unusual coherence and vibration, usually with bluish hue. When placed together they form an energy grid. Elemental Effect: Rarefying, Aligning, Elevating.

Key 1: Grid of Light (Wasteland of the Soul <> Fertile Grounds) I am bringing star-light into my aura. I manifest sacred space.

Quartz (Strawberry)
Love Elixir Stone. Elemental Effect: Inspiring, Balancing.

Key 1: Love Elixir (Heart-Ache <> Freedom to Heal) I connect to my inner heart, which heals me.

Quartz (Tabular) *Great River Stone.* Tabular Quartz has been used as a Rigidity Remedy. Elemental Effect: Expanding, Stimulating.

Key 1: Widened Focus (Rigidly Narrow-minded <> Openly Flexible) I widen my focus, allowing myself to perceive the wider picture of my situation.

Key 2: Ego Detachment (Reactive Mind <> Observing Mind) I interact easily with people. I take nothing personally.

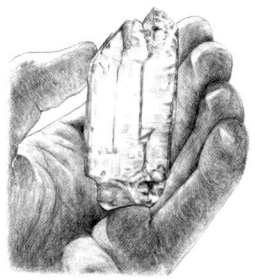

Tantric Twins Crystal.

Quartz (Tangerine) *Conflict Resolution Stone.* Tangerine Quartz has a thin natural tangerine (orange-red) coloured veil covering its surface. Elemental Effect: Stimulating, Purifying.

Key 1: Benevolent Relationships (Animal Urges <> Conscious Creation) I am the conductor and the composer of my life experience.

Quartz (Tantric Twins) *Soul Mate Stone.* Elemental Effect: Stimulating, Purifying.

Key 1: Divine Union (Freedom to relate <> Co-dependency) I am balanced and even-minded in all my relationships. I find divine unity in all people, and in all things.

Quartz (Time-Link) *Time Travel Stone.* Elemental Effect: Elevating, Expanding.

Key 1: Time Travel (Expanded Consciousness <> Limited Mind) I am the sum of all my experiences; it is up to me to attach pain or joy to them.

Quartz (Tower Crystal) Tower Crystals have been
used as a *Crisis Remedy*. Tower Crystals have their base or tip broken off. Their effect is similar to the Tarot Card: *The Tower*. Elemental Effect: Transforming.

Key 1: The Unknown (Resistance to Change <> Flexible) I am embracing change with joy and curiosity knowing therein lies my gift of Love.

Quartz (Transformer) *Transformer Crystal* has areas on
its body that are transformed, manifesting an entirely new crystal formation. Elemental Effect: Transforming.

Key 1: Metamorphosis (The Known <> The Unknown Potential) I invite the unknown potential to manifest. I step out into the unknown, trusting the highest good to be with me.

Quartz (Transmitter) *Telepathy Stone*. Elemental Effect: Elevating, Expanding.

Key 1: Transmission (Shutting Out <> Listening). I am mindful of what each moment holds. I am listening and communicating.

Quartz (Window) *Seer Stone*. Elemental Effect: Inspiring, Opening.

Key 1: Perceptive Awareness (Ignorance <> Seeing) I allow the unknown to guide me to see a Higher Good.

Quartz Wands *Energy Mastery Crystals.* A matched pair
of Quartz Crystal Wands may move energy in the hands of a shaman or healer. Citrine or Smokey Quartz is also used. Elemental Effect: Inspiring, Purifying, Elevating.

Key 1: Energy Mastery (Unaware of Potential <> Energy Movement) I open my channels to heal.

Quartz yellow *Belly Balancer Stone*. Elemental Effect: Absorbing, Transforming.

Key 1: Assimilation (Constipation <> Regularity) I accept the food I eat as true nourishment.

Rhodochrosite
pink-white bands *Inner Child Stone.* Elemental Effect: Balancing, Purifying.

Key 1: Inner Child (Abandoned/Abused <> Loved) I love all parts of myself. I prepare my heart as a place for love. I let go and let G-d.

Rhodonite
medium-pink with black *Processing Stone & Hate Remedy.* Note: This stone is especially helpful for some men (and women, too) as it calls for action rather than just being passive and reflective. Elemental Effect: Balancing, Purifying, Grounding.

Key 1: Processing Emotion (Aggression <> Conflict) I am grounded in Love and Compassion.

Rose Quartz
Self-Love Stone. Elemental Effect: Inspiring, Transforming, Elevating.

Key 1: Compassion (Self-Hate <> Self-Love) I love myself, inviting beneficial thoughts and feelings about myself.

Key 2: Worthiness (Self-Criticism <> Self-Esteem) I am worthy of Love. I am appreciating myself and who I am.

Rose Quartz (Elestial)
Core of Love Stone. This is the energy of the Tarot Arcanum: *The World.* Elemental Effect: Illumining, Penetrating, Stabilizing.

Key 1: Core of Love (Worthiness <> Self-Hate) I love myself. I have compassion for my past mistakes.

Rose Quartz (Girasol)
Self-Created Chaos Remedy. Elemental Effect: Inspiring, Balancing, Elevating.

Key 1: Loving Kindness (Hate <> Love) I extend my loving to all beings. I know only friends.

Rose Quartz (Star)
Star Rose Quartz vibrates for dissolving the 'need' for others. Then we can be with others unencumbered by co-dependency. Elemental Effect: Inspiring Purifying, Elevating.

Key 1: Focus on Love (Essence of Love <> Romance) I release my need for another. I love myself. I attract people who also love themselves.

Ruby *magenta Stone of Passion.* Elemental Effect: Purifying, Stimulating, Elevating.

Key 1: Beauty (Pain <> Vibrant Health) I am nurturing my spirit, bringing Beauty and Love into my life.

Key 2: Passion (Longing <> Gratification) My passionate longing leads me to Spirit. I am joyful union.

Ruby (Elestial) *Core of Passion Stone.* Elemental Effect: Opening, Transforming, Illumining.

Key 1: Core of Passion (Ecstasy <> Pain) My heart is a place of joy. I open my heart.

Ruby (Star) *magenta Stone of Passion.* The star in Ruby is inclusion of Rutile, which makes Star Ruby a particularly active stone to work with. Elemental Effect: Purifying, Stimulating, Elevating.

Key 1: Fulfilment of Passion (Ideal <> Afflicted) I am clearing the way for passionate enthusiasm.

Ruby in Zoisite *magenta and green Stone of Passionate Involvement.* Elemental Effect: Purifying, Stimulating, Elevating.

Key 1: Immortal Beauty (Old <> Youth) I am the beauty of the immortal spirit within.

Rutillated Quartz *Energizer Stone.* Elemental Effect: Stimulating, Transforming.

Key 1: Life-Force-Cornucopia (Physical Energy <> Spiritual Radiance) I am gifting all life I touch with vibrant and loving energy.

Ryolite (Rainforest) *Forest Elemental's Stone.* Elemental Effect: Balancing, Absorbing.

Key 1: Canopy of Life (Nurturing <> Exploiting) I attune to nature to sustain myself. I am cared for by Mother Earth.

Sacred Seven (Super Seven™) *All Chakra Stone.* Sacred Seven is also called 'Melody' Stone and contains seven minerals: Amethyst, Cacoxenite, Goethite, Quartz, Lepidocrocite, Rutile, Smokey Quartz. Elemental Effect: Transforming, Purifying, Elevating.

Key 1: Authentic Self (Hiding <> Naked Self) I am my true authentic Self, a source of joy to others and myself.

Key 2: Transformation (Uneven <> Balanced) I am allowing my divine core to be in charge of my being.

Sapphire blue *Self-Sufficiency Stone.* Elemental Effect: Inspiring, Elevating, Purifying.

Key 1: Empowered Abundance (Co-dependency <> Self-sufficiency) I am simplifying my life, being clear about what I actually need. I honour the sacredness of my being.

Key 2: Divine Wisdom (Lack of direction <> Knowingness) I am in communication with Spirit, receiving all I need to know.

Sard brown See: Chalcedony, Gaia Agate

Sardonyx see: Chalcedony, Sard, Onyx

Scolecite white *Artists' Block Remedy.* Elemental Effect: Inspiring, Elevating.

Key 1: Creativity (Artists' block <> Inspirational Joy) I am allowing inspiration and Joy to come to me, providing me with a fountain of light and happiness.

Sedona Red Rock *Sacred Earth Stone.* Elemental Effect: Grounding, Opening, Aligning.

Key 1: Conservation (Vibrant Energy <> Dead Matter) I respect the sacredness of the earth. I am part of sacred Earth.

Selenite white clear *Stone of Light Activation*. Elemental Effect: Aligning, Elevating, Balancing.

Key 1: Light Activation (Dense Body <> Light Body) I am transformed forever as I breathe in the liquid Light of Spirit.

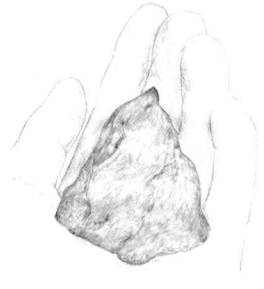

Shungite.

Seraphinite black with light star bursts *Divine Matrix Aligner*. Elemental Effect: Absorbing, Stabilizing, Rarefying.

Key 1: Life-Force (Health <> Illness) I am flowing with Divine Energy to restore myself. I am a vessel of the Divine.

Key 2: Divine Matrix (Individual <> Tribe) I am an expression of Divine Radiance and Health. I am one with the Divine Field of Life. I align with nature's creation to activate my part.

Seriphos Quartz (with Hedenbergite inclusions) Seriphos Quartz are sweet tiny crystals like small nature devas. One may immediately feel the magnetism of nature radiating from them. Elemental Effect: Strengthening, Balancing, Rarefying.

Key 1: Nature Devas (Tone <> Silence) I am in tune with my environment. I am assisted to reach my full potential

Serpentine pale green *Spirit Earth Stone*. It is also called The Joy Ball and New Jade. Elemental Effect: Stabilizing, Elevating.

Key 1: Joy (Lost dreams <> Realized dreams) I am living my dream.

Key 2: Subconscious Connection (Aggression <> Loving) I am the path between my heart and ego.

Key 3: Life Journey (Nature <> Spirit of Earth) I am a living being with role to play. I am more than my physical body.

Serpentine banded black and green *Shamanic Connection Stone.* Banded Serpentine (Zebra Stone) is a magnesium silicate mineral. Elemental Effect: Absorbing, Elevating.

Key 1: Shamanic Connection (Yearning for Nature <> Nature-wise) I am honing my abilities to perceive other realities.

Shadow Quartz *Witness Stone.* Shadow Quartz, also called Phantasy Quartz, has inclusions of Chlorite and other minerals. Elemental Effect: Moving, Purifying.

Key 1: Witness (Perspective <> Lack of Directions) I have the perspective to see where I am going.

Shattukite dark blue *Introspection Stone.* Elemental Effect: Purifying, Blending, Penetrating.

Key 1: Depth (Introspection <> Self-awareness) I allow my pain to teach me about myself. I am fully embracing life.

Shungite black *Waste Transformer Stone* Elemental Effect: Absorbing, Purifying.

Key 1: Detoxification (Energy Pollution <> Rarefied Space) I am purified and clear. I am clearing myself energetically.

Smithsonite green *Soul Connection Stone.* Smithsonite is a soft zinc carbonate manifesting in botryoidal layers. Elemental Effect: Balancing, Elevating.

Key 1: Soul Connection (Sensation <> Perception) I am training my psychic abilities. I am becoming aware of my High Heart, the seat of my Soul.

Key 2: Gentleness (Crisis/Drama <> Support) I remain gentle with others and myself.

Smithsonite pink *Gentleness Stone.* Elemental Effect: Balancing, Elevating.

Key 1: Stillness (Upset <> Calm) I am the source of calmness and peace.

Key 2: Soul Connection (Is that all? <> 'All that is') I come to the gentle well of Love that is hidden in the heart of my Soul.

Smithsonite purple *Spiritual Practice Stone.* Elemental Effect: Inspiring, Elevating.

Key 1: Discipline (Yearning <> Effort) I am committed to my Spiritual Practice each day. My practice becomes my anchor and support. I am unifying my mind and my heart towards spiritual connection.

Smokey Quartz *Fearfulness Remedy Stone.* Elemental Effect: Grounding, Inspiring.

Key 1: Grounded/Centred (Unbalanced <> Centred) I am grounded. I am centring myself each moment.

Key 2: Happiness / Belonging (Fearful <> Safe) I am safe as I invite the unknown. I am gentle with myself.

Sodalite blue *Logic Stone.* Elemental Effect: Grounding, Absorbing, Expanding.

Key 1: Understanding (Mental chatter <> Mental order) I am learning about the nature of myself in relationship to the universe.

Key 2: Truth (Fear of retribution <> Voicing concerns) I allow myself to speak from how I feel. I connect how I speak, to who I really am. I am encouraged to be truthful at any time.

Sphalerite orange-red to black *Relationship Stone.* Sphalerite can be used as a Co-dependency Remedy. Elemental Effect: Purifying, Stabilizing.

Key 1: Healthy Relationships (Co-dependency <> Co-creation) I relate to the loved ones in my life, with loving-kindness.

Key 2: Commitment/Creative Vision (Unfinished projects <>

Completed projects) I am gathering the energy to complete any project I start with Joy.

Spinel ruby red *Vibrancy Stone.* Elemental Effect: Purging, Elevating, Absorbing.

Key 1: Purification (Energized <> Holding Back) I am transforming inner inertia into vibrant energy. I am creating inner beauty and vibrancy by using what I already have.

Spirit Quartz (drusy formation on cluster) *Soul Community Stone.* Elemental Effect: Aligning, Inspiring.

Key 1: Soul Community (Belonging <> Exile) I am connecting with my Soul's family, accepting all the gifts of the Universe.

Staurolite (Fairy Cross) *Christ Consciousness Stone.* Elemental Effect: Grounding, Elevating.

Key 1: Spiritual Mission/Purpose (Isolation <> Free) I am fully aligned with my Angel Guide. I am free and serve my purpose.

Stibnite silver-grey *Exhaustion Remedy.* Elemental Effect: Grounding, Stimulating.

Key 1: Physical Energy (Tiredness <> Alert) I allow the earth's replenishing energy to rise in me.

Key 2: Energy Management (Energy Vampire <> Energy sufficient) I am grounded. I develop healthy bonds with other people. I am mindful of my boundaries, letting only loving bonds form with others.

Stichtite see: Magenta Stone

Stilbite tan peach *Joy in Action Stone.* Stilbite is a Zeolite (Na Ca hydrous Al silicate) Elemental Effect: Aligning, Stimulating.

Key 1: Placement of Joy (Gentle Joy Flowing <> Being in the past) I flow with joy, letting the old subside.

Sugilite magenta *Right Relationship Stone/War Remedy.* Elemental Effect: Strengthening, Inspiring, Rarefying.

Key 1: Cause and Effect of Love (Thought <> Feeling) I am thinking and feeling Love. I trust my intuition.

Key 2: Right Relationships (Searching Mr/Ms Right <> Being Soul Mates) I am committed to long loving relationships on every level.

Sulphur yellow *Digestion Stone.* Elemental Effect: Strengthening, Purifying.

Key 1: Wisdom of the Body (Addiction/Stress <> Listening) I am connecting my gut to my brain, feeling what my body is telling me.

Sulphur in Quartz yellow hue *Digestive Wisdom Stone.* Sulphur in Quartz has been used to gain understanding of bodily cycles. Elemental Effect: Absorbing, Calming.

Key 1: Buffering (Stressful Energies <> Calm Energies) I am bubble of calmness pausing before I respond. I am listening to my body's needs.

Sunstone orange flash *Solar Alignment Stone.* Sunstone is a hematite oligoclase feldspar. Elemental Effect: Stimulating, Aligning.

Key 1: Movement (Inertia <> New Beginnings) I am activating the Light within me. I energize my ability to move forward. I allow new beginnings to sprout.

Tanzanite blue *Immortal Beauty Stone.* Elemental Effect: Transforming, Rarefying.

Key 1: Youth (Circulation/Action <> Decay) I am the beauty I seek. I am a radiant vessel of the Divine.

Tektite *Spirit Communication Stone.* Elemental Effect: Stimulating, Elevating.

Key 1: All is One (Relying on Tradition <> Open to Guidance) I am communicating with Guidance. I am accepting wisdom from wherever it comes. I am fully present in this moment.

Tektite gold *Spirit Communication Stone.* Elemental Effect: Inspiring, Rarefying.

Key 1: All is Light (Source <> Dis-located) I am a messenger of Light; all I need is to listen. I am home when I turn on my inner light.

Tempest Stone see: Pietersite

Temple Stone *Surrender Stone.* Temple Stones are artefacts of rocks & clay from ancient sites and ruins. Elemental Effect: Absorbing, Inspiring.

Key 1: Ultimate Surrender (Attachment <> Selfless Creation) I am giving myself over to life, letting all parts of myself be part of the Oneness.

Thulite green *Sensitivity Enhancer Stone.* Thulite belongs to the Zeolite family. Elemental Effect: Stabilizing, Blending

Key 1: Mental Integration (Observant <> Sensitive) I am observant to what is happening. I respond wisely.

Thulite pink *Far Reaches Stone.* Thulite belongs to the Zeolite family. Elemental Effect: Strengthening, Expanding.

Key 1: Mental Integration (Inspirational <> Despondent) I am inspired to reach my goal. I act appropriately.

Tiger-eye yellow *Stone of Strength.* Elemental Effect: Grounding, Strengthening.

Key 1: Physical Mastery (Weakness/Lack <> Strength/Abundance) I am strong and flexible. I manifest authentic power where it is needed.

Tiger-eye (Bull's-eye) red *Root Strengthening Stone.* Elemental Effect: Grounding, Stabilizing.

Key 1: Emotional cycles completed (Shame <> Self-Acceptance) I am adaptable, flowing with the tides of my life. I am grounding the life force within me.

Tiger-eye (Hawk's-eye) blue *Male Balancer Stone.* Elemental Effect: Strengthening, Stabilizing.

Key 1: Perspective on Ego (Power struggles <> Selfless Insight) I stand strong and am willing to express myself without fear. I use inner strength to move me in the direction I choose. As a warrior I am strong and patient, waiting for correct timing of rapid action.

Tiger Iron see Hematite, Jasper and Tiger-eye

Topaz clear/silver *Judgment Remedy.* Elemental Effect: Purifying, Elevating.

Key 1: Judgment (Deeds <> Effects) I am in control of my emotions. I am listening with compassion, hearing all aspects of my being. I accept all beings as they are, equally.

Topaz (Imperial Golden) *Abundance Stone.* Golden Imperial Topaz grows inside clay and is easily extracted from open pit mines. Elemental Effect: Purifying, Elevating.

Key 1: Abundance (Poverty <> Wealth) I am creating all the abundance I need. I am expressing my creative power in abundance and joy.

Topaz blue *Justice Stone.* Elemental Effect: Purifying, Elevating.

Key 1: Justice (Wronged/Judged <> Accepting what is) I accept justice for all. I accept what is. I am free to move.

Topaz purple *Spiritual Wealth Stone.* Elemental Effect: Transforming, Elevating.

Key 1: Selfless Abundance (Spiritual Poverty <> Spiritual Wealth) I am a cornucopia, abundant with life energy. I am giving and receiving abundantly on all levels.

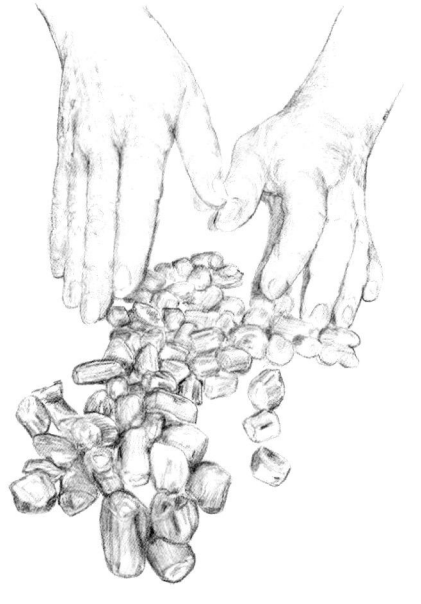

Rubillite Crystals.

Tourmaline (Dravite) golden *Stone of Nobility.* Golden Tourmaline has been used as a Shame Remedy. Elemental Effect: Purifying, Aligning.

Key 1: Nobility (Shame <> Dignity) I am holding myself in esteem. I am a noble being acting for a higher good.

Tourmaline (Indicolite) blue *The Singer's Stone.*

Has been used as a Dishonesty Remedy, and for presenting one's voice. Elemental Effect: Purifying, Aligning.

Key 1: Activation of Voice (Dishonesty <> Truth) My voice carries beauty and truth. I am living in the moment. I listen to the voice of Spirit.

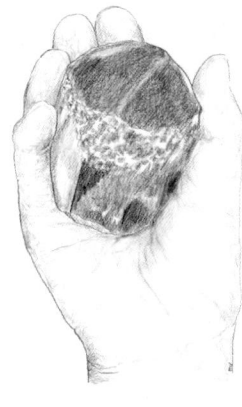

Black Tourmaline.

Tourmaline (Rubillite) pink *Love Activator Stone.*

Elemental Effect: Purifying, Stimulating.

Key 1: Activate Peacefulness (Heart-Ache <> Feeling Loved) I am an expression of unconditional Love. I open my heart to receive loving energy. I am letting my heart feel peaceful.

Tourmaline (Schorl) black *Spiritual Warrior Stone.*

Black Tourmaline is also called Warriorite and has been used as a negativity remedy. Elemental Effect: Grounding, Aligning, Purifying.

Key 1: Active Clearing (Negativity <> Strength) I am clear and strong. I am grounded and clear, feeling the connection to the universe.

Key 2: Grounded Protection (Aggression <> Tough Love) I am protected by the pure life force grounded within me. I am centred and present to experience all facets of life.

Tourmaline (Verdite) dark to light green *Power Infusion Stone.* Elemental Effect: Stimulating, Grounding.

Key 1: Moving with Life force (Lack of Energy <> Energized) I am balanced and strong, flexibly moving with energy.

Tourmaline (Warriorite) see: Tourmaline black

Tourmaline (Watermelon) *Heart of Heart's Stone.* Watermelon Tourmaline has been used as a Betrayal Remedy. Elemental Effect: Aligning, Purifying.

Key 1: Active Balance of Love-Wisdom (Betrayal <> Feeling Loved) I let go and trust. I flow with loving emotions, giving and receiving without resistance.

Tourmaline yellow *Obstacle Remover Stone.* Elemental Effect: Purifying, Transforming.

Key 1: Clearing (Obstacle <> Catalyst) I am finding new ways to act. I am creatively abundant.

Tourmaline in Quartz *Clarity and Grounding Stone.* Elemental Effect: Grounding, Focussing.

Key 1: Dispersion (Movement <> Stuck) I am able to move forward. I am clear to act.

Turquoise *Master Healers Stone.* Elemental Effect: Purifying, Aligning.

Key 1: Healing (Dis-ease <> Aliveness) I am a clear channel guided through the Heart. I am healing myself.

Unakite pink and green *Birthing Stone.* Unakite is epidote feldspar. Elemental Effect: Stimulating, Balancing.

Key 1: Birth (Sterility/Barrenness <> Fertility) I embrace birthing with true love. I give birth to the vision of what I am.

Urbanite *Wastefulness Remedy Stone.* Urbanite is drusy man-made formation of organic material and rocks found in cities and urban centres. Elemental Effect: Absorbing, Grounding.

Key 1: Immortal Resources (Disposable <> Wasteful) I am becoming aware of resources and wastefulness in my life. I am letting go of material attachments. I see everyone and everything as part of the cosmic whole.

Vanadinite orange *Blame Remedy Stone.* Elemental Effect: Inspiring, Purifying.

Key 1: Alive Connection with Others (Seeing Faults <> Seeing Perfection) I am energizing my relationships with trust.

Vesuvianite pink-green *Temper Tantrum Stone.* Elemental Effect: Purifying, Aligning.

Key 1: Freedom to Feel (Emotionally Suppressed <> Violent Temper) I allow myself to feel the richness of life.

Vesuvianite amber-green Has been used as a *Sexual Frustration Remedy.* Elemental Effect: Purifying, Aligning.

Key 1: Natural Expression (Creative <> Depressed) I open my creative potential. I transform frustration into art. I love my body and its potential to express joy and ecstasy.

Zoisite green to blue *Immortal Beauty Stone.* Zoisite is the birth mineral of Tanzanite. Elemental Effect: Purifying, Grounding Elevating.

Key 1: Rejuvenation/Beauty (Age <> Youth) I rejuvenate my body. I feel young, healthy and vibrant. I allow my inner healer to emerge. My life is a beautiful poem.

Mini Lingams.

Notes:

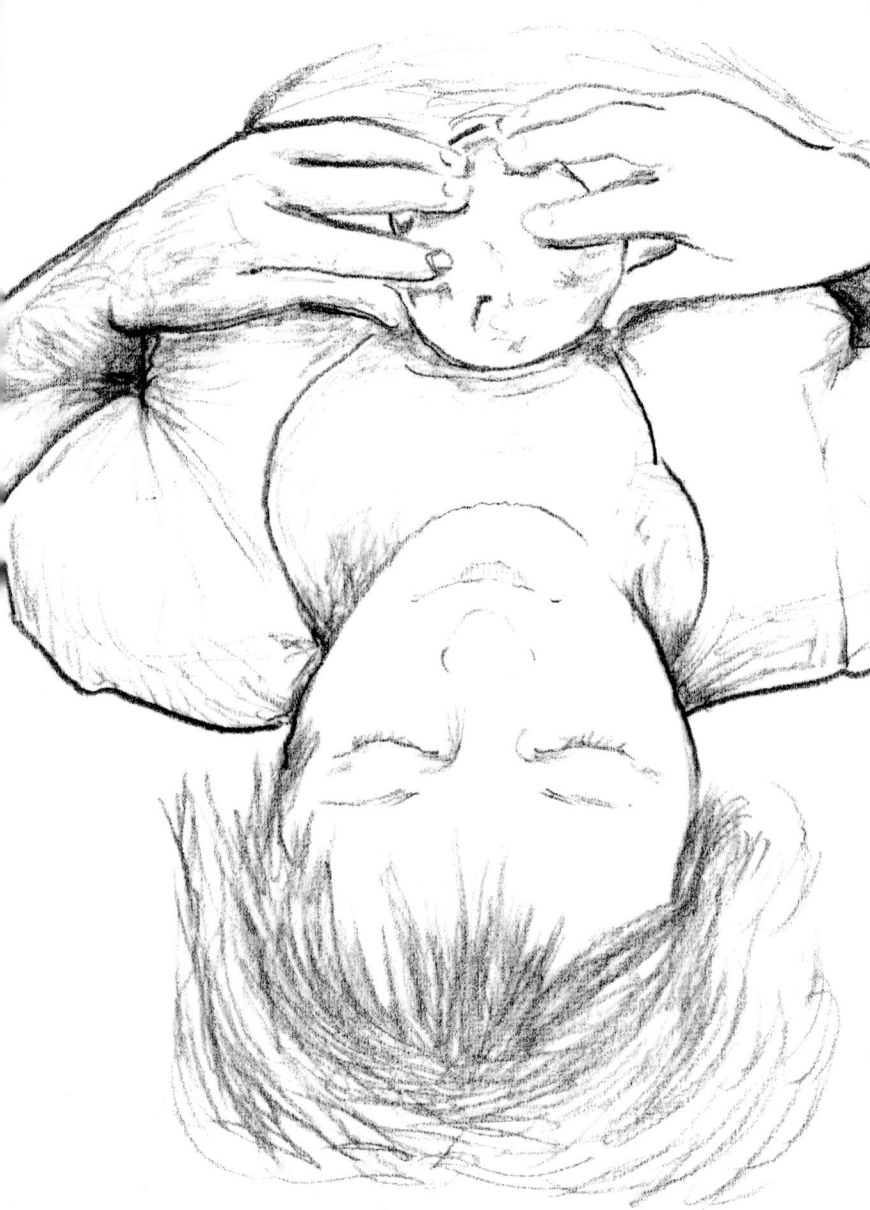

Figure 133 Whitin a healing session the healee may have direct experience of his or her subtle anatomy, and how a crystal assists with balancing or releasing of energies. The drawing shows a large raw Rose Quartz placed on the heart.

Appendix

Healing Session Overview

This is a list of what might be included in a crystal healing session:

Preparation before a session:
Preparing Tools (clean and cleared)
Preparation for space (tidy and cleared)
Preparation for self

Healing Session Techniques:
Centring & Grounding
Light Invocation (stating intention for session)
Guided Breath for client (for example the *Dual Flow Breath*)
Body Scan (dowse to determine location for the work)
Applying Crystal Modalities (*Layout, Installation* etc.)
Healing Hands (moving energy)
Auric Sweep (combing, moving or aligning energy)
Completing (time for integrating and rest)

Interactive Healing Processes:
General Verbal Interaction
Client Interview (to establish client's intention for session)
Addressing energy blocks (identified by the body scan)
Tracing root cause
Working with archetypes (inner child, the victim etc.)
Identifying and addressing detrimental thought-forms
Installing new intentions (reprogramming)
Maintenance program

After session:
Clean up
Client records
Follow up

List of Crystal Modalities

Included in this list are examples of modalities presented in this book:

In-session:
Laying on of Stones, Crystal Layouts
Crystal Grids (temporary or permanent)
Gem Elixirs (maintenance)
Sphere Massage (to assist relaxation)
Crystal Wand (aura combing, investing energy, locating auric energy forms)
Crystal Installation (addressing blocks)
The Crystal Orb (training tool for visualization for manifestation and letting go, incinerator portal for foreign entities and subtle matter)

Maintenance:
Crystal Talisman (for maintenance practice)
Crystal Grids (house grid, bed grid etc.)
Crystal Spas (specialized grids)
Crystal Yoga (the use of crystals, visualisation, breath and movement for personal practice)

Basic Crystal Healing Kit

The basic Crystal Healing Kit consist of 33+ healing stones. In order to make it easier to learn and gradually approach the stones, the crystals have been divided into the levels and then put together as chakra layouts. Literally hundreds of stones can be used in a healing session, so how does one begin knowing what to do? Not all people are fully intuitive yet. The levels presented appeared to be most helpful method for me. I was taught the importance to place stones on all the 8 chakras to assist the process, and that is still true for me.

O. The Chakra Clean Layout (Hematite) is used to ground us and remove already released energies, see page 172.

I. The Chakra Balancing Layout (Coloured Quartz) is used to balance and synchronize our chakras, see page 175.

II. The Activating Layout (Tourmaline). Here we introduce stimulating stones using the two triangles in the star tetrahedron. Rising triangle: hip points (with green Tourmaline) and heart point (Rubillite). Descending triangle: Earth Star (black Tourmaline) and hip points (green Tourmaline). By moving the stones, up ward or down ward as the session progresses, energy in the body may move as well (several small double terminated quartz can be added to facilitate this flow).

III. Purging (Purification) Layout (Coppers) Here we propose to delve deeper to let stagnant energies, primarily emotions be released in the healing session. The four subtle bodies are addressed with crystal placement. It is only with great care we should use this level of stones as the healee should be ready, and the facilitator skilled enough to assist. With proper facilitation the copper minerals act in a purging way allowing for rapid progress. See *Purging Layout* on page 325.

IV. Inter-dimensional Travel Layout (Apophyllite). Here the work with the dream body is explored. See *Inner Journey Practice*, page 206.

V. Here the facilitator is composing his or her own layout that may include one or more master crystals such as the Elestial and the Laser Wand.

Placement	Level 0	Level I	Level II	Level III	Level IV
Crown	Hematite	Clear Quartz	Clear Quartz	Clear Quartz	Angelite or Petalite
Hair Line	Pyrite			Copper Combo	
Brow	Hematite	Amethyst	Sodalite	Azurite	Apophyllite
Throat	Hematite	Blue Lace Agate	Indicolite	Turquoise	DT Quartz
Heart	Hematite	Rose Quartz	Rubillite	Rose Quartz	Danburite
Solar Plexus	Hematite	Aventurine	Green Jade	Malachite	Prehnite
Navel	Hematite	Citrine	Rutillated Quartz	Yellow Tiger-eye	Yellow Jasper
Sacral	Hematite	Carnelian	Red Jasper	Red Pietersite	DT Quartz
Hip Points			Green Tourmaline		
Root	Hematite	Smokey Quartz	Smokey Quartz	Smokey Quartz	Black Obsidian
Earth Star			Black Tourmaline	Black Tourmaline	
Facilitator					Obsidian Sphere

Figure 134 The Basic Crystal Healing Kit. The table shows the crystals and placement in each progressive layout. In Level V you may select and design your own layout with the inclusion of Master Crystals. Not shown is the four pieces of Hematite for the Hematite Grid. It is essential to learn how to apply and integrate these layouts by attending a crystal healing course.

List of Causes

This list includes examples of some of the phenomenons that one may become aware of in a healing session:

Blocked Energy, may be an emotional memory (of a traumatic event) that was experienced but not integrated yet. Pockets of accumulated energy in the body may cause pain.

Etheric Holes, where energy may seep out and be lost. Subtle body holes, or wounds might be caused by trauma or by drug use. Such holes may surface as a physical or mental-emotional weakness of some kind.

Foreign Matter, may include toxins, inert matter and implants. Such matter can be physical or ethereal.

Foreign Energy Blocks, may consist of: thought forms of others or group of others that individuals have taken on and now believes is their own.

Foreign Entity, such as virus, bacteria or parasites may inhabit part of the body or organ, or totally possess a person.

Soul Fragments, of others, or internally disassociated part of self, created by traumatic event.

Mental-emotional Cords, to past events. They may be located and traced back to its source, such cords are generally fairly easy to deal with when they are discovered.

Protective Shields, created by self or others. A person may be ready to remove such shields when the trust for the process is established. Shields from others might have been placed for the other person to be safe. When a shield is released, other people may be free to put down their shields too.

Genetic Cords. Our genes that may be activated to manifest dis-ease. Perhaps most people have dormant genes for all kinds of illness, but they do not have the circumstances to have them activated.

Hereditary Cords, are said to be inherited and learned patterns passed down from our family. A changed detrimental belief makes a big difference to make healing possible. A person may be attracted to a certain family situation in lieu of what needs to be learnt. When such life lesson is integrated the hereditary problem is no longer needed.

Covenants, Contracts & Agreements, from the past may be identified and dissolved when obsolete. A promise of 'poverty' in the past might affect a person's life situation drastically now. When abundance are sought after but never attained, an old agreement might be a source.

Silver-Gold Cord Damage. This is our connection to the earth and to our source, maintenance of them is essential for vital functioning. Exercise, yoga movement and spiritual practice might be applied to recover their functioning.

Archetypal Pattern. Patterns of conditioned behaviour (scripts) that can be described as "actors in a play". For example: victim, abuser, inner child, mother, martyr, and saint etc. Several archetypal patterns may be in effect at the same time within a person.

Anatomy Test Chart

Name: _____Date:___

Locating Areas			
PHYSICAL BODY SYSTEMS:			
Skeletal System: structure			
Muscular System: movement			
Digestive System: assimilation			
Nervous System: messaging			
Cardiovascular System: circulation			
Endocrine System: hormonal control			
Respiratory System: respiration			
Lymphatic System: fluid balance			
Excretory System: excretion			
PHYSICAL ORGANS:			
Sensory Organs: Skin, Tounge, Nose, Ear, Eyes			
Yang Organs: Colon, Ovaries/Testes, Intestine, Pancreas, Spleen			
Yin Organs: Kidney, Stomach, Liver, Lung, Heart			
Endocrine Glands: Gonads, Adrenals, Pancreas, Thymus, Thyroid, Parathyroid, Hypothalamus, Pituitary, Pineal			
SUBTLE LEVELS:			
Spiritual Bodies			
Mental Body			
Emotional Body			
Etheric Body			

Body Scan Template

Name: _____Date:___

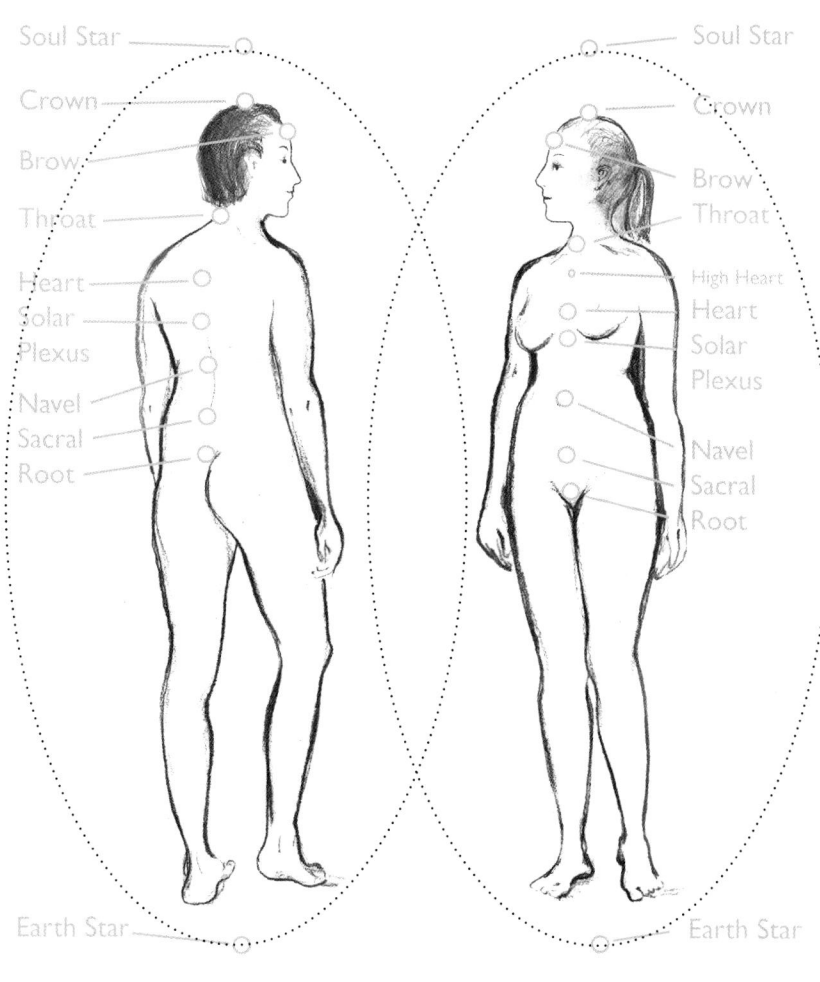

Soul Star

Crown

Brow

Throat

Heart

Solar
Plexus

Navel

Sacral

Root

Earth Star

Soul Star

Crown

Brow

Throat

High Heart

Heart

Solar
Plexus

Navel

Sacral

Root

Earth Star

Notes:

Gem Elixir Session

Gem Alchemist:_____

Date:_____

Client:_____

Problem/Situation: _____
_____
_____
_____

Intent: _____
_____

Affirmation: I am _____
_____

Crystal(s): _____

Time for infusion in sun light, dowsed to be:_____

Guideline: At least 11 minutes up to 8 hours for water, 24-48 hours for oil.

Clearing Method: _____

Guideline: by intent, smudge, Reiki, other.

Gem Water (mother solution):_____

Guideline: single multiple daily doses or continuous sipping from water bottle during the day.

Gem Elixir Tincture: _____

Guideline: indicate # of drops per dose and how often.

Duration of regiment with Gem Elixir: _____ days/ weeks

Guideline: You may decide to do a 40 day practice with good benefits. To really gain understanding and integrate using a Gem Elixir at least 7 days practice is recommended.

Notes and summary of effects: _____
_____
_____

One can use this template for daily recording in a Gem Elixir Journal.

Pendulum Query Template

Session Name: _____

Date:_____

Describe Query: _____

_____

_____

_____

Flowing List: _____

_____

_____

Organize List:

	Pendulum:
1. _____	Yes No O
1.1_____	Yes No O
1.2_____	Yes No O
1.3_____	Yes No O
1.4_____	Yes No O
2. _____	Yes No O
2.1_____	Yes No O
2.2_____	Yes No O
2.3_____	Yes No O
2.4_____	Yes No O
3. _____	Yes No O
3.1_____	Yes No O
3.2_____	Yes No O
3.3_____	Yes No O
3.4_____	Yes No O
4. Other	Yes No O
4.1_____	Yes No O
4.2_____	Yes No O
4.3_____	Yes No O
4.4_____	Yes No O

O = Not Available Now

Crystal Orb Assembly

To make a successful Crystal Orb you need to select the kind and size of wire you prefer, most bigger hard ware stores carry plain copper wire which can be used.

1) Select the size of Crystal Orb you'd like to make. Measure the circumference and add allowance for the loops then cut 4 lengths of wire.
2) Straighten the wire.
3) Trim the wires to the exact same length.
4) Bend the ends to create the loop.
5) Join into four circles.
6) Make the circles lay flat and make sure they are circular.
7) When you have four equal flat circles mark six equal distances on each circle.

Look on the instruction for the paper Orb, each circle is added outside of the one you start with. Join each node with wire and an optional node crystal. There are 12 nodal points.

To activate: place your Crystal Orb on a tray, include an item for each of the elements. Then proceed to state your clear intentions that was worked out in the Crystal Orb process, see page 94 for further details.

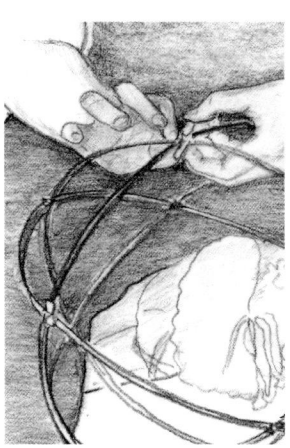

Crystal Orb Chart

Name: _____Date:___

List of wishes:

1._____
2._____
3._____
4._____
5._____
6._____
7._____
8._____
9._____
10._____

Group similar items:

_____

_____

_____

_____

Prioritize:

1._____

2._____

3._____

4._____

Name Projects:

1._____

2._____

3._____

4._____

Bibliography

For further reading and research in the field of self awareness, human energy field, healing and crystals, please consult the following books:

Andrews, Lynn V., *Crystal Woman, The Sisters Of The Dreamtime*, Warner Books Inc., NY, 1987.

Andrews, Carol, *Amulets of Anscient Egypt*, British Museum Press, Great Britain, 1994.

Andrews, Ted, *Animal-Speak The Spiritual & Magical Powers of Creatures Great & Small*, Llewellyn Worldwide, MN, 1998.

Artress, Dr. Lauren, *Walking the Sacred Path, Rediscovering the Labyrinth as a Spiritual Tool*, Riverhead Books, New York, 1995.

Ashley-Farrand, Thomas, *Healing Mantras*, Ballantine Publishing Group, USA, 1999.

Ashley-Farrand, Thomas, *Mantra Meditation*, Sounds True, Boulder CO, USA, 2004.

Atkinson, William Walker, *Thought Vibration*, written in 1906, ebook, see: www.ManifestationMeditation.com, 2008.

Bailey, Alice A. & Djwhal Khul, *Ponder on This*, Lucis Publishing Company, 1971.

Bailey, Alice A. & Djwhal Khul, *The Seven Rays of Life*, Lucis Publishing Company, 1995.

Barks, Coleman and Michael Green, *The Illuminated Rumi*, Broadway Books, NY, 1997.

Benjamin, Ben E. and Cherie Sohnen-Moe, *The Ethics of Touch* The Hands on Practitioner's Guide to Creating a Proffesional, Safe and Enduring Practice, SMA Inc. Az., USA, 2008.

Berger, David Aubrey, *Living Education: god sits before me*, The Living University, Toronto, Canada, 2002.

Bien Julianne, *Golden Light* A Journey with Advanced Colorworks, Specrahue Light, & Sound Inc. Ont. Canada, 2004.

Bien Julianne, *Color Awakening the Child Within*, Specrahue Light, & Sound Inc. Ont. Canada, 2006.

Bonewitz, R.A., & Lilian Verner-Bonds New *Cosmic Crystals* , Thorsons, HarperCollinsPublishers, UK, 2000.

Booth, Claudia, *Aura-Soma Colour Essence* Broschure, Aura Soma Products Ltd., England.

Booth, Mike, *Aura Soma Handabook*, Aura Soma Products Ltd., England 2000.

Borax, Mark, *2012 Crossing the Bridge to the Future*, Frog Books, CA, USA, 2008.

Brennan, Barbara Ann, *Hands of Light* A Guide to Healing Through the Human Energy Field, Bantam Books, NY, 1987.

Brennan, Barbara Ann, *Light Emerging* The Journey of Personal Healing, Bantam Books, NY, 1993.

Bruyere, Rosalyn L., *Wheels of Light*, Simon& Shuster, New Yourk, 1994.

Calverley, Roger, *Ancient Mysteries Tarot*, Lotus Press, Twin Lakes, WI, 2004.

Calverley, Roger & Margherita, *The Crystal Yoga Workbook*, The Crystal Lotus, 2006.

Calverley, Roger, *Crystal Yoga One*, Lotus Press, Twin lakes, Wisconsin, USA, 2006.

Calverley, Roger, *The Healing Gems*, Rock of Ages Distributors Inc., Kleinburg, ON, 1983.

Cameron, Julia, *The Artists Way,* Jeremy P. Tarcher/Penguin, New York, USA.

Cameron, Julia, *Finding Water - The Art of Perseverance*, Jeremy P. Tarcher/Penguin, New York, USA, 2006.

Carroll, Lewis, *Alice in Wonderland,* first published in 1865.

Cheng, R.H. & Lena Hammar, *Conformational Proteomics of Macromolecular Architecture* Approaching the Structure of Large Molecular Assemblies and Their Mechanisms of Action, World Scientific Publishing Co Pte. Ltd., Singapore, 2004.

Chesterman, Charles W., *The Audubon Society Field Guide to North American Rocks and Minerals*, Alfred A. Knopf, Inc. N.Y., 1978.

Chia, Mantak, *Chi Nei Tsang chi Massage for the Vital Organs*, Destiny Books, Rochester Vermont, 1993, 2007.

Chia, Mantak, *Darkness Technologies* Darkness Techniques for Enlightenment, Universal Tao Publication Thailand, www.universal-tao.com.

Chips, Dr. Allen, *Clinical Hypnotherapy* A transpersonal approach, Transpersonal Publishing Inc, Goshen, VA, 2006.

Choa, Kok Sui, *Pranic Crystal Healing*, Institute for Inner Studies Publishing, CA, 2000.

Clarson, Laura E., *Tarot Unveiled*: The Method To its Magic, US Games Systems Inc., Stamford, CT, 1988.

Dale, Cyndi, *New Chakra Healing* the Revolutionary 32-Center Energy System, LlewellynWorldwide, MN, 1996, 1999.

Dannelly, Richard, *Sedona Power Spot, Vortex, and Medicine Wheel Guide*, Published by Richard Dannelley, (1989), 1991.

D'Ascenzo, Lori E., *From a Little Acorn*, how to grow a triving business when you are starting out small, MediaArt, Niagara Falls, Ontario, Canada, 2003.

Davidsson, Dr Marcia Foley et.al., *Illuminating Physical Experience*, Holistic Wellness Foundation II, Kansas, 2000.

Donna Eden, *Energy Medicine*, Jeremy P. Tarcher/Putnam, NY, USA, 1998.

Donnelly, Ignatius, *Atlantis: the Antediluvian World*, Harper & Brothers, New York, 1882.

Dow JaneAnn, *Crystal Journey: Travel Guide for the New Shaman*, Santa Fe, NM, Journey Books, 1994.

Dow, JaneAnn, *Crystal Journey Cards*, Journey Books, Santa Fe, NM, 1995.

Dwoskin, Hale, *The Sedona Method* Your Key to Lasting Happiness, Success, Peace and Emotional Well-being, Sedona Press, AZ, USA, 2003.

Dzubian, Peter Francis, *Consciousness Is All*, Now Life Is Completely New, Blue Dolphin Publishing, Inc., CA, 2006, revised ed. 2008.

Emoto, Dr. Masaru, *The Hidden Messages in Water*, Beyond Words Publishing, Inc, Oregon, 2004.

Emoto, Dr. Masaru, *The True Power of Water*, Beyond Word Publishing, Oregon USA, 2005.

Fernie, William Thomas, M.D., *The Occult and Curative Powers of Prescious Stones*, Harper & Row Publishers, (originally published in 1907), 1973.

Finlay, Victoria, *Colour Travels through the Paintbox*, Hodder & Stoughton, London Great Britain, 2002.

Flem-Ath, Rand & Colin Wilson, *The Atlantis Blueprint*, Warner Books, Great Britain, 2001.

Franklin, Anna, *The Sacred Circle Tarot, a Celtic Pagan Journey*. Llewellyn Publications, St Paul MN, 1999.

Fraser, Sylvia, *The Green Labyrinth* Exploring the Mysteries of the Amazon, Thomas Allen Publishers, Toronto, Ontario, 2003.

Freke, Timothy & Peter Candy, *The Hermetica*, The Lost Wisdom of the Pharaos, Judy Piatkus (Publishers) Ltd., 1997.

Gach, Michael Reed, Acu-Yoga *The Acupressure Stress Management Book*, Japan Publications, Inc., 1981.

Gach, Michael Reed, *Acupressure's Potent Points*, A Guide to Self-Care for common Ailments, Bantam Books, 1990.

Garudas, *Gem Elixirs and Vibrational Healing* vol. II, Cassandra Press, CA, 1986, 1989.

Gerber, Richard, *Vibrational Medicine* New Choices for Healing Ourselves, Bear & Company, Santa Fee, (1954) 1996.

Gienger Michael, *Crystal Power Crystal Healing* The Complete Handbook, London, UK, 1998.

Goswami, Amrit Ph. D., with R. E. Reed and M. Goswami, *The Self- Aware Uniwerse* How consciousness creates the material world, Tarcher/Putnam, NY, 1995.

Goswamis, Syam Sundar, *Laya Yoga* The Definitive Guide to the Chakras and Kundalini, Inner Traditions, VT, 1999.

Govinda, Lama Anarika, *Foundations of Tibetan Mysticism*, Century Hutchinson Ltd., London, Enland, 1960, 1987.

Grumbacher Inc., *Colour Wheel*, N.Y., 1977.

Gurmukh with Cathryn Michon, *Eight Human Talents*, Cliff Street Books, HarperCollinsPublishers, NY, 2000.

Hadingham, Evan, *Circles and Standing Stones* An Illustrate Exploration of Megalith Mysteries of Earky Britain, Anchor Press/Doubleday, NY, 1976.

Haich, Elisabeth, *Wisdom of the Tarot*, Aurora Press, Santa Fe NM, 1984.

Hansard, Christopher, *The Tibetan Art of Living*, Hodder &Stoughton, London, England, 2001.

Hay, Louise L., *Heal Your Body*, The Mental Causes for Physical Illness and a Metaphysical Way to Ocvercome Them, Hay House, Inc., CA, 1982, 1984.

Hill, Sally, *Tarot Affirmation Cards*, US Games Systems Inc., Stanford, CT, 2001.

Jansen, Eva Rudy, *Singing Bowls* A Practical Handbook of Instruction and Use, Binkey KoK Publications, Holland, (1990) 1994.

Johari, Harish, *Chakras, Energy Centers of Transformation*, Inner Traditions, Vermont, USA .

Johnson, Dr Beverley, *Muscle Testing in the 21st Centuary*, The Canadian Institute of Natural Health Inc. , Midland, Ontario, 2000.

Johnson, Dr. Beverly, *Mind over Matter*, Part II, Vol. 1 The Language of Energy, The Canadien Institute of Natural Health Inc., Midland, Ontario, 2006.

Johnson, Larry, *Gemstone Prescriptions*, White Elephant Monastery, Crestone, Colorado, 2001.

Joly, Nicholas, *Wine from Sky to Earth*, Growing & appreciating Bio-dynamic Wine, Acres Publishers, Austin, Texas, translation from French, 2005.

Judith, Anodea PhD., *Wheels of Life* A Users's Guide to the Chakra System, Llewellyn Worldwide, MN, 2002.

Kaminoff, Leslie, *Yoga Anatomy*, Human Kinetics, USA, 2007.

Khalsa, Virochana , *Cultivating a Body of Nectar, Kriya Yoga and Tantric Foundations*, Books of Light Publishing, Creston, Co, 2001.

Khanna, Madhu, *Yantra* the Tantric Symbol of Cosmic Unity, Inner Traditions, Vermont, USA, 1979.

Kircher, Nora, *Gemstone Reflexology*, Healing Arts Press, Vermont, 2004, 2006.

Krieger, Dolores, Ph.D. , *The Therapeutic Touch* How to use your hands to help or to heal, Prentice Hall Press, 1989, 1992.

Kulvinskas, Viktoras, *Survival into the 21sth Century* Planetary Healers Manual, Omangod Press, PO Box 77, Woodstock Valley, Ct. 06262.

Kunz, Barbara & Kevin, *Reflexology Health at your fingertips*, DK Publishing, Inc. N.Y., 2003.

Kushi, Michio, *Your Face Never Lies* An Introduction to Oriental Diagnosis, Avery Publishing Group Inc., 1976.

Kynes, Sandra, *Gemstone Feng Shui*, Creating Harmony in Home & Office, Llewellyn Worldwide, Minnesota, 2002.

Lewis, Roger, *Color and the Edgar Cayce Readings*, A.R.E. PressVirginia Beach VA, 1973.

Lincoln,Michael J., *Messages from the Body, their Psycological Meaning*, Talking Hearts, USA, 1991 & 9th version 2008

Little, L. G., Van Auken. J., Little, L., *Mound Builders*, Eagle Wing Books, TN, USA, 2001.

Lucier, Katherine S., *Notes from The Living Tarot Workshop*, 1999.

Mandarino, J. A. and M. E. Back, *Fleicher's Glossary of Mineral Species 2004*, Mineralogical Records Inc. , Az, 2004.

Margherita, *Crystal Healing Manual for Beginning Courses*, Library of Crystals (II), Toronto, 2001.

Margherita, *Tarot & Crystals* A Journey through the Major Arcana with Crystals, The Crystal Lotus, 2005.

Margherita, *The Crystal Keys - An Affirmation Workbook*, The Crystal Lotus, Kyirong Village, 2005.

Margherita, *Crystal Moon Mandala Cards*, The Crystal Lotus, Kyirong Village, Ontario, Canada, 2007.

Martin, Art, *Your Body is Talking: Are You Listening?* Personal Transformation Press, CA, 1997.

McCreight, Tim, *The Complete Metalsmith* An Illustrated Handbook, Davis Publications, Inc., MA, 1991.

McCullough, David Willis, *The Unending Mystery* A Journey through Labyrinths and Mazes, Pantheon Books, Random House, 2004.

McLaren, Karla, Y*our Aura & Your Chakras* The Owner's Manual, Samuel Weiser In., ME, 1998.

McTaggart, Lynne, *The Field* The Quest For The Secret Force Of The Universe, Harper Collins, NY, 2002

Meditation on the Tarot, A Journey into Christian Hermeticism, Penguin Putnam Inc. New York , NY, 1985.

Melchizedek, Drunvalo, *Living in the Heart* How to enter into the Sacred Space within the Heart, Light Technology Publishing, AZ, 2003.

Melody, *Love is in the Earth*: A Kaleidoscope of Crystals, EarthLove Publishing House, Colorado, 1995.

Melody, *Love is in the Earth - Crystal Tarot*. Earth-Love Publishing House, Wheat Ridge CO, 2000.

Melody, *Love is in the Earth* - the Crystal & Mineral Encyclopedia, Earth Love Publishing House, Colorado, USA , 2007.

Mitchell, James R., *Gem Trails of Arizona*, Gem Guides Book Co, CA, 1995.

Modi, MD, Shakuntala, *Remarkable Healings* A Psychiatrist Discovers Unsuspected Roots of Mental And Physical Illness, Hampton Roads Publishing Co, Chalottesville, VA, 1997.

Myss, Caroline, Ph.D., *Anatomy of the Spirit* Seven Stages of Power and Healing, Three Rivers Press, Crown Publishers, Inc.,1996.

Myss, Caroline, Ph.D., *Why People Don't Heal And How They Can*, Harmony Books, New York, 1997.

Myss, Caroline, Ph.D., *Sacred Contracts* Awakening to your divine Potential, Harmony Books, NY, 2001.

Narby, Jeremy, T*he Cosmic Serpent*, Jeremy P. Tarcher/Putnam Inc., N.Y., 1998.

Norbu, Chögyal Namkhai, Rinpoche, *The Crystal and the Way of Light*, Snow Lion, (1986), 2000.

Norbu, Chögyal Namkhai, Rinpoche, *Yantra Yoga*, Snow Lion, 2009.

Osho, *The Book of Secrets*, Osho International Foundation, St. Martin Griffin, New York, 1974.

Ozaniec, Naomi, *The Illustrated Tarot*, Sterling Publishing Co., New York, NY, 1999.

Pellant, Chris, *Rocks and Minerals* The visual guide to more than 500 rocks and minerals around the world, Dorling Kindersley Inc., NY, USA, 1992.

Price, Monica and Kevin Walsh, *Bergarter och Mineral*, Albert Bonniers Förlag, Sweden, 2005.

Raphaell, Katrina, *Crystal Enlightenment*, Aurora Press, Santa Fe, 1986.

Raphaell, Katrina, *Crystal Healing*, Aurora Press, Santa Fe, 1987.

Raphaell, Katrina, *Crystalline Transmission*, Aurora Press, Santa Fe, 1990.

Raphaell, Katrina, *Crystalline Illumination, The Way of the Five Bodies*, The Crystal Academy of Advanced Healing Arts, Hawaii, 2010.

Rawlinson, Philip, *Sacred Tibet*, Thames and Hudson, London, 1991.

Richardson, W.& J. and Huett, Leonora, *The Spiritual Values of Gem Stones*, DeVoss & Co, Marina del Ray, CA, 1980.

Richmond, Lewis, *Work as a Spiritual Practice*, Broadway Books, NY, 2000.

Rossbach, Sarah & Lin Yun, *Living Color*, Master Lin Yun's Guide to Feng Shui and the Art of Color, Kodansha America, Inc., NY, 1994.

Rotolo, Domenic, *Empowerment through Crystal Consciousness,* Privatly printed compendium.

Scholten, Jan, *Homoepathy and Minerals*, Stichting Alonnissos, The Netherlands, 1993, 1996.

Sha, Dr Zhi Gang, *Power Healing*, the four keys to energizing your body, mind and spirit, HarperCollins Publishers Inc., San Francisco, USA, 2003.

Shesso, Renna, *Math for Mystics*, Red Wheel/Weiser, LLC, CA, 2007.

Simmons, Robert & Naisha Ahsian, *The Book of Stones*, Heaven and Earth Publishing , East Montpelier, VT, 2005.

Small Wright, Machaelle, *MAP: The Co-Creative White brotherhood Medical Assistance Program*, published by Pereleandra Ltd, VA.

Sohnen-Moe, Cherie M., *Business Mastery* A Guide For Creating a Fulfilling, Thriving Business and Keeping it Successful, Sohnen-Moe Associates, Inc., AZ, 2008.

Sorrel, Charles A., *Minerals of the World*, Golden Press, WI, 1973.

Sperling, Renate, T*he Essence of Gem Stones*, Bluestar Communications Corp., CA, 1995.

Stuber, William C, *Gems of the 7 Color Rays*, Llewellyn Publications, St. Paul MN, 2001.

Tayler, Rosemary, *Homeopathy for Pregnancy & Childbirth*, The Ottawa School of Homeophathy, 2000.

Tedeschi, Marc, *Essential Anatomy For Healing & Martial Arts*, Weaterhill, Shambala Publications, Boston, MA, 2000, 2007.

Temple-Thurston, Leslie, *The Marriage of Spirit* A manual for the practice of clearing the shadow and transcending duality, NM, 1996.

The Audubon Society, *The Audubon Society Field Guide to North American Rocks and Minerals*, Alfred A. Knopf Inc. N. Y. 1978.

The Findhorn Community, *The Findhorn Garden*, Turnstone Books & Wildwood House Ltd, UK, 1976, 1977.

Twintrees, *The Heart of Matter* Awakening to Earth's Wisdom through Stones, Tree House Press, AZ, 1996.

Twintrees, *Stones Alive*, Tree House Press, Tuscon, AZ, 1999.

Twintrees, *Stones Alive 2*, Ahhhmuse, Silver City , NM, 2005.

Twintrees, *Stones Alive 3*, Ahhhmuse, Silver City , NM, 2008.

Walker, Richard, *BODY* an amazing tour of the human anatomy, DK Publishing, N.Y. , 2005.

Wangyal, Tenzin, Rinpoche, *Healing with Form, Energy and Light* The Five Elements in Tibetan Shamanism, Tantra, and Dzogchen, Snow Lion Publications, NY, 2002.

Wanless, James, *New Age Tarot: A Guide to the Thoth Deck*, Merrill-West Publishing, Carmel CA, 1987.

Warner, Tom, *High speed cameras allow detail of lightening*, ZT research, article in USA Today, Feb. 23, 2009.

Wauters, Ambika, *Chakras and their Archetypes*, Uniting Energy Awareness and Spiritual Growth, The Crossing Press, CA,1997.

Weyler, Rex, *The Jesus Sayings, The Quest For His Authentic Message*, House of Anansi Press, Toronto, Canada, 2008.

Wilcox, Joan Parisi, *Masters of Living Energy*, Inner Tradition, Vermont, USA, 2004.

Wood, Ernest, *The Seven Rays*, A Quest Book, The Theosophical Publishing House, Ill., 1925.

Yogananda, Sri Sri Paramhansa, & Swami Kriananda, *The Essence of the Bhagavad Gita*, Crystal Clarity Publishers, Nevada City, CA, 2006.

Yogananda, Sri Sri Parmahansa., *Where there is Light,* Self-Realization Fellowship, California, USA , 2000.

Young, Meredith Lady, *Agartha* A Journney to The Stars, Stillpoint Publishing, New Hampshire, 1984.

Zain, C.C, *The Sacred Tarot* The Brotherhood of Light Lessons, The Church of Light, Los Angeles, CA, 1987.

Endnotes

Chapter 1. Beginning the Journey

1. The sutra of Shiva is named *Vigyan Bhairav Tantra*: it includes over one hundred techniques for enlightenment training. This is mentioned by Osho in his work, *The Book of Secrets.*

2. The three Hindu Gods: Brahma, Vishnu and Shiva represent the three aspects of God's omniscience: creation, preservation and destruction.

3. Sakyamuni Buddha, the historical Buddha.

4. Ego is the integrating consciousness, or lower self that manages our personality.

5. Such seeds are also called "Samskaras" (Sanskrit) or grooves, upon which the soul is acting.

6. A thought-form is a type of memory that is stored in the body. It consists of mental-emotional imprints, like a groove on a vinyl record. When accessed, it plays up the same scenario or thinking that created it and causes a reaction inside. Reactions can be positive (like that of pleasure when being kissed lovingly) or negative (becoming angry when a partner misplaced the keys again).

7. Reference to Lewis Carroll's books: *Alice in Wonderland,* first published in 1865, and the sequel, *Through the Looking Glass.*

Chapter 2. Why Use Crystal?

1. See Sal Rachel, *"Life on the cutting edge"* p. 119.

2. Galileo was born in 1564, quote from: http://galileoandeinstein.physics. virginia.edu/lectures/gal_life.htm

3. Shown by Dr. Masaru Emoto in his book *Messages from Water.*

4. Katrina Raphaell describes the Record Keeper crystals in detail in her book, *Crystal Enlightenment.*

5. Exodus 28:15-21; 39:8-14, *King James Bible.* The 12 stones of the Breast plate of Judgement. First row : Sardious, Topaz, Carbuncle. Second row: Emerald, Sapphire, Diamond. Third row: Ligure, Agate, Amethyst, Fourth row: Beryl, Onyx, Jasper.

6. The technological advances in our time of history are now so perfect that some lab-grown materials are "more" perfect than the natural gem.

7. This phenomena is called "dichroism."

8. This phenomena is called the "piezoelectric effect," whereby electricity is produced by mechanical pressure on certain crystals (notably quartz or Rochelle salt); alternatively, electrostatic stress produces a change in the linear dimensions of the crystal. From: http://wordnetweb.princeton.edu/perl/webwn?s=piezoelectric%20effect

9. In honour of my friend Helen Sladden, who introduced the lighthouse as a spiritual symbol for me.

10. Light spectrum or a range of light frequencies.

11. Nicholas Joly writes about using Quartz, Feldspar and other minerals in the biodynamic production of wine grapes in his book, *Wine from Sky to Earth.*

12. The "Channelling Crystal" was named so by Katrina Raphaell. See her book, *Crystal Healing.*

13. Middle English corusible, from Medieval Latin "crucibulum," earthen pot for melting metals, from 15th century.

Chapter 4 Ground Zero

1. Formulated by Sir Isaac Newton (1642-1727), mathematician and physicist. He was one of the foremost scientific intellects of his time.

2. The chakras, or energy wheels, and the central channel called "Susumna" with its two side channels, "Ida" and "Pingala," relating to the left and the right side.

3. Swedish researchers have presented evidence to support their new theory about the structure of the Earth's core. "We found that the body-centered cubic structure of iron is the only structure that could correspond to the experimental observations," says Börje Johansson, Professor of Condensed-Matter Theory at Uppsala University. From Science Daily, Feb. 11, 2008. http://www.sciencedaily.com/releases/2008/02/080208091314.htm

4. Hematite was continuously used to grid the space for healing during my studies with Katrina Raphaell.

5. Katrina Raphaell taught about Black Obsidian's protective ability when dealing with hostile entities. She also describes it in her book, *Crystal Enlightenment*.

6. The Soul Star is the upper entry point into our immediate aura facing the sky. This centre or chakra is an energy organ located within the system of subtle bodies of living human beings. The Earth Star centre is the lower entry point on the bottom of our immediate aura, facing the Earth. The Soul Star and Earth Star were identified and named by Katrina Raphaell.

Chapter 5 Crystal Touch

1. This type of massage is not the same as "hot stone massage", which uses heated flat rocks.

2. For more detail regarding Reflexology and specific reflex points please refer to: *Reflexology, Health At Your Fingertips* by Barbara & Kevin Kunz.

Chapter 6 How did I arrive here?

1. Refers to *The Artist's Way* by Julia Cameron, where she describes the process of writing three "morning pages" each day, to deal with personal issues and blocks to creativity.

2. Julia Cameron's new oasis, *Finding Water,* is a book which is encouraging me to still persevere in my efforts to bring my own writing work to completion. I am indebted to Julia for her amazing pioneering in the field of correctly supporting artists.

3. Hara means "belly" in Japanese, and is an energy centre located in the gravitational centre of the body, near the navel.

4. This Tiger-eye practice was first mentioned in the *Crystal Yoga Work Book* published by The Crystal Lotus (now out of print).

Chapter 7 Mastering Manifestation

1. Cubatahedron: Dr. Derald Langham, a plant geneticist, discovered this structure in the 1940"s when working with and observing how cells divide and grow. He saw that it reflects the cellular pattern of embryonic growth of all earthly life forms at the stage of the third cell division, where eight cells have formed from the original fertilized cell. From this point, life can expand in any direction. He coined the phrase "Genesa" (registered trademark) to describe a family of shapes he found to symbolize the growth patterns through which life energy flows. From: The Genesa Foundation, 4702 San Jacinto Terrace, Fallbrook, CA 92028.

Chapter 9 Working with Nature

1. See: *The Celestine Prophecy* by James Redpath, where he relates energy-raising activities such as talking to plants or surrounding them by people praying, thereby creating prayer fields to affect a beneficial outcome.

2. See: *Wine from Sky to Earth* by Nicholas Joly.

3. Machaelle Small Wright describes in detail the energy processes relating to harmonious plant growth in her work: *The Garden Workbook I* and *The Garden Workbook II*.

4. The word "deva" is used here to describe Nature Intelligences, but the word is also used to name beings in the "God" realms (in the Buddhist teachings) and to describe fully enlightened beings.

5. See: *The Findhorn Garden*, Angel of Sound 3 July 1963, p. 173.

6. "Devic Temples" or houses for devic beings, were first described by Katrina Raphaell.

7. The "Azez" beings were first made known through Naisha Ahsian.

Chapter 10 Covered by Masks

1. Ego is another term for the integrating consciousness of a person. Art Martin calls ego the inner file manager who serves the lower self, see his book, *Your Body is Speaking: are You Listening?*

Chapter 11 Love Illusion

1. A Talisman, from the Arabic word tilsam (meaning a "magical figure") via the Middle Greek word telein ("to initiate into mysteries"), is an object producing apparently magical or miraculous effects. The person making the talisman concentrates power and energy in it by intention. The crystals included in the talisman simply hold and reflect that energy to the person wearing it.

2. From *Survival into the 21sth Century-Planetary Healers Manual* by Viktoras Kulvinskas.

3. "Collective psyche" means in this context a thought form or several linked

thought forms that are shared by many people or even nations.

4. Dowsing can be done with a pendulum, or by inner attunement. It is the process with which one can receive inner guidance. See chapter *Pendulum Basics*. One should adhere to medical treatment prescribed by a licensed professional. The use of gem elixirs works on the existing thought patterns within a person, and not on the physical chemical level that is used in conventional medicine.

5. "Mukti" (Sanskrit) meaning "liberation."

6. Donna Eden describes the thymus thump in her book: *Energy Medicine*.

Chapter 12 The Lions Roar

1. An example of negating is to engage in shouting derogatory names and using foul language.

2. See the practice of the *Moon Mandala Journey* in the chapter "New Horizon."

3. See, *The Artist's Way* by Julia Cameron, regarding "Morning Pages." I have tried this, and it works wonders as it empties our inner built-up storage bin of unsorted, emotionally-loaded communications. Here we have the additional help of the Gem Water.

4. If you do not have any of the stones, find a picture of the stones or alternatively write the name and colour on a card and place under the carafe as: Blue Aquamarine - the Stone of Truth, or Coral Calcite - the Stone of Joy.

5. The sounds or letters are called "mantrika units", or components of mantra.

6. "Chakra" is Sanskrit for "wheel (of energy)." Seven major chakras are used in the Vedic system: Base, Sacral, Solar Plexus, Heart, Throat, Brow and Crown.

7. Om (AUM) and chakras, see Syam Sundar Goswamis book, *Laya Yoga, The Definitive Guide to the Chakras and Kundalini.*

8. See: Parmahansa Yogananda"s book, *Where There Is Light.*

9. "Issues" may be seen as karmas (Sanskrit) or results of earlier actions that have to be worked out.

10. See, Art Martin's book, *Your Body is Talking, are You Listening?*

Chapter 13 The Mystery of Energy

1. This explanation refers to the Buddhist teaching about the three "Kleshas" (Sanskrit), or obstacles for attaining enlightenment.

2. See: *Vibrational Medicine,* by Richard Gerber.

3. "Chakra" (Sanskrit) for "wheel", or "wheel of energy. "

4. Earth and Soul Star chakras are located at the top and bottom of our immediate aura.

5. See, *Hands of Light* and *Light Emerging* by Barbara Brennan.

6. Crystal Acupressure, see: *Gemstone Prescriptions* by Larry Johnson.

7. See also: *Crystalline Illumination, The Way of the Five Bodies* by Katrina Raphaell.

Chapter 16 New Horizons

1. You may glean insight on this topic by reading, *The Green Labyrinth* by Sylvia Fraser, exploring shamanic journeys with Ayahuasca, a psychoactive plant medicine, and as well, *The Cosmic Serpent* by Jeremy Narby.

2. Vincent van Gogh (1853-1890) was a Dutch painter who during his lifetime never reached abundance or fame. His truly masterful works fetch

millions of dollars today.

3. "Tingshas" are small cymbals giving a distinct sound that clears the air.

4. "Mesa" is a Spanish word for "altar" or "table."

5. Joan Parisi Wilcox describes the Q'ero Indians of Peru, the lineage holders of the Andean Tradition, and the use of Mesa in her book, *Masters of Living Energy*.

6. I had the privilege to collaborate with Roger Calverley regarding the stones in the Master Mesa, during the writing of his book, *Crystal Yoga One*.

Chapter 17 Light & Crystal Colour

1. The idea of study of various sciences to learn about colour comes from, *Color Compass* by M. Grumbacher Inc. N.Y, 1977, p.7.

2. The nine specific emotions depicted in the drawing of the 'emotional iceberg' are presented in detail in, *The Sedona Method* by Hale Dwoskin.

3. The symbolic use of colour, in discussing colour rays, is put forth by Virochana Khalsa in his book, *Eternal Yoga*.

4. Bibliography for the article about Mount Kailash: *A Mountain in Tibet*, Charles Allen, Rupa and Co, Calcutta, 1992. *La Méditation Créatrice*, Lama Anagarika Govinda, Albin Michel, Paris, 1993. *Himalaya A Practical Guide*, Major H.P.S Ahluwalia & Manfred Gerner, *Himalayan Books*, New Delhi, 1985. *Tibet, A Guide to the Land of Fascination*, Trilok C Majuparia & Indra Majupuria, S. Devi, Lashkar, 1988. *The Tibet Guide*, Stephen Batchelor, Wisdom Publications, London, 1987.

5. The origin of clockwise or counterclockwise circumambulation originates, according to dzogchen teacher Chögyal Namkhai Norbu, in which side of oneself would show the most respect. If one consider the right side more important, then the respectful way would be to move in clock wise fashion.

Chapter 18 The Crystal Grid

1. See: *Vibrational Medicine,* by Richard Gerber, p.126.

2. See: *Vibrational Medicine,* by Richard Gerber.

3. Another person's emotional field can be dowsed, or simply detected by our hands by moving them through the auric field. You can begin to practice by moving your hands over a hot element closer and further away. You will detect the heat quite easily. The emotional field is much subtler than that of heat and has some 'thickness' to it that the hands can detect.

4. Quote from *Thought Vibration* by William Walker Atkinsson, published in 1906.

5. See: Barbara Hand Clow's book *Journey through the 9 Dimensions.*

6. Albert Einstein (1879-1955), information from: *Body* by Richard Walker, p 28.

7. See: Amit Goswanmi et. al., *The Self-Aware Universe, How Consciousness Creates the Material World.*

Chapter 19 Crystal Mandala

1. The Chartres design is reproduced with permission from: www.labyreims. com

2. The List of Crystals for Lunar days was first published in the *Crystal Yoga Work Book,* by Roger Calverley and Margherita.

3. The technical part of the *Heart Map Process* was inspired by the methodology of the so called "Mind-Mapping Technique" introduced by Tony Buzan. The intuitive process of the Hearth Map was given by inner guidance.

Chapter 24 Pendulum Basics

1. "Akasha" (Sanskrit) meaning the element of space or ether, from the root word "kash, " meaning "to radiate", "to shine".

2. See: Notes from Toronto Dowsers meeting, October 14, 2008. With permission from Toronto Dowsers.

3. See: *Indestructable Truth* by Reginald A. Ray, (Shambhala, Boston & London , 2000), page 30.

4. For your own sake, keep your work impeccable, and ask only about things regarding how you best can serve in the process of healing. Respect other people's privacy. Safest is to ask what you can do about your own situation and how you may change your own situation.

5. When applying a crystal remedy that as a practitioner, you are in no way prescribing or diagnosing illness. This is for the medical profession to do, and is outside of this practice. The crystal practitioner (including certified crystal healers) can work on the non-physical realms, as counsellors or energy workers. Responsibility must be clearly stated so that each prospective client who receives crystal therapies and healing, does so by his or her own accord and must take responsibility for his or her own healing.

6. See: Notes form Toronto Dowsers meeting, October 2006. With permission from Toronto Dowsers.

7. To find out your dominant hand, separate your hands about hip width with the palm facing each other. Your thumbs should point to the ceiling and fingers spread flat. Close your eyes and then put the palms together quickly, interlacing your fingers as if in prayer. Notice which thumb is above. That hand is considered your dominant hand.

Chapter 25 Crystal Healing

1. A new national survey finds that most medical students think that knowledge of complementary and alternative medicine could help western doctors do a better job. Complementary and alternative medicine, or

CAM, includes such therapies as acupuncture, yoga, massage and herbal treatments. Published by: HealthDay News, on Jan. 20, 2010.

2. Regarding practice and the natural production of DMT, see: Mantak Chia *Darkness Technology,* www.universal-tao.com, and about DMT studies see: www.RickStrassman.com

3. See: *Vibrational Medicine* by Gerber.

4. The Buddha observed that a person is a result of all his or her actions in the past. What is done now is to become the future.

5. To learn more about forgiveness practice, see the *Dioptase Grid.*

6. I remember being in the presence of the Dalai Lama in 1999, together with 5000 other people. The entire space was filled with such exquisite feeling that seemed to radiate from the stage where he was seated. I did not understand what was said as it was in Tibetan, but I felt transformed.

7. Time Link Crystals were so named and described by Katrina Raphaell.

8. The *Healing Hands* practice is similar to Reiki but not the same. The energy channelled, however, is in my view very similar, but it depends on how well you attune to your guidance/source. If you do this on your own, you do not have a teacher's attunement to rely on. Therefore, seek to receive this. I received this attunement spontaneously by an accomplished person who on an occasion touched the palms of my hands. I felt like two huge portals opened in that moment with the result that a huge amount of energy started to flow in and out. Some time after I received several attunements from my Reiki teachers.

9. The focussed intention of invoking "the angelic team of true protection" was formulated by Margherita, with the same intention in mind as a much longer prayer included in Dr. Modi"s book: *Remarkable Healings, A Psychiatrist Discovers Unsuspected Roots of Mental And Physical Illness.*

10. Ho'oponopono (ho-o-pono-pono) is an ancient Hawaiian practice of reconciliation and forgiveness. Similar forgiveness practices were performed on islands throughout the South Pacific, including Samoa, Tahiti and New

Zealand. Traditionally ho'oponopono is practiced by healing priests or kahuna lapa'au among family members of a person who is physically ill. Modern versions are performed within the family by a family elder, or by the individual alone. (from Wikipedia).

11. I highly recommend Ben E. Benjamin & Cherie Sohnen-Moe's book on ethical considerations for any healing practice: *The Ethics of Touch.*

Chapter 26 Crystal Spas

1. See: *Cultivating a body of nectar, kriya yoga and tantric foundations* by Virochana Khalsa, page 211.

2. See: *Cultivating a body of nectar, kriya yoga and tantric foundations* by Virochana Khalsa, page 215.

Note! Our intention has been as accurately as possible to detail all sources. If there are any mistakes or inconsistencies, please contact the publisher.

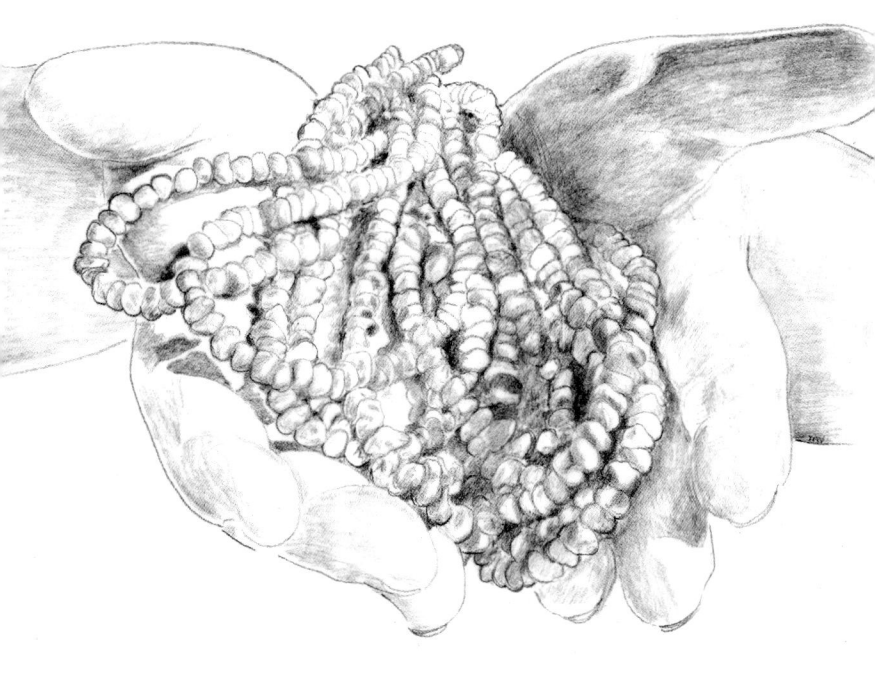

Turquoise Beads, each one can be seen as a seed of healing wisdom.

Index

Amethyst Ball

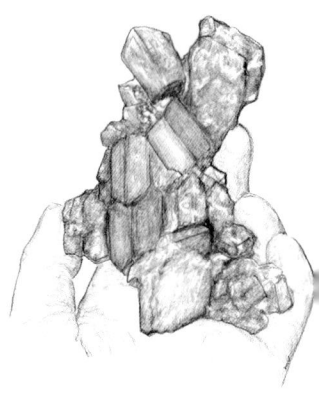

Sugar crystals

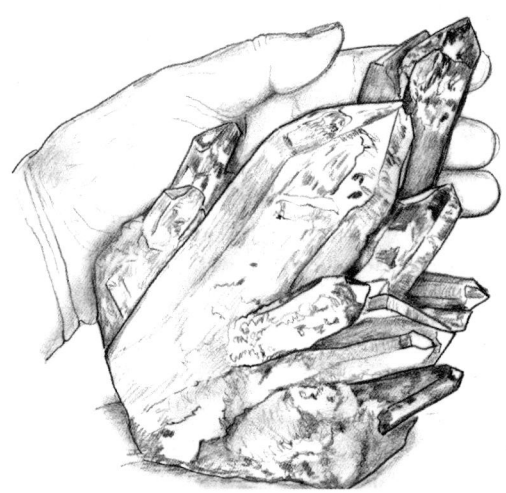

Quartz Cluster

I open my heart...

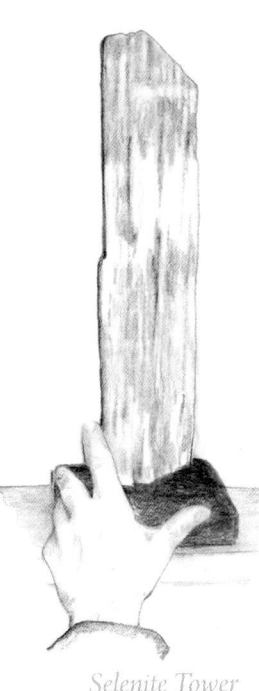

Selenite Tower

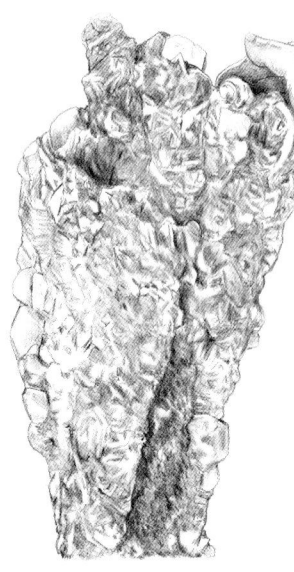

Mica Cluster

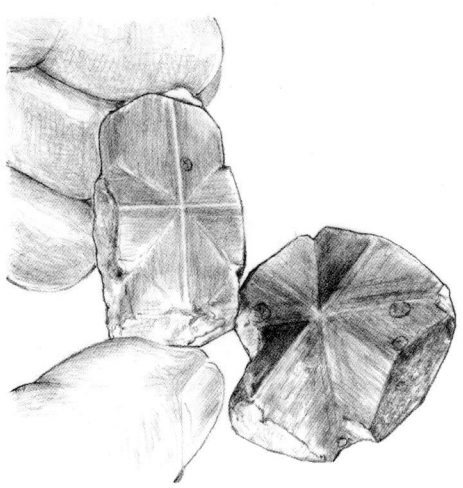

Staurolite crystals with tiny Garnets:
"I am free and serve my purpose."

Copper Spiral Wand Charoite and Scolecite: "I clear the way for my spiritual evolution."

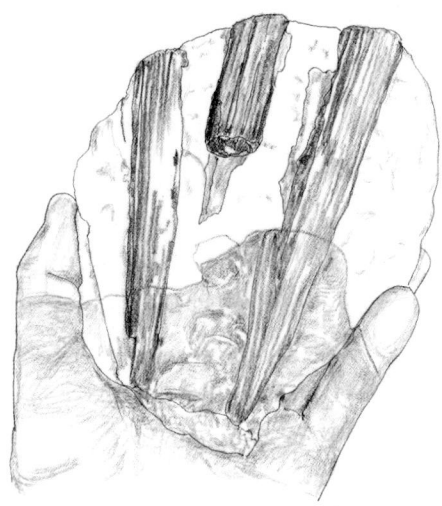

Tourmaline in matrix

Cool Girls taking a break... we got got this far in this book after all.

The painting "Crystal Lotus" on the cover was painted by intuitive healer, artist and life long friend **darinka blagaj**, through her skill and perceptive vision of the purpose for the crystal work. She also took the photographs of the author on back cover and page 608.

The landscape photographs were taken by dear friend and professional photographer, **Jiri Vondrak** as a result his real life adventure trips (including fending off polar bears and not getting extinguished by molten lava).

Page 88 (Lysefjorden, Iceland)
Pages 252-253, Air (Cloudy Herdubraid Volcano)
Pages 258-259, Earth (Thingvellir and the continental divide)
Pages 254-255, Fire (Storm Gathering over Askja Volcano)
Pages 256-257, Water (Fjällssjökull Glacier)
Pages 260-261, Natural Mandala (Landmannalaugar)
Pages 269, Background (Kjolur Route)
Pages 250-251, Space (From Spitsbergen: Svalbart)
Page 606, (Gamblin Valley)

The 'Condor flying into the Sun' photo (page 248-249) was taken by artist, writer, editor, and photographer, **Hilary Slater,** in South America.

The image of the 'Love Tree', (page 163) was painted by gifted artist **MiSun Kim-Hunter**, she shared that it was an expression of the love she felt between herself and her husband.

About the Images

Drawings. The drawings were made by the author, based on her own photographs, in order to highlight a particular focus that not readily be seen in a photograph alone. It required dedicated single focus and patience for many hours. The result of this process created further insight into the energy of each stone (and the person holding them). Materials used were Pentax Optio M20 digital Camera, graphic art pencils and ink pens on opaque paper. In addition, several free hand ink illustrations are also included.

Crystal photographs, all by the author, were carefully selected to illustrate each topic. The Tarot images was created in 2005, as part of the booklet and cards: *Tarot & Crystals. A Journey through the Major Arcana with Crystals.*

About the Author

Margherita has practiced and taught the art of Crystal Healing since 1997. Crystal Healing is a traditional, non-intrusive, holistic modality utilizing gem and mineral specimens, whereby one may be assisted in healing by becoming conscious of underlying patterns and beliefs. Margherita's foundation was in Katrina Raphaell's ground breaking work, and she is an Advanced Graduate of Katrina's Crystal Academy in Hawaii.

Foremost an artist and intuitive, specializing in the ancient art of *Gem Weaving*, Margherita creates intricate crystal combinations made into *Crystal Talisman* necklaces and pendants, which have proven profoundly transformative when actively worked with, and she shares this art with others through creating *Healing Jewellery* courses. As well, she has realized the value of other crystal healing modalities including *Gem Elixirs*, another traditional art she teaches. This is a simple and gentle modality, accessible for anyone with sincere intent.

Margherita also has a profound interest in Labyrinths and Sacred Circles. In 2003, she took the initiative together with a team of friends to construct several Labyrinths, including the 91-foot wide fieldstone *Kyirong Labyrinth*, which follows the "Chartres" design. She is also the co-creator of *Crystal Yoga*, which is a form of personal spiritul practice utilizing crystals to facilitate the expansion of consciousness. Subsequently she created the *Crystal Moon Mandala Cards*, to assist such practice. *The Crystal Lotus* was founded in 2001 as a vehicle for her work.

Margherita was born in Sweden, holding degrees in Mathematics and Chemistry from the University of Stockholm. She currently resides at Kyirong Gardens, restoring a traditonal family farmstead to include healing arts, with her husband Karish and their two pets: a kitten named Kitten and the dog Akita.